REFORM NATION

Best wishes!

Advance Praise for *Reform Nation*

'There are books (and papers) on the Indian economy and reforms. They tend to be dry and academic. It is not Gautam Chikermane's style to be dry and academic. That's the reason his writings are so refreshingly different, and this book is no exception. On exploring India's economic policymaking, this is his second book. The first primarily looked backwards. This volume primarily looks at the present and the future, not the past. Using the lenses of ease of living and ease of business, the first part of the book gives the GPS map of the destination, while the second portrays the journey travelled so far. A delightful read.'

—Bibek Debroy, chairman, Economic Advisory Council to the Prime Minister of India

'Gautam Chikermane has written an important book. Youngsters and students of Indian economic history will find it very useful to understand how far India under PM Modi has travelled from its starting point in 1947. His emphasis on creating industrial, manufacturing and services enterprises at scale is very welcome. India needs policies that encourage enterprises to grow rather than remain dwarf-like. How to achieve that is explained in his earlier joint work, *Jailed for Doing Business*. Together, they provide the policy blueprint and the political roadmap for policymakers across the national geography to make India a socially cohesive economic giant by 2047. *Reform Nation* is an essential read for students of Indian economic policymaking.'

—V. Anantha Nageswaran, chief economic adviser to the Government of India

'*Reform Nation* is a brilliant account of how India found its wings to fly. I belong to a generation that was born and raised in the pre-liberalization era. It was an era where waiting for a decade for a new scooter or telephone connection was the norm, companies needed a licence to expand their production and a watch or cycle was considered luxury. The landmark reforms in 1991 and each reform afterwards have laid the foundations for one of the largest economies in the world. Gautam Chikermane has not only captured the three decades of India's reforms engagingly, he also gives a glimpse of a new India riding on these reforms.'

—Arundhati Bhattacharya, chairperson and CEO of Salesforce, India; former chairperson of the State Bank of India

REFORM NATION

From the Constraints of P.V. Narasimha Rao to the Convictions of Narendra Modi

GAUTAM CHIKERMANE

HarperCollins *Publishers* India

First published in India by HarperCollins *Publishers* 2022
4th Floor, Tower A, Building No. 10, Phase II, DLF Cyber City,
Gurugram, Haryana – 122002
www.harpercollins.co.in

2 4 6 8 10 9 7 5 3 1

P-ISBN: 978-93-5629-004-4
E-ISBN: 978-93-5629-012-9

Typeset in 10.5/14.3 Adobe Caslon Pro at
Manipal Technologies Limited, Manipal

Printed and bound at
Thomson Press (India) Ltd

FSC MIX Paper FSC® C010615

This book is produced from independently certified FSC® paper
to ensure responsible forest management.

To India's entrepreneurs, who refused to die.

Contents

PART III: THE JOURNEY OF REFORMS

Preface

Largely a bystander.
Often a beneficiary.
Always a believer.

Driving on these three wheels, the journey of my career as a writer has run in parallel with India's economic reforms. Many of us, who began our jobs in 1991 and 1992, call ourselves 'children of liberalization'. Before our eyes, our country changed for the better, as did our fortunes.

As a bystander, I have witnessed India's economic reforms, and engaged with innumerable stories about and around them. I have watched the expression 'economic reforms' itself come out of nowhere and become part of the virtuous vocabulary of India's economic policy lexicon. I have seen companies emerge from thin air, create value, multiple jobs and build wealth. I have tracked global investors as they rediscovered India as the land of capital opportunity, set up bases here and grew—from a trickle in the early 1990s to the open floodgates today. Appended to them I have followed the related opportunities that reforms have offered Indian workers and entrepreneurs.

Who in 1991 would have imagined that Infosys Technologies Ltd, whose IPO was undersubscribed in 1994,[1] would be one of India's top wealth creators within a decade? That companies would be offering packages of Rs 1 crore to B-school graduates.[2] That with 50,000 start-ups, India would have the third largest entrepreneurial ecosystem in the world.[3] That India would see a stupendous growth in the number of cars produced, a rise of almost 13 times in the quarter century between 1994–95 and 2018–19, while that of two-wheelers would rise 9.6 times.[4] Across sectors, industries and firms, economic reforms have delivered value, growth and prosperity.

As an analyst, I have tracked the impact of economic reforms through the flowering of the Indian economy. This change in the economy, from one that had been shackled by laws, rules and regulations to one where we see a far greater economic freedom, is not only in terms of reducing government control. To me, the bigger transformation is the breaking out of policy from the philosophical-ideological bars that had imprisoned wealth creation—an idea foreign to the modern history of independent India. Sector after sector has been opened up, policy after policy has supported entrepreneurs, process after process has been relaxed. This remains a work in progress.

From capital markets to pensions and competition to real estate, new regulators have become the institutional mechanism for regulatory oversight. Most of them have performed well—India today has one of the world's lowest-cost mutual funds because of the Securities and Exchange Board of India (SEBI) and the lowest data tariffs thanks to the Telecom Regulatory Authority of India (TRAI), while the Competition Commission of India (CCI) has ensured that there is no abuse of dominant position. On the other side, real estate regulators in states are teetering on the edge, and the Insurance Regulatory and Development Authority of India needs to be freed from industry capture.

As a beneficiary, I have seen my salary rise at a rate that has exceeded India's GDP growth over the past thirty years. India's GDP has risen by ten times, at a rate of 8 per cent per annum. When I joined the workforce as a trainee, little did I know that writing and editing was a sustainable job, leave alone a career. My salary was Rs 1,650 per month; today, trainees in the same job function get more than twenty times that amount as starting pay. In hindsight, I marvel that even though I had joined a low-paying profession, I am financially comfortable while doing what I want to. Along with me, millions of other Indians saw their career trajectories evolve for the better and their and salaries rise. Managers, technicians, doctors, builders, drivers, accountants, government servants, teachers, judges ... We were sitting in a boat that was rising with the high tide of reforms that nourished us.

Reforms also reduced poverty. From 63.1 per cent in 1977, poverty—defined by the World Bank[5] as living on less than $1.90 a day (2011 Purchasing Power Parity)—in India stood at 47.6 per cent in 1993. This 15.5 percentage point fall was accomplished in sixteen years. Since then, it has continuously fallen, touching 39.9 per cent in 2004 (a fall of 7.7 percentage points in eleven years), 32.8 per cent over the next five years (2009), and 22.5 per cent over the next two years (2011).[6] While poverty has fallen, the decline in inequality has lagged. In 1993, the income share of the highest earning 20 per cent of Indians was 41.1 per cent. At 44.4 per cent in 2011, it has remained more or less the same.[7]

For decades, India was home to the largest number of the world's poor. That changed in 2018, when it fell below Nigeria; estimates suggest that in 2020, the number fell further, moving below the Democratic Republic of Congo. In absolute terms, the number of poor in India is estimated to be less than 60 million, half of that number in 2017, a third of what it was in 2015, and less than a quarter of what existed in 2012.[8] Moving forward, in the pandemic year 2020–21 extreme poverty was at its lowest level ever—0.8 per cent of the population. Further, as early as 2016–17, extreme poverty had reached a low 2 per cent level.[9]

As a result, I am a believer in economic reforms. The pay, perks and pensions of government servants have risen exponentially. As have wages of workers, and returns to entrepreneurs. The minimum wage that was Rs 35 in 1995, for instance, stood at Rs 178 in 2020, a five-fold rise in twenty-five years.[10] I would argue that there is not a single constituency in India that has not seen its economic well-being rise over the past three decades of reforms. And yet, there are some who remain blind to these spectacular changes. I call them data atheists.

The most high-profile statistic expressing economic reforms is the BSE (formerly known as the Bombay Stock Exchange) Sensex. While daily fluctuations can be taken in stride and can often mislead on a point-to-point analysis, when seen on an average annual basis, the Sensex has jumped by more than twenty-six times in the past thirty years, from below 2,000 to above 50,000, or a compounded annual growth rate of 11.5 per cent. Economic reforms have also created disruptions in the market. Of the thirty companies that comprised the Sensex in 1991, only six—Hindustan Unilever, ITC, L&T, Mahindra and Mahindra, Nestle, and Reliance Industries—remain today. ACC, Bombay Dyeing and Century Spinning are out; HDFC Bank, Sun Pharmaceuticals and TCS are in.[11]

Structure of the Book

This book is a reference on India's economic history since Independence. It is the story of India's economic reforms, its rise as a regional power, its aspiration to rid itself of poverty, create wealth, jobs, healthcare, education, prosperity. It is a saga of independent India, viewed through the prism of economic policies.

The book opens with the contradictions of the party that should be taking credit for reforms but has turned into its biggest opposer. Of course, politics is at play here. But this U-turn shows that the essential DNA of the Indian National Congress (INC) remains steeped in the 'povertarian' policies designed by prime ministers Jawaharlal Nehru, Indira Gandhi (who was also her predecessor's daughter) and Rajiv Gandhi (Indira's son) between 1947 and 1989. Here, I also examine what reforms are and attempt a new definition that coalesces around power. Although I began the book keeping as base the thirtieth anniversary of India's economic reforms that began in 1991, the book eventually began to take me along on a course that seemed to be of its own choosing. But exploring three decades of reforms did provide an intellectual anchor around which to carve out ideas, study actions and examine outcomes.

To see how important Prime Minister P.V. Narasimha Rao was to India's economy, the book forced me to go through and endure the frustrations of reviewing how we reached that critical point when reforms were thrust upon the country, and the financial, regulatory and moral crises were fixed. As a result, the book goes on to talk about how, captured by the political narratives of ideological entrapment, India was boxed into a wealth-shunning economic policy regime. This is a story full of sadness and melancholy, of lost opportunities and wasted time, of seeing the rest of the world fly ahead, of millions of women and men being closeted in hutments of scarcity, of smothered aspirations, of an India condemned to abjectness.

The Left-dominated politics that had deeply captured the minds of India's leaders, policymakers and even economists of the time, created a narrative that looked at all entrepreneurs and wealth creators with contempt, draining the creative energies of enterprises into blackholes of self-aggrandizement. It made me angry—still does. It may have the same effect on readers. But reading this part of the story is important so that in the future, no leader dares to travel on this path of entitlement, dynastic privileges and power-grabbing at the cost of citizens. There are many reforms that need to peel off these taxpayer-funded excesses, grabbed by individuals in the name of institutions of the state.

The economic decline of India can be traced back to Prime Minister Jawaharlal Nehru, whose first economic policy vehicle, Resolution 1948 (See Chapter 6), I argue, laid the policy foundations for the next forty-three years of keeping India poor. The lack of a strong opposition, both politically and individually, gave him even more confidence to abuse the system. He then further choked the economy, depriving it of jobs, wealth and economic freedom through the Industrial Policy Resolution 1956 (See Chapter 7). While part of the moral base of these policies was the intellectual direction of the Bombay Plan (See Chapter 4), picking the worst ideas from it was Nehru's doing.

This smothering of private enterprise did not abate under his daughter Prime Minister Indira Gandhi. She continued with the 1956 policy and made tiny changes in her 1973 policy (See Chapter 8). By now, the economic repression had trickled down across the political landscape. So, when Prime Minister Morarji Desai unseated Indira Gandhi, the faces changed but the policies remained the same. Morarji Desai's 1977 policy (See Chapter 9) too echoed the squalor of the policy prisons of the past. When Indira Gandhi returned to power three years later, she delivered the Statement on Industrial Policy 1980 (See Chapter 10), with insignificant changes functioning within the same paradigm of state control and the Licence–Permit–Quota Raj. There is a ridiculous policy vacuum in the data vaults of the government as far as the policies of Prime Minister Vishwanath Pratap Singh are concerned; his 1990 industrial policy (See Chapter 11), again, was more of the same; it changed the language but retained the repressive essence.

Nobody likes a financial crisis—not households, not companies, and certainly not nations. But when the macroeconomic crisis hit India between 1990 and 1991, the resultant reforms were worth the pain. Not only did the economy open up, it laid the foundations for the prosperity that today's young, born after 1991, take for granted and often shun. The next chapter, therefore, lays out and celebrates the next Prime Minister P.V. Narasimha Rao's opening of these prison doors, behind which the Indian economy lay imprisoned. It talks about the constraints on the Indian economy and the resultant policy compulsions placed on the establishment.

There are three policies (See Chapter 12) here that have been opened out. First, the Statement on Industrial Policy 1991. Second, the Union Budget 1991–92. And third, the policy measures for small-scale industries. The first two were unveiled on 24 July 1991, the last on 6 August 1991. While the last policy can be ignored as a necessary political appendage, the first two have decisively changed the face of India—economically of course, but also socially when we examine other indicators such as education or healthcare. I see them as the roads on which future policies have been rolled out—policies that have simultaneously driven on and widened the reforms road. In other words, 1991 created a policy infrastructure for subsequent reforms, even the ones being implemented today. The policies have brought reforms into India's economic discourse permanently and, despite attempts to stop it, irreversibly.

Part III explores the specific reform journeys over the past thirty years. Crafted by six prime ministers, this is an analytical listing of sixty-nine most important policy reforms over thirty years, between 1991 and 2021. These include but are not restricted to trade (free trade agreements), finance (partial convertibility of the rupee), governance (the creation of several regulators), taxation (reduced rates of taxation on direct taxes and consolidation of indirect taxes into the Goods and Services Tax), foreign investment limits, poverty eradication schemes, education and healthcare.

The concluding part of the book throws up ideas for future reforms.

The Work Ahead

Stepping back, I see this book not merely as a text of independent India's dramatic history of economic policies peppered with tragedies and victories, but as a precursor to several future scholarly works. It provides a view that challenges some of the extant ideas. For instance, it debunks the fake narratives that prime ministers Indira Gandhi and her son Rajiv Gandhi were reformers—what some scholars have argued as 'reforms' were, I argue, incremental tinkerings; the hard reforms came under Prime Minister P.V. Narasimha Rao. Of course, while the sources presented are etched in facts, the views expressed are mine alone.

There is enough scope to make counterarguments that use the same set of sources to reach the opposite conclusions. But those conclusions have been reached before already, and I believe that any addition to them would be extremely marginal to the wider debate.

This entire book rests on the use of data tributaries that emanate from policies. Every policy has outcomes and any scholar with a strong data sense can analyse the past seventy-five years of India through policies.

Then, there are entire themes to be explored. Poverty and its several solutions, of course. But equally, prosperity and its struggle. Or, deological traps and getting freedom from them. And the out of sync political capture of essential economic policy.

An entire series can be done on sectoral analyses and their policy intersections. For instance, it is interesting to consider why one sector would lag the foreign direct investment (FDI) curve, while another would flourish. Could it be that the philosophical restrictions of Jawaharlal Nehru, Indira Gandhi and Rajiv Gandhi continued partly through the tenures of P.V. Narasimha Rao and Atal Bihari Vajpayee, in their allowing foreign investments?

Infrastructure is another book. Every curious mind is sure to wonder if India could have grown faster had economic policy concentrated on it in the first forty-four years, between 1947 and 1991. Is it under constraints because the prices of land have multiplied? How can the digital infrastructure of the future that is well entrenched today be leveraged for a better tomorrow?

In all these and more, I see several opportunities, hundreds of papers, dozens of books. In that context of future research, I visualize this book as a baton passed from one scholar to another. How you take this work forward, at what pace and in which direction, are for you to decide.

While these scholarly debates will continue till eternity, the bigger beneficiaries of this book will be entrepreneurs. To them I say: Read it, understand what the three generations of entrepreneurs faced before you, construct your business plan, and take India forward. Create wealth, but also jobs; follow valuations, but also share them with employees; break barriers of innovation, but also stay green. The twenty-first century India offers all these opportunities and more.

Above all, I offer this book to our political leaders. They need to know the errors their predecessors made and not repeat them. They also ought to see what has worked, and what has failed. Economic history is as much a rear-view mirror that alerts as it is a springboard that helps conquer greater policy heights, offers new directions and crafts new prosperity.

In the writing of this book, I tried to speak to the leaders of the INC. I got no response. The office of former Prime Minister Manmohan

Singh told me he was not keeping well and hence couldn't speak. Senior INC leaders told me that INC President Sonia Gandhi 'will never speak', the general secretary who is Sonia Gandhi's daughter was 'unreachable', and her brother, the current face and possibly the future president, Rahul Gandhi was 'inaccessible'.

I thought it was something to do with me; meeting me, perhaps, was not worth the trouble. But when I saw the INC steer clear of the celebrations of the thirty years of economic reforms on 24 July 2021, I felt it had nothing to do with anything but with the INC party politics recaptured by a dying ideology. It is a disowning of a glorious past, and arguably the one crown of policies, the one huge and positive contribution of the INC, in an otherwise decaying economic policy junkyard.

The party that had done the heavy-lifting and authored the 1991 reforms was now stepping back from its ownership. I spoke to a few Congressmen I respect at a personal and intellectual level. But beyond that, there is an INC-sized hole in this book. I hope a future scholar will get access to the INC leadership so the country can get a clearer picture of their stance. Right now, keeping in mind the party's opposition to the three recent farm laws, which were part of its own manifesto in the 2019 elections, India will need to look beyond the INC for continued reforms. Politically, perhaps, India will also need to search for an Opposition beyond the INC.

During the same time, I had also reached out to the serving Prime Minister Narendra Modi for his views on reforms. The dominant narratives told me that Narendra Modi is not open to criticism, that he is not a reformer, that for him everything is politics, not economics. I took my chances. It worked. And I got time from him.

In the two-hour-long conversation that followed, he held forth on several economic reforms, from the theory of reforms to their policy expression. He also made life very difficult for me as a writer. First, because I approached him from a position that stated he is not a reformer. And second, because in the few months that followed, he pushed the reforms accelerator so hard that it has been difficult to keep pace. Prime Minister Narendra Modi may not have authored an 'industrial policy' the way Prime Minister Jawaharlal Nehru (in 1948 and 1956), Prime Minister Indira Gandhi (in 1973 and 1980), Prime Minister Morarji Desai (in 1977), Prime Minister V.P. Singh (in 1990) or Prime Minister P.V. Narasimha Rao (in 1991) did. But in the several reforms since 2014, he has shown a strong conviction for, and ability to deliver, them.

I believe that just as the 1991 reforms have inspired and pushed subsequent leaders to deliver reforms, each powering the conviction of the next, the reforms between 2014 and 2024 too will influence the next government, irrespective of its leanings. There is no going back to bankruptcy, poverty and uncertainty.

Me: I remain a bystander–beneficiary–believer.

PART I

Introduction

1

A Tale of Two Protests
Challenges to India's Economic Reforms

Circa 2021.

Weaponization of tractors.[1] A tragic death.[2] Farmers block Delhi.[3] Police show restraint.[4] Threats the precursor.[5] Violence the currency.[6] Playbooks of protests.[7] A foreign hand.[8] Globalization of anarchy.[9] Self-appointed saviours: singer,[10] activist,[11] former adult star[12] and activist.[13] And amid all this, the desecration of the Tiranga,[14] the Indian flag, on Red Fort and a ghastly display of brutality.[15] And after standing firm for fifteen months, an unexpected policy reversal.[16]

Not a freedom movement, not a fight against fascism, no oppressed people. Violence has unfortunately become the overarching image of protest against, and opposition to, what is seen to be the biggest reforms initiative by India in three decades. Thirty years ago, the 1991 reforms powered industry and brought India close to becoming a #3 trillion economy. Enacted in September 2020, three new legislations had the potential to transform agriculture the way the three polices in 1991—Statement on Industrial Policy 1991, Union Budget 1991–92, and Policy Measures for Promoting and Strengthening Small, Tiny and Village

Enterprises—had pushed industry to a new growth and innovation trajectory. It could have been a bigger reform because, at 54.6 per cent of India's total workforce, agriculture impacts the maximum number of people.[17] Instead, it backfired.

Circa 1991.

It is not that the 1991 reforms had a smooth sail. There were voices of dissent, just as there were in 2021. The opposing voices were of entrenched industrialists—few of them are industry leaders today—who functioned under excessive control and adapted themselves to make the best of those distortions. The entry of Foreign Direct Investment (FDI) into sectors had been protected until then. Allowing it meant not only greater competition for existing businesses but also potential loss of management control for the industrialists. To fight foreign companies in the marketplace, Indian firms would need to dilute their stakes in their family businesses. Which, in turn, meant the end of using inheritance as a tool to get the CEO's job or management control.[18] This resulted in protests from what was known as the Bombay Club.[19]

It is surprising that despite seeing the fruits of economic reforms—both as a requirement from the outside (as the 1991 industrial reforms were), or an expression of domestic aspirations (like the 2020 agricultural reforms were)—industrialists have been, are and will continue to be, opposed to them. The two ends of India's thirty-year journey of the economic reforms story, the reforms of 1991 and 2021, have been the most opposed, because they are the most impactful.

But it isn't these reforms alone that have run into opposition; every smaller reform in this sojourn has also left a small sliver of constituents unhappy. Some oppositions, such as those to the 1991 industrial reforms, did not have political clout and died behind the scenes; others, like the 2021 agricultural reforms, have significant political weight, and have wreaked havoc and worked to smother reforms. This chapter examines the nature of protests in the journey of India's economic reforms.

First Pushback: The Bombay Club, 1993

Despite the overall prosperity that economic reforms have delivered, the underlying position is that they are good as long as they impact 'them', not 'us'. The two biggest economic reforms in the history of India stand at two ends of its three-decade-long journey—industrial reforms of 1991 and agricultural reforms of 2020.

There are other important reforms that have been carved out in the middle. These include but are not restricted to the introduction of regulators such as the Securities and Exchange Board of India (SEBI, See Reform 6 in Chapter 13) in 1992, the Telecom Regulatory Authority of India (TRAI) in 1997 (See Reform 15 in Chapter 13) and the Competition Commission of India (CCI, See Reform 31 in Chapter 13) in 2002. The reimagined Companies Act of 2013 (See Reform 47 in Chapter 13) is another major rethink. A national identity tool, Aadhaar in 2016 (See Reform 53 in Chapter 13) is one more reform that has become a hugely enabling tool for state service delivery providers. Most important has been the introduction of the Goods and Services Tax (GST) in 2017 (See Reform 57 in Chapter 13) that has changed the face of indirect taxes.

All big reforms will hurt some incumbents—SEBI hit the opaque practices of stockbrokers, the GST plugged tax leakages and held evaders accountable, and the CCI is breaking business cartels. Most of all, they have adversely impacted the fortunes of rent-seeking government officials.

While most reforms do negatively impact some group or the other, nothing can match the shock and awe produced by the Statement on Industrial Policy 1991 (See Chapter 12) and the three farm laws of 2020.

As far as evidence goes, the 1991 economic reforms—through opening up the economy, deregulating sectors, cutting tariffs, reducing the licence-permit infrastructure and allowing FDI—have had the biggest impact on India's prosperity. In hindsight, these reforms, brought into force on 24 July 1991, are the reason why India is the world's sixth-largest economy today[20] and will be the third-largest within this decade.[21]

They have changed the texture of the economy. The share of agriculture to India's value, added as a percentage of GDP, fell to 18.3 per cent in 2020 from 27.3 per cent in 1991. While this fall is in tune with global trends (the share of agriculture has come down to 5.5 per cent in 2020, from 9.8 per cent in 1994), the extent is lagging—with agriculture contributing less than 1 per cent to the GDP of the US, Germany and the UK, 7.7 per cent to China, and 1 per cent to Japan. The share of industry has fallen marginally, from 26.4 per cent in 1991 to 23.2 per cent in 2020.[22]

The foresight of the authors who crafted these reforms was as bold as it was risky. It was bold because the Statement on Industrial Policy 1991 was not merely a change in the administrative stance of reforms choices and their economic governance. Its audacity lay in the fact that after decades of shunning entrepreneurs and wealth creators, it provided the first moral support for doing business. It followed the Industrial Policy Resolution of 1956 (See Chapter 7), the Industrial Policy of 1973 (Chapter 8), the Industrial Policy of 1977 (Chapter 9), and the Statement on Industrial Policy of 1980 (Chapter 10). It was risky because it contained within it the seeds of the destruction of those who had benefited from the infamous licence raj.

Prime among the adversely impacted was the world of incumbent businesses, especially those directly affected, through their associations—the Confederation of Indian Industry (CII), Federation of Indian Chambers of Commerce and Industry (FICCI), the Associated Chambers of Commerce of India (ASSOCHAM). Within two years of the Statement on Industrial Policy 1991 being drafted, a new and informal group that the press informally called the 'Bombay Club' came into being.

The Club sought protection through a 'level playing field'. Their key arguments against the opening up were the potential destruction of India's indigenous industry, particularly capital goods. As a result, tariffs should be brought down slowly and foreign investment should be limited, the Club argued.[23]

The political weight of the Bombay Club was inadequate for several reasons. First, protectionism as an economic strategy was the norm rather than the exception. Sri Aurobindo:[24]

> I am not afraid of being thought a heretic with regard to economics, if I say that I think we need Protection to enable our industries to reach their growth. The economic history of Germany and America shows that there is a stage in the growth of a nation when Protection is necessary… A high wall of tariffs has secured to American manufactures the home market as an undisputed field for their own development; and India, maimed, and helpless as she has been, may expect that relief from her beneficent Government.

Second, though protectionism was part of the swadeshi politics of the largest Opposition party, the Bharatiya Janata Party (BJP), the number of seats were not enough to stall reforms. The BJP had 120 seats, against the INC's 244. By tying up with smaller parties, the INC formed the government, with P.V. Narasimha Rao as prime minister.

Third, in the social atmosphere that saw wealth creation as evil and wealth creators as economic sinners, there was little public sympathy that could be galvanized politically. The only constituency that the Bombay Club could have harnessed, the labour force and trade unions, had an adversarial ideological relationship with capital and a class conflict. Dwijendra Tripathi:[25]

> The vigour of the multinational invasion alarmed not only isolated groups of politicians and intellectuals, too attached to the old *swadeshi* concept, but also some captains of the Indian industry, who until yesterday were crying hoarse against the excessive governmental control. The leaders of the group of industrialists, the so-called Bombay Club, wanted the government to create what they called a 'level playing field'. They wanted the government to regulate the multinational

> entry in such a manner that they, with their vast resources, did not swamp the Indian producers of goods and services. Among them ironically was Ratan Tata, whose predecessor, J.R.D. Tata, had continued to lament the excessive presence of the government on the nation's economic horizon throughout his life.

The argument for a level playing field had a strong basis. If Indian industry had been shackled for decades, how could it compete against global players overnight? Surely, an India-first policy should precede globalization. In other words, open the Indian market to Indian companies before allowing foreign companies in. This argument was economically logical but politically inconsequential. The high cost of power, the long turnaround time on ports, the harsh labour laws, an inefficient and scattered indirect taxes system, the high cost of money ... all were barriers to Indian entrepreneurs. This is other than the licence-permit system, under which bureaucrats controlled what businesses could produce, in how much quantity, and to be sold at what price. How could economic actors functioning in a compressed regulatory system that thrived on and celebrated shortages be expected to fight those accustomed to open markets without a lead time?

The problem with the Bombay Club was that it was motivated by the practical impact on their businesses—it was not a principled stance. Selectivity underlined its philosophical signature, firm-level interests drove support of or objections to policy choices, and promoter interests reigned supreme. On deregulation and delicensing, for instance, there was wide support. The opening up of the economy had been something the industry had been seeking for more than a decade. On trade liberalization, there was selective support. The industry supported a lowering of tariffs on products that were inputs to industry; but when tariffs were lowered for competing products, the same Club opposed it. Finally, on the relaxation of FDI there was no support.

The lobbying by the Bombay Club was not heard and trade barriers were scaled down. Ajay Shah:[26]

> Customs collections as [the] per cent of merchandise imports dropped first from the worst value of 61.6% in 1987–88 to 37.5% in 1992–93, and stagnated to 30.85% in 1996–97 as lobbying by industry resurged. When a tariff goes from 100% to 30%, there is still a lot of fat for local producers; but progress from 30% to zero arouses greater opposition from local producers. In Yashwant Sinha's period, the tactic of cutting the 'peak rate' by five percentage points every year broke through these political barriers. India's pernicious quantitative restrictions (QRs) were removed through the WTO process. The average customs collection then crashed to 8.09% in 2008–09. Nominal imports (in rupees) grew 60-fold in 21 years!

The Bombay Club may have been snubbed in the early years of reforms. But its pushback did not end. Five years later, it was still active. On 14 December 1998, the Ministry of Industry released new guidelines 'pertaining to approval of foreign/technical collaborations under the automatic route with previous ventures/tie-up in India'. The guidelines converged on the idea that if an MNC wanted to enter the country on its own, it would have to convince the government that its existing collaborators would not be hurt. Essentially, there were three clauses.

First, the automatic route for FDI or technology collaboration would not be available to those who have or had any such agreement in the same or allied field in India. Second, foreign investors of technology would have to seek government approvals and give detailed circumstances for the necessity of a new agreement. And third, the onus was on foreign investors to provide requisite justification and proof to the government that the new proposal would not jeopardize the interests of the existing joint venture. A final line: 'It will be at the sole discretion of FIPB/PAB to either approve the application with or without conditions or reject in toto duly recording the reasons for doing so.'[27] Effectively, the spirit of control and command put the balance of power back in the hands of bureaucrats, and by adding the word 'discretion' opened the doors to selectivity and corruption.

But the doomsday situation that the Bombay Club had envisioned simply did not materialize. 'There was no calamity,' writes Shah and gives five reasons why. One, the competitive advantage of a nation is an agglomeration of several inputs: if the cost of electricity and capital was high, that of labour was low. Two, removal of trade barriers often leads to a currency depreciation, which makes exports cheaper and imports expensive. Three, opening up, as the Bombay Club had warned, did lead to the closure of some industries, but not all; it rearranged the capital–labour utilization. Four, competition and survival in the market helped firms restructure and reinvent themselves by offering new products, using new technologies and investing in talent. And five, Indian companies began to lobby for and use the same liberalized policies for their benefit; these included ending restrictions on coal imports and debt capital, and pushing for infrastructure such as highways and telecom.[28]

Besides, the objections of the Bombay Club were out of sync with the larger forces of reforms. The Statement on Industrial Policy 1991 was in reaction to macroeconomic dangers, notably the potential balance of payments crisis. Giving a concession here or a loophole there didn't matter much. Today, Indian businesses are taking larger strides, reaching global scales and serving global markets. From finished products such as automobiles and commodities like iron ore, to technologically powered payment systems and delivering quality healthcare, India is attaining both a reputational as well as executional credibility.

The Bombay Club also failed to gather political momentum due to its composition—it was essentially a group of wealthy incumbents. This, at a time when society looked down on money and enterprises. The anti-wealth sentiment in films like *Roti Kapda aur Makaan* (1974), *Trishul* (1978) and *Kala Pathar* (1979), which showcased the rich as evil, and their box office success is not insignificant. They simultaneously reflected and powered the underlying political angst against businessmen through creative narratives. *Kala Pathar*, for instance, was released following the nationalization of coal mines, which took place in batches in 1971, 1972, 1973 and 1975. In an earlier work I explained this development as follows:[29]

> First, the Coking Coal Mines (Emergency Provisions) Act of 1971 took over the management of coking coal mines and coke oven plants pending nationalization. The Coking Coal Mines (Nationalization) Act of 1972 followed, and on 1 May 1972, the government nationalized coking coal mines and coke oven plants (excluding Tata Iron & Steel Company Ltd and Indian Iron & Steel Company Ltd) and brought them under a new PSU, Bharat Coking Coal Ltd. The next year saw the enactment of Coal Mines (Taking Over of Management) Act of 1973, under which the government took over the management of coking and non-coking coal mines in seven states. Finally, all these mines were nationalized, following the enactment of Coal Mines (Nationalization) Act on 1973, under Coal Mines Authority Ltd. In November 1975, the government formed Coal India Ltd as a holding company. In this bout of takeover, the government nationalized 937 mines: 226 coking coal mines and 711 non-coking coal mines.

Left with little room for manoeuvre, the Bombay Club could reach only a small sliver of constituents. One of those was the BJP. Political scientist Atul Kohli captures this small but somewhat effective opposition to reforms, in an essay that expresses his concern about the problems posed by India's current pro-business model of development:[30]

> The nationalist element in Indian business's protests found a strong echo in the swadeshi politics of India's main opposition party at the time, the BJP. A variety of more diffuse issues—such as intellectual property rights and rapid opening of trade in commodities and services—also fed the nationalist wrath of India's political class. The BJP mobilized these sentiments effectively in the mid-1990s, putting the ruling Congress government on the defensive. The early momentum of reforms thus got bogged down in the nearly normal complexities of India's democratic politics.

No two economists agree on a single point. So to expect all of them to support economic reforms is expecting miracles. Nonetheless, even if the arguments of the Bombay Club against the sudden reforms versus gradualism had some economic logic, their politics stood on a feeble footing. They had no mass support. Their narrative was out of sync with the dominant anti-rich attitudes of the day. The Bombay Club made its point, sailed on a few tributaries of success, but as an idea, it finally drowned in the bigger tide of economic reforms.

Last Pushback: Farmers, 2021

Thirty years later, on the other end of the reforms spectrum stands agriculture—a sector yearning for efficiency, productivity and economic freedom. But when agricultural reforms were put in place through three farm laws that give farmers greater flexibility to sell their produce, leaving all other institutions untouched, the pushback was unexpected and unprecedented.

In comparison to the protests against the 1991 industrial reforms, those against the 2021 agricultural reforms were an inversion—this time the economic arguments against reforms were weak but the force of politics was strong. Such is the illiteracy about these laws and there are so many fake narratives crafted around the vacuum of facts that several of those commenting on the laws are unable to articulate what's wrong with them, or worse, even name the three laws. The protests seem only political.

The first law—the Farmers' Produce Trade and Commerce (Promotion and Facilitation) Act, 2020[31]—offers farmers the flexibility to sell their produce outside predesignated mandis, thereby breaking the monopsony of the Agriculture Produce Marketing Committees (APMCs). This is a reform that should have happened several decades ago. The APMC, an institution run by state governments, was created during the economy of shortages and had hitherto insisted that farmers sell their outputs only through mandis. In an economy of surpluses, there is no space for APMCs. These opaque institutions, created by state governments and behaving like the state, but accountable to none, need to be shut down.

This law, however, did not do away with them. It merely expanded the ambit of sale to farmers, gave them more choices to sell to other institutions. In other words, farmers would be free to sell their output in APMCs or elsewhere, across states, thereby creating a single national market for every farmer, who currently is forced to sell only within a restricted geography mandated by APMCs. If a farmer is selling outside the APMC areas, the law prevents the latter from charging any market fee, cess or levy—a logical corollary. There is no clause anywhere in this eight-page law that prevents farmers from continuing with the status quo and selling to APMCs.

Sections 3 and 4 of Chapter II of this law enabled new choices for sale by farmers. Section 6 of Chapter II prevented APMCs from charging a fee if the sale was outside APMC areas, including through electronic trading and transaction platforms. Sections 8, 9 and 10 of Chapter III put in place a dispute resolution mechanism to prevent potential exploitation of the farmer. The burden of resolution was placed on the sub-divisional magistrate (SDM), with the collector as the appellate authority. Under the Constitution, agriculture is a state subject,[32] but food is a national market. The law enabled farmers to access a national market while legally remaining within the confines of state laws.

The second law—the Farmers (Empowerment and Protection) Agreement on Price Assurance and Farm Services Act, 2020[33]—flows from the first and protected farmers when they dealt with non-APMC buyers such as agri-business firms, processors, wholesalers, exporters or large retailers. It created a legal framework of agreements within which farmers could engage with companies and wholesalers. Section 2(g) under Chapter I in the law defined a farming agreement. Sections 3 to 12 under Chapter II provided the details of the farm agreements. Finally, Sections 13 to 15 under Chapter III created a dispute resolution on the lines of the mechanism in the previous law.

Effectively, this law provided legal oversight on all components of an agriculture transaction—pricing, transparency, payment mechanisms, manner of delivery and disputes. It placed compliances on quality and standards (Section 4 under Chapter II), a power held by the middlemen in APMCs and to which the small farmer has no questioning recourse. It introduced new quality markers in farm practices, such as, climate, pesticide residue and food and safety standards. Of crucial importance was the protections given to farmers through Section 8 under Chapter II. Here, companies, processors or wholesalers were clearly prohibited from acquiring ownership rights or making permanent modifications on farmers' land or premises. In other words, whatever the nature of dispute, the law prohibited them from acquiring ownership rights or making permanent modifications on farmers' land or premises.

The third law was an amendment to an extant legislation. By reducing controls on the production and distribution of agricultural commodities, the Essential Commodities (Amendment) Act, 2020[34] brought a twentieth century law in tune with twenty-first century realities, flexibilities and aspirations. Primary among them was the reduction in food wastage, as the amendment enabled cold chains to store perishables and sell them after the harvest period, something the Essential Commodities Act of 1955 prevented.[35] The 2020 Amendment helped the storage of fruits and vegetables—and had no impact on rice and wheat.

Section 2 of this law deregulated the prices of cereals, pulses, potatoes, onions, edible oilseeds and oils. Controls, the amendment stated, would come into effect 'only under extraordinary circumstances which may include war, famine, extraordinary price rise and natural calamity of grave nature'.[36] These 'extraordinary circumstances' was specified too—a 100 per cent increase in the retail price of horticultural produce,[37] or 50 per cent increase in the retail price of non-perishables.[38] The time period was also specified—the prevailing price over the preceding twelve months or average retail price over the preceding five years. This short, two-page amendment opened the doors to food efficiencies.

It is not that these reforms have been harvested out of the blue. Over the past two decades, there have been at least seventeen reports (See Table 1.1) authored by Parliamentary Standing Committees, expert committees, task forces, Farmers' Commission, and economic surveys that have studied the sector and made recommendations that the three legislations brought into force. Table 1.1 lists out some of these reports. Gautam Chikermane:[39]

Table 1.1: Twenty years of debate behind the three farm laws

Year	Report	Chairperson/Head
2001	Expert Committee on Strengthening and Development of Agricultural Marketing[40]	Shankarlal Guru
2001	Report of the Task Force on Employment Opportunities[41]	Montek Singh Ahluwalia
2001	Inter-Ministerial Task Force[42]	R.C.A. Jain
2003	Model APMC Act created[43]	N.A.
2004	National Commission on Farmers: First Report[44]	M.S. Swaminathan
2005	National Commission on Farmers: Second Report[45]	M.S. Swaminathan
2005	Towards an Indian Common Market: Removal of Restrictions on Internal Trade in Agriculture Commodities[46]	F.A.O.
2005	National Commission on Farmers: Third Report[47]	M.S. Swaminathan
2006	National Commission on Farmers: Fourth Report[48]	M.S. Swaminathan
2006	National Commission on Farmers: Fifth Report—Volumes I[49] and II[50]	M.S. Swaminathan
2007	Model APMC Rules, 2007[51]	N.A.
2012	Economic Survey 2011–12[52]	Kaushik Basu
2013	Final Report of Committee of State Ministers[53]	Harshvardhan Patil
2013	Economic Survey 2012–13[54]	Raghuram Rajan
2014	Economic Survey 2013–14[55]	Arvind Subramanian
2019	Standing Committee on Agriculture (2018–2019)[56]	Hukmdev Narayan Yadav
2021	Economic Survey 2020–21[57]	Krishnamurthy Subramanian

Among all the reports above from either task forces, committees or commissions, the one that stands out in the context of the three reformist laws is the Parliament's Standing Committee on Agriculture (2018–2019).[58] On 3 January 2019, the Committee came down heavily on the problem farmers faced and made some hard-hitting observations and recommendations. Excerpts from the Committee report that comprised members across parties:[59]

> The Committee notes that Agriculture Produce Market Acts (APMC Acts) which were enacted in various State Governments with the objective to ensure an environment for fair play for supply and demand forces thereby resulting in an effective price discovery for farm produce, to regulate market practices and attain transparency in transactions has become hotbed of politics, corruption and monopoly of traders and middlemen. The Committee observes that APMC markets across the country are not working in the interest of farmers due to various reasons such as limited numbers of traders in APMCs markets thereby reducing competition, cartelization of traders, undue deduction in the name of market fee, commission charges etc. The Committee was also informed that provisions of the APMC Acts are not implemented in their true sense. Market fee and commission charges are legally to be levied on traders, however, the same is collected from farmers by deducting the amount from farmers net proceed.
>
> […]
>
> The Committee feel that scarcity of marketing platforms for agriculture produce and mismanagement and corruption in APMC markets have created a situation where farmers are being deprived of fruits of their hard-earned labour leading to low price realization for farm produce.[60]
>
> […]

> The private markets should be treated at par with the existing APMCs.[61]
>
> [...]
>
> The Committee observe that there is urgent need for radical reform in APMC Act in the country, if we intend to provide justice to the farmers. Remunerative pricing for the farmers cannot be ensured unless number of marketing platforms for farm produce are enhanced and functioning of APMC markets is made democratic and transparent.[62]

In other words, and to use economic jargon, there is a market failure in the agriculture sector. Unlike the Statement on Industrial Policy 1991 that was ushered in due to the compulsions of a macroeconomic crisis, the farm laws of 2020 were being pushed through with conviction, keeping farmers' interests in mind. It offered them an additional venue to sell their produce rather than be stuck with corrupt monopsonies.

This is what the Standing Committee pointed to. Who were the members of this Standing Committee? Including Chairperson Hukmdev Narayan Yadav, the committee had thirty members. Of these, fourteen were from the BJP, and an additional one each from NDA (BJD and JDU). The rest were from parties that currently comprise the Opposition. These include members from SAD, AIDMK and Shiv Sena. In other words, the ratio of governing coalition members versus those in the Opposition was 16:14.[63] The irony is that most of the large parties who later opposed these crucial reforms were signatories to the report. There are no dissent notes, no words of caution from any of the members in the report.

With political opportunism being the driving force,[64] what rich incumbent farmers and middlemen had going for them was the power of mobs that have displayed that they are not afraid to use violent means to subvert democratic procedures.

In three decades, the tables have been turned in regard to the reform and its discontents. While the Bombay Club had some arguments (gradualism) but little political support (small murmurings aside), the rich farmers-middlemen opposing agricultural reforms have strong political support (of the Opposition) but not a single economic argument. In all this, the interests of the small and marginal farmer community, in whose name the entire protest is being packaged and global sympathy and funding raised, are conspicuous by their absence, while vested interests are having a field day. Gautam Chikermane:[65]

> The political economy of this bandh, this protest, is really the politics of vested interests that is steamrolling over farmer economics. Every reform has to pass through and either co-opt or side-line vested interests—the incumbents who resisted foreign entry into Indian businesses in 1991, the brokers who resisted electronic trading in 1994, the unions that have resisted the entry of private banks (and still do), the traders who resisted FDI in retail (and still do), the companies that found loopholes in the Insolvency and Bankruptcy Code (IBC) law such that it has had to be amended several times, the corrupt tax officials that have turned the goods and services tax into a compliance nightmare rather than a catalyst of convenience…the list of vested interests coming in the way of economic reforms is long.

In the case of farm laws, by using violence, street protests and brutal murders, these vested interests drew political victory. Modi was forced to repeal the three laws. He said he wasn't able to communicate the benefits of the three laws to farmers. And on 19 November 2021, 'in the spirit of holy Gurupurab', he announced that the three laws would be repealed:[66]

> … such a sacred thing, absolutely pure, a matter of farmers' interest, we could not explain to some farmers despite our efforts. Agricultural economists, scientists, progressive farmers also tried their best to make them understand the importance of agricultural laws… Today I have come to tell you, the whole

> country, that we have decided to withdraw all three agricultural laws. In the Parliament session starting later this month, we will complete the constitutional process to repeal these three agricultural laws.

Modi is among India's strongest political communicators. For him to say that he could not explain to farmers the advantages of the three laws is difficult to believe. It seems more like wealthy farmers working with the Opposition and allied media created and disseminated fake narratives (such as the withdrawal of the minimum support price).

The Supreme Court did not say the laws were unconstitutional but told the government to put them in abeyance, and thus gave more strength to the violent protesters. Instead, rather than the executive (union government) or the legislature, it was the farmer unions who told the judiciary to get off; they refused to meet the committee appointed by the Supreme Court.

It is a sad commentary on the direction India's democracy is taking. It is telling vested interests to block roads, harm the police, brutally kill innocent bystanders, raise the pitch to national security—and for petty interests, undermine the state in general and Parliament in particular.

On 2 December 2021, the laws were repealed. The politics of rich farmers and middlemen won, the economics of poor farmers lost.[67] Nobody could tell us what was wrong with the laws—not farmers, not the Opposition, not the media. The best those opposing the laws could come up with was that the laws weren't discussed in Parliament (certainly not the first such enactment, nor the last).

If the sole idea of smothering a reform that would have helped poor farmers get flexibility to engage with corruption-free infrastructure was to defeat Modi, rich farmers and middlemen along with the Opposition parties supporting them have won. But lost in the celebrations and victory marches of farmers was the bitter irony of India's political economy. India will have to wait for a quarter century (one generation of politics) before these crucial reforms are initiated again. This victory of entrenched interests of the rich is a sad defeat for the poor farmers of India.[68]

Reforms Pushbacks Ahead

India's opposition to reforms is not limited to the Statement on Industrial Policy 1991 or the farm laws of 2020. Almost every reform in the thirty years between these two iconic reform attempts has faced objections and protests by incumbents.

A series of scams had plagued the capital markets in the 1990s. The incentives of the incumbent broker-owned, broker-managed Bombay Stock Exchange were in conflict with investors that had embraced it in the 1980s. The reform was the introduction of a competitor through the corporatized National Stock Exchange, incorporated in 1992 and operationalized in 1994. This was an electronic exchange that differentiated ownership from trading. The incumbent stockbrokers tried to stall this reform. The Narasimha Rao government did not stop. The rest is history.

Here's another pushback to reforms. In August 2020, when the Narendra Modi government attempted to bring reforms in the tax administration, such that corruption and overreach by tax officials ended through the introduction of a faceless system, it saw opposition from another set of incumbents: Income Tax Employees Federation and the Income Tax Gazetted Officers' Association.

The faceless implementation is simple and will be underlined by technology through a National e-Assessment Centre (NeAC) and a network of Regional e-Assessment Centres (ReACs):[69]

> There is no discretion in selection of assessment cases, while earlier, case selection used to happen manually. In place of single territorial jurisdiction, we now have automated random allocation of cases. While notices used to be issued both manually and on the system, issue of notices will now be done through a

> central mechanism (by NeAC) in electronic mode. There shall be no physical meetings between taxpayers and officers. Wide discretion and subjective assessment are being replaced by team-based assessment and a system wherein [a] draft order is issued in one city, review is done in another city and finalization is done in yet another city. This thereby leads to an objective, fair and just assessment order, said the Principal Chief Commissioner.

There is no doubt that a faceless system of tax administration is superior to one where an official has the flexibility to demand tax, seek bribe or harass the taxpayer. The idea was to ease compliances for taxpayers.[70] This is one component of ease of doing business.[71] It would also increase transparency, reduce litigation, standardize processes and improve the ease of doing business. On the taxpayers' side, part of the excess tax demand has to be paid upfront, which locks capital. A faceless interaction is not only digitized, with a date-time stamp on it, but also pinpoints the official raising issues and is, therefore, a more accountable system.

But the Income Tax Employees Federation and Income Tax Gazetted Officers' Association opposed the move. Their reasons, as mentioned in a letter to the chairman of Central Board of Direct Taxes, include 'displacement of employees and their families' and children's education.[72] Such shallow responses from those tasked with such great responsibilities is telling:[73]

> Sir, you must appreciate that it is an exercise which if not implemented in a thoughtful manner may result in massive displacement of manpower from one station to another. Any ill-conceived diversion of posts may lead to exodus of posts and thereafter displacement of employees and their families, particularly in mofussil charges. Further, any large-scale diversion of posts and consequent transfer of promotee officers and officials among different states under the jurisdiction of one PCCsIT charge, may result in complex problems, eg., children's

education, unmanageable operational difficulties in the residual charges, etc.

The conclusion is staring India in the face: Irrespective of the party in power or the ideology in vogue, economic reforms in India have been, are and will continue to be accompanied by protests from incumbents for reasons that boggle the mind. Managing them will be a core skill for reformist leaders in twenty-first century India—the country cannot be held hostage, indefinitely, to the personal benefits of the few.

2

The Philosophy of Economic Reforms

In Hindi, there is an undated but timeless *muhavara* (proverb): *Jiski lathi, uski bhains* (He who wields power decides what's what). Not facts, not logic, not even truth—it is power, the *muhavara* states, that sets the agenda.

The story of global economic reforms is not very different.

The source of the expression 'economic reforms' as well as its explanation and policy tributaries lie in the narratives stitched together in the world's most powerful nation, the United States of America. In the twentieth and twenty-first centuries, economic reforms have been crafted by the interests of the US. In the nineteenth century, they were cleverly endorsed and morally pushed by the UK, which cynically used Christianity to brutally get China to open its opium trade.

All have had their moral justifications. All through, it has been the shifting sands of power that have defined what is good, what is reform and what has been pushed with violent enthusiasm in the interests of those wielding power. And in the twenty-first century, with democracies facing the pressure of the people and multiple interest groups, the Chinese authoritarian narrative on reforms is gathering momentum.

This is a technical chapter that attempts to answer a key question: What is the definition of economic reform?

Actions by governments across the world over varying ideologies and political systems bring us to a simple definition that pivots around power. Behind this simplicity, and in the process of reaching this conclusion, lies a review of economic and financial literature as well as policy actions. The question is important because giving prescriptions, sitting in the citadels of unaccountable global institutions is one thing; having skin in a game that has players outside pure economics quite another.

As it is, the definition of what constitutes economic reform is fuzzy; what's worse, it keeps changing. To put it positively, it is a dynamic definition that is based on actions rather than on theory. In turn, the theory of economic reforms has been extracted from the jaws of success. If the West is wealthy and followed a certain path to prosperity, the rest must walk on the same path to attain the same level of riches, goes the argument. If political systems get in the way, if cultural uniqueness raises a barrier, they need to be set aside, even crushed, so that success, as defined by the successful and for the successful, is attained.

There is almost a religiosity in the way economic reforms have been defined. As though there is only one path to prosperity—that of the successful. But the histories of nations are coloured by diversities that monetary success cannot imagine. The sad part is that academia, which is supposed to celebrate such diversities of ideas and their infinite expressions, has fallen prey to that one path to one God: Success.

Part of this push is because superpowers have the itch to police the world and remodel it to serve their interests, as the US has shown earlier and China is now exhibiting. The economic legitimacy of the Chinese model with its fast growth and technological edge is no longer in question. The hurdle before the dragon is its political authoritarianism; its lack of credibility in making deals around the Belt and Road Initiative (BRI); its trust deficit with neighbours in the South China Sea, India and Bhutan; its debt trap diplomacy in various countries; and now its corporate implosion that's creating a unique uncertainty for its own companies. The success of China may be an attractive, even enviable, idea. Many democracies, particularly in the European Union, are bending to its will. But finally the method to get there lacks acceptance among them, and it will either change to accommodate legitimacy or implode under its own weight.

At scale, that leaves India with the US model of growth and reform. Here lies the root of all discussions and debates on reforms. A brief timeline explains it.

1918: Point III from President Woodrow Wilson's Fourteen Points echoes in the global economic discourse till today: 'The removal, so far as possible, of all economic barriers and the establishment of an equality of trade conditions among all the nations consenting to the peace and associating themselves for its maintenance.'[1]

1930: Against an agrarian distress due to falling farm prices and political calls for protection, the US Congress passes and President Herbert Hoover signs the Tariff Act of 1930, also known as the Smoot-Hawley tariff. The objectives of this law: to 'provide revenue, to regulate commerce with foreign countries, to encourage the industries of the United States, to protect American labour, and for other purposes'.[2] The trading partners of the US retaliate and in a beggar-thy-neighbour race to the bottom, drive down world trade by 66 per cent between 1929 and 1934.[3]

1932: Franklin D. Roosevelt is elected US President. The next year, Roosevelt introduces the New Deal and undertakes several reforms on the assumption that the power of the federal government was needed to get the country out of the depression. These include banking reform laws, emergency relief programmes, work relief programmes and agricultural programmes.[4] A Second New Deal follows and includes the Social Security Act and programmes to aid tenant farmers and migrant workers.

Here's what the New Deal delivered. It addressed unemployment; attempted to promote recovery, by checking unbridled competition; tried to stabilize wages, prices, and working hours through detailed codes of fair competition; attempted to stabilize agricultural prices by paying farmers to produce less; gave workers the right to collective bargaining; introduced a social security plan for retirement pensions; created the Securities and Exchange Commission and Federal Deposit Insurance Corporation; and separated commercial banking from investment banking.[5]

The thing about ideas is that they can come from anywhere. Roosevelt rejected Keynes. But the idea of reforms stuck. Half a century later, in 1989, reforms had their revenge and made a major comeback through what is known as the Washington Consensus. British economist John Williamson's list of ten actions—aimed at Latin American countries—placed the word 'reforms' firmly and irreversibly in the jargon of economists:[6]

1. Budget deficits ... should be small enough to be financed without recourse to the inflation tax.
2. Public expenditure should be redirected from politically sensitive areas that receive more resources than their economic return can justify ... towards neglected fields with high economic returns and the potential to improve income distribution, such as primary education and health and infrastructure.
3. Tax reform ... So as to broaden the tax base and cut marginal tax rates.
4. Financial liberalization, involving an ultimate objective of market-determined interest rates.
5. A unified exchange rate at a level sufficiently competitive to induce a rapid growth in non-traditional exports.
6. Quantitative trade restrictions to be rapidly replaced by tariffs, which would be progressively reduced until a uniform low rate in the range of 10 to 20 per cent was achieved.
7. Abolition of barriers impeding the entry of FDI.
8. Privatization of state enterprises.

9. Abolition of regulations that impede the entry of new firms or restrict competition.
10. The provision of secure property rights, especially to the informal sector.

These ten points remain the classic definition of what constitutes economic reforms today, which the rest of the world has swallowed whole. Essentially, over the past thirty years, this stream of thought and definitional direction of reforms has espoused for more liberalization, more privatization and more globalization. Several scholars have redefined and fine-tuned the expression but the essential thread echoes some aspect or the other of Williamson's points. A sample:

On liberalisation, Leonardo Baccini and Johannes Urpelainen:[7]
We define economic reform as policies that liberalize profitable activities in various sectors of the national economy. Not limited to trade reform, this definition captures many reforms in services, finance, and investment.

In India, the abolition of licensing (See Chapter 13, Reform 1), the deregulation of interest rates (Chapter 13, Reform 8) and the abolition of 'Monopolistic and Restrictive Trade Practice under Act 1969 (MRTP) Houses' (Chapter 13, Reform 5) fall under this category.

On the focus on markets, David H. Bearce and Daniel C. Tirone:[8]

Broadly defined, economic reform refers to policy change directed at creating and opening markets, including reduced barriers to international exchange, decreased government intervention in and regulation of the national economy, more secure private property rights, and improved 'law and order'. Our assumption concerning the effect of market creating/opening economic reform is that such policy changes will positively influence economic growth and development, albeit with some lag.

The free trade agreements signed with several countries and groups of countries (See Chapter 13, Reform 38), the convertibility of the rupee on the capital account side (Chapter 13, Reform 14) and the allowing of 100 per cent FDI in defence and several other sectors (Chapter 13, Reforms 2, 45 and 64) all fall under this category.

Similarly, on structural reforms, Aurelia George Mulgan:[9]

> In economic policy, structural reform means market-oriented reform, that is, moving economies in the direction of freer and more transparent markets by introducing or strengthening the market mechanism. In more general policy contexts, structural reform encompasses not only the idea of market reform, but also notions of smaller and more efficient government. In addition to reforms such as deregulation, trade liberalization, strengthened competition policy and financial sector restructuring, it also includes reforms of the state sector such as privatization, fiscal and tax reform, and welfare and pension reform. In sum, it refers to a package of interrelated policy 'correctives' aiming at more efficient resource allocation, higher productivity and increased growth prospects for states.

The disinvestment of shares in several public sector enterprises (See Chapter 13, Reform 4) in general and the recent privatization of Air India in particular,[10] one of the most troubling policy decisions ever, the ending of the Controller of Capital Issues and replacing it with the Securities and Exchange Board of India (Chapter 13, Reform 6) and the use of the JAM (Jan Dhan account, Aadhaar and Mobile connectivity) trinity (Chapter 13, Reform 49) to deliver financial inclusion fall under this category.

On macroeconomics or regulatory changes, Jos Mooij:[11]

> The term 'reforms' can be used in different ways. It can refer to macroeconomic changes regarding fiscal, monetary and financial policies, but it can also refer to changes in sectoral policies (in

> the agriculture, industry or social sectors) as well as to changes in the system of administration or mode of governance (White and Masters, n.d.). In the broad sense, reforms refer to almost all the policy changes that have taken place and that politicians and policy-makers choose to present as 'part of the reform process'. Both understandings make sense, and there is no best way to define reforms. Rather, it is an interesting question in itself why some economists, policy advisors, politicians or bureaucrats in certain circumstances work primarily with a narrow definition, while other people, or the same people in different contexts, broaden its connotation and include a much wider set of policy changes in the term 'reform'. I will not go into this question in this introduction, but can refer to Chakraborty's papers in this volume, which discuss questions of discourse and presentation. In this introduction, I will use the term in the broad sense. Reforms refer to all the macroeconomic and other (sectoral or governance) policy changes that are sometimes labelled as part of the reform process.

The Statement on Industrial Policy in general (See Chapter 12), the enactment of the Fiscal Responsibility and Budgetary Management Act (Chapter 13, Reform 35) and even the paradigm shift in India's indirect tax policy by enacting the GST (Chapter 13, Reform 57) fall under this category.

On policy, Leonardo Baccini and Johannes Urpelainen:[12]

> We define *economic reform* as policies that liberalize profitable activities in various sectors of the national economy. Not limited to trade reform, this definition captures many reforms in services, finance and investment.

The outsourcing of sectoral regulation by the government to independent regulators such as the Insurance Regulatory Development Authority of India (See Chapter 13, Reform 24), the Pension Fund Regulatory and

Development Authority (Chapter 13, Reform 33) and the Competition Commission of India (Chapter 13, Reform 31) fall under this category.

Whether the packaging of policy actions determines the definition of reforms or reforms drive policy actions remains open to debate. Even as policymakers struggle to deliver political outcomes to voters, and academics and thinkers follow, influence and often sell these ideas, the definition of reforms continues to evolve.

Although the Washington Consensus has lost credibility in terms of practice, the power of the reforms theory has remained strong. All the ideas presented by Williamson hold merit today. If anything, it is the executive arms of the Bretton Woods institutions, particularly the role of the International Monetary Fund (IMF) and the World Bank in placing lending conditions 'not only on reasonable fixes to macro problems but also on privatization, trade and capital market liberalization and other structural policies, leaving aside the supportive institutional matrix to an extent that in many countries turned out to be politically toxic'.[13] Nancy Birdsall, Augusto de la Torre and Felipe Valencia Caicedo:[14]

> The sense of disenchantment with the Washington Consensus deepened dramatically in the late-1990s and early-2000s when the region was hit by a wave of financial turbulence that pushed several countries into crippling twin (banking and currency) crises, including Ecuador (1999–2000), Argentina (2001–2002), Uruguay (2002) and the Dominican Republic (2003). Not surprisingly, during 2001–2003 per capita income growth in the region was negative even as other regions in the world enjoyed positive growth.
>
> As the region entered the new millennium not only did the Washington Consensus lose support but it also generated vibrant opposition in many quarters. With societies disappointed by the outcomes, policy makers found little or no ground to mobilize the political coalitions needed for additional doses of Consensus-style reforms. Not surprisingly, the region entered into a period

of structural reform fatigue, as economic reforms stalled in most Latin American countries around 1997.

As one of the chief architects and global chief public relations officer of economic reforms, the World Bank noted a dissonance. As an institution that has authored several stories of economic reforms across the world, an honest introspection of its work has yielded more questions about what reforms are, what their effectivity is and what the way forward should be—a shift away from one-size-fits-all to country-specific factors. Gobind Nankani et al.:[15]

> The central message of this volume is then that there is no unique universal set of rules. Sustained growth depends on key functions that need to be fulfilled over time: accumulation of physical and human capital, efficiency in the allocation of resources, adoption of technology, and the sharing of the benefits of growth. Which of these functions is the most critical at any given point in time, and hence which policies will need to be introduced, which institutions will need to be created for these functions to be fulfilled, and in which sequence, varies depending on initial conditions and the legacy of history. Thus we need to get away from formulae and the search for elusive 'best practices', and rely on deeper economic analysis to identify the binding constraints on growth. The choice of specific policy and institutional reforms should flow from these growth diagnostics. This [is a] much more targeted approach requires recognizing country specificities, and calls for more economic, institutional, and social analysis and rigour rather than a formulaic approach to policy making.

This, according to Dani Rodrik, is the World Bank's *mea culpa* moment. There are five learnings from the World Bank's introspection, he writes. First, the conventional package of reforms was too obsessed with reaping efficiency gains and did not pay enough attention to stimulating the dynamic forces that lie behind the growth process.

Second, the encapsulation of the Washington Consensus into a stability–privatization–globalization trinity does not translate into a unique set of policy actions. Third, without understanding the complex contexts within which countries function, copying solutions often ends in failure. Fourth, the proclivity to exaggerate the advantages of rules over discretion in government behaviour does not work—discretion by the government is an important component of success. And fifth, reforms need to take 'binding constraints' of economic growth into account rather than following a tick-box method of translating the Washington Consensus. Nankani et al.: [16]

> ... different contexts require different solutions to solving common problems. Enhancing private investment incentives may require improving the security of property rights in one country but enhancing the financial sector in another. Technological catch-up may call for better or worse patent protection, depending on the level of development. This explains why countries that are growing—the report cites Bangladesh, Botswana, Chile, China, Egypt, India, Lao PDR, Mauritius, Sri Lanka, Tunisia, and Vietnam—have such diverse policy configurations, and why attempts to copy successful policy reforms in another country often end up in failure.

Rodrik then expands the scope of the Washington Consensus to ten new points—corporate governance; anti-corruption; flexible labour markets; WTO agreements; financial codes and standards; 'prudent' capital-account opening; non-intermediate exchange rate regimes; independent central banks/inflation targeting; social safety nets; and targeted poverty reduction. He calls them second-generation reforms that are heavily institutional in nature. Dani Rodrik:[17]

> Often, this work has taken a form that may be called 'institutions fundamentalism'—to relate it to (and distinguish it from) the earlier wave of 'market fundamentalism'. Getting the institutions right is the mantra of the former, just as getting prices right

> was the mantra of the latter. The Augmented Washington Consensus derives its academic support largely from this work on the primacy of institutions.

Having crafted an elegant design for 'others', it is amusing to see that the US itself has been found wanting on several counts. 'Washington does not always practice what it preaches,' Williamson writes, and lists out corruption and fraud, excessive fiscal deficit in the 1980s, exchange rate policy, and finally trade policy that has 'discouraging lurches toward protection despite all the pledges to the contrary'.[18]

Now that there is a new contester to the US and contender to changing the economic reforms narrative, a China-specific definition is taking birth. Dwight H. Perkins:[19]

> In the context of China and in this chapter, economic reform is defined as elimination of the institutions of a command economy and replacement of them with the institutions of a modern market economy similar to those in most of the high-income countries of the world. It is assumed that this transformation has had and continues to have a positive impact on GDP growth. This definition, however, does not include all institutions and policies that impact the rate of GDP growth. Growth can be, and often is, affected by investment strategies or by the level of research and development expenditure, for example, but that would be as true in a command as a market economy.

This definition, and most similar definitions by Chinese or China-leaning scholars, are spurious at best. The actions of the Chinese Communist Party, to which a country called China is attached, are beyond comprehension—and carry none of these characteristics. This is a rising power with no ethics. For instance, we are now seeing how China has captured the World Bank and has been caught manipulating Doing Business rankings;[20] the rankings have been stopped.[21] Unfortunately, the power of money, an intellectual capture by the Left and now by

China ensures that these academic narratives continue to hold up as truisms. Trying to replace the US as the new reforms narrative setter, scholars are pitching the Chinese model of growth to other countries, including India. Yi Wen:[22]

> What has prevented India so far from emulating China and detonating an industrial revolution? Is it the lack of access to technology? No. India is already capable of sending spaceships to Mars. Is it the lack of democracy? No. India is the largest democracy on earth. Is it the lack of property rights? No. India has had private property rights in place for thousands of years. Is it the lack of the rule of law? No. India inherited English law in the 18th century. Why then does India choose to import toys instead of producing them on its own? To answer this question, we must forget about the rhetoric of extractive and inclusive institutions or the law of comparative advantages. We must think about market coordination failures. It is the lack of a well fermented market and intermediaries to organize India's massive number of autarkic and anarchic peasants to form organizations based on the principle of the division of labour that has led to India's failure to create its own supply of toys. It is this lack of market creators and state-backed powerful intermediaries that has prevented agrarian India from replacing small-scale autarkic artisan workshops with mass-production factories. In one word, India lacks *proto-industrialization* to jump start its own industrial revolution, to create and nurture a large and powerful merchant class, to raise the demand and purchasing power of its grassroots population, to transform its rural population into an organized work force, and to promote the division of labour and form supply chains and distribution networks nationwide.

Prior to the rise of China was the rise of the Soviet Union. Like China today, the Soviet Union of twenty-three years ago was no different in creating narratives. 'The strength of socialism lies in the diversity and richness of international experience,' former Soviet Union President Mikhail Gorbachev said, in an attempt to capture the diversity of reforms. In an 11 May 1988 speech at the Czechoslovak-Soviet Friendship Meeting, reported by *Pravda* and cited by L.V. Palei and K.L. Radzivanovich, he said:[23]

> The majority of the socialist countries have adopted a policy of renewal, and an intensive search is going on for the model of economic management which is most appropriate for socialism. There is no single, uniform point of view in the socialist countries on the aims and methods of carrying out economic reforms, nor even on their necessity.

From macroeconomic stabilizations and fiscal adjustments to the transition of economic institutions, and from being state-led to market-led, the trajectory of economic reforms has also been reforming. While most countries continue to grapple with macroeconomic indicators, and some with the component of public sector in their GDP, a new tributary of what constitutes reforms has emerged in the form and nature of what constitutes public goods and how much of it needs to be the responsibility of the state versus private entities in the market. Finally, in times of serial crises—no longer Black Swan events but almost like the regular and natural rise and fall of tides—reforms that hold the economy together are falling back on the state. Experts may call it a solution to 'market failure', but from China to the US the greater involvement of the public sector and the government in economic affairs is there for all to see.

The osmosis of political ambitions with the economy makes these seemingly innocent, even logical, interventions part of the grand strategies of nations that aspire for regional or global hegemony—the US, the former Soviet Union, and now China. Defining a reform, therefore, is as much an expression of domestic economic systems as it is of geopolitical outreach. Why, for instance, Scandinavian socialism is celebrated and its 'welfare state' aspired for within democratic moorings, but Soviet or Chinese socialism condemned because of their authoritarian stance, remains a question that can be answered only politically, not economically.

We get some clarity on the matter only when we view it through the prism of power, particularly against the rise of China. Thus far, economic reforms have mainly been conceptualized and pushed through by the US. Their export, through Bretton Woods institutions such as the IMF and the World Bank, by placing harsh conditionalities on developing economies, has been the driving force, the power behind the reform idea. Now that China is emerging as a successful alternative, both in terms of high growth performance, poverty reduction and technological prowess, as well as in the manner in which it is exporting this model, through its aggressive Belt and Road Initiative (BRI), the contestations of the idea of what constitutes economic reforms is gathering currency, particularly in Central Asia and parts of Europe.

Some academics with propagandist leanings term the BRI 'as a global ecosystem for long-term symbiosis'. Peter Ping Li:[24]

> The final point is that the notion of a 'second home' approach is salient in the three-stage pattern of BRI applicable to all the firms involved. First, both Chinese and European businesses must firmly establish themselves in each other's region as their second home with the status of local insider, rather than external intruder. Second, Chinese and European firms must establish themselves in the regions or countries along the BRI route in the same way. Third, all firms in the world in the future must firmly establish themselves in other regions in this manner. This is the *deep-level substance of BRI as a global ecosystem for long-term symbiosis.*

Others showcase the BRI as a journey of wild imagination, public relations and anti-India rhetoric masquerading as profound scholarship. Yiwei Wang:[25]

> Other places still live in darkness, like India; 300 million Indians suffer from shortage of electricity and live in darkness. India is the biggest democracy but a democracy in darkness, so how can the people access electricity to get industrialization? The Belt and Road Initiative wants to do that, and by following that, India will get access to the Internet.

Essentially, we return to the point made at the beginning of this chapter. Not the power of arguments, not the force of ideas, not the empirical evidence of facts and data—it is hard power and the success it crafts that has determined and continues to define reforms. When data is backed by good ideas, the venture can mushroom, lead to a soft power export, as countries embrace them. Further, if the data, in terms of GDP growth, poverty reduction or jobs created powers the idea, then countries must adopt it. In the rapidly contracting post-COVID world of today, there is much that India can take from these ideas, without being blinded by the contexts, while exporting its own success in tackling this Made in China pandemic.[26]

Stepping back from all these, we could also capture the reforms definition through the prism of aspirations and outcomes. Stuti Khemani:[27]

> 'Reform' from the perspective of economics refers to changes in government policies or institutional rules because status quo policies and institutions are not working well. Further, reforms refer to alternative policies and institutions that are available that would most likely perform better than the status quo to achieve economic goals. The main question examined in the political economy of reform literature has been why reforms are not undertaken when they are needed for the good of society.

We have seen this play out in India, as the country freed itself from the repressive clutches of ideas pushed through and absorbed whole by prime ministers Jawaharlal Nehru (See Chapters 6 and 7), Indira Gandhi (Chapters 8 and 10) and then Rajiv Gandhi, and began to breathe the fresh air of economic freedom with prime ministers P.V Narasimha Rao (Chapter 12), Atal Bihari Vajpayee, Manmohan Singh and Narendra Modi. Rao opened the gates of growth, Atal Bihari Vajpayee sailed several ships through it, Manmohan Singh managed to keep the direction of reforms but lost momentum, and incumbent Narendra Modi is now in reforms acceleration mode. The baton of reforms has passed through several leaders. The texture of reforms has changed. But the journey of reforms has continued.

From the Nehru–Gandhi economic approach of import substitution and commanding heights to Narendra Modi's idea of less government, more governance and Atmanirbhar Bharat, for instance—both functioning within the same democratic constraints—India's economic reforms have walked the thin line that allows and invites several contexts and ideas to merge. To that extent, the philosophy of economic reforms lies in engaging with poor outcomes and seeking change, not merely in inputs or strategies but equally as a function of aspirations of the people.

Through its various experiments, India has been both a consumer as well as a creator of economic reforms ideas. As it becomes the world's third-largest economy within this decade, its economic strength will give it the power needed to add its weight to the still-evolving theory of economic reforms, particularly for emerging, and poor- to middle-income democracies. And that's why, understanding the past thirty years of India's economic reforms is a crucial conversation for the world to witness, comprehend and learn from.

PART II

FROM REPRESSION TO REFORMS

3

How We Got Here
Eight Preludes to 1991

How a Wednesday became *the* Wednesday

In the 2008 Neeraj Pandey film, *A Wednesday*, a 'common man' (Naseeruddin Shah) chooses a Wednesday to threaten the city of Mumbai, pushing Police Commissioner Prakash Rathod (Anupam Kher) to launch a counter-operation. The film captures four hours of the day, between 2 and 6 p.m., during which a cat and mouse game between the common man and Rathod plays out. An engrossing and relevant film, it did well at the box office,[1] got 14 nominations,[2] and found resonance among film critics as well.

Seventeen years earlier, the announcement of the 1991 reforms had followed a similar script. There were two major announcements, both made on that Wednesday. The first at 12.50 p.m., the other at 5 p.m.—a gap of 4 hours and 10 minutes. If the 1991 reforms were a film, and evaluated as one, it is India's biggest policy box office hit on every parameter, from economic growth to markets to poverty reduction. It is equally the most lauded policy among observers.

If India's economic reforms had a single and defining timestamp, a dull and boring, mid-week day (a Wednesday) on the 24 July 1991 would be it. The two policy documents released on this day have changed the face of India, placed it on an alternative political trajectory, and created the foundations of an economically strong and globally powerful nation. While the 1991 policies were a packaging of priorities that attempted to fix a faltering economy teetering on the edge of default, we need to give Prime Minister P.V. Narasimha Rao credit for the courage to go through with reforms. Above all, Rao deserves praise for choosing Manmohan Singh as finance minister and giving him the freedom to articulate the policies and stand as the face of those reforms.

Reaching that Wednesday was not an easy task. It took forty-four years, eleven prime ministers, and eight industrial policies to get there. In between, there were several obstacles, from ideologies to politics, both resonating with and influencing the aspirations and philosophies of the time. Examining them with the power of a 20/20 hindsight, the resulting policies were a bunch of complex, confused and counterproductive grand treatises resting on the mantle of 'public good' but driving private interests, in the political and the business spaces.

In the run-up to and since Independence there have been eight major attempts at changing the direction of the Indian economy. Most scholars have examined the Big 5—the Resolution of 1948 (See Chapter 6), the Industrial Policy Resolution of 1956 (Chapter 7), the Industrial Policy of 1973 (Chapter 8), the Industrial Policy of 1977 (Chapter 9), and Statement on Industrial Policy of 1980 (Chapter 10). Few have explored the Industrial Policy Statement of 1990 (Chapter 11). Apart from government policies, there was one bold, and perhaps the only since, statement from private visionaries, popularly called the Bombay Plan of 1944 and 1945 (Chapter 4), parts of which have infused intellectual vigour into India's economic discourse. Finally, three years before Independence, there was the Statement on Industrial Policy 1945 (Chapter 5).

This part examines these eight preludes to that nation-changing Wednesday of 1991.

4

Prelude 1:
The Bombay Plan: 1944–1945

Four years before independent India's first government officially released the country's first economic direction, a group of private individuals with experience in running large corporations, working with the government and having a stake in India's growth envisioned a plan for prosperity. Popularly known as the Bombay Plan, this is the first document that captured the contours of the economic journey of India. The plan failed to take off in the manner it was envisaged. It was rejected by the political economy of the day. But its influence ran deep into the planning process of India.

Authored by Purshotamdas Thakurdas,[1] J.R.D. Tata,[2] G.D. Birla,[3] Ardeshir Dalal, Shri Ram,[4] Kasturbhai Lalbhai, A.D. Shroff[5] and John Mathai, the document known as the Bombay Plan is officially titled 'Memorandum Outlining a Plan of Economic Development of India'.[6] These magnificent seven authors had rich credentials, both in terms of what they had achieved and the legacies they had inherited.

Thakurdas was president of the East India Cotton Association, a director of the Reserve Bank of India, and ran several organizations as chairman and/or director. Tata was the head of the Tata Group, while Dalal, Shroff and Mathai headed various companies of the Tata Group. Dalal, an Indian Administrative Service officer, was in charge of Tata Iron and Steel Co. Ltd (TISCO); Shroff was the head of Investment Corporation of India and Tata Oil Mills; and Matthai led Tata Chemicals, was vice chairman of TISCO and Tata Engineering and Locomotive Company (now renamed Tata Motors), the first president of NCAER, and had served the government as minister of railways, commerce and industry, and finance. Birla headed the Birla Group, then known as Birla Brothers; Shri Ram was the chairman of DCM Group and the director of the RBI; and Lalbhai was a textile manufacturer and another director of the RBI.

Despite the rich historicity of the document and the importance the ideas hold even today, the Bombay Plan is not easily available. The research effort undertaken to procure this document was way beyond necessary, becoming almost an information-seeking adventure. I finally found it in a book published by Penguin. I faced this challenge while seeking the 1945 policy (See Chapter 5), the 1990 policy (See Chapter 11) and across several policy-pages while writing an earlier book.[7] Documents like these must be easily accessible to a lay person and scholars alike. This is a perennial problem and needs to be fixed; I seek the indulgence of our leaders to make good this information shortfall.

The Bombay Plan was uncovered in two parts. The first part placed the context and laid emphasis on production, growth and finance, and was drafted in January 1944. The second part examined redistribution, the state and economic organization and was published in January 1945. In other words, the first looked at wealth creation, the second at wealth redistribution. Between the two, Dalal was appointed Member for Planning and Development in the Government of India; the second part, therefore, is authored by the same group but without Dalal.

Part I had 99 sections, divided into five parts—Introductory had eight sections; Requirements of a Minimum Standard twenty-six; Economic Plan Explained forty-three; Sources of Finance eleven; and

Stages of Development eleven.[8] Part II had forty-eight sections, divided into three parts—Introductory had three sections; Distribution of the National Income thirty; and the State and Economic Organization fifteen.[9]

The micro-detailing in the Bombay Plan combined with a macro-direction of the economy may sound perplexing. How, for instance, could India's biggest industrialists and their seniormost executives demand an overarching role of the state in economic affairs? Or, being wealthy, how could they seek greater taxes on the rich? Or, talk about inequality?

The answer leads us to three speculations. First, the dominant thought at the time was to step away from the UK model; socialism as the other end of the spectrum was a ready alternative. The economy functioning within this model was, therefore, an ideological shift. Second, for countries either getting out of World War II or becoming newly independent nations, private enterprises did not have the resources, financial or operational, to negotiate the future. As a result, the role of the state as the driver of the economy gained currency. And third, the profit motive alone may not have guided these corporate leaders in public policy intersections. To view them through the limiting lens of vested interests would be an error. They were as patriotic and cared as much for the Indian economy and nation building as politicians and civil servants did, even if the lack of conflict of interest makes us have more confidence in the latter than the former. Seventy-seven years later, this faith and faithlessness is a disease that continues to plague the Indian mind.

If the authorship of the Bombay Plan was not known, it could be a document drafted by a statist government official. Some basic pointers as to what it contained include:

- Double India's per capita income in fifteen years. Keeping population growth in mind, this would mean trebling the national income in the same period.[10] In 1944, a minimum standard of living entailed a per capita income of Rs 74, against the reported per capita income of Rs 65. 'It is, therefore, necessary to increase our national income above the present level by a substantial margin even if we aim at nothing more than to secure for our people their bare requirements as human beings.'[11]

- A minimum standard of living that would include food, clothing and shelter on the basic side and provisions for medical relief and education on the other.[12] Under education, the document delves deep and breaks it down to primary education,[13] adult education,[14] secondary education,[15] university and technical education, and scientific education and research.[16] Preventive healthcare, including vaccinations and sanitation.[17]
- Classify industries into two—basic industries and consumption goods industries.[18] Basic industries would include power (electricity); mining and metallurgy (iron and steel, aluminium, manganese); engineering (machinery of all kinds, machine tools); chemicals (heavy chemicals, fertilizers, dyes, plastics, pharmaceuticals); armaments; transport (railway engines and wagons, shipbuilding, automobiles, aircraft); and cement.[19] And consumption goods would include, among others, textiles (cotton, silk and wool); glass; leather goods; paper; tobacco; and oil.[20]
- The idea of small-scale industry got seeded in the document as an employment generator and scarce capital meant for basic industries. But the authors conceded that it would be difficult to define which industries to place where.[21]
- It proposed agriculture reforms with the objective to increase agricultural production by 130 per cent, readjust the cultivation of different crops to feed the nation,[22] and intensify farming through the instrument of cooperative farming, which increases output and yield per acre[23] without compromising ownership.[24] Irrigation,[25] model farms[26] and capital for agriculture were the other reforms the document proposed.[27]
- It had detailed designs for transport and communications, from railways[28] and roads[29] to shipping[30] and their costs.[31]

- The entire section on sources of finance gives us, twenty-first century readers in an independent India, a deep insight into the state of the economy in the run-up to Independence.[32]
- The foundations of this framework were change with stability. It laid the groundwork for free enterprise but 'enterprise which is truly enterprising and not a mere cloak for sluggish acquisitiveness. It must ensure at the same time that the fruits of enterprise and labour are fairly apportioned among all who contribute to them and not unjustly withheld by a few from the many.' The production push discussed in Part I, therefore, would be 'meaningless unless it is directed towards the eradication of poverty'.[33]
- It saw economic equality as a tool for growth: 'The large increase in production which is postulated in the plan will be difficult to achieve if the present disparities in income are allowed to persist. To this extent, therefore, equitable distribution is necessarily implied in a plan for increased production. A policy which specifically aims at securing this object should have a double purpose: i) to secure to everybody a minimum income essential for a reasonable standard of living and (ii) to prevent gross inequalities in the incomes of different classes and individuals.'[34]
- In the context of inequality and its reduction, the Bombay Plan sowed the seeds for industry to be dominated by the public sector: 'Control by the State, accompanied in appropriate cases by State ownership or management of public utilities, basic industries, etc., will also tend to diminish inequalities of income.'[35]
- But it did not completely do away with private initiative. It said that a complete abolition of inequality would not be in the interest of the country. 'Subject to the provision of a basic minimum, it is desirable to leave enough scope for variations in income according to ability and productivity.'[36]
- In terms of incentives and rewards to the three factors of production—labour, land and capital that yield wages, interest and profits—the Bombay Plan proffered a strange and confused

mix. This lack of clarity is telling in a document that was otherwise very clear about the direction of India. 'As a general rule, these rewards, viz. wages, interest and profits, should continue to be determined on the basis of demand and efficiency as at present, subject to the overriding consideration that wages should not fall below a certain minimum and that interest rates should be controlled with a view to maintaining full employment. Profits should be kept within limits through fixation of prices, restriction of dividends, taxation, etc. But care should be taken to leave sufficient incentive for improvement in efficiency and expansion of production.'[37]

- The reason for this confusion could be that Part II of the Bombay Plan was focused on redistribution and welfare. The measures to increase the general level of income that followed need to be seen in this perspective. It had a fivefold path—provision of full employment; increase in efficiency; improvement in urban and rural wages; security of agricultural prices and development of multi-purpose cooperative societies; and reform of the land system.[38]
- It is here that the idea of a minimum wage was planted in the Indian economy. The document not only sought a physical minimum wage; it equally focused on the process of devising an industry-specific minimum wage through a Standing Committee for each industry, comprising representatives of employers and workers and a few independent persons.
- The memorandum recommended that a planned movement of the economy was necessary, and state intervention was inherent in planning. But it rejected the idea that planning necessarily has to be done in a non-democratic manner, as in Soviet Russia and Germany. 'If democracies can successfully plan and organize their resources for waging wars,' the Plan argued resolutely, 'it stands to reason that they can do so equally for fighting social evils such as poverty, disease and ignorance.'[39]

- It argued for a balance between individual economic freedom on the one side and state intervention to prevent abuse of that freedom on the other. 'We believe that capitalism, in so far as it affords scope for individual enterprise and the exercise of individual initiative, has a very important contribution to make to the economic development of India. We believe at the same time that unless the community is endowed with powers for restraining the activities of individuals seeking their own aggrandizement regardless of public welfare and for promoting the main objectives of economic progress, no plan of economic development will succeed in raising the general standard of living or promoting the common good.'[40]
- The role of the state would centre around ownership, control and management of economic enterprises; this laid the foundations for a large public sector in India. Of these, the Plan laid the highest emphasis on control; that is, even private enterprises should play a role in delivering social welfare. 'A widening of the economic functions of the State in these directions is advocated on the ground that unrestricted private enterprise under the capitalistic system of production has not served the interests of consumers and of the community generally as satisfactorily as it should have.'[41]
- This control would be exercised over all aspects of economic activity—production, distribution, consumption, investment, foreign trade and exchange, and wages and working conditions. That these were, and still are, happily embraced by the state and the resultant economic laws that have been drafted on the basis of 'state control' shows how strong this economic idea was to India's politics.[42]

The two parts of the Bombay Plan seem to have been authored by almost two different minds. Part I focuses on production; Part II on redistribution. Part I leans towards incentives, freedom and capitalism; Part II seems to be weighed down by lofty, noble and blinkered socialist objectives. Part I is clear; Part II is fuzzy. Could the missing link in Part II be Ardeshir Dalal, who, in the interim, had been appointed as member for Planning and Development in the Government of India? We will never know. Effectively, like the Indian state over the past seventy-five years, the framework of the Bombay Plan envisioned the country as a mixed economy and influenced serial prime ministers to set their political economy agendas.

Some insights from the Bombay Plan remain relevant. The moral and practical equation between finance and what it can do, for instance. (Wall Street could take some lessons here.)[43]

> It is necessary to emphasize that in a planned economy we are primarily thinking in terms of commodities and services. Money or finance is therefore completely subservient to the requirements of the economy as a whole and must be treated merely as a means of mobilizing the internal resources of the country in material man-power.

Or, take the issue of inequality. Writing in 1944, the authors of the Bombay Plan were conversant with the importance and implications of the idea, an issue the world is examining closely and grappling with in 2022:[44]

> The per capita average itself varies from Rs 51 (£3:16:6) to Rs 166 (£12:9s.) in rural and urban areas respectively. In 1931–32 one-half of the total urban income was in the hands of less than 10 per cent of urban workers and 'even among the comparatively well-to-do class, whose annual incomes exceed Rs 2,000 (£150) a year, 38 per cent of their number could claim only 17 per cent of their total income, while a little more than 1 per cent were in possession of as much as 10 per cent of their total income'. In rural areas, the income of the majority of the people must have been less than the average of Rs 51 (£3:16:6). This is because farmers holding less than 2 acres of land form a large proportion of the cultivating class. Moreover, the agricultural labourer,

> whose wage is sometimes as low as 2 to 3 annas (2d. to 3d.) a day, and the cultivator, are generally without any work for 3 to 6 months in the year. The increase in population since 1931 must have considerably increased the pressure on this class.

Another debate that India is engaging with in 2022, and which had been discussed in the Bombay Plan, is the one around the increase in direct taxation. Despite the authors being beneficiaries of wealth, inherited or earned, Section 31 (Taxation of Income) of the document highlighted two controversial and counterintuitive issues—higher direct taxes, and taxes on inheritances:[45]

> Further, in the taxation of personal incomes, distinction should be made between earned and unearned income, so as to make the latter taxable at a higher rate. As a means of correcting the existing inequalities of wealth, the device of death duties, which has been successfully utilized in other countries, might also be adopted. The advisability of taxing inherited estates more severely at the second and later transfers than at the first would be a further step in the same direction. It is obvious that India's fiscal system will have to place more and more reliance on direct taxation in future if the increase in the cost of administration which planning will involve is to be met and if provision is to be made for free social services like education, medical treatment, etc., and subsidies for essential utility services.

But simultaneously, the Bombay Plan also sought a higher accountability of the high taxes from the government in Section 33 (Conditions for Heavy Taxation):[46]

> Taxation on the scale we have proposed will place a very heavy burden on the country and will be justified only if its utilization for the purposes for which it is intended is fully guaranteed by

> a national government responsible to the people of the country. It is necessary to emphasize this fact because, as experience has often shown in the past, it is a dangerous thing to vest large powers of taxation in a foreign government bred in traditions of imperialistic exploitation. Both our plan of development and our proposals for meeting its cost imply the existence of a responsible national government as an essential condition.

Despite a vision that leaned on the people and private initiative, the Bombay Plan canvassed for controls. These were selectively and enthusiastically accepted by the government in 1956. Section 46 talks about six kinds of control—production, distribution, consumption, investment, foreign trade and exchange, and wages and working conditions. A student of India's economic history can see several strands of law and regulations that have Section 46 of the Bombay Plan as its roots. These include but are not restricted to the Controller of Capital Issues, 1947, the Minimum Wages Act, 1948, or the Factories Act, 1948. Its reverberations went on till the Essential Commodities Act, 1955, Monopolies and Restrictive Trade Practices Act, 1969, and the Foreign Exchange Regulation Act, 1973.

The authors of the Bombay Plan may not have received their due credit from the Nehru government. But the public was struck by the vision. Frank Moraes:[47]

> So widespread was the public interest stirred by the initiative of these private planners that for a while New Delhi tried to delay publication of their report in an attempt to steal their thunder. Despite this the sponsors succeeded in releasing the plan at an appropriate time and the report attracted considerable attention and aroused controversy shared strangely by the conservative British Government on the one hand and the extreme left-wing elements on the other.

What went on in the minds of the authors of the Bombay Plan? Clearly, they looked at the country ground up. Poverty was so rampant in India and the condition of the nation so abject that no decision-maker or influencer could look away. Having worked closely with Mohandas Karamchand Gandhi, the influence of poverty and its alleviation impacted G.D. Birla and found reflection in the document. In his 4 March 1944 speech on Part I of the document at the annual session of the Federation of Indian Chambers of Commerce and Industry, he expounded on India's poverty malaise. G.D. Birla:[48]

> The poverty of India is proverbial. The people have got neither sufficient food to eat nor sufficient cloth to wear nor adequate accommodation to live in. They are half-starved, ill-clothed and living the life virtually of a dog or a cat. In education they are most backward. The health of the people is extremely poor. Mortality rate is extremely high. Out of every 1,000 children born, 167 are dead before they achieve the age of one year. The average income of an Indian is Rs 65 against Rs 980 for an Englishman. The expense of an average Englishman on cigarettes alone is as much as the total yearly income of an average Indian.

Taking inputs from the country's poorest and carting it to the highest echelons of India's planning fraternity, the Bombay Plan influenced the creation of the Planning Commission. Former Governor of the Reserve Bank of India and civil servant H.V.R. Iengar:[49]

> Indeed, there seems little difference between the basic approach of the Bombay Plan and the approach of the Planning Commission of the Government of India and it would by no means be far-fetched to say that the Planning Commission actually got its inspiration from the Bombay plan. And the interesting point is that A.D. Shroff accepted this approach in 1944 and was, indeed, one of its principal proponents.

The Bombay Plan also influenced the First Five Year Plan. The more the politics of the day consolidated itself around a mirage called socialism and redistribution—two themes the document explored and exhorted—the lesser became the space for private partnership in the growth of the nation. Medha Kudaisya:[50]

> However, while the first Five-Year Plan in form seems similar to the Bombay Plan, it ran contrary to the spirit of the Bombay Plan, which lay in the idea of a partnership between state and business. As the Nehruvian regime secured political legitimacy through the national elections of 1952 and 1957, the autarchic features of economic policy-making became more pronounced. Private enterprise became increasingly wary and defensive, no longer looked upon by the state as stakeholders in nation-building. The promise of partnership receded, only to see a revival in 1990s post-liberalization, when India faced the overwhelming challenges of integration into the global economy.

Sixty years after the Bombay Plan was published, a future prime minister of India would laud its vision. As finance minister during India's economic reforms, this particular prime minister gave India the key to open up, liberalize and push economic growth. That prime minister was Manmohan Singh:[51]

> As a student of economics in the 1950s and later as a practitioner in government, I was greatly impressed by the 'Bombay Plan' of 1944. In the conceptualization of this document, JRD [Tata] played an important role, along with G.D. Birla, Purushottamdas Thakurdas, Ardeshir Dalal and John Mathai. When we read it today, nearly 60 years later, we see how relevant many of the central propositions of the Bombay Plan remain. In those days, it was an unprecedented document. It is worthy of emphasis that nowhere in the developing world had a group of businessmen come together to draw up such a long-term plan for a country.

> The Bombay Plan laid great emphasis on public investment in social and economic infrastructure, in both rural and urban areas, it emphasized the importance of agrarian reform and agricultural research, in setting up educational institutions and a modern financial system. Above all, it defined the framework for India's transition from agrarian feudalism to industrial capitalism, but capitalism that is humane, that invests in the welfare and skills of the working people. In many ways, it encapsulated what all subsequent Plans have tried to achieve.

But why this 60-year-long gap between the publishing of the plan and granting it credit? Neither the government nor political parties—not even the business fraternity—pushed for the implementation of the plan. Amal Sanyal gives us four reasons for it, of which two are key—the approach of the Indian National Congress and the Left parties.[52]

First, the Left parties of India claimed the plan was irrelevant to the people because it did not address redistribution. The criticism seems ideological rather than factual because even after Part II of the plan was published, the Left parties refused to change their stance. Labelling it 'a blueprint for building capitalism with the aid of the state', the Left simply ignored Part II, where all its concerns were addressed.

And second, the Indian National Congress and the government pretended the plan did not exist. 'Like the communists, Congress too was in a position from where they could neither accept the Plan nor reject it. To be seen as toeing the line of big industrial houses at this point would seriously damage its claims at home and abroad. Congress was therefore in no position to acclaim the Plan.' The ideas of wealth and business had been debased. As a result, 'the closeness of Mr. Birla to Mahatma Gandhi and a faction of Congress remained a point of embarrassment and a reminder that the party was close to industry and business. Congress as a party would like to wipe out these sources of embarrassment and distance itself from the Plan and its authors'.[53] We will get a glimpse of this struggle in 1991 as well.

Such was the hostility to the Bombay Plan that in a 12 August 1944 letter, G.D. Birla wrote to J.R.D. Tata expressing his disappointment:[54]

> I wonder if you agree with me regarding that the real hostility is not against the plan so much, but against the businessman in general. The main target of attack is the businessman and the critics treat yourself and myself as a symbol of the business community. The Communists, the Socialists, the British vested interest and our own Government all seem to be on common ground ... There is as it were a plan to discredit businessmen. Their patriotism, integrity and good motives are questioned. People are told that schemes for more Tatanagars and Birlanagars are afoot. First iconoclasm and then the next step, that is the technique of these critics. We should, therefore, tackle the root cause and not merely beat about the branches and bushes.

There was also an element of colonial politics in taking the steam out of the Bombay Plan. Dalal's appointment as Member of Planning and Reconstruction of the Viceroy's Executive Council was not an innocent choice. It was done 'to take the wind out of the sails of the planners'.[55] But Dalal wouldn't play the game and resigned within a year of his appointment. Dietmar Rothermund:[56]

> The immediate cause of his resignation was an unsuccessful mission to London, where he had pleaded for British aid to Indian industry. Dalal insisted that such aid should be given only to purely Indian companies and not to British companies operating in India. The British government stated that it was unable to discriminate against British firms that had got themselves registered in India in order to benefit from the protective tariffs granted to India in the 1930s. These firms had seen to it that their rights were enshrined in the Government of India Act of 1935, and thus the government was indeed handicapped in this respect. This proved to the Indian capitalists once more that their only

> hope was an independent government of India, as the British were pledged to uphold British interests. When Dalal saw that by remaining a member of the Viceroy's council he would only provide an alibi to these British interests without being able to do anything, he decided to quit.

Other objections to the plan rode the political-ideological wave. Reading the anti-business climate that was slowly but surely emerging in India, even the business community did not lend support to the plan. But frustration and a sense of loss was in the air. 'The British have gone and the princes and the zamindars are in the background,' wrote G.D. Birla to Home Minister Govind Ballabh Pant, in an October 1948 letter, four years after the Bombay Plan was released. 'The Congress accustomed to a target for its hatred, is now finding only one target, that is the capitalist.'[57] Sanyal:[58]

> Bombay Plan was forgotten not because it was worthless or faulty or lacked vision. It was dropped out of memory for strategic reasons. Not mentioning it was the best strategy in the fifties for all the important players.

Those strategic reasons were really political and ideological. India's downward economic journey since then can be and must be pinned to the politics of poverty that began here. Unfortunately, despite more than seven decades behind this unfortunate turn of India's consciousness against business and wealth, the remnants of this disease linger on.

5

Prelude 2: Statement of Industrial Policy 1945

Following the Bombay Plan and in the run-up to Independence, the government proposed a policy that attempted to give India a direction for industrialization. This Statement of Industrial Policy 1945,[1] along with the Bombay Plan, can be seen as the intellectual foundations of several future industrial policies. At some points, the 1945 industrial policy is in tune with the Bombay Plan, at other points, it steers away; but all through it remains a precursor to future industrial policies.

Over the years, several ideas on the roles of the state and the private sector for industrial development merged into one another. It is almost as if there was a dominant thought across the post-war world into which India was embedded. And this 21 April 1945 statement was one such step in the evolution of India's industrial policy.

Like the Bombay Plan, this document too is difficult to find. It does not exist in the archives of the Indian government. The search for this document led me to several black holes of research. The one door that finally opened and presented this policy was Appendix I in Sharad S. Marathe's 1986 book, *Regulation and Development: The Indian Policy Experience of Controls Over Industry*. Thirty-five years ago, Marathe had faced the same challenge: 'The text of Statement of Government's Industrial Policy is now not readily available and is, therefore, reproduced in Appendix I at the end.'[2] The other place where this policy has been reproduced is a PhD thesis by Raghabendra Chattopadhyay, in Appendix III.[3]

While we are grateful to Marathe and Chattopadhyay for having the foresight to print the document, the callousness with which successive governments of India have handled and continue to manage information remains a frustrating experience for researchers. The 1945 policy, for instance, is part of 'Planning and Development Department', the intellectual inheritance of which must surely exist in some file, in some vault tightly guarded by some government bureaucrat.

The ideas contained in the 1945 Industrial Policy, framed two years before Independence, were experimented with in the 1948 Policy (See Chapter 6) and solidified in the 1956 Policy (Chapter 7). Thus, not just the Bombay Plan (Chapter 4), even the 1945 Policy found expression in the containment of Indian business and wealth creation. This underlying, outdated and counterproductive political psychology continues to putrefy in the minds of several policymakers in 2022. The 1945 Policy found itself tuned to international post-war economic thought of reconstruction, coordinated development of large industries, dominance of the state and licensing as a tool for that control, which in turn, due to the powers imparted to them, laid the foundations of a rent-seeking bureaucracy.

The Statement of Industrial Policy 1945 was the first time that the federal government (broadly equivalent to the Union government of today) intruded into the mandate of provincial governments (broadly, the state governments). As per the structure of the Government of India Act, 1935, industry and commerce were the domain of provinces.[4] But the Act also had a provision that enabled the development of certain industries by the federal government. 'No such Act has, in fact, been passed by the Central Legislature with the consequences that the development of industries is at the moment wholly a provincial subject,' the 1945 Policy stated, right at the outset.[5] The Policy took time to explain this intrusion and gave two reasons. Sharad S. Marathe:[6]

> In the first place, the general economic policy pursued by the Government of India under their own constitutional powers exercises a profound influence over industrial development. It is a matter of history, for example, that the cotton textile, the iron and steel and the sugar industries have made rapid strides in India largely as a result of the fiscal policy pursued by the Central Government. In the second place, the progress of planning has made it abundantly clear that certain industries must be taken over under Central control in the interests of co-ordinated development.

The intrusion justified and institutionalized, the Policy listed twenty industries that would be centralized, subject to consultations with 'the Provinces and leading Indian States'. These included iron and steel, automobiles and tractors, heavy machinery, cement, electric power and coal. See the full list here.[7] The thrust was clear. These were either infrastructure industries or those that needed large capital outlays or 'of vital importance to the country's development'. The participation of the state in business had already begun with railways, public utilities and ordnance factories being largely state owned and state managed. This list expanded the scope of industries where the government would play a larger role.

Nationalization, that pretence of a policy solution for all ills in the 1950s to 1980s, was born in this 1945 Policy. It exerted itself first in 1953 with the nationalization of Air India and eight other airlines.[8] It then followed through with nationalizations of life insurance in 1956;[9] banks in 1969 and 1980;[10] coal mines in 1971, 1972, 1973 and 1974;[11] general insurance in 1972;[12] textile mills in 1974;[13] and Maruti Udyog in 1980.[14] 'It is contemplated also that Government may take over certain industries in which the tax element is much more predominating than the profit element and it is necessary and convenient for the State to take over the industry,' the Policy stated, citing salt manufacturing as an example.[15]

'All other industries will be left to private enterprise under varying degrees of control.' These controls would be fair conditions for labour, free competition, and stricter controls for industries of a 'semi-monopolistic nature'.

The other side of the state control of industries was the state support to industries. This came by way of the development of transport facilities, power, mineral resources, scientific and industrial research, and technical education and skilling; the sixth was financial support.

The government, the Policy stated, would either give loans or subscribe to share capital in industries considered important to the country's development. In turn, the government sought representation on the board, and whose sanction would be important for 'incurring certain types of expenditure and for certain appointments'.[16]

Other than debt or equity, the Policy also provisioned 'guaranteeing a minimum dividend on capital or undertaking to meet revenue losses for a fixed number of years, subject to the condition that Government would have a voice in the management and that a ceiling will be fixed for the return on capital'. Further, the government would encourage industry by 'buying its products in preference to others'.[17]

The approach to tax in the Policy was balanced—it proposed to secure social justice and national budgetary interests on the one side, while ensuring that the tax doesn't become a deterrent before development.[18]

The role of the state in the 1945 Policy didn't stop at controls or finance. The government, it said, would give 'adequate financial support to research organizations set up by Industrial Associations representing organized industries' and provide research grants to universities.[19] It also assured expertise to industry.[20]

As far as procurement of capital goods by industrialists was concerned, the Policy proposed to set up an organization in the UK and in the US, thereby controlling vital equipment sales from those countries to India,[21] and ensuring economic imperialism when political imperialism was ending. Geoeconomics was thriving in this industrial policy—of course, no surprises there.

Further, the Policy suggested that three things would ensure the economic recovery of post-war India and set out to enable them. First, a focus on expanding the economy by the maximum exploitation of the country's resources. Second, a strategic emphasis to make the country better prepared for defence. And third, a high and stable level of employment. The Policy also took an ideological U-turn on how to look at wealth by focusing on socially equitable redistribution. In tune with the reconstruction efforts of the post-war West, the Policy formally shifted from laissez-faire towards a regulated economy:[22]

> The attitude of Government towards industry in the past was, for many years, one of laissez faire. Till the war of 1914–19 this policy was maintained in the belief, which was in accordance with the current economic doctrine, that industrial progress was best achieved by unregulated private enterprise. This attitude underwent some modification after the last war through the adoption of the policy of discriminating protection.[23]

The most dominating shadow of regulation was licences. The government concluded and the Policy conferred powers to grant licences to industry.[24]

> They [the government] have [at] present no power except for emergency wartime controls, to regulate the growth of industry; normally a person may set up a factory wherever he likes and may manufacture in it whatever commodity he chooses. One effect of this unregulated freedom to promote industrial enterprise has been the concentration of industry in certain areas, for instance, the manufacture of cotton textiles has been concentrated in Bombay and Ahmedabad; sugar in the United Provinces and Bihar; paper in Bengal.

The policy effort to fix the geographical concentration of industries was driven by the spectre of war and ideated by strategy. 'It seems unsound from the strategic point of view that so large a proportion of industry should be concentrated in a few cities which might well be vulnerable to attack.'[25]

Other reasons for deconcentrating industries included 'housing problems', creating a geographically diversified economy, and some anti-freedom gobbledygook: 'Even where concentration appears relatively cheap on the basis of financial costs of production and distribution, it would, in many cases, be found in the long run, both socially and economically cheaper to disperse industry, if regard is paid to the benefits of a widely spread industrial structure and its integration with agriculture.' Figure that out.

But in terms of incentives, worse was still to come. Not only did the government want to control licences, geographies or industries, it turned incentives that drove entrepreneurs into an ethical-moral chokehold that trickled down into future policies, notably the ones drafted in 1948, 1956, 1973, 1977, 1980 and 1990. Although the policy of 1991 did attempt to break this hold, the damage created in 1945 continues to dog India's political economy even today. This one section captures all future anti-profit, anti-wealth streams that place moral control and public interest over economic freedom and entrepreneurial ingenuity:[26]

> Control over development would be necessary from another point of view. In an unregulated industrial economy there is likely to be a tendency for capitalists to go in for schemes which promise quick returns. This will lead to lopsided development—a scramble for some industries, with the danger of overproduction and excessive competition and inadequate attention to other industries which are equally necessary in the national interest. To overcome this difficulty, it would be necessary to fix targets, to allocate them on a regional basis, and to see that these targets are achieved.

Imported from the moral hollowness and economic debris of World War II reconstruction and the rise of socialism in its aftermath, the planned economy began to settle down in and infect India. Atop its licensing drive, the 1945 Policy added objectives that pushed for state intervention in six areas. First, in securing balanced investment in industry, agriculture and social services; second, in securing a fair wage, decent working conditions and security of tenure for industrial workers; third, in preventing 'excessive profits to private capital'; fourth, in the standardization of quality; fifth, in preventing the 'unhealthy concentration of assets in the hands of a few persons or of a special community'; and sixth, in technical training and extending the benefits of such training to minorities and backward communities.[27]

Like the Bombay Plan, the Statement of Industrial Policy 1945 could not move forward. 'Since the said policy was drafted in haste so it could not satisfy the new leaders of independent country,' write Babita Thakur, Rozika Gupta, and Rajesh Singh.[28] 'All the scanty efforts made by the British Government to develop industry in the country took [a] back seat, and [a] new revolution in industry was sought by the planners.' Announced three years prior to Independence, this policy was politically doomed right in the beginning—no political party would openly accept a colonial inheritance of economic policy.

Although the authorship of the policy has been granted to the Planning and Development Department, there are speculations about its link with the Bombay Plan. H.K. Paranjape:[29]

> A clearer indication of the consensus in the matter of future economic policy is provided by the Statement of Industrial Policy issued by the Government of India in April 1945 when Sir Ardeshir Dalal, who obviously represented Indian business interests, was in charge of development planning in the Government of India. Many of the important points in the post-Independence industrial policy are to be found in this Statement which was obviously endorsed—or at least not objected to—by the British rulers.

Whether that link is causal or correlational, we will never know. What we do have is a fair idea of the time, the geography and the politics. Here's a sample of the economic objectives laid down by countries in the same space, around the same time (all countries named as in the United Nations report):[30]

Burma: Increase public wealth, improve material conditions of the people, raise their cultural level, consolidate the independence of the Union, and strengthen its defensive capacity. Lay the foundations of a balanced economy and increase national wealth in a manner which will secure for the villager a higher standard of living and create an economy which will ensure that a fair share of the fruits passes on to the common man.

Ceylon, Malaya, and British Borneo: Increase economic stability by reducing their precarious dependence upon factors outside their control, and broaden and diversify the economies.

China: Improve people's livelihood and bring about a balanced, equitable and democratic economy.

India: Raise the standard of living of the people by increasing production by all possible means side by side with measures to secure equitable distribution.

Indonesia: Improve living standards, social justice and a balanced economy.

Pakistan: Improve standard of living of the people by harnessing the forces and treasures of nature in the service of the people, provide gainful and legitimate employment, and assure freedom from want, equality of opportunity, dignity of labour and a more equitable distribution of wealth. Formulate industrial policy to ensure the building up of a sound and healthy economy.

The Philippines: Extensively develop the country's resources, structural adjustment to free the national economy from too

> great a dependence on a few export crops, fortify it better against the severe fluctuations in demand and prices of these crops in the foreign markets by increasing the local production of foodstuffs.

There are similarities as well as differences between each of the countries listed above. If India wanted to raise the standard of living, so did China, Pakistan, Indonesia and Burma. If Indonesia sought social justice, so did India, China and Pakistan. As far as differences or unique requirements went, each country had its own. The Philippines focused on agriculture, Pakistan on natural resources, Burma on raising cultural levels, and Ceylon, Malay, and British Borneo on reducing dependence on factors outside their control.

These are neither coincidences nor correlations nor causalities. They are part of a concerted action plan by what was known as the Economic Commission for Asia and the Far East (ECAFE), formed under the United Nations through a 28 March 1947 Resolution,[31] which twenty-seven years later morphed into the Economic and Social Commission for Asia and the Pacific.[32]

Twelve territories comprised the ECAFE. These were British North Borneo, Brunei and Sarawak, Burma, Ceylon, China, India, Indo-Chinese Federation, Hong Kong, Malayan Union and Singapore, Netherlands Indies, Philippine Republic, and Siam. The objective: economic reconstruction. India's 1945 Policy, therefore, was not merely the Indian state taking charge of its economic affairs, it was a coordinated strategy in the area, and was as much a product of the time as of geography, politics—and almost as an afterthought, economics.

6

Prelude 3: Resolution 1948

In India's economic literature, there is no primary source document called the 'Industrial Policy Resolution of 1948'.[1] In the *Gazette of India*, under the Ministry of Industry and Supply, the policy is simply titled, 'Resolution'.[2] How this Resolution became the Industrial Policy Resolution 1948 is a mystery that perhaps a future scholar can investigate.

This investigation would be important not merely to correct the semantics of economic reforms; it will be an illustration of how even basic facts, upon which analyses, scholastic excursions and opinions rest, can be and often are incorrect. Over a period of time these attain scale and become a compounding of errors.

That said, like the Bombay Plan of 1944 and 1945, and the Statement of Industrial Policy, April 1945, this is a document that's almost impossible to find in the data mines of the government. If the objective was to distance the text and the ideas it contained from India's policymaking process, it has been a success. If the intention was to create an ideological divide between Prime Minister Jawaharlal Nehru and the large corporations in particular and business in general, hiding the document has turned into a resounding victory. Of course, these are speculations of a researcher, who neither has time-travel skills nor engages in historical psychology.

Signed by S.A. Venkataraman, Secretary, Ministry of Industry and Supply, the 6 April 1948 Resolution, in turn, drew inspiration and direction from the 1944 and 1945 Memorandum Outlining a Plan of Economic Development of India or what is informally and popularly known as the Bombay Plan (See Chapter 4), and the pre-Independence 1945 Statement of Industrial Policy (Chapter 5).

Planning the dominant economic fashion statement, government control its tool and curtailment of economic freedom its political expression, the 1948 Resolution followed the post-war reconstruction trends then prevalent in the West. With one difference: the economically developed West, as well as its political opponent, the Soviet Union, went about this government-led, government-driven, government-managed reconstruction on the strength of affordability, India from a position of poverty.

The average per capita income of India in the 1941 to 1949 period, using a centre ring of 1945, was estimated at between Rs 246 ($51.79) and Rs 274 ($57.68). The estimates were made by four economists. H.C. Arora and K.R.R. Iyengar (together) gave three estimates; K. Mukerji made two estimates; and S.J. Patel made one estimate.[3] The conversion rate has been taken as Rs 4.75 to the US dollar. According to Suphan Andic and Alan T. Peacock, India's per capita income in 1949 was $57.[4]

On the other hand, the per capita incomes in the West, against which India's economic policies were being benchmarked, were multiples of India's—at $124, Spain's per capita income was double that of India's, Italy's $235 was more than four times higher, France's $482 was 8.4 times higher, the UK's $773 was 13.5 times higher, and the per capita income of the US ($1,453) was 25.5 times higher.[5] The corresponding multiples today are worse—Spain's absolute per capita income is 14 times India's, Italy's 16 times, France's 20 times, the UK's 21 times and the US's 33 times. On a PPP basis the multiples range from 6 to 10.[6] Clearly, India's povertarian policies have made India relatively poorer.

Adopting a policy that mindlessly mimics economic giants, without the equivalent financial, institutional or human wherewithal to manage it, shows an acute lack of political and intellectual confidence on the part of India's leaders. It's like a weakling attempting to lift a mace, which would obviously crush the lifter. It could be forgiven then—it's a big jump from fighting for and getting political freedom to devising economic policies. Unfortunately, the copy-pasting of economic narratives set by the West and/or by the Soviet Union, which change every few decades as per their interests, continues to infect India even today.

It is against the backdrop of one such narrative—that there was a global shift away from laissez-faire to a more regulated architecture in order to heal post-war wounds, since arguably only the state could provide the healing needed—that India's first prime minister Jawaharlal Nehru introduced this Resolution in 1948. Of course, itchy fingers of new politicians and bureaucrats to grab control of every aspect of citizens' lives added to the administrative-economic excesses. Between the Resolution of 1948 and the Industrial Policy Resolution of 1956, the Union government pretty much established control over anything and everything that could be controlled or was worth controlling, leaving crumbs for private businesses.

Holy statements aside, Nehru's Resolution began with the role of the state as the central actor in the play of economic forces. The overall objectives were to increase national wealth and improve the economic conditions of the country in order to redistribute resources to the poor. Noble as these objectives may sound and virtuous their politics, the Resolution made a fatal error. It failed to recognize the role of the entrepreneur as a factor of production. The policy focussed on expansion of output, agricultural and industrial, but suffixed it with political rhetoric and granted the government undue control over economic freedom—even while recognizing its constraints:[7]

> There can be no doubt that the State must play a progressively active role in the development of industries, but [the] ability to achieve the main objectives should determine the immediate

> extent of State responsibility and the limit to private enterprise. Under present conditions, the mechanism and the resources of the State may not permit it to function forthwith in Industry as widely as may be desirable. The Government of India are taking steps to remedy the situation; in particular, they are considering steps to create a body of men trained in business methods and management. They feel, however, that for some time to come, the State could contribute more quickly to the increase of national wealth by expanding its present activities wherever it is already operating and by concentrating on new units of production in other fields, rather than on acquiring and running existing units. Meanwhile, private enterprise, properly directed and regulated, has a valuable role to play.

The one-page preamble containing three sections established the backdrop. From Section 4 onwards, the Resolution reimagined wealth creation in the newly-independent India in a manner that placed the state, within it the executive, and within the executive the Union government, at the core of economic activity and managing large enterprises. Overnight, political leaders and bureaucrats, whose role was to create a regulatory structure within which individuals could express themselves and grow, became managers of industries, with neither the experience, nor the knowledge, the ability, or the incentive to do so.

It is easy to understand the control of the Union government in sensitive areas. The troika of industries under the 'exclusive monopoly of the Central Government'—manufacture of arms and ammunition, the production and control of atomic energy, and the ownership and management of railway transport[8]—can be argued as strategic. But the policy took several other steps that put barriers to economic freedom.

The government, the Resolution stated, 'would always have the power to take over any industry vital for national defence'. Further, it identified six industries where the state, defined as 'Central, Provincial and State Governments and other Public Authorities like Municipal Corporations', will be exclusively responsible for the establishment of new undertakings. These were coal; iron and steel; aircraft manufacture; shipbuilding; manufacture of telephone, telegraph, wireless apparatus, excluding radio receiving sets; and mineral oils.

The 1948 Resolution raised the bogey of 'public interest' sky-high—and plunged economic freedom to depths unseen. A condescending tone set the pitch, almost as if the government was doing entrepreneurs and businesses a favour by nationalizing their companies after a ten-year gap and not immediately:[9]

> While the inherent right of the State to acquire any existing industrial undertaking will always remain, and will be exercised whenever the public interest requires it, Government have decided to let existing undertakings in these fields develop for a period of ten years, during which they will be allowed all facilities for efficient working and reasonable expansion. At the end of this period, the whole matter will be reviewed and a decision taken in the light of circumstances obtaining at the time. If it is decided that the State should acquire any unit, the fundamental rights guaranteed by the Constitution will be observed and compensation will be awarded on a fair and equitable basis.

Seven decades later, these industries have been reclassified as infrastructure, and have given rise to uncomfortable questions. What has been the outcome of government control? Where are India's aircraft manufacturing and shipbuilding industries on the global map? Where was the telecom industry until it was opened up to the private sector? Like the introduction to the Resolution, the questions are rhetorical and the respective answers—inefficient use of scarce resources; nowhere; and in the homes of the rich and powerful, respectively—are visible to even the blind. If this is the texture of national interest the Resolution pursued, it's time to redefine the phrase.

All three are potentially strategic industries. But the idea that their control should be in the hands of the government, however, was deeply flawed. Worse, this policy stance stretched itself through the years, and created a nation of, by and for the entitled. In other words, Nehru's 1948 Resolution ended up infecting the economy with the lethargy of the entitled, an apathy towards the people, and with no accountability to match. Even the fundamental premise, that strategic industries should be under the control of the government, was a copout in its execution. Instead of encouraging domestic industry to build them, India began to import the most sensitive industry of the lot—defence. Apparently, importing defence equipment made by foreign manufacturers was fine, but defence equipment manufactured by Indian companies was not. Who gained from this? Certainly not India.

Even if we take key strategic sectors out of the picture, Nehru's anti-industry stance was clear. For instance, in industries where the private sector was allowed to function, not only could the state participate and therefore compete with the might of taxpayers' funds behind it, it would not 'hesitate to intervene whenever the progress of an industry under private enterprise is unsatisfactory'. Thus, the government embarked on enterprises like large river-valley projects, such as the Damodar Valley Scheme, the Kosi Reservoir, and the Hirakud Dam. It didn't stop here: the Resolution enabled the entry of government production of fertilizers and essential drugs. Further, it placed eighteen industries, including cotton and woollen textiles, sugar and machine tools, under 'Central regulation'. The complete list,[10] it stated clearly, was not exhaustive.

Within private enterprise, the Resolution introduced cottage and small-scale industries as sectors of priority. The reason was not economic but social, such that it increased the 'scope for individual, village or co-operative enterprise, and means for the rehabilitation of displaced persons. These industries are particularly suited for the better utilization of local resources and for the achievement of local self-sufficiency in respect of certain types of essential consumer goods like food, cloth and agricultural implement.'

Inspired by Mohandas Karamchand Gandhi and pushed through by Jawaharlal Nehru, this focus on cottage and small-scale industries found resonance not merely in the 1948 Resolution but in subsequent polices too. The First Five Year Plan, for instance, devoted two chapters to them—Chapter 24 focused on Village Industries, and Chapter 25 on Small Industries and Handicrafts.[11] For both, the Planning Commission recommended reservations as a policy, state purchase as a tool to help them, and imposition of cess and capacity constraints on large-scale industries, effectively using tax policy to control economies of scale and promote inefficiencies of the small.

Citing the December 1947 Industrial Truce Resolution, under which both employers and workers agreed to refrain from lockouts, strikes and slow-down tactics,[12] Jawaharlal Nehru's 1948 Resolution of good intentions created a huge hurdle before industry—labour. It provisioned the setting up of a series of committees and sub-committees, by both the Central and state governments, 'for each major industry'.

The governance structure, rooted in socialist planning, ensured that Indian industry was overburdened by compliances. It ended up creating a complex web of controls by those who had zero skin and no stakes in the idea of how jobs are generated, value built, wealth created—but were themselves protected by permanent employment with inflation indexed pensions and no accountability. Except for the Works Committees and the Production Committees, which would comprise representatives of employers and workers only, all other committees would be tri-partite, with representatives of government, employers and workers.[13]

> The machinery which [the] Government propose[s] to set up will function at different levels, central, regional and unit. At the Centre there will lie a Central Advisory Council, which will cover the entire field of industry, and will have under it Committees for each major industry. These Committees may be split up into sub-committees dealing with specific questions relating to the industry, e.g., production, industrial relations, wage fixation, and distribution of profits. The regional machinery under the Provincial Governments will be Provincial Advisory Boards which, like the Central Advisory Council, will cover the entire field of industry within the province; they will have under them Provincial Committees for each major

> industry. The Provincial Committees may also be split up into various sub-committees dealing with specific questions relating to production, wage fixation and industrial relations. Below the Provincial Committees will come the Works Committees and the Production Committees attached to each major industrial establishment.

The arguments and stances in the 1948 Resolution gave moral power to enact several laws. The Minimum Wages Act, 1948 was enacted 'to provide for fixing minimum rates of wages in certain employments'.[14] The Factories Act, 1948 was enacted 'to consolidate and amend the law regulating labour in factories'.[15] The Industries (Development and Regulation) Act, 1951 was enacted 'to provide for the development and regulation of certain industries'.[16] The Essential Commodities Act, 1955 was enacted 'to provide, in the interest of the general public, for the control of the production, supply and distribution of, and trade and commerce, in certain commodities'.[17] All these Acts were further fortified by laws, rules and regulations, and accompanying compliances and filings, devised by state legislatures and governments. All of them placed restrictions on doing business in India.

The Resolution also gave teeth to further consolidate control—the nationalization of nine airlines including Air India;[18] the creation of the Planning Commission as an extra-Constitutional executive authority that usurped some of the powers of the Finance Commission (a Constitutional body created later in 1956) and which reported to the prime minister;[19] the failed development finance institutions,[20] which are curiously being resurrected in 2021–22.[21] The Industrial Disputes Act, 1947,[22] enacted 'to make provision for the investigation and settlement of industrial disputes, and for certain other purposes', and which has been critiqued as a law that 'entrenched regulation and strangled development' was already in force before the 1948 Resolution was unleashed.[23]

The controllers of the India narrative being the same set of individuals, reflections of the 1948 Resolution can be found in the

Directive Principles of State Policy in the Constitution of India that was adopted by the Constituent Assembly of India on 26 November 1949 and became effective on 26 January 1950. 'The State shall strive to promote the welfare of the people by securing and protecting as effectively as it may a social order in which justice, social, economic and political, shall inform all the institutions of the national life.'[24]

With minor edits, the Irish Constitution of 1937 influenced the Indian Constitution of 1950. Compare the statement from the Indian Constitution with the Irish Constitution here: 'The State shall strive to promote the welfare of the whole people by securing and protecting as effectively as it may a social order in which justice and charity shall inform all the institutions of the national life.'[25]

From this grand political stance flowed the economic stand, again borrowed from the Irish Constitution:[26]

> The State shall, in particular, direct its policy towards securing—
> (a) that the citizens, men and women equally, have the right to an adequate means of livelihood;
>
> (b) that the ownership and control of the material resources of the community are so distributed as best to subserve the common good;
>
> (c) that the operation of the economic system does not result in the concentration of wealth and means of production to the common detriment;
>
> (d) that there is equal pay for equal work for both men and women.

In an inverted manner, therefore, the economic part of the Constitution was influenced by the 1948 Resolution and in a circular way, the Directive Principles of State Policy were cited for the drafting of future economic policies. To clarify, the Directive Principles were recommendatory, not legal: 'The provisions contained in this Part[27] shall not be enforceable by any court, but the principles therein laid down are nevertheless fundamental in the governance of the country and it shall be the duty of the State to apply these principles in making laws.'[28]

Already an ill-conceived notion, the 1948 Resolution was stretched and twisted beyond recognition in subsequent industrial policy statements, the adverse implications of which will be discussed in the next few chapters. Examining it in that light, along with the Bombay Plan from which economic positions were selectively gleaned, we can conclude that Jawaharlal Nehru put the Indian economy on a path that was visibly anti-industry, anti-entrepreneur, anti-wealth.

In his mind, perhaps, he walked the road of good intentions. Perhaps he bowed before politics rather than economics, votes instead of wealth, and democracy in place of prosperity. Or perhaps, the Resolution, as argued earlier, was a function of the age and reflected the time. But once the idea of self-interest overcame national interest (the bogey of 'national interest' has been used four times in this Resolution, that of 'public interest' once—without defining what those interests are) and the echo chambers of self-serving officials got a whiff of the power and intellectuals of influence, it was impossible to pull this train back.

Forty-three years later, the 1991 reforms initiated by Prime Minister P.V. Narasimha Rao, therefore, were not merely necessary, essential or radical—they were courageous and needed moral strength to overrule entrenched interests. The Resolution of 1948 held the reins of the Indian economy for eight years, until the Industrial Policy Resolution of 1956 that consolidated economic repression was crafted, and which we examine in the next chapter.

7

Prelude 4: Industrial Policy Resolution 1956

If the Resolution of 1948 laid the foundations of India's economic wrong turn, the Industrial Policy Resolution of 1956 (IPR 1956) built upon it a superstructure that ensured the cages created for businesses by the 1948 Resolution were narrowed, industries suffocated, and companies as an essential, job-creating, growth-inducing and tax-paying element of India's democracy socially and morally criminalized. The political success of the Resolution of 1948 reflected in the deluded sense of smugness in IPR 1956. Questions: Didn't the planners and leaders of India know that they were taking the Indian economy downhill? Didn't they understand that political freedom must ignite and not trample on economic freedom? Didn't they envision a prosperous and poverty-free India? Didn't they learn any lesson from the failure of the 1948 Resolution? Possibly not, as the very first paragraph of IPR 1956 suggests:[1]

> The Government of India set out in their Resolution dated 6 April 1948 the policy which they proposed to pursue in the industrial field. The Resolution emphasized the importance to

> the economy of securing a continuous increase in production and its equitable distribution, and pointed out that the State must play a progressively active role in the development of Industries. It laid down that besides arms and ammunition, atomic energy and railway transport, which would be the monopoly of the Central Government, the State would be exclusively responsible for the establishment of new undertakings in six basic industries—except where, in the national interest, the State itself found it necessary to secure the cooperation of private enterprise. The rest of the industrial field was left open to private enterprise though it was made clear that the State would also progressively participate in this field.

Here, the Jawaharlal Nehru government celebrated the three steps to a slowing GDP growth. First, it revelled in having legitimized the primacy of the state in private affairs. Second, it rejoiced in the creation of state-owned, state-managed and state-ruined industrial monopolies, and set the stage for their expansion. And third, it placed a threat on the remaining businesses so that the entire might of the state could compete with the resources of individual entrepreneurs to produce and distribute products; and if it could not win in the marketplace, it would nationalize private industries. In December 1954, it harped on about the virtues of planning, the First Five Year Plan, the Constitution of India and within it the Directive Principles of State Policy—all authored by the same set of people, and dominated by a deluded dissonance—and above all, the acceptance by Parliament of the socialist pattern of society. 'Industrial policy, as other policies, must therefore, be governed by these principles and directions,' the IPR 1956 stated.[2]

IPR 1956 continued to emphasize and justify a greater role of the state in business and classified industries into three categories while warning that, 'It should also be remembered that it is always open to the state to undertake any type of industrial production.'[3] It also adopted a condescending tone carrying an underlying threat towards the private sector reeks of an ideological stance rather than an economic policy statement:[4]

> In the first category will be industries the future development of which will be the exclusive responsibility of the State. The second category will consist of industries which will be progressively state-owned and in which the State will, therefore, generally take the initiative in establishing new undertakings, but in which private enterprise will also be expected to supplement the efforts of the State. The third category will include all the remaining industries, and their future development will, in general, be left to the initiative and enterprise of the private sector.

IPR 1956 expanded the span of state control over industries by multiples. It began slow. From three industries (manufacture of arms and ammunition, the production and control of atomic energy, and the ownership and management of railway transport) as the exclusive monopoly of the state in the Resolution of 1948, it expanded the list by one to include air transport.[5]

But against six industries in the Resolution of 1948, where the state would be exclusively responsible for establishing new units (coal; iron and steel; aircraft manufacture; shipbuilding; manufacture of telephone, telegraph, wireless apparatus, excluding radio receiving sets; and mineral oils), the IPR 1956 expanded the list almost three-fold to seventeen, under Schedule A. Here, private entities already functioning would be allowed to continue and given permissions to expand, 'when the national interests so require'. The new industries in this list included generation and distribution of electricity, aircraft, and air transport.[6] Remember, given that nine airlines had already been nationalized two years earlier in 1953,[7] the tone of the policy carried the threat of nationalizing other industries in words—and followed through in deeds.

Schedule B listed out twelve industries in the second category.[8] These would be industries where the state would establish new undertakings.

The patronizing tone remained: 'At the same time, private enterprise will also have the opportunity to develop in this field, either on its own or with State participation.'[9] The third category would be whatever was left. 'It is expected that their development will be undertaken ordinarily through the initiative and enterprise of the private sector, though it will be open to the State to start any industry even in this category.'[10]

In IPR 1956, the policy of state dominance didn't end with state reservation or state monopolies. 'Industrial undertakings in the private sector have necessarily to fit into the framework of the social and economic policy of the State and will be subject to control and regulation in terms of the Industries (Development and Regulation) Act and other relevant legislation,' the policy stated. This law 'entrenched regulation and strangled development, and a series of similarly wrongheaded laws that enshrined what Rajaji called the "licence-permit-quota Raj"'.[11]

In fact, to read IPR 1956 in isolation, without examining the Industries (Development and Regulation) Act of 1951[12] (IDR 1951) would be an error. Enacted on 31 October 1951, IDR 1951 came into force three years after the Resolution of 1948 and five years before the IPR 1956. It took inspiration from the former and executed control on the latter. Again, the tool used to suppress economic freedom and consumer choices was, ironically, 'public interest', an idea that Indian citizens, given their voting behaviour, were happy to embrace: 'It is hereby declared that it is expedient in the public interest that the Union should take under its control the industries specified in the First Schedule.'[13]

The First Schedule comprised thirty-eight industries,[14] from boilers[15] and machine tools[16] to household equipment[17] and photographic raw film and paper.[18] Within these industries, products were situated. To illustrate the difference and its complexity, the item 'Industrial Machinery' had three sub-items—major items of specialized equipment used in specific industries containing eleven products, such as jute machinery or tea machinery; general items of machinery used in several industries, such as the equipment required for various 'unit processes' containing fourteen sub-items such as evaporators and mixers and reactors; and other items of industrial machinery containing three sub-items (ball, roller and tapered bearings; speed reduction units; and grinding wheels and abrasives).[19] In total, twenty-eight items.

Nightmare? There's more. Chapter II of the law created 'development councils' that would, under the Second Schedule comprising sixteen functions, would effectively choke all enterprise. To illustrate, let's take just one, Item 7, under this schedule:[20]

> Promoting or undertaking inquiry as to materials and equipment and as to methods of production, management and labour utilization, including the discovery and development of new materials, equipment and methods and of improvements in those already in use, the assessment of the advantages of different alternatives and the conduct of experimental establishments and of tests on a commercial scale.

That the Indian inheritors of power from the British had so much time and devoted so much attention to such detail shows the depth to which India's leaders had stooped in their tirade against industry, entrepreneurs and wealth.

The IPR 1956 read in conjunction with IDR 1951 suddenly made the Resolution of 1948 seem benign. Benjamin Zachariah:[21]

> Social justice, to some extent, was something for which the Nehruvians believed they could plan. From 1955, the Congress had declared, and Parliament had accepted, a commitment to a 'socialistic pattern of society'. The 1956 Industrial Policy Resolution replaced the gentler-on-private-entrepreneurs Industrial Policy Resolution of 1948—it envisaged the dominance of the public sector, and a complementary private sector preferably organized on cooperative lines. Rapid economic growth through industrialization, especially through the development of heavy industries was set as the goal.

At a time when the country was still experiencing political freedom and the intoxication of that success was on a high, instead of diverting that energy towards powering economic freedom, growth and prosperity, Jawaharlal Nehru's IPR 1956 smothered India's industrial ambitions. While bringing corporations that could help India leapfrog growth under state control, IPR 1956 indulged in the large politics of the small by promoting cottage, village and small industries. In itself, promoting small is not a problem; doing so at the cost of large is. Again, while misleading the people by saying it would create jobs (nobody asked what sort of jobs, at what wages and under what conditions), the underlying political sales pitch was so naive that it would give Communist leaders a run for their failures:[22]

> The Government of India would, in this context, stress the role of cottage and village and small scale industries in the development of the national economy. In relation to some of the problems that need urgent solutions, they offer some distinct advantages. They provide immediate large scale employment; they offer a method of ensuring a more equitable distribution of the national income and they facilitate an effective mobilization of resources of capital and skill which might otherwise remain unutilized. Some of the problems that unplanned urbanization tends to create will be avoided by the establishment of small centres of industrial production all over the country.

Controls on production and higher taxation on the large combined with financial assistance and subsidies to the small[23] crushed India's industry, even as smaller nations such as South Korea raced ahead. The vision of industrial cooperatives was another step in the same direction. As was the attempt to copy-paste the idea of income redistribution into industrial redistribution.[24]

The entire policy environment of the time reeks of a political, economic and administrative set-up becoming captive to a povertarian ideology that characterizes the remarkable failure of Jawaharlal Nehru and his intellectual descendants. Instead of catalysing it, his policies prevented prosperity from embracing India. And unfortunately, despite four other industrial policies in the interim—one each in 1973 (See next chapter), 1977 (Chapter 9), 1980 (Chapter 10) and 1990 (Chapter 11)—the IPR 1956 continued to corrode the Indian economy. This went on for three and a half decades till P.V. Narasimha Rao rescued the nation in 1991.

8

Prelude 5: Industrial Policy 1973

On 2 February 1973, what may have gone through as a small regulatory change by the government was packaged as 'Industrial Policy—Government Decisions of February 2, 1973—Key Provisions.'[1] In 252 words, this 'industrial policy' sharpened the teeth of a 1969 law and an earlier 1970 policy that had placed restrictions on companies that were labelled 'large industrial houses'. The law was the Monopolies and Restrictive Trade Practices Act, 1969, and the policy was the Industrial Licensing Policy of 1970.

The 1969 law was enacted by Parliament to prevent 'concentration of economic power to the common detriment', and to prevent the creation and proliferation of monopolies. Titled, the Monopolies and Restrictive Trade Practices Act, 1969,[2] this law once again leaned on the anti-corporation rhetoric and the crutch of 'public interest'—a phrase, defined for the first time, that has been used twenty times in the law, and whose implications were embedded in an eleven-headed hydra of definitions.[3]

If the working of a firm was found to be 'prejudicial to public interest', or worse '*likely to lead to* [emphasis mine] the adoption of any monopolistic or restrictive trade practices', the law provisioned imprisonment that could go up to five years. In other words, a company need not break any law for its officials to be imprisoned. While the law was in tune with regulatory practices across the world that attempted to prevent restrictive trade practices and abuse of monopoly power, its Indian version was steeped in an anti-success, anti-size and anti-growth stance. Countries across the world were fixing the problem administratively to help their companies grow fairly; India was using the problem ideologically to demonize scale and keep its private firms small.

Report after report was commissioned and crafted to condemn size and scale. Such was the ideological power, so intense the political capture, and so astounding the extreme control over private enterprises by the government that it needs a book in regressive political psychology to analyse it. What follows in the next three paragraphs is just one of several examples of the manner in which the economic freedom of entrepreneurs and private enterprises was subjugated by the self-serving politics of drift and the bureaucracy of suppression. To think that the government of the day devoted so much of its time to ideologies and virtue signalling rather than concentrating on economic growth, poverty reduction and original policy thinking within India-centric frameworks makes one pull one's hair out in despair.

Between January 1956 and December 1966, the total number of business licences issued were 10,016, while 7,477 applications were rejected.[4] In conjunction with policies, introduced through the previous resolutions and statements, the licences were broken up into five types—new undertaking (3,102 or 30.9 per cent), substantial expansion (3,601 or 35.9 per cent), new article (1,904 or 19.0 per cent), carrying on business (1,366 or 13.6 per cent), and shifting (226 or 2.3 per cent). As the years progressed, the enthusiasm for even these crumbs of opportunity began to diminish.

In the first five years of this period, that is, between 1956 and 1960, the number of licences granted tripled to 1,890 from 585. In the last six years, they fell from 1,388 in 1961 to 423 in 1966, a 70 per cent drop—and 28 per cent lower than what India started out with following the Industrial Policy Resolution of 1956. The grip of the state was beginning to choke private enterprise.

But even this was not enough power in the hands of an unquestioned political leadership and an unaccountable bureaucracy. The licences were further classified into nine categories—seventy-three large houses, second tier of large houses, large independent companies, other foreign companies,[5] other companies,[6] individuals,[7] other non-corporate bodies,[8] public sector,[9] and cooperatives.[10] These were handed to entrepreneurs by eight 'progressing authorities'—Directorate General of Technical Development or DGTD (7,079 licences); Textile Commissioner (1,098); Coal Controller (390); Sugar and Vanaspati Directorate (262); Iron and Steel Controller (209); Jute Commissioner (101); Ministry of Petroleum and Chemicals (32); and Ministry of Defence (5).[11]

The twenty 'larger industrial houses' were of much concern to the government of Prime Minister Jawaharlal Nehru (and subsequently, Prime Minister Indira Gandhi).[12] The problem being that these conglomerates managed to procure a larger chunk of licences than others. Industrialists belonging to 'Large Industrial Sector' were looked upon with suspicion when they sat on the boards of financial institutions. Rather than addressing and combating the problem of conflict of interest, the idea of the time was to get rid of them altogether, replacing them with people who neither had the skills to negotiate businesses nor any skin in the game:[13]

> While it is necessary that these institutions should have available to them the advice of persons with experience and knowledge of industry, it is preferable that these persons should not be associated with Large Industrial Houses. It would be more useful to rely on professional experts such as Engineers, Economists, Accountants and Managers.

Within the twenty larger houses, the Birla Group got extra attention:[14]

> The pace of Birla's advance was moderate in 1957 and 1958, considering that it was the second largest group in size and already had the largest number of companies, more than 300. The build-up of momentum started in 1959 and the breakthrough came in 1960. There has been no looking back since then. Over these 9 and a half years, the Birlas applied for 228 new articles, 267 substantial expansions and 443 new undertakings (all gross of some multiple counting) and received approvals for 102, 149 and 124, respectively.

The approach to factors of production remained confined to a theoretical framework—land, labour, capital and their control. The most important factor of production, the entrepreneur who brings all the other factors together into a cohesive whole to deliver the harmony of enterprises, was smothered. If the Birla Group was more dynamic than others, why penalize that dynamism and the resultant production remains unanswered. In any case, the result was that the capitalist was boxed into becoming the industrialist, controlled by bureaucrats and technocrats, while entrepreneurs were relegated to the fringes of the economy.

The idea of scale was devalued:[15]

> We think it necessary that some Governmental agency should be entrusted specifically with the task of collecting information about the Large Industrial Sector so that it would be easily possible to identify concerns belonging to it. This is specially important in view of our recommendation that licences in the middle sector should ordinarily be refused to concerns belonging to the Larger Industrial Houses and foreign concerns. The list of such Houses and information about their composition must be kept up-to-date for this purpose. This may also be of use in the working of the proposed Monopolies Commission.

Already in the making, the term 'core sector' was given a body here. The definition of the Planning Commission 'involving significant investments or foreign exchange'[16] was expanded to include 'all the basic, strategic and critical industries, and no single criterion such as that of foreign exchange requirements should govern the definition of the core sector. It is also obvious that the core cannot remain fixed for [all] times.'[17] An interesting aside here on the intellectual scam of circular citing. The Industrial Licensing Policy Inquiry Committee cited the draft Fourth Five Year Plan to define 'core sector' in its report; the Final Five Year Plan cited the same report, to make the same point.

In their justification of the draft Monopolies and Restrictive Trade Practices Bill, 1965, the K.C. Das Gupta Committee bared its ideological bias. First it cited that the proposed law was in tune with Article 39 under the Directive Principles of State Policy. And then went on to condemn wealth creators using concentration of economic power even while playing victims.

Examined politically, these worthies attempted to strengthen the 'money is bad and those holding it evil' narrative, conveniently forgetting that it is only big businesses and large corporations—not the tiny, village or small industries—that create jobs in tune with compliance requirements under the various other laws (the Factories Act, 1948, the Minimum Wages Act, 1948, or the Industries [Development and Regulation] Act, 1951, for instance). This narrative plays out in different forms even today, so it is a good exercise to study this playbook of policy-defining narratives.

First brand big business as evil ...[18]

> We are aware of the strong feeling of aversion and antipathy for these industrial empires. We are also not unmindful of the unhealthy effect these industrial colossi may have on the political and social fields, *even where they do not indulge in conduct which are clearly shown to be harmful in the economic sphere* [emphasis mine]. In a previous portion of the Report we have mentioned the risk of the power big business has to corrupt political democracy.

> We have discussed also at some length the evil social effects that the concentration of wealth produced by concentration of economic power does produce. The temptation to solve this even by dismembering the existing industrial empires and to curb the formation of future empires of this nature is great indeed. It may indeed not even be difficult to evolve measures for this purpose.

... and then, right in the next paragraph, display political victimhood of the government hand being forced by what is now a necessary evil:[19]

> We are however of opinion, in the light of experience of other countries and having regard to the urgent need of the country's industrial development that diversification with its necessary concomitant country-wise concentration of economic power, *even though an evil in some respects* [emphasis mine], is a necessary evil in the economic interests of the country. It would not be right at the present stage of our industrial development to attempt to place any curb on diversification (which in turn gives rise to country-wise concentration) that may result in a slowing down of the pace of such development.

In a country that needed production, jobs and wealth, the demonization of industry, job and wealth creators was accelerating at a pace unseen. In no way is anyone—least of all the author of this book—justifying concentration of economic power. I believe such power cannot and will not happen within the confines of a deep and rich democracy like India—it could and it did happen in the US, but in India it can only happen in exceptional cases. India first needed to stand on its own legs and industrialize before allowing those who had zero skin in the game to control the country's enterprises.

Even when defending industries around concentration of economic power, the underlying theme was that size is guilty until proven innocent. An excerpt from the Note of Dissent by R.C. Dutt:[20]

> While it is true that individual pioneers in the field of industry have by their zeal and initiative made invaluable contributions to the process of industrialization, I hold that concentration of economic power has been an unfortunate, though perhaps not [an] entirely un-intentional, by-product of these efforts. In any case, it is not concentration which has contributed to the economic betterment of the country. Concentration must be distinguished, in this context from bigness of individual industrial units. Every big industrial unit does not necessarily have concentrated economic power. Big industrial units are necessary for efficient production, and those who have had the initiative and enterprise to set up such units certainly deserve credit. In the process of setting up large industrial units, or as a result thereof, concentration of economic power may have been achieved, and those in whom such power is concentrated may have contributed to the process of development. And yet, the fact of concentration as such cannot be regarded as responsible for such development. My point can be illustrated by an analogy drawn from the political field. There are instances in history of benevolent dictators doing good to their countries. In the process of doing good, some persons may have achieved dictatorial powers and they may have continued to benefit the country even after achieving such power. The conclusion cannot, however, be drawn therefrom that the institution of dictatorship is beneficial to the countries concerned or that the same good could not have been achieved by some other form of Government.

The idea of keeping Indian businesses small didn't go through without pushback. 'We believe that the entire apparatus of control is by and large restrictive and harmful to the growth of Indian economy,' said Member of Parliament M.R. Masani.[21] 'I find it difficult to think of a control which either does not plug the springs of production or obstruct the flow of it,' said economist B.R. Shenoy.[22] 'Licensing has not tended to democratize, but has tended to strengthen these monopolies,' another economist, S.K. Muranjan, said.[23] None of them were heard. The wealth creators were smothered. The MRTP law was enacted. And the rest, as they say but with a cruel twist, is poverty.

It is in this context, and the overall anti-industry, anti-money and anti-wealth narratives, that India's 'Industrial Licensing Policy of February 18, 1970' combined with the 'Industrial Policy—Government Decisions of February 2, 1973' need to be read. Together, the policies placed restrictions on undertakings belonging to large industrial houses, defined as those with assets exceeding to Rs 35 crore, subsequently changed to Rs 20 crore to harmonize with the MRTP law. I believe, most of the 'policy' work was accomplished earlier through the law and the comedown on large industries. The rise of small industries began here, with preferences, encouragements and exemptions.

Here's the two-paragraph policy:[24]

> The Industrial Licensing Policy of February 18, 1970 had placed certain restrictions on undertakings belonging to the large industrial houses defined on the basis of assets exceeding to Rs 35 crore. In 1973, the definition of large industrial houses for industrial licensing restrictions was adopted in conformity with that in the Monopolies and Restrictive Trade Practices Act (MRTPA) 1969 on the basis of assets exceeding Rs 20 crore to provide more effective control on concentration of economic power. A consolidated list of industries that were of basic, critical and strategic importance for the growth of the economy and that had long term export potential were specified in Appendix I. MRTP companies and foreign concerns were eligible to participate in Appendix I industries that were not reserved for production in the public sector (Schedule A of IPR, 1956) or the small scale sector (involving investment in plant and machinery up to Rs 7.5 lakh and up to Rs 10 lakh for ancillary undertakings). Preference would be given to small and medium entrepreneurs over the large industrial houses and foreign companies in the setting up of new capacity. Cooperatives, small and medium

> entrepreneurs would also be encouraged to participate in the production of mass consumption goods.
>
> Exemption from licensing provisions for substantial expansion and new undertakings of up to Rs 1 crore by way of fixed assets in land, building and machinery was specified though for MRTPA and foreign companies this exemption would not apply. Exemption from licensing would also not apply to existing licensed or registered undertakings having fixed assets exceeding Rs 5 crore.

While the size of the policy is short, its impact on preventing Indian businesses from growing has been huge. Further, this policy cannot be seen in isolation. Between the Industrial Policy Resolution of 1956 and the 1973 policy, there was a spate of government actions that undermined Indian industry. These include but are not restricted to the nationalization of life insurance companies in 1956,[25] nationalization of banks in 1969,[26] nationalization of coal mines in 1971, 1972, 1973 and 1974,[27] raising the marginal rate of personal income tax to 93.5 per cent in 1971,[28] nationalization of general insurance in 1972,[29] and enacting the Foreign Exchange Regulation Act in 1973.[30]

The Nehru–Gandhi ideological stranglehold on the economic freedom of India, at a time when it needed it the most, bordered on the criminal. Policy after policy debated whether they wanted their governments to be seen as virtuous (and therefore demonize wealth creators) or tax-paying entities (for development works that delivered votes).

For instance, the underutilization of licensing capacities became a matter of concern in 1970—it was 83.8 per cent for cranes (other than mobile), 83 per cent for S.G. (spheroidal graphite) castings, 80 per cent for asbestos cement product making plants, 77.1 per cent for cranes, 74.5 per cent for building and construction machinery, 72.7 per cent for railway wagons, 66.4 per cent for petrol kerosene engines, 62.2 per cent for cast iron and spun pipes, and 58.4 per cent for agricultural implements.[31] The capacity utilization was 2 per cent for road rollers, 3 per cent for diesel engines (vehicle type), 4 per cent for diesel engines (stationery), and 5 per cent for weighing machinery.[32]

Anyone expecting any other outcome from this top-down, politically-dominated and bureaucratically executed system of economic governance would either be aligned to the Nehru–Gandhi ecosystem, or trapped in ideological fantasies. Either way, they were part of a system that was choking the Indian economy. And not learning, leave alone changing. Instead of fixing or reforming these choke points, the government and its bureaucrats made small concessions in the 1970 policy, but continued to mislead Parliament and the people by the dominant rhetoric, as this reply, that is misleading and meandering, to the Lok Sabha Estimates Committee by then Secretary of Ministry of Industrial Development shows:[33]

> It can be said that any restriction on anybody wanting to get up industry in the country would retard the rate of industrial growth. But I would submit we have to take Industrial Policy Resolution as a whole. It does lay emphasis on economic development and all that. It also prescribes certain other objectives which Government have (in view) … It is the question of how much weightage you give to various objectives that you have in the Industrial Policy Resolution.
>
> I would submit that there is bound to be a period in which while you are trying to develop entrepreneurial skills in a large number of smaller people … The rate of growth may not be so fast as one would wish it to be … It may take two years, three years or four years. Gradually, that kind of expertise is bound to spread out into a wider section of people and that would be good for the country.

Technically, this short policy stayed alive for four years until 1977, when a new, and first non-Congress, government brought a new policy. But its impact, particularly the MRTP and the Foreign Exchange Regulation Act (FERA), the shunning of large groups into industrial outcastes, alongside nationalization of industries, the strengthening of the Industries (Development and Regulation) Act, and the intensification of licence-permit-quota infrastructure of rent seeking, lingered on and fed off entrepreneurs for much longer.

9

Prelude 6: Industrial Policy 1977

In 1977, the politics of India changed for three years. So did the leadership. As did the Congress monopoly on economic policy. But on the policy side, it was an opportunity lost. Prime Minister Morarji Desai's approach to the economy under the Janata Party was more of the same. Nine months into his two years and three months long tenure, Desai introduced the 'Industrial Policy—Government Decisions of December 23, 1977—Key Provisions'.

The policy tried to differentiate itself from its predecessors' policies, made some noises about the implementation problems, but reconfirmed the decaying politics of economics as anti-business, anti-large, anti-rich, anti-ostentatious, to be driven towards becoming an economy of the small, by the small, for the small—under the large, entitled and controlling state, infested with micro-compliances and swarms of inspectors. A policy that ensured the Indian economy remained small and Indians poor.

Morarji Desai's economic virtue-signalling around poverty and its moral force continued to keep India poor. The 1977 policy talked about changes but ended up merely tinkering with what he inherited as administrative structures and ideological biases. It sought to remove 'distortions' in the Industrial Policy Resolution of 1956 but refused to look beyond. Desai's economic policy,[1] it can be said, was effectively a Nehruvian-povertarian economic policy Part IV—Part 1 was crafted in 1948 (See Chapter 6), Part II drafted in 1956 (Chapter 7), and Part III as inheritance by his daughter Indira Gandhi (Chapter 8). This policy came at a time when the new government, brought in with new political enthusiasm against the tyranny of the Emergency, new hopes and new economic directions, was expected to deliver a course correction to, if not a complete rethink of, economic policy. Essentially, the policy turned out to be an accelerated sense of historic sameness, a dud.

The ideological stances and outdated ideas of wealth creation overrode economic corrections. So far deluded was Morarji Desai by the legacy of the recent past and the weight of leaders before him that, like prime ministers Jawaharlal Nehru and Indira Gandhi before him, he forgot India was a poor nation that needed to build enterprises to create jobs and wealth, before engaging with redistribution and welfarism. These were his remarks to businesses:[2]

> Power always is corrupting, as wealth is corrupting. Therefore, do not think that only power is corrupting. Please do not forget that wealth also is a great power and it is that which has got to be borne in mind. But when wealth and power combine, God help the country. This is where we have to be careful. Of course, power force and wealth force have to combine themselves.
>
> In all your business transactions if you have purity of means, I shall have absolutely no hesitation in saying that there can be no objection to earning wealth, there can be no objection to getting as much work as possible both by yourself or by others. The purity of means will mean that whatever we get, whatever we earn, whatever we accumulate, is not only for our use, but it is for the use of the society, which has enabled us to earn it. That is why Gandhiji had appealed to all business communities to be trustees.

If Morarji Desai's words are to be taken seriously, it shows the absolute capture of the Indian politicians' minds by the Soviet Union.

Irrespective of the textures of India's politics, the influence of this socialist nation remained deep and wide. Socialism its marketing arm, India its laboratory, they watched how the Indian leadership swallowed the anti-capitalist rhetoric whole. While defence equipment was the crucial key to India-Soviet relations, oil, trade and large projects strengthened it and 'created a vested interest in the continuance of the connexion'.[3] While the Janata Party had an opportunity to course correct the economic direction of the Indian economy, the lack of any original thought, the poverty of ideas and the non-existence of an India-centric focus underlined Morarji Desai's policy actions. His policies were frozen in his own rhetoric:[4]

> I want to recall how in the first ten years of this century, Mahatma Gandhi and Leo Tolstoy became friends. They shared the belief that the progress of any society lay in the happiness and quality of life of its peasantry. We are still inspired by this vision of the Mahatma. We have no attraction for the luring example of affluent consumer societies. We are more concerned with satisfying basic needs and removing inequalities. Our success will rest on what we may be able to do to transform our villages, give productive work to our people and to assure them a better standard of living.

The change of government from Indira Gandhi's Congress to Morarji Desai's Janata Party[5] couldn't deal with the internal contradictions of India's first coalition experiment. When Charan Singh took charge as prime minister,[6] the move remained a political power play, with no change in the approach to the economy—the focus on small business, the suspicion of large corporations and the threat of nationalization continued to loom large.[7]

> For a country like ours with its endemic economic and social problems, there is no escape except to encourage by every possible means, the establishment of small economic units both in industry

> and in agriculture. This does not mean that my Government has any reservations about the role of big industries as a matter of principle. Whenever necessary, big industries will continue to be established and, wherever national interest so demands, they will be established in the public sector. Not only that, in special cases even existing private industry will be nationalized.

The 1977 industrial policy focused on four areas. First, it almost tripled the list of industries exclusively reserved for the small-scale sector to 500 items from 180; and redefined the tiny sector.[8]

> The list of industries exclusively reserved for the small scale sector was expanded from 180 items to more than 500 items. It provided for an annual review of this list in view of new products and new processes of manufacture that emerge. Within the small scale sector, a tiny sector was also defined with investment in machinery and equipment up to Rs 1 lakh and situated in towns with a population of less than 50,000 according to 1971 census figures, and in villages. Special legislation to protect cottage and household industries was also proposed to be introduced.

Second, it reworked the areas where large corporations could function:[9]

> (a) basic industries that are essential for providing infrastructure and for the development for small and village industries, such as steel, non-ferrous metals, cement, oil refineries;
>
> (b) capital goods industries;
>
> (c) high technology industries that require large scale production and that are related to agricultural and small scale industrial development such as fertilizers, pesticides and petro-chemicals; and

(d) other industries that are outside the list of reserved items for the small scale sector, such as machine tools, and organic and inorganic chemicals.

Third, it tinkered with the treatment of companies that came under the Foreign Exchange Regulation Act, 1973, and eased the rules for remittance of profits and repatriation of capital.[10]

> It was also clarified that foreign companies that diluted their foreign equity up to 40% under the Foreign Exchange Regulation Act (FERA), 1973 would be treated on par with Indian companies. A list of industries was issued where no foreign collaboration, financial or technical, was considered necessary since indigenous technology was fully developed in the field. For all approved foreign investment, complete freedom for remittance of profits, royalties, dividends and repatriation of capital (subject to rules and regulations common to all) was provided. Only in highly export oriented and/or sophisticated technology areas fully owned foreign companies were to be permitted.

And fourth, it removed compulsory export obligations for new industrial capacity, focused on 'balanced regional development' by not issuing new industrial licences if the projects were located close to large metropolitan cities, and reworked how management takeovers of sick units by the government would happen (... resorted to only selectively in view of the large amounts of public funds pumped into sick units that have been taken over but which continue to make losses which have to be financed by the public exchequer).[11]

The 1977 policy, thankfully, did not adhere to the Janata Party's election manifesto, which among several other things, was a hotchpotch of rhetoric that sounded virtuous but would have led the country's economic growth nowhere:[12]

> Economic Charter
>
> The Janata Party's Economic Programme envisages:
>
> (1) Deletion of property as a fundamental right;
> (2) Affirmation of the right to work and a full employment strategy;
> (3) Stress on Gandihan (sic) values of austerity, 'antyodaya' and a decentralized economy;
> (4) An end to destitution within ten years;
> (5) Appropriate technology for self-reliance;
> (6) New planning priorities, notably the primacy of agriculture, agrarian reforms and more favourable terms of trade and higher allocations for the rural sector;
> (7) Narrowing down of rural-urban disparities and a new rural-urban nexus;
> (8) Emphasis on wage goods production for mass consumption;
> (9) Statutory reservation of spheres of production for small-scale and cottage industries;
> (10) A wage and price policy; raising the minimum tax exemption limit to Rs 10,000 and exemption of land revenue on all holdings below 2.5 hectares;
> (11) Redistributive taxation and excise in lieu of sales tax;
> (12) Formulation of a national water policy and a national energy policy;
> (13) Environmental care …

The political change of government was an opportunity to change the economy. Freedom from political repression was expected to deliver freedom from economic excesses. Expectations from economic actors, within and outside India, included a taming if not an outright end to the deadly licence-permit-inspector trinity. Sol W. Sanders:[13]

> Yet we may well be approaching the time that so many have prophesied, when a basic change in the economic environment of India, brought on by increasing poverty for the great mass of the population and a mushrooming of communications, will

> produce political developments such as have never been seen on the Subcontinent before—including peasant revolution. This is why it will be important in the next few months to monitor Prime Minister Morarji Desai's attempt to put an end to the permit-licence raj.

The Janata Party couldn't use this opportunity and economic repression continued. Further, Morarji Desai didn't see consumption as an idea to be nurtured. Bringing down the consumption of the rich and middle class as the driving force, the tax system in various budgets ensured that being wealthy or spending money was looked down upon, not just socially but economically. The expression Finance Minister H.M. Patel used to deliver this in his Budget 1977–78 was 'egalitarianism in consumption':[14]

> A large part of the increase in consumption arises from the demonstration effect of the high standard of living of the wealthy and the well-to-do in our society. To neutralize all this, greater egalitarianism in consumption needs to be practised. Our tax system has to be so reoriented as to discourage ostentatious living and promote the habit of savings. However, austerity cannot be ushered in merely through tax reform. We must arouse public opinion against a life style inconsistent with the harsh economic realities of a poor country such as ours.

The structural contradictions within the Janata Party, based on both personal political ambitions as well as ideological contestations, continued to simmer. This was a coalition whose constituents expressed diverse and conflicting interests. Congress (O) had no faith in social and economic equality, while the Bharatiya Lok Dal believed in taking the cake of economic development to the villages and the farmers there without disturbing the pattern of ownership of the land. The Swatantra Party advocated private ownership of the means of production and was against the public sector and advocated free trade, while the socialists' talk leaned on distribution of land to the tiller, encouraging the public sector, attacking private businesses, taking away the privileges of big business, winding up multinationals.[15]

While the Janata Party was the first flush of successful political grouping after a quarter century of the Nehru–Gandhi monopoly, it had little experience in managing the diversity of interests and was unable to put administration before ambitions or work towards creating common governance goals. The lust for power often got the better of their statements, and exposed their raw ambitions, including preying on another's death.[16] Outside the party, citizens were not unaware of these clashes. But the memory of the Emergency loomed large, and a sense of hope ruled high. India had voted a political change and was now hoping for a new stability. Romesh Thapar:[17]

> Watching the goings on in the Capital, one wonders whether we are in the fact witnessing the birth pangs of a new continental party. It will be torn by dissensions, alignments and counter-alignments. It will assume the consensus techniques of the old Indian National Congress, throwing out those who do not adjust. It will attempt to carry out corrections in political, economic and social policy which the former ruling party lost sight of in its obsession with 'the leader'. If these assumptions prevail (and the 'if' remains rather large!), we could be on the edge of a major change—and for the better.

That hope did not materialize. The Janata Party got political success too soon. And the success was based on opposing the repression unleashed by the Emergency. To the extent that it was able to reverse Indira Gandhi's attempted authoritarianism, the coalition worked. But it could not sustain that entry to power and give a new economic direction to the country. The disparate fleet of personal interests could not navigate this success in the high seas of hard governance and economic policy. The glue binding this coalition's cohesion came more from the compulsions of office than from any conviction in or source of informal fellowship: 'What accounts for the strength of the ruling party is the convenient combination of tightly knit domains of support mobilized by these components and the additional support from allied parties.'[18]

The three reforms the Janata Party managed to usher in were, again, around the politics of corruption and the legislative momentum of the past. First, it attempted to curb unaccounted for wealth by demonetizing high-denomination currency notes by passing the High Denomination Bank Notes (Demonetisation) Act, 1978,[19] under which notes of Rs 1,000, Rs 5,000 and Rs 10,000 ceased to be legal tender from 16 January 1978 onwards. Second, it attempted to fix gold smuggling by commencing the sale of the yellow metal from the stocks held by government.[20] Executed through six auctions, the scheme 'proved a dismal failure, with gold prices shooting above Rs 1,100 for 10 ounces against the preauction level of around Rs 630'.[21] And third, after seven Constitutional amendments—First Amendment in 1951, Fourth (in 1955), Seventeenth (1964), Twenty-Fifth (1971), Thirty-Ninth (1975), Fortieth (1976), and Forty-Second (1976)—were brought in by successive governments and all of them struck down by the Supreme Court, it was with the Forty-Fourth Amendment, enacted by Parliament during the Janata Party years, that the right to property was reduced from a fundamental right to a legal one, with one exception—minority institutions.[22]

But overall, its economic policy had degenerated into managing the 'politics of nonissues'.[23] In 1977, Indian voters had rejected Indira Gandhi's Emergency. But apart from a political change, the economic course remained the same. Even though the Janata Party experiment worked irreversibly to extinguish all authoritarian tendencies in India forever, its governance system failed to deliver. In 1980, therefore, the nation voted Congress back to power and thus began Indira Gandhi's second term as prime minister,[24] and the incremental recrafting of India's economic policies, which I explore in the next chapter.

10

Prelude 7: Statement on Industrial Policy 1980

The return of Indira Gandhi as prime minister following the first failed experiment of a non-Congress coalition through the Janata Party somewhat reduced the intensity of her anti-business economic policies. Perhaps the electoral defeat in 1977 and learnings from political repression through the Emergency in its run-up trickled down to reducing economic repression three years later. But while political repression ended with one straight election, the economic repression, despite all attempts by the intelligentsia to whitewash it, didn't—it merely slowed down. Looking beyond the confines of her industrial policy, we see the same mindset, the same approach and a higher degree of political as well as personal self-aggrandizement.

Titled 'Statement on Industrial Policy July 23, 1980—Key Provisions', Indira Gandhi's second industrial policy is not available in its complete form anywhere. For the purpose of this chapter, therefore, I have had to use the base policy as has been placed on the Department for Promotion of Industry and Internal Trade website,[1] and taken the rest from the *Gazette of India*[2] under the subsection that contains the

32nd Annual Report of Industrial Finance Corporation of India, and a Written Answer in Parliament by the Minister of State for Industry Charanjit Chanana on 17 December 1980.[3]

A casual reading the 1980 policy indicates how its phraseology was not different from all other policies of the past, displaying a drafting perfection that economic bureaucrats had attained. The political signalling was completely in place. While overtly and unambiguously leaning on the Industrial Policy Resolution of 1956, drafted by her father Prime Minister Jawaharlal Nehru, Prime Minister Indira Gandhi's 1980 industrial policy stood on eight legs, none of which showed any creativity in handling the changing times:[4]

(i) Optimum utilization of installed capacity;
(ii) Maximum production and achieving higher productivity;
(iii) Higher employment generation;
(iv) Correction of regional imbalances;
(v) Strengthening of the agricultural base through agro-based industries and promotion of optimum inter-sectoral relationship;
(vi) Promotion of export-oriented industries;
(vii) Promotion of economic federalism through equitable spread of investment and dispersal of returns; and
(viii) Consumer protection against high prices and bad quality.

But reading between the lines, in the 1980 policy there is a distinct shift towards the practical management of the economy along with the ideological mumbo-jumbo that repressed business operations and investments. It focused on plucking the low-hanging administrative fruits rather than sowing more economic repression. The very first socio-economic objective, an innocuous phrase around optimum capacity utilization, shows that Indira Gandhi's new government had possibly begun to take data into account and listen to voices on the ground. The restrictions by the state on industry had begun to choke the economic energies of the nation, and the 1980 policy acknowledged it. Take capacity. Jagdish Bhagwati:[5]

> Few outside India can appreciate in full measure the extent and nature of India's controls until recently. The Indian planners and bureaucrats sought to regulate both domestic entry and import competition, to eliminate product diversification beyond what was licensed, to penalize unauthorized expansion of capacity, to allocate and prevent the reallocation of imported inputs, and indeed to define and delineate virtually all aspects of investment and production through a maze of Kafkaesque controls. This all-encompassing bureaucratic intrusiveness and omnipotence has no rationale in economic or social logic; it is therefore hard for anyone who is not a victim of it even to begin to understand what it means.

In other words, if a company produced more than the capacity granted to it by a bureaucrat, it would be breaking the law. The fact that an entrepreneur would produce more because there was a higher demand escaped the minds of the governance system that was protected by a penalty-free, accountability-free tenure with no skin in the game. In that respect, when the 1980 policy eased capacity constraints, it was a big move at the time, though for those conversant with, and practitioners of, market economy would find this quota system puzzling and against India's economic interests. Indira Gandhi not only took this step but pushed further. Sumit K. Majumdar:[6]

> In the early 1980s the ratification of surplus capacity as part of actual capacity commenced. While no radical departures from existing policy mindsets were forthcoming in regime 4, the need to use existing capacity in place was well-recognized by her senior advisers. 1982 was declared as the Productivity Year, and in that year a scheme of re-endorsement of capacity was introduced. Till then, existing capacity in place could not be

> used to meet production quotas, even if market demand existed, if such capacity was in excess of authorized limits. Now, such excesses were allowed to be used for productive purposes.

Data coming out of the capacity debate revealed conflicting conclusions. 'The Industrial Licensing System (IIS) is, on the one hand, restrictive and, on the other, a permissive mechanism,' a 1983 report by the Indian Institute of Public Administration stated.[7] Within the framework of an economy dominated by micro-control of entrepreneurs, the results of the survey the study based its analysis on were 'contrary to some of the widely held beliefs and assumptions of Indian policymakers'. Sample these seven, for instance:[8]

> After the issuance of industrial licences there seems to be no machinery to ensure that licences do get implemented. Licensees are often able to keep the licences unimplemented for years together without facing the prospect of revocation.
>
> A comparison of the actual level of production reported by the licensees with the capacities licensed reveals that in over 20 per cent of the total cases, no production had taken place. In another 25 per cent cases, production was less than 25 per cent of the licensed capacity.
>
> Just as the installed capacities do not always correspond to the licensed capacities, the production levels reported by the large, corporate sector do not fully relate to the capacities installed. In nearly two-thirds of the cases production was less than 50 per cent of the installed capacity. Only one-fourth of the licences are being utilized fully, i.e. at levels of more than 75 per cent of the installed capacities.
>
> The Indian public sector has often been criticized for poor efficiency. But if one compares the performance of the two sectors in terms of capacity utilization, one finds that the performance of public sector was far better than that of the large private sector. Out of the total of 131 Central Government Public Enterprises,

> 47 per cent of the units had a capacity utilization rate of more than 75 per cent. The proportion of licences falling in the same category was only 24.5 per cent in the case of the large private corporate sector.
>
> The performance of the companies belonging to the two largest houses of the country, namely, Tatas and Birlas, is also not found to be any better. For instance, 75 per cent of the licences held by the Tata companies covered in the Survey and 58 per cent of those held by the Birla House companies studied were not being utilized even to the extent of 60 per cent.
>
> It is an interesting feature of the operation of the ILS that while in a large number of products of the Scheduled Industries the utilization of industrial capacities is extremely poor, the very licensees responsible for this often produce far in excess of the authorized capacities in respect of some other products. This suggests that there could have been considerable diversion of resources and raw materials, obtained in the name of one licence to the production of items being produced under another licence.
>
> Violations of the ILS have been frequent and many specific cases have been brought to Government notice by committees like the ILPIC and the Hathi Committee. But no one has ever been penalized for the violations. The government is reported to be helpless in dealing with such cases as the violations have been detected after more than one year and thus penal action has been time barred.

Step back and what we see is that the ideological drive to control the Indian economy and shackle it to the whims of politics and rent-seeking by bureaucrats created a regulatory infrastructure that choked production but did little else. India wasted its first three decades of political freedom in shackling economic freedom. Building imaginary and ideological castles was one thing; creating state capacity to deliver the executive foundations, howsoever repressive they be, was quite another and sorely missing. It neither delivered the growth required, nor created the jobs needed, nor fixed the geographical inequality. And even when companies were found violating capacity licences, the state was administratively incompetent.

The entire edifice of the industrial licensing system, rightly called the license raj—as in, a kingdom of institutionalized rent-seeking by individuals holding various offices in the political and administrative set-up—had become a den of corruption hiding in plain sight, wearing the garb of 'institutions' under the benign shadow called 'the system'. Part of the problem lay in the inability of policymakers to define, much less execute, what that system was. Backed by the Industries (Development and Regulation) Act, 1951,[9] the language of the law and the resultant approach to entrepreneurs was one of outright hostility by the state.

As in the previous policies, notably 1956 (See Chapter 7) and 1973 (Chapter 8) but also brushes of 1977 (Chapter 9), the broad expectations from this system were to ensure the economy was in tune with the Five Year Plans and Directive Principles of State Policy. There was an industrial management balance between the public and private, large private and small private, and cooperative sectors. All these were relegated to officials, with fuzzy objectives, such as preventing concentration of wealth, peppering the assault. To imagine that such an infrastructure would turn India into an independent and self-reliant economy would have been a joke had it not been so cruel, and so devastating for the nation.

All the seven points the report raised as breaches were, in fact, creative actions of and economic incentives for those who had skin in the game. Why would a licensee hoard a licence? There could be several reasons. It could be due to a lack of capital to invest when the licence was granted. It could also be the outcome of a cold evaluation of the opportunity cost of that capital. Or it could even be a change in market dynamic between the time the licence was applied for and granted.

Why would the level of production be less than what the licence had permitted? Because the real demand could have turned out to be less than that planned by government controllers. Why would the capacity utilization of public sector companies be higher than those of the private sector? Because exchequer-funded salaries and incentives of public sector employees were not linked to performance—more production does not necessarily translate into more sales. All PSU executives need to do is follow the government policy; private entrepreneurs need to be at least self-sustaining if not profitable, a far more difficult objective.

Finally, on the other side, why would companies create capacities greater than assigned? Because they planned for a higher demand a few years down. Or, because the plant they were importing had a higher capacity. Or, a second-hand plant was going cheap. Why would raw materials be diverted? Because once the money was down, there is a cost of that money and a price for the warehousing of that material, so it's better to utilize the raw material to generate cash flows now than to store it for a theoretical future.

In other words, the state through the Planning Commission, filled with friends, economists and academics, could not understand the mechanics of markets and entrepreneurs. It could not figure out the idea of risk, the potential of returns, the importance of turning money over, the criticality of cash flows. They were in sublime ignorance of the philosophy of wealth. It is not surprising, therefore, to see Indira Gandhi's 1980 policy dish out more of the same. Recognizing that it is 'desirable to allow private sector undertakings to develop in consonance with targets and objectives of national plans and policies but shall not permit the growth of mono-politic [I think this is an error, the word could be "monopolistic"] tendencies or concentration of economic power and wealth in a few hands.'[10]

Above all and ironically so, the political and administrative mechanism only took further what the business community, through the Bombay Plan (See Chapter 4), had sought, leaving us, even in the twenty-first century, with lessons to think well, think deep, and think data before seeking a government intervention—be careful what you ask for, you might get it. Goyal et al.:[11]

> In India, the need for planning was indeed argued by Captains of private industry in the document, A Plan of Economic Development for India, generally known as the Bombay Plan, in

> 1944. The Indian industrialists had not taken the view (at least in the pre-Independence era) that the state should not intervene in the economic life of the country. Quite contrary to the position many in the private sector may take now, the Bombay Plan suggested establishment of a Supreme Economic Council under the Central Government. Indian industrialists, therefore, cannot be said to be wholly opposed to an active and direct role of state in planning or to the philosophy of industrial licensing. The criticism of the ILS from the private sector has, however, been on the question of (i) long delays in granting approvals; (ii) avoidable, cumbersome and time-consuming procedures; (iii) large amounts of unnecessary information being asked for; and (iv) excessive bureaucratic discretion against which no appeal could be made.

As analysts, we are all familiar with the expression 'political economy', the infiltration of politics into economics through ideas, people, processes and institutions, and changing outcomes for consumers, entrepreneurs and finances. While the field has been carefully tamed into a set of complex abstractions and random theories compounded by incrementalism of citations, the facts on the ground are simpler. Apart from using politics to execute economic policies, the expression is equally a proxy for the use, and misuse, of institutional power gathered through a democratic process for personal political survival. The incentive abstraction of economics blends smoothly into the power abstraction of politics. Indira Gandhi typified the conversion of both these abstractions into a private power fief.

Be it industrial licensing …[12]

> Through industrial licensing, Gandhi was able to harness the financial power of the private sector to aid her in sustaining her precarious voting base. For example, in one case, Gujarati oil barons funded the Congress Party's 1974 election campaign in Uttar Pradesh in exchange for industrial deregulation. Similarly, a 1988 government study (published when Rajiv Gandhi, who

> adopted much of his mother's approach, was prime minister) found that the government had used industrial licenses to dissuade private industry from investing in non-Congress states.

... allocation of government finances ...[13]

> To shore up her unstable voter support, [Indira] Gandhi also made strategic use of at least two important sources of government finance: the Planning Commission and the nationalized commercial banks. The money allocated through these government bodies was used for a variety of purposes, including the establishment and expansion of protected industries. The prime minister was able to use these outlays as a source of patronage to build her support base among both state governments and private actors.

... the institutional breakdown ...[14]

> The political system which Indira Gandhi did so much to create in the 1970s made it hard to initiate reforms in the 1980s. Tendencies towards, or actual authoritarianism, in this context, was not the means of creating a 'developmental state'—as it had seemed to be in the 'Newly Industrializing Countries' of East Asia—but rather the response of an ideologically and politically bankrupt ruling elite which was entangled in its own populist rhetoric.

... or, the personal motivation to stay in power, which created an economic incentive that smothered the Indian economy. This singular, selective and brazen narrative drove India's political economy in the first three decades of independent India. Of course, Indira Gandhi only accentuated these fault lines and raised them to a level of never-seen-before impunity. The seeds of these abominations existed long before her and were planted during her father Jawaharlal Nehru's tenure.

With a greater thrust on digitalization of the Indian economy, which, among other things, has raised the risk of being exposed and despite the impunity works against incumbents politically, these abominations are slowly crumbling, though stray remnants continue to find salience.

But the returns from repression have a limited, perhaps even a one-time, shelf life. As Indian democracy has shown, an autocratic tendency can play its part just once and Indira Gandhi took that chance with the Emergency. Once used, the marginal utility of self-serving political manoeuvrings begins to decline. The 1977 elections proved that. As a result, when Indira Gandhi returned to power in 1980, she came armed with new survival lessons.

A small part of these lessons, touted as huge reforms then, expressed itself in enhancing capacity utilization, or let's just say removing obstacles to efficiency, a recurrent theme in Indira Gandhi's second term. She revised her 20-Point Programme on 14 January 1982 to include ease of doing business: 'Liberalize investment procedures and streamline industrial policies to ensure timely completion of projects. Give handicrafts, handlooms, small and village industries all facilities to grow and to update their technology.'[15] The next month, on 7 February 1982, she also made the revised 20-Point Programme the core of the Sixth Five Year Plan.[16]

Ten days later, President Neelam Sanjiva Reddy pushed the capacity utilization idea further with his 18 February 1982 President's Address, a speech in Parliament that is the government's point of view on various issues of the day:[17]

> In order to maintain the tempo already generated in industrial production and accelerate economic growth, the year 1982 is being observed as 'Productivity Year' and we shall have an intensive drive to maximise utilisation of capacities available in all sectors of the economy.

This low-hanging fruit of capacity utilization dominated the policy. Focusing on core and export-oriented industries, the policy permitted companies to expand their capacities by 5 per cent per annum or 25 per cent in a five-year plan period. Further, 'Requests for setting up 100 per cent export oriented units and for expansion of existing units for purposes of export would also be considered sympathetically.'[18] The definition of 'sympathetically' is as fuzzy as 'national interest'.

On a different note, if you accused her 1980 policy of being futuristic and one that dared to look beyond the predictable, you won't be too far off the track. In the policy's last paragraph was a provision of adding alternative energies and backing it up with subsidized finance. This provision, imagined four decades ago after a return to power, is an idea that the rest of the world is grappling with today:[19]

> Industrial processes and technologies aimed at optimum utilization of energy or the exploitation of alternative sources of energy would be given special assistance, including finance on concessional terms. Similar benefits would be given to activities that contribute directly to the improvement of the environment and reduce the deleterious effects on pollution of air and water.

But beyond that, Indira Gandhi's 1980 industrial policy offered little. By now, the notion of a state-controlled, state-directed and state-managed public sector had crystallized in the minds of the planning fraternity comprising the political leadership, the bureaucratic execution, the economic advisory industry, academia and the media. Indira Gandhi further strengthened this process and articulated it as much in the policy:[20]

> Noting the erosion in people's faith in the public sector, it was decided to launch a drive to revive the efficiency of public sector undertakings through a time bound programme of corrective action on a unit by unit basis. Effective steps would also be taken to develop the management cadres of public sector undertakings in functional fields such as operations, finance, marketing and information system.

The other components of the 1980 policy included the 'elimination of artificial distinction of conflicting interests between small and large scale industry', the creation of 'nucleus plants' in backward districts to promote the concept of 'economic federalism', and an increase in the investment of small-scale industries and tiny sector units.

Despite all attempts to term these as the first flush of economic reforms, upon which Indira Gandhi's son Prime Minister Rajiv Gandhi brought in his policies, which in turn are claimed to be the basis of Prime Minister Narasimha Rao's 1991 momentous and true reforms, the fact is that the 1980 policy was a continuation of the past, with minor diversions. Kalpana Kochhar, Utsav Kumar, Raghuram Rajan, Arvind Subramanian, and Ioannis Tokatlidis:[21]

> The paradox of Indian manufacturing in the early 1980s is thus that of a labour-rich, capital-poor economy using too little of the former, and using the latter very inefficiently. The reason, simply put, was perverse policy.

The most perverse aspect of Indira Gandhi's politics was the slogan coined by Congress President D.K. Barooah in 1974: 'Indira is India, India is Indira.'[22] That she revelled in it and encouraged the Congress party, which she had captured, to turn it into a political legend was one thing. But worse, even after returning to power in 1980 following a three-year exile, she did nothing to change it. This abominable slogan delivered a shameful and despotic policy brimming with conflict of interest, but whose unintended consequences have delivered to the Indian economy far more than she could have imagined. The worst of these policies was pandering to her son Sanjay Gandhi's 'dream' and nationalizing his private company, Maruti.

About the time that Indira Gandhi returned to power, her son Sanjay Gandhi, whom she was grooming for a political career at the time, died in an air crash on 23 June 1980. Almost a decade earlier, in June 1971, his company Maruti Motors Ltd had received a licence to manufacture cars, the first conflict of interest. After his death Indira Gandhi set out to fulfil her son's dream by nationalizing his company with a law[23] and prevented its liquidation and winding up, the second conflict of interest. This is the only time in India's history that a private company, owned by the prime minister's family, has been nationalized. The issue was much debated in Parliament then. But little came of it—Indira Gandhi went ahead with it.

Even though the policy reeked of nepotism, corruption and self-aggrandizement, the unintended consequences have been spectacular. Gautam Chikermane:[24]

> Maruti shows how a private limited company was first nationalized, then disinvested in parts, then turned into a public limited company, in the process creating wealth for the Indian government, a huge auto market in India, and a company that makes more cars in India than in Japan and whose value and profits are greater than its promoter's.

Prosenjit Datta, writing in the Congress newspaper:[25]

> The birth of Maruti which was allowed collaboration with Suzuki, allowed to set an initial production capacity of 100,000 cars (when others were producing 20,000 or so) and forced to indigenize 75 per cent of the auto components by 1988 helped create the modern auto component vendor ecosystem that later entrants who came in after the reforms of 1991 could capitalize on. The fact that Maruti also got a protected domestic market for almost a decade helped it complete its task. (This is not to take anything away from the excellent management it had.)

The policy that started out as an expression of an immoral political economy has turned into a catalyst of an entire industry of enterprises and ancillaries, creating domestic markets and serving exports, and jobs and wealth. But this was a happenstance of accident, not policy by design. It was a political capture for private gains that somehow blundered its way to success.

That the public gained in the bargain was a by-product. Pulling back, we realize that this was not a one-off benign accident; this was the policy of the time. These were economic choices made by the Indian establishment that drove India to build industries that other countries at comparable levels shy away from. Kochhar et al.:[26]

> In this cloud of distortion may well have resided a silver lining—in creating capabilities that did not exist in the typical poor country, India may have created potential sources of growth that would allow it to follow a different growth path from other countries as policy distortions were removed. Put another way, unique distortions may well have created unique sources of comparative advantage that allowed India to follow a different path.

Around this time, new entrepreneurs were coming up and questioning the status quo of the past being applied to industries of the future. To apply the licence-permit constraints to a new business, technology, that was innovating and changing its capacity-price texture faster than ever exposed the chasm between the Indian state and Indian entrepreneurs. Montek Singh Ahluwalia:[27]

> The system was particularly unsuitable for areas where technology was changing rapidly. N.R. Narayana Murthy, the iconic co-founder of Infosys, told me of his personal experience in 1983, when Infosys wanted to import a Data General MV/8000 computer, with three removable disk drives with a capacity of 200 MB each. They had to make several trips to New Delhi to get the import licence. By the time they got the licence, a new disk drive with a capacity of 300 MB had become available, 30 per cent cheaper. Naturally, they wanted to import the latest model. However, the original licence specified the model number and several additional visits to Delhi had to be made to modify

> the licence. In an area where technology was changing rapidly and timely delivery of export orders was crucial, long delays in getting equipment was fatal for exporters.

Irrespective of the grand statements her 1980 industrial policy made, and despite all political narratives, media whitewashing and wishful scholarship, the fact is Indira Gandhi had not changed. The disgraceful Maruti nationalization aside, her stance against private enterprises continued as before. In fact, nationalization had become her biggest continuing assault on businesses.

The first few rounds of nationalization were authored by Jawaharlal Nehru. In 1953, under the Air Corporations Act, 1953, Nehru had nationalized nine airlines[28]—Air India Ltd, Air Services of India Ltd, Airways (India) Ltd, Bharat Airways Ltd, Deccan Airways Ltd, Himalayan Aviation Ltd, Indian National Airways Ltd, Kalinga Airlines, and the Air India International Ltd—and replaced them with Indian Airlines and Air India International. The success of this first nationalization set the course for more, notably life insurance in 1956.[29] When Indira Gandhi took charge of the dynastic mantle, she nationalized general insurance in 1972,[30] coal mining in 1971, 1972, 1973 and 1974,[31] textile mills in 1974[32]—and banking in 1969 and 1980.[33]

If the momentum of repression had ended when Indira Gandhi returned to power in 1980, as several scholars claim, the second round of bank nationalization would not have happened. Her 1970 law, that came into force retrospectively in 1969, had nationalized fourteen banks—Central Bank of India, Bank of India, Punjab National Bank, Bank of Baroda, United Commercial Bank, Canara Bank, United Bank of India, Dena Bank, Syndicate Bank, Union Bank of India, Allahabad Bank, Indian Bank, Bank of Maharashtra and Indian Overseas Bank. Returning to power in 1980, she nationalized another six banks: Andhra Bank, Corporation Bank, New Bank of India, Oriental Bank of Commerce, Punjab & Sind Bank and Vijaya Bank.[34]

Clearly, the political lessons learnt were sketchy and the will to manipulate public money for political gains overrode economic principles. To say, therefore, that in her second innings as prime minister, Indira Gandhi had brought in reforms that in turn influenced her son Prime Minister Rajiv Gandhi's reforms, which in turn enabled Prime Minister P.V. Narasimha Rao to deliver the 1991 reforms is a misleading narrative. It is equally false to claim that 'a more consistent shift towards prioritizing economic growth and embracing the private sector began after Indira Gandhi returned to power in 1980'.[35] The brutal facts of history tell another story—Indira Gandhi continued with the putrid policies her father Jawaharlal Nehru had framed and only bridled, not ended, the underlying repression. Everything else was political, including inflation management. Atul Kohli:[36]

> Among the short-terms changes, it must have been clear to Indira Gandhi by 1980 that the politics of garibi hatao was running out of steam: anti-poverty policies like land reforms had proven difficult to implement; ineffective socialism had hurt economic growth; and by contrast, putting the weight of the state behind private producers had helped agricultural production, leading to the green revolution in the 1960s. The economic lessons must have been hard to ignore. Politically too, Indira Gandhi and her advisors might have calculated that a realignment with big capital may not be too costly, in part because the poor were already loyal to her, but also because state support of business may lead to higher growth and thus to lower inflation, an outcome that India's largely poor electorate may appreciate.

After Indira Gandhi was assassinated by her bodyguards on 31 October 1984, her son Rajiv Gandhi became Congress president. In the ensuing elections, he brought the Congress party to power and followed her footsteps as India's next prime minister. During his term, he attempted to reshape India's economic policy.

One can look at Rajiv Gandhi's policies as a bridge that had one foot in the past and one in the future. He continued with the political-economy repression of Indira Gandhi but opened the boundaries a bit to give entrepreneurs a little breathing space. His first few speeches continued with the rhetoric of his mother, simultaneously celebrating both, her political as well as economic repression, to the extent of crediting her for 'seed bed of modernization', while justifying her political repression of the Emergency in his speech at the Congress's centenary session in 1985:[37]

- To meet an unprecedented threat to the nation's stability, an emergency was proclaimed in 1975.
- Generations will remember with gratitude the decisive direction Indira Gandhi gave to India's industrialization and technological advance. She set exacting tasks for the public sector, which responded with enthusiasm. Through the exertions of the working class and talented managers and technologists, it became the pivot of India's industrial progress. All branches and sectors of industry grew with speed, placing India among the major industrial nations of the world. The enormous range and depth of industrial progress, centred on the public sector, has served the nation well. Today, if we are poised for faster technological growth, the credit goes to Indiraji who prepared the seed bed of modernization.

While whitewashing the economic failures of his grandfather Prime Minister Jawaharlal Nehru and his mother Prime Minister Indira Gandhi as grand visionaries of India continued to dominate his speeches and plans, possibly as a political imperative to sustain and brand the Gandhi dynasty as saviours of India—a malaise that continues with the Congress party even today—lurking beneath this rhetoric was a man who wanted to do some good for the country, modernize it, reform it. So, while continuing with the thrust on agriculture, small-scale and village industries, he also began to understand and attempted to fix the problems of industry through efficiency, infrastructure and technology:[38]

> In the Seventh Plan, we shall establish new parameters of efficiency. Infrastructural shortages will be remedied.

> Appropriate investments will be made in energy, transport and critical materials. We have reached a watershed in our industrial development. We must now move to a new phase, when the focus must be on increasing efficiency, reducing costs and improving quality. With industry trapped in outdated technology, we cannot achieve self-reliance. The thrust of policy will be for absorption of new technology, modernization, reduction of costs and greater competition. Lower costs will bring industrial products within the reach of the masses, raising their standard of living. This will further stimulate industrial growth.

Despite being reined in by the Congress baggage of political, personal and the Gandhi brand interests, Rajiv Gandhi's purpose seemed beyond doubt. He assembled several teams headed by experts, the most high profile of them being the inventor Sam Pitroda, who convinced him about the importance of telecom for India's economic development.[39] He embraced technology, not merely in spirit and rhetoric but in policy actions that took it from a protectionist, statist establishment to a private sector-oriented model.[40] On the governance side, Rajiv Gandhi called out the corruption and leakages in the system, saying that only 15 paise out of every rupee allocated by the government actually reached the poor.[41] He identified the pent-up India demand story and reduced indirect taxes on consumer goods.[42] He saw the virtues of a reduced and simplified income tax regime.

In the very first Union budget after Rajiv Gandhi took charge as prime minister, he oversaw a series of easing to industry on the production side and shoppers on the consumption side. In his March 1985 budget speech, Finance Minister (who later became prime minister) Vishwanath Pratap Singh brought in several policy changes that reduced the costs to industry and tax on earners, while keeping Rajiv Gandhi's goal of self-reliance in mind:[43]

- Delicensing several industries to create additional capacity.

- Allowing the corporate sector to mobilize resources from the market by raising the maximum interest rate to 15 per cent from 13.5 per cent.
- Easing listing norms, creating new instruments such as convertible cumulative preference shares.
- Reducing the rate of duty on project imports from 65 per cent to 45 per cent ad valorem.
- Exempting from customs duties certain advanced type of computer imports, reducing customs duty on four important components of computers from 75 per cent to 25 per cent ad valorem, and exempting computers from excise duty.
- Abolishing export duties on twelve items—iron ore, manganese ore, raw cotton, chromite ore and concentrate, cotton waste, animal feed, manganese dioxide, de-oiled groundnut oilcake, raw wool, kyanite and bridge mica.
- Reducing the number of income tax slabs for individuals from eight to four, while reducing tax rates, and cutting corporate tax rates by 10 percentage points to 55 per cent.

The attempts to turn these small changes in the 1980s, first by Indira Gandhi and then by Rajiv Gandhi, into a decisive agenda-setting and reforms-friendly change in the direction of the Indian economy by scholars having little exposure to India read more like papers of hope than scholarships that endure. Click-bait headlines rather than factual analysis and communal titillations rather than secular studies define their scope. Dani Rodrik and Arvind Subramanian display this abject intellectual poverty in their IMF paper titled, 'From "Hindu Growth" to Productivity Surge: The Mystery of the Indian Growth Transition':[44]

> India's growth transition began in the early 1980s, rather than after the crisis of 1991. The performance of the 1980s cannot be explained by Keynesian pump priming, because there is a variety of time-series and cross-section evidence pointing to trend improvements in productivity indicators. Equally, this transition

> was not triggered by implementing the conventional litany of Washington Consensus reforms, because the transition occurred a full decade before such reforms were initiated. It appears to have been triggered by a perception on the part of the private sector that the government's attitude toward it had changed, a perception that was subsequently (in the mid- to late-1980s) mildly validated by piecemeal reforms of the industrial licensing system. The attitudinal shift signalled by the Congress Party governments in the 1980s elicited a large productivity response, a phenomenon facilitated by the fact that India was far away from its income-possibility frontier.

As if generalities of abstractions garnished in jargon were not enough, they cite Maruti as an example of liberalization. Thankfully, they don't embarrass themselves further and conclude that, 'Allowing a single foreign firm, Suzuki, to enter the domestic car market under existing conditions of limited external liberalization (and subject to local-content requirements) is very different from opening the domestic car market to all foreign producers, which is the normal liberalization strategy and the approach adopted in the 1990s.'[45] Again, this reads like a whitewashed version of the fundamental policy distortion for personal benefit (economic and political): the nationalization of a private company, belonging to a prime minister's son, in order to fulfil his 'dream'. I am aghast.

And I'm not alone. T.N. Srinivasan critiques the Rodrik–Subramanian narrative, with rich data and hard arguments:[46]

> The economy in the 1980s was virtually closed to imports of manufactured consumer goods, and high tariffs and quotas restricted imports of intermediates and capital goods. Until the mid-1980s, there was no real exchange depreciation either. There was excess capacity in the industrial sector (though it is hard to quantify), which in itself was a reflection of the draconian control regime. Liberalizing the use of this capacity at the margin as

> well as imports of intermediates created the potential for output growth. However, the demand for output had to be generated largely from domestic resources, since export growth was limited. Fiscal expansion raised domestic demand. The external resources needed for additional demand for imports of intermediate goods and replacement equipment as capacity utilization increased was financed by borrowing abroad from private creditors. This way of generating growth was obviously not sustainable. The authors [Rodrik–Subramanian] dismiss this explanation of 1980s growth by derisively calling it 'Keynesianism run amok'. Their dismissal is 'ignorance run amok' of the essential features of the Indian economy of the 1980s.

We can sympathize with such [Rodrik–Subramanian] narratives. We can even look at their authors as victims of good intentions. Incapable of capturing on-ground politics into their spreadsheets and policy posits, they were unable to understand, leave alone analyse, an India captured by dying ideologies and dynastic supremacy. However fast he wanted to move, Rajiv Gandhi remained gridlocked to the deadload of poor incentives of the party he was leading. Outside the entrenched power confines of the Congress, the desire for economic freedom was creating an economic policy vacuum among scholars as well as yearnings for economic growth among wealth creators. As a result, the policy crumbs the youthful prime minister's tenure threw were taken up with great fanfare and celebration by entrepreneurs and turned into fake reform myths by wide-eyed scholars.

The truth lay elsewhere. Following decades of economic repression, Rajiv Gandhi may have opened the reforms door a small crack. But this looks more like policy atonement than economic conviction. And the results may have seemed like 'policy reforms' but in fact were 'policy repairs'. Rajiv Gandhi's finance minister and successor Prime Minister Vishwanath Pratap Singh made another attempt to take India in a new direction. But like Rajiv Gandhi, he too could not envision a future beyond the past. We examine his policy in the next chapter.

11

Prelude 8: Industrial Policy 1990

There has been no dearth of laudable, larger-than-life objectives wearing the garb of India's politically rich and economically poor industrial policies. Likewise, there has been no scarcity of systemic policy actions that smother such objectives on factory shop floors. Between the two stand India's politicians and bureaucrats, across hierarchies, all using these moral objectives to expropriate personal power and private rent-seeking. So when Prime Minister Vishwanath Pratap Singh announced industrial growth to ensure employment generation in his 1990 industrial policy, nobody could quarrel with it.

But in its execution, the economic and administrative direction of his policy was not much different from those designed by the industrial policies of Jawaharlal Nehru in 1948 (See Chapter 6) and 1956 (Chapter 7), crafted by Indira Gandhi in 1973 (Chapter 8) and 1980 (Chapter 10), or repackaged by Morarji Desi in 1977 (Chapter 9). Coming to power on the basis of two electoral propositions—anti-corruption stance against Rajiv Gandhi and reservations for Other Backward Classes—and carting the political and intellectual baggage of having served as finance minister in Rajiv Gandhi's Cabinet, Prime Minister Vishwanath Pratap

Singh's policies, like his politics, were largely extensions of the past and confined to archaic playbooks of power.

One part of this approach can be laid on politics and the other on poor leadership. V.P. Singh was prime minister for a year, from 2 December 1989 to 10 November 1990,[1] a turbulent time not just in terms of the economy but also in the internal contradictions and power rifts within the minority National Front government, particularly between V.P. Singh and Deputy Prime Minister Devi Lal. In order to checkmate Devi Lal, V.P. Singh unilaterally implemented the Mandal Commission, which recommended a reservation quota of 27 per cent in central government jobs for Other Backward Classes in addition to the existing reservations for Scheduled Castes and Scheduled Tribes. But Devi Lal was not the sole causal entity for the fall of the National Front government; both the Bharatiya Janata Party and Communist parties that were giving outside support to the government withdrew that support following V.P. Singh's decision without consensus.[2]

Despite such shaky political foundations, or perhaps because of them, V.P. Singh pushed through an industrial policy. Titled, 'Industrial Policy 1990: Policy Measure for the Promotion of Small Scale and Agro-Based Industries and Changes in Procedures for Industrial Approvals', V.P. Singh's policy, again, is not available in the public domain. We are, therefore, grateful to Arvind Panagariya who has provided it in full as an appendix[3] in his 2008 book, *India: The Emerging Giant*. This 31 May 1990 statement is the shortest-lived industrial policy; it lasted less than six months. The policy was not only transient, it was also insipid; and even that was not executed. However, there were four clauses in it that show an attempt to change the texture of Indian industry.

First, under Section 5 (viii), V.P. Singh correctly identified the regulatory overreach on businesses by the state. The licence-permit-quota raj that had been unleashed by his predecessors had attained monstrous dimensions. The change he proposed was in the right direction (reduction of processes) but for limited reasons (complaints by small businesses), which I explore in the third part of this book. Panagariya:[4]

> One of the persistent complaints of the small scale units is their being subjected to a large number of ACTs/Laws, being required to maintain a number of registers, submit plethora of returns and face an army of Inspectors, particularly in the field of labour legislations. These bureaucracy controls will be reduced so that unnecessary interference is eliminated. Further, procedure will be simplified and paper work cut down.

These reductions of inspectors and simplifications of paperwork came as part of what the earlier industrial policies had etched into India's policy design—the supremacy of small over large. V.P. Singh's policy, while granting these concessions to small businesses, attempted to expand the list of 836 items reserved for them; it also promised that 'encroachment and violation by large-scale units into areas reserved for small-scale sector will be effectively dealt with'.[5]

Second, the policy partially addressed delicensing, again with a thrust on small businesses:[6]

> All new units up to an investment of Rs. 25 crores in fixed assets in non-backward areas and Rs. 75 crores in Centrally notified backward areas will be exempt from requirement of obtaining [a] licence/registration.
>
> For the import of Capital Goods, the entrepreneur would have entitlement to import up to a landed value of 30% of the total value of plant and machinery required for the unit.

Third, it understood and attempted to partially fix the resultant raw material requirements:[7]

> For imports of raw materials and components, imports will be permissible up to a landed value of 30% of the ex-factory value of annual production. The ex-factory value of production will exclude the excise duty on the item of production. Raw materials and components on OGL will not be included within

> this 30 per cent limit. For all licensable items of raw materials and components, import licencing procedures will continue to operate.

And fourth, it eased the mechanics of technology transfers in foreign collaborations:[8]

> In respect of transfer of technology, if import of technology is considered necessary by the entrepreneur, he can conclude an agreement with the collaborator, without obtaining any clearance from the Government, provided that royalty payment does not exceed 5% on domestic sales and 8% on exports. If, however, lump sum payment is involved in the import of technology, the proposal will require Government clearance, but a decision will be communicated to the entrepreneur within a period of 30 days.

Panagariya finds that the political rhetoric and lip service paid to small entrepreneurs aside, V.P. Singh's policy was a prelude to the 1991 reforms and 'found a place in the package adopted by the Narasimha Rao government a year later'.[9] In particular, Panagariya illustrates seven points—raising the investment ceiling in plant and machinery for small-scale industries to Rs 60 lakh from Rs 35 lakh; no licence requirement for new units with investments up to Rs 75 crore in fixed assets in backward areas and Rs 25 crore in other areas; entitlement of 30 per cent for import of capital goods; permission to import raw materials and components up to a landed value of 30 per cent of ex-factory value; automatic permission of up to 40 per cent equity investment in technology inflows; coverage of deregulation for all expansion and not restricted to new units; delicensing up to investment of Rs 75 crore in 100 per cent export-oriented units and units to be set up in export-processing zones; and companies on which the MRTP and FERA laws were applicable to be covered by the above but would need clearances under the provisions and regulations of these two Acts.[10]

Panagariya is being kind. He is also granting the Indian policymaking fraternity fig leaf narratives. Among them is the idea of gradualism in the evolution of India's economic policy in general and economic reforms in particular. This is a point that he illustrates with the trade liberalization in P.V. Narasimha Rao's initiatives in 1991. In banking, for instance, the 'norms for income recognition, asset classification, and provisioning were introduced, and have been gradually raised toward international standards. Norms for the recognition of non-performing assets were gradually tightened.'[11]

Further, he is a proponent of gradualism and has argued that 'India should move toward capital account convertibility gradually, while simultaneously deepening its financial markets. In particular, it should not commit itself to a specific timetable and milestones.'[12] He is consistent in his gradualism argument and has argued for it in the case of export subsidies,[13] observed it in the trimming for small-scale industries reservations,[14] the shift from autarkic policies of the 1970s,[15] the expansion of the tax net to cover hard-to-tax groups,[16] and recommends that India's shift to a system of direct cash transfers should also be gradual.[17]

His gradualism argument is elegantly encapsulated here:[18]

> … the policy changes in India have been gradual and largely predictable. Within the complex democratic setup of India, even relatively modest policy changes are usually preceded by the appointment of committees or commissions and extensive discussions. The process is, of course, often used by vested interests, including politicians and bureaucrats, to substantially delay or even block the necessary change. In turn this contributes to low productivity. At the same time, however, it insulates the system from unexpected shifts in policy. When a change is actually made, it is rarely unanticipated.

Panagariya is not alone in extolling the virtues of gradualism. The most high-profile thought leader in the Congress reforms execution,

Montek Singh Ahluwalia, has explored the theme intellectually as well as in action. 'The impact of ten years of gradualist economic reforms in India on the policy environment presents a mixed picture,' he concluded a decade after the 1991 reforms had been introduced.[19] 'Gradualism,' he writes two decades later in his 2020 book …[20]

> … made sense at the start of the reform process because we were not sure how the economy would respond to economic reforms. We now know that it can respond well. The case for faster change is also reinforced by the fact that growth is bringing about structural change in the economy at an accelerated pace and these changes pose new challenges that must be addressed with urgency.

Citing Chile and Poland as examples of 'shock therapy', versus the poor record of some other East European countries, scholar Baldev Raj Nayar compares the two approaches.[21] Mainstream economists, he argues, prefer shock therapy or what is known as big bang reforms:[22]

> They believe it delivers better results since it sweeps away the debris of the previous system with all its accumulated irrationalities […] On the other hand, the gradualist approach is less well regarded because it is believed that it retards the process of economic policy reforms after the first flush of enthusiasm as lobby groups mobilize to defeat change that would affect their narrow interests, even if it is beneficial for the country as a whole.

In the area of privatization of public sector enterprises, Devesh Kapur and Ravi Ramamurti argue, 'Gradual privatization is the international norm and rapid privatization is the exception.'[23] Examining the politics behind reforms, they see slow pace of privatization as a tool that gives opponents (employees, labour unions, bureaucracies, and opposition parties) time to organize resistance:[24]

> Any misstep on the government's part provides a particularly good opportunity for opponents to derail the programme, as happened in 1992, after the first block of shares in SOEs (State-Owned Enterprises) were sold to government-owned mutual funds and became embroiled in a major financial scandal (the Harshad Mehta scam), and again in the mid-1990s after the fiasco with auctioning the telephone licenses. Each such misstep was followed by a lull in privatization.

While this debate continues to date, new political stances have been adopted in support of incrementalism and against big bang reforms. The idea of seeking 'consensus' stands out in recent reform attempts; the farm laws, discussed earlier, for instance.[25] But unlike Switzerland, India's democracy is not a policy-by-policy expression of the majority. And even if the majority vote in favour of a particular policy it doesn't mean that will become the policy; it usually has to go through a process of judicial scrutiny. The ideal world, when 'in a single stroke, the statement of industrial policy dated July 24, 1991, did away with investment licensing and myriad entry restrictions on the MRTP firms' or 'ended public sector monopoly in many sectors and initiated a policy of automatic approval for foreign direct investment up to 51 percent' has been forgotten.[26]

Coming from that perspective, I believe and tend to agree with Ahluwalia that we need to give up on gradualism and seek out big bang reforms. And as such, what is being defined as 'reforms' in V.P. Singh's 1990 policy, in Indira Gandhi's 1980 policy (See Chapter 10), or even in Rajiv Gandhi's endeavours of the mid- to late-1980s, is really the ascent of incrementalism. They functioned in the coalition politics of the day. They were also laced with regressive and outdated ideologies. They attempted to stand on two boats together, one leg in the failed policies of a past adrift and the other in a future of aspirations dynamic. And they may have cleared space for reforms.

But the space they created needed to be filled with policy courage. What India needed was simply to look out and examine the high growth models that were shaping the prosperity of East Asia, notably South Korea, Taiwan, Hong Kong and Singapore through the 1950s, 1960s and 1970s, or China from the 1980s. It needed to break out of its policy lethargy or incrementalism and move with the world towards a new dynamism, deliver a higher standard of living to citizens while catalysing wealth creation. It needed to unshackle the Indian economy. It needed to end economic repression. None of that happened. It took a major macroeconomic crisis and a committed leader called P.V. Narasimha Rao along with his high-intellect team to pull the ship of Indian economy out of the low tide of indolence, inertia and stagnancy and steer it into the high seas of vitality, dynamism and growth. We examine this pathbreaking policy in the next chapter.

12

The Beginning of India's Economic Reforms, 1991

Two documents out of three, all crafted and made public in 1991, have changed the policy playbook of the Indian economy over the past three decades. These documents were brought together by a courageous and risk-taking prime minister, a knowledgeable and experienced finance minister, and a sharp team of politicians, economists and bureaucrats. Such teams may have existed in policy constructions of the past, but other than the political leadership, they were conspicuous by their absence from the public sphere. In relation to the 1991 policies, each of these shared credit, held forth on, and continues to influence, India's economic policy, directly or through their ideas, even today. Not one, not two, not three ... There are several authors of this policy in the public space.

While the then prime minister P.V. Narasimha Rao was the political anchor of this policy, his finance minister Manmohan Singh became the public face. Manmohan Singh oversaw and argued for the reforms delivered and the economic freedom unleashed from 1991 onwards. Other key political players were politicians and ministers P. Chidambaram and

Jairam Ramesh, both of whom continue to endorse and strengthen these ideas, mostly in tune with the increasingly Left-leaning and outdated politics of their party, the Indian National Congress. Technocrat economists led by, but not limited to, Montek Singh Ahluwalia and Rakesh Mohan, now part-time member of Economic Advisory Council to the Prime Minister, continue to power their policy actions of the past even now, with books, papers and speeches that question the present and influence the future; both remain credible economists. All of them have given due credit to the economic bureaucrats of the time, notably then Cabinet secretary Naresh Chandra and then principal secretary Amar Nath Verma.

The year 1991 was a magical moment in the intellectual journey of India's economic policymaking. It was a coming together of the time, the people, the need and the change—all bound together by a looming balance of payments crisis. This was never seen before and has not been experienced since. In fact, there is an entire book to be written about how this team functioned, the challenges it faced, the steps it took and the impact it has had on the country's GDP growth, poverty reduction, markets. Given these numbers and in fact driving them, the impact on the political psychology of the nation through its wealth creators has been explosive. Placed against the restraints of the previous forty-four years of economic repression, the freedom these policies granted have helped entrepreneurs soar over the next three decades. In the process, millions of jobs have been created, and hundreds of millions have been pulled out of poverty.

The India consumption story has gained unimagined traction among the middle class. Products and services have expanded to create a market deep enough to support international capital, both through direct and financial investments. The economic strength these policies powered has made us the world's fifth-largest economy in thirty years; India is soon to be the world's third-largest economy within this decade. This growing economy has been accompanied by a global influence on the high table of international affairs, notably its weight in G20, Quad, and BRICS. This growth has also invited challenges from the increasingly roguish and hegemonic nation, China; the scale of a nation's adversary tells you a lot about the strength of a nation.

The 1991 policy framework can also be seen as a platform that has enabled five successive prime ministers to deliver reforms. To illustrate, we can look at it as a road project, on which different leaderships have driven innumerable reforms, both in the Union and in states. Although this book has identified seventy most impactful reforms (See Chapter 13), this is barely skimming the surface. Beneath each big reform lies many smaller steps. A reform enacted in Parliament through a new law, for instance, has many rules and often is delivered at the level of states, each of which adopts the reform to serve its specific constituents.

Until the next industrial or mega policy framework is devised, the 1991 policy troika will remain the guidebook of India's economics. It has been, and will continue to be, the benchmark against which economic policy will be measured. For any policy devised, the contours of analysis will lie in the ideas and frameworks this paradigm shift created. Of course, the sophistication of policy tools has jumped several rungs in the past three decades. But just as the political foundations remain rooted in the socialist pattern of society, the reference point for arguments in the economic domain are, and will remain in the foreseeable future, anchored to 1991.

A 20/20 hindsight showcases the impact of 1991 as a year of great change. But this transformation becomes even sharper when contrasted with the ills of the previous forty-four years that culminated in the macroeconomic and balance of payments crisis of 1990. Politics is partly to blame. Two unstable Union governments, the first led by Prime Minister Vishwanath Pratap Singh and supported by the BJP for eleven months (2 December 1989 to 10 November 1990) and the second by Prime Minister Chandra Shekhar with the support of the INC for seven months (10 November 1990 to 21 June 1991), ensured that all conversations on and around the economy were not untouched by politics.

Around the time V.P. Singh took charge as prime minister in end 1989, he inherited an economy that was already teetering and 'was truly a crisis foretold. The current account deficit in the BOP (balance of payments) had averaged 1.5 per cent of GDP in the first half of the 1980s and increased in the second half, reaching 2 per cent in 1989–90. However, while the government inherited a festering problem, it was squarely its responsibility to take corrective action and it failed to do so.'[1]

The numbers were screaming in agony. India's import cover of reserves had been consistently falling. From almost ten months in 1977–78, the import cover had fallen to less than two months by 1989–90. This was not the first financial stress India faced from outside. It was the fifth, after the devaluation of 1966, the first oil shock of 1973, the second oil shock of 1980, and the third oil shock of 1990. It would not be the last either. Following the external payments crisis of 1991, India has faced and come out fairly safe from two financial ricochets—the Y2K crisis of 2000, and the Trans-Atlantic economic crisis of 2008.

But none of these matched the financial havoc of the 1990 crisis. When Saddam Hussein invaded Kuwait on 2 August 1990, it not only doubled the prices of crude oil to $34 per barrel in November 1990 within four months, it also hit India's remittances, as 1,50,000 Indian citizens were evacuated and brought back to India. Around this time, Vishwanath Pratap Singh resigned as prime minister and Chandra Shekhar took charge. Amid a well-intentioned mismanagement of the economy, India's foreign exchange reserves fell to $1 billion (on a GDP of $270 billion)[2] in June 1991, covering barely two weeks of imports.[3]

Apart from problems that had their fulcrum outside India, there was economic mismanagement on the domestic side too. India's fiscal deficit had risen to a mind-boggling 9.4 per cent in 1990–91, about three percentage points higher than the average of 6.3 per cent in the first half of the 1980s. Apart from the second oil shock and agricultural subsidies, defence expenditure had increased and direct taxes reduced. Unable to contain government expenditure, the Union budgetary deficit was higher by 30 per cent in 1989–90, while the RBI credit to government was double of that in the previous year. These led to severe consequences. Reserve Bank of India:[4]

> First, to the extent that this entailed recourse to the Reserve Bank, the deficit turned out to be the principal factor propelling high rates of monetary growth, which, in turn, fuelled inflationary pressures and expectations. Second, the greater recourse by the government to borrowing from the commercial banking system as well as directly from the households claimed a higher proportion of household savings for government expenditure, leaving a lower proportion for use in directly productive sectors, such as industry and agriculture. Third, the mounting stock of public debt led to mounting interest payments on the government's revenue account, which exacerbated the problem of continuing revenue account deficits and pre-empted an increasing fraction of the government expenditure to meet such debt-service obligations. Finally, the high deficit spilled over into the BoP gap, with the resultant drawdown of foreign exchange reserves.

Had it not been for the gold sales by the Chandra Shekhar government—when Finance Minister Yashwant Sinha authorized the State Bank of India to sell 20 tonnes of gold from the government's stock, which had been confiscated from smugglers, to the Union Bank of Switzerland for $200 million in April 1991—and negotiations for pledging 47 tonnes from gold reserves to raise another $405 million from the Bank of England, India would have defaulted. The government also sought emergency bilateral assistance from Japan ($300 million) and Germany ($60 million).[5] Montek Singh Ahluwalia:[6]

> Though the Chandra Shekhar government was criticized for 'selling the family jewels', these were actually bold decisions indicating that the government was willing to take unpopular steps to stave off default. Dr [Manmohan] Singh later went out of his way to praise Sinha for this action because it created credibility that India could take tough action if necessary.

Elections followed, Rajiv Gandhi was assassinated, the Indian National Congress came to power and P.V. Narasimha Rao was made prime minister.

In a nutshell, the economy Rao inherited was in shambles. The inflation rate was 13.9 per cent, second only to 1974's 28.6 per cent. Lending rates stood at 17.9 per cent, while real interest rates were 3.6 per cent. The annual growth rate stood at 1.1 per cent. India's per capita income was $303 on absolute basis and $1,230 on a purchasing power parity (PPP) basis. Almost half the population faced poverty, spending less than $1.90 a day in PPP terms, against 36 per cent for the world average. Life expectancy at birth was 58.3 years, compared to the world average of 65.6 years.[7]

Selling or pledging gold, obviously, was not enough. The overvalued rupee since the late-1980s had made Indian products less competitive than the rising Asian Tigers, now roaring their way to growth. Devaluation of the rupee was not only needed, it became a macroeconomic imperative. But apart from delivering an economic shock to the economy, devaluation was equally a political weapon. Bringing his vast administrative experience in government to the policy plate, Finance Minister Manmohan Singh implemented the devaluation policy through the Reserve Bank of India in two steps—the first, on 1 July 1991, involved the testing of waters and finding them shallow enough; the second two days later, on 3 July 1991. The two devaluations reduced the value of the rupee by 18.7 per cent in dollar terms. Working in tandem, the RBI raised policy rates and term deposit rates to prevent inflationary fires.[8]

But these were merely operational steps. They did not and could not fix the underlying malaise of the Indian economy. So dire was the situation and so alarming its financial consequences that it took the same institution that destroyed the Indian economy over the previous four and a half decades, politics, to put it back together. Within politics, it took the same party that had smothered and repressed the Indian economy—Indian National Congress—to free and fix it.

The 1991 story is, therefore, one of economics defeating ideology. It is a saga of the victory of national interest over virtue-signalling. It is a tale of the rise of economic freedom over state control. But above all, it is an argument for economic survival and future prosperity that came after an entire array of failed policies of the past. Alongside the 1991 balance of payments crisis, this was equally a political-ideological crisis seeking an alternative model of development, poverty alleviation and GDP growth.

The reforms P.V. Narasimha Rao brought in or set in motion were economic in their expression, but political in their stance. The economy was the body, politics the mind. Standing between them, and setting the course for prosperity, the Statement on Industrial Policy 1991 became a rendezvous where a changed ideology, a courageous politics and an economic crisis came together to meet time, talent and tasks. That tryst with change has stood strong for thirty years.

The Groundwork and Intellectual Frameworks

To understand the on-ground realities of how difficult it was to do business in pre-1991 India, here is an excerpt from a book by Rakesh Mohan, one of the technocrat-drafters of the 1991 policy. The macroeconomic problems that faced the nation in their compounded form were aggregated from the microeconomic difficulties entrepreneurs faced:[9]

> Prior to the sweeping industrial policy reforms of 1991, the establishment and operation of an industrial enterprise in India required approval from the central government at almost every step. Before making an investment, an entrepreneur had to obtain an 'in principle' approval from the Ministry of Industry. The granting of this approval resulted in the issuance of a 'Letter of Intent' (LoI), which usually included a requirement for a phased manufacturing programme (PMP) aimed at progressive indigenization of the manufacturing process. Armed with this

> LoI, the entrepreneur could then tie up other requirements for setting up the project. If he needed to import capital goods, he had to obtain a capital goods import licence from the Chief Controller of Imports and Exports (CCI&E), in the Ministry of Commerce. The approval for the import, however, was given by a committee set up in the Ministry of Industry. If there was also a need for a foreign collaboration agreement, as there usually was, the entrepreneur had to obtain a specific approval for this, an 'FC' approval, from a committee chaired by the finance secretary, but serviced by the Ministry of Industry, which then enabled the allocation of foreign exchange from the RBI. In order to raise funds for the project, if an entrepreneur wanted to go to the capital market, he needed separate approval from the Controller of Capital Issues (CCI) in the Ministry of Finance. For import of raw material and components, separate licences had to be obtained on an annual basis from the CCI&E, with the list each year having been determined by the requirements of the PMP. In each case, an essentiality and indigenous non-availability clearance had to be given by the technical wing of the Ministry of Industry, the Directorate General of Technical Development (DGTD). Once everything was tied up and the unit was about to go into production, the entrepreneur had to go back to the Ministry of Industry for an Industrial Licence, and then approach the government-owned development finance institutions for funding. In this whole approval process, the DGTD was the linchpin as it alone was supposed to possess the technical knowledge needed to process the approvals at this stage.

Parts of these distortions worked their way through what was being alleged as economic reforms. That is, use the expression 'economic reforms' as a branding exercise to legitimize and 'satisfy the "aid-givers", whether from the World Bank, or from the richer countries like the US, West Germany and Japan, from whom the Indian government and big business are seeking assistance', wrote H.K. Paranjape in a sharp paper seeking liberalization from the 'vice-like grip of parasitic "rent" seeking politicians and bureaucrats':[10]

> This manner of liberalization in doses, sometimes small, sometimes large, also serves the purpose of keeping the discretionary powers of the government largely intact. Every time a basic structural change which would lay down clear-cut guidelines and rely on macro-instruments has been suggested, those in power have defeated it. Whether it was the Dutt Committee in 1969–70, or the Narasimhan Committee in 1983–84, the bureaucracy makes sure that its power and authority do not suffer; and those in political authority agree, for they benefit probably even more as a result.

Keeping this as background and the macroeconomic crisis as trigger, there are three men (the 1991 economic reforms story has no women characters) who prepared the intellectual groundwork for the Industrial Policy 1991. One end saw veteran politician Pranab Mukherjee deliver resounding rhetoric but refrain from moving away from the past. In the middle was young politician Jairam Ramesh who tried to bridge the past and the present to guide the future. And on the other end, technocrat Montek Singh Ahluwalia, with a clearer mind, advocated for shedding the past to drive a new future.

First, Jairam Ramesh, who prepared 'A discussion paper on new industrial policy initiatives' in September 1986. His ideas were lucid, his arguments strong. But he devised the recommendations in that present, keeping one foot in the regressive ideas of the past and one in the potentially bright but invisible-yet future. Some of his pointers and recommendations:[11]

- The swing from one extreme of controls and regulations to the other extreme of permitting a 'free for all' in many technology-intensive industries has resulted in fragmentation of capacities that would result in high costs. An appreciation of market structure would involve acceptance of an oligopoly in many technology-intensive industries. This simply means that a few (between five and eight) procedures would control the market and would aggressively fight it out for establishing market share.

- We should be actively allowing a large company to grow. For this major modifications will have to be introduced in the MRTP Act to permit large companies to become truly international giants.
- On market development, Ramesh offered specific proposals—legal changes for cement, easier credit for commercial vehicles, procurement policy for capital goods.
- To remove infrastructural bottlenecks, his advice was to make states the stakeholders: each State must have an industrial location policy of its own—a policy that is clear in terms of the types of industries it wants to attract and how these should be dispersed within the State.
- He was in favour of sector-specific liberalization versus an across-the-board approach.
- On capital markets, his approach was in the right direction (expanding investors, for instance) but he could not let go of state control ('with proper pricing at least 50 per cent more capital can be raised from the public').

Read together, it seems Ramesh knew what needed to be done but keeping the political proclivities of his party in mind, was exercising self-restraint. Despite calls to open the economy he continued with an underlying layer of controls. Of course, a full-blown crisis was yet to emerge. Another way to look at his recommendations is that while they attempt to fix the economy, his approach is that of a pragmatic gradualist rather than a big banger. If he had drafted this paper three or four years later it would have looked different.

Second, Montek Singh Ahluwalia, whose 34-page note to Prime Minister Vishwanath Pratap Singh titled 'Restructuring India's Industrial, Trade and Fiscal Policies' put together key changes needed for the economy. Informally called the 'M Document', the June 1990 note sought the following (paraphrased):[12]

- Reduce fiscal deficit.
- Contain defence expenditure, and food and fertilizer subsidies.
- Restructure ministries to reduce staff by 10 per cent.
- Do not push expenditure commitments such as the Right to Work until resources situation improved.
- Public sector reforms: partial privatization, exclude PSUs from the definition of 'state' under Article 12, shut down unviable PSUs, reserve strategic and mineral resources for PSUs, end preferences to PSUs in purchases, and make wage negotiations on the basis of the ability to pay rather than uniformity.
- Expand the coverage of liberalization.
- Ease FDI norms.
- End import licensing for a wide range of products.

'It was clear to me that the central economic challenge for India was how to break out of the low-growth trajectory and ensure that higher growth would benefit lower-income groups in sufficient measure. In India, there was a tendency in public debate to denigrate growth on the grounds that it did not help the poor,' writes Ahluwalia, capturing the povertarian ideas of the nation, whose echoes continue to linger aimlessly in policy corridors even today. 'But our problem was not that growth did not trickle down to the poor, rather that the rate of growth itself was too low.'[13]

And third, Pranab Mukherjee whose February 1991 note on the economic situation for a meeting of the Congress Working Committee was general in its approach and poetic in its push: 'Congress Working Committee firmly believes that before the end of this century this last decade of the nineties can be the decade of transformation for [the] Indian economy—transformation from sluggishness to dynamism, transformation from stagnation to growth and transformation from "closed economy" to "open economy.'" Perhaps the word 'transformation' of the Indian economy that has been incessantly used by all governments post 1991 has its rhetorical roots here.

Mukherjee, the epitome of Indian politics, remained guarded and restrained about critiquing the past and the party. He made some interesting observations, but refrained from embracing change:[14]

- He began with courage and hope: The immediate task before the government is to remove the sense of panic and frustration and to restore confidence in the system.
- But without batting an eye, he pulled out the dark spirit of the 1970s: The psychology of scarcity should be removed and stringent measures taken against hoarders, black marketeers, smugglers and profiteers who want to exploit the situation.
- Then, he got political, as all leaders are inclined to be: There is no doubt that the panic reaction of the erstwhile Janata Dal Government and its failure to locate alternative sources of crude oil supply since the beginning of the Gulf crisis created the dislocation in availability of diesel, kerosene and petrol.
- A loyalty statement followed: Although in growth rate terms, the performance in the eighties has been very dynamic it did create some major weaknesses and structural imbalance. Mainly because of the failure of public sector enterprises [not policies, ideologies or politics, but PSEs under the control of the same government, which could not even defend themselves]. Our public sector has failed to exhibit the quality needed to cope with the fast pace of change.

Mukherjee remained rooted in the policies and approaches of the past and stayed a loyal articulator of the Gandhi family. Above all, despite being one of the most knowledgeable leaders of the Indian National Congress, with access to all information and experiential knowledge about the nuances of the economy, he remained the quintessential Congressman—a devoted statist.

Other than Jairam Ramesh, Montek Singh Ahluwalia and Pranab Mukherjee, there were others who added their weight to this discussion at various points in time. In a 1 July 1991 statement titled 'Agenda for Economic Reform', P.N. Dhar, I.G. Patel, M. Narasimham and R.N. Malhotra bemoaned the fact that the nation had 'got used to living beyond our means, our persistently high fiscal deficits and current account deficits are testimony to the firmly-grounded belief that social and economic responsibility carries no penalty'.[15]

Apart from holding forth on bringing efficiencies in the public sector, freer induction of foreign investment and fiscal adjustment, they were clear about the underlying requirement of economic reforms—courage. 'Vigorous growth will not come from doing more of what we have done before. A bold programme of setting free initiatives and capabilities will have to be put in place. For this, resolution and courage are needed. But, more importantly, shedding of dogma is indispensable.'

In addition, they not only supported going to the International Monetary Fund and accepting its conditions, they pushed for the expected conditionalities irrespective: 'We need indeed, self-imposed conditionality in the three major areas where the IMF also is likely to ask for reform, viz in correcting the fiscal deficit, in having an appropriate and competitive exchange rate and in moving towards an open economy.'[16]

Eight days later, in ideological odds of more than eight-to-one, 35 Leftist economists offered a collective response. On 8 July 1991, they issued a statement consisting of six paragraphs titled 'Structural Adjustment: An Alternative Viewpoint'.[17] As part of a well-oiled playbook of arguments, or rather substantively poor but morally rich rants, they accused the government of fashioning domestic policies 'in keeping with the requirements specified by the IMF':[18]

> In a peculiar effort at a two-stage devaluation of the rupee, its value has been reduced by around 20 per cent relative to most

> leading currencies. And judging by statements by government spokesmen, a major liberalization of the trade regime, the financial structure and industrial policy, as well as a substantial reduction in subsidies on food and fertilizer are in the offing.

Devaluing the rupee would mean inflationary pressures on the economy due to the import bill or fiscal pressures at a time of high fiscal deficit. Unable to envision the changes happening around the world and unwilling to look beyond the Leftist eat-the-rich rhetoric, they proposed higher direct taxes—no lessons learnt from the expropriative tax rates of the 1970s. Finally, they recommended 'a carefully modulated reform programme, wherein the highest priority is given to raising the productivity of all the Indian workers, through better education, while the system is de-bureaucratized and strengthened before subjecting it to international competition in a fundamentally iniquitous world system'.

P.V. Narasimha Rao did not waver, ignored these rants and went ahead. Backed by a smart and enthusiastic team, the kind we have never seen before or after, in the middle of a crisis that could have seen the Indian economy fall off the fiscal cliff with all the accompanying financial bruises, he took all such attacks on his chin and bravely went ahead with reforms. The rest is not only history but historic.

That his party, the Indian National Congress, would disown him or smother his legacy doesn't shock us. That the nation till date doesn't give him the credit he should have got does—lesser and destructive prime ministers have received India's highest award, the Bharat Ratna, but P.V. Narasimha Rao hasn't. The constraints under which he ushered in economic reforms is the reason why leaders who followed him could move forward with confidence and take India ahead. He built the reforms road on which five subsequent prime ministers—Atal Bihari Vajpayee (two terms), H.D. Deve Gowda, Inder Kumar Gujral, Manmohan Singh (two terms) and incumbent Narendra Modi (serving in his second term)—were (Modi still is) able to drive change. Between the two ends of the time spectrum, from P.V. Narasimha Rao's compulsions to Narendra Modi's convictions, lies a thirty-year-long journey that has irreversibly transformed India.

India needed a political pact to fix the economy. That accord—call it India's 'new deal'—fell in place on 24 July 1991, three weeks after the rupee devaluations. The devaluations of the rupee, having passed the test of politics in favour of economics, gave P.V. Narasimha Rao the confidence to push down on the reforms pedal. It wouldn't have been an easy task. Several of his own party colleagues, led by Pranab Mukherjee, were against economic reforms. Irrespective, in the larger swathe of history, thankfully these oppositions did not matter. Thirty years later, 24 July 1991 can be called the Wednesday India's economic repression ended and business breathed the air of freedom.

A Political Preamble as Cover Fire

Despite being a bold and big bang reform, Prime Minister P.V. Narasimha Rao's Statement on Industrial Policy 1991 could not escape paying obeisance to the Family. This statement, the exact opposite of all past industrial policies, could not get past the gate of the Gandhis without turning the administrative excesses and pathetic outcomes into a virtue, and crediting those policies with a Triple-A rating on outcomes. Something like a Preamble to the Policy, this is a small but significant price paid to whitewash the regressive policies of the past, even as the foundations of freedom were being rebuilt; anything else would have been career debilitating. It can also be seen as giving cover fire to reform warriors as they dismantled the now-collapsing economic infrastructure from within.

First, it credited Prime Minister Jawaharlal Nehru and termed an economy on the brink of disaster as 'a major industrial nation of the world'. Effectively, it saw economic repression as a major contributor to India's performance. It sang praises and justified Nehru's Resolution 1948:[19]

> Pandit Jawaharlal Nehru laid the foundations of modern India. His vision and determination have left a lasting impression on every facet of national endeavour since Independence. It is due to his initiative that India now has a strong and diversified industrial base and is a major industrial nation of the world.

... as well as his Industrial Policy Resolution 1956:[20]

> In 1956, capital was scarce and the base of entrepreneurship not strong enough. Hence, the 1956 Industrial Policy Resolution gave primacy to the role of the State to assume a predominant and direct responsibility for industrial development.

The justifications continued, this time to pay homage to Prime Minister Indira Gandhi, the expander of, among other evils, nationalization and the tightening of the licence-permit-quota raj. Both her policies were lauded. First the 1973 policy ...[21]

> The Industrial Policy Statement of 1973 [under Indira Gandhi], inter alia, identified high-priority industries where investment from large industrial houses and foreign companies would be permitted.

... and then, the 1980 policy:[22]

> The Industrial Policy Statement of 1980 [again under Indira Gandhi] focussed attention on the need for promoting competition in the domestic market, technological upgradation and modernization. The policy laid the foundation for an increasingly competitive export base and for encouraging foreign investment in high-technology areas. This found expression in the Sixth Five Year Plan which bore the distinct stamp of Smt. Indira Gandhi. It was Smt. Indira Gandhi who emphasized the

> need for productivity to be the central concern in all economic and production activities.

Lest the Family feel that one of theirs had been left out, the policy credited Indira Gandhi's son Prime Minister Rajiv Gandhi with 'increasing productivity, reducing costs and improving quality'. Rajiv Gandhi did not bring out any industrial policy but some of his insipid policy actions and higher economic growth—that brought fiscal excesses along with them—were being packaged as foundations of the 1991 economic reforms:[23]

> A number of policy and procedural changes were introduced in 1985 and 1986 under the leadership of Shri Rajiv Gandhi aimed at increasing productivity, reducing costs and improving quality. The accent was on opening the domestic market to increased competition and readying our industry to stand on its own in the face of international competition. The public sector was freed from a number of constraints and given a larger measure of autonomy. The technological and managerial modernization of industry was pursued as the key instrument for increasing productivity and improving our competitiveness in the world.

A veteran politician, Prime Minister P.V. Narasimha Rao could not get away with just crediting the Family without acknowledging the participation of non-Family leaders in these policy excesses. To create some credibility and a little respectability, a surprising but insignificant line on Prime Minister Morarji Desai's inconsequential 'Industrial Policy—Government Decisions of December 23, 1977—Key Provisions' too found its way into the statement:[24]

> The Industrial Policy Statement of 1977 laid emphasis on decentralization and on the role of small-scale, tiny and cottage industries.

While the small leftover of credit was thrown at Prime Minister Morarji Desai, not a crumb was wasted on Prime Minister V.P. Singh's Industrial Policy Statement 1990, which, as discussed earlier, has been disowned by the state and even its last remnants are not available. Although Vishwanath Pratap Singh's policy offered nothing new, whether his exclusion from this credit-largesse was because he had raised charges of corruption against Rajiv Gandhi or defeated him in elections, is unclear.

'It is a miracle that Indian economy grew at all over the long period of forty years since 1950,' writes Rakesh Mohan.[25] 'The failure of Indian planning and economic policy was that it did not adapt to the changing circumstances as the country grew, and the industrial economy became more complex, and the international environment changed from the relatively stable period of the 1950s and early 1960s to an environment that was characterized by rapid change on a regular basis.'

That complexity can be seen as the changing dynamic of increasing productivity, greater scale of enterprises and freer flows of global capital. You need to be made of a special DNA to remain a bystander while these nation-changing forces take over and you watch other countries race ahead and keep yours poor. India's political leaderships, administrative structures and institutions, and academic thought leaders ... all seemed to be trapped in the inertia of the past, frozen into economic submission, wrapped by indolence.

And then, suddenly, P.V. Narasimha Rao happened.

The Statement on Industrial Policy 1991

'I beg to lay on the Table a statement (Hindi and English versions) on Industrial Policy.'[26]

At 12.50 p.m. on 24 July 1991, with this simple statement—the format for laying all statements in Parliament—the then minister of state in the Ministry of Industry, P.J. Kurien, found his place as a footnote in history. In the course of normal business, such a statement would be preceded by an hour-long speech of great fanfare and rhetoric today. But it did not on that Wednesday. Perhaps it was because of the time, perhaps the fear of reactions from political opponents, or perhaps the uncertainty of it all. Irrespective, the statement permanently etched Prime Minister P.V. Narasimha Rao's place in India's economic history.

Those who had worked hard on it for years were rightly disappointed by its flat, almost apologetic unveiling. Jairam Ramesh:[27]

> That was it. A bland sentence to usher in a radical transformation of Indian enterprise. The occasion was made more ironic by the fact that the junior minister's heart was not in the revolutionary contents of the new industrial policy. In fact, I had reason to believe that lobbying by some prominent figures of industry—nervous about foreign direct investment—had delayed the approval of the new industrial policy.

Howsoever downplayed the mechanics of the announcement, it could not restrain the impact. Among other things, the policy illustrated that P.V. Narasimha Rao understood that the autarchy-like approach to growth had failed the nation, and India's policy design had to take a U-turn. The ideas expressed and the words used would have sent the thrill of adventure down the spines of India's entrepreneurs. India, the policy stated, had to grow 'as part of the world economy and not in isolation'.[28] It talked about a policy framework that would encourage entrepreneurship, dismantle the regulatory system, and develop capital markets.[29] The policy further stated that it would welcome foreign investment.[30]

While these were all forward-looking changes on the economic side, the policy was not bereft of politics. The public sector, it stated, will play its 'rightful role in the evolving socio-economic scenario of the country', will be run on 'business lines', and will continue to lead in 'strategic areas of national importance'.[31] It let go of using investments as the principal instrument for 'controlling the commanding heights', and shifted that control to fiscal and monetary instruments on the one side and state-owned banks on the other.[32] To manage potential opposition, it co-opted labour and announced that it would protect their interests, enhance their welfare, and make them equal partners in progress and prosperity.[33] All these it captured in a single line: 'Government's policy will be continuity with change.'[34]

The politics of continuity announced, P.V. Narasimha Rao was now free to detail out the economics of discontinuity. 'All sectors of industry, whether small, medium or large, belonging to the public, private or cooperative sector will be encouraged to grow and improve on their past performance,' the policy stated.[35] The details were placed under five heads.

1. Industrial Licensing Policy, or Freedom to Invest

The 1991 policy changed the 44-year-old decaying system of industrial approvals by giving entrepreneurs the freedom to invest. Further, it announced a changed role of the government. From a policy that had exercised control over private enterprises, it shifted focus to 'providing help and guidance by making essential procedures fully transparent and by eliminating delays'.[36] Of course, as every entrepreneur worth her enterprise knows, this part hasn't played out that smoothly; the government and its innumerable agencies continue to test the patience of entrepreneurs by delaying or stalling projects. But it was still a start and a breath of fresh air.

Outside the policy, the inclusion of the private sector into areas traditionally reserved for the public sector had been waning. This was on an opaque 'case-by-case' system. Inside, the policy, a disruption was taking place:[37]

> ... industrial licencing will henceforth be abolished for all industries, except those specified, irrespective of levels of investment. These specified industries (Annex-II), will continue to be subject to compulsory licensing for reasons related to security and strategic concerns, social reasons, problems related to safety and over-riding environmental issues, manufacture of products of hazardous nature and articles of elitist consumption.

> The exemption from licencing will be particularly helpful to the many dynamic small and medium entrepreneurs who have been unnecessarily hampered by the licensing system.

Cautious politics, however, continued to underline the policy's bold economics. The phrase 'elitist consumption' seems to have been put forward to tame objections to freedom. The specificity of these proposals to small and medium enterprises, while confessing failure, appears to have been placed to prevent small business political rhetoric from exploding.

The context in place, the policy detailed out the changes. It abolished industrial licensing for all projects except for a short list.[38] This expanded the span of expression for entrepreneurs. But not completely. The policy continued to reserve industries for the small-scale sector.[39] If an entrepreneur needed to import capital goods, automatic clearance was ensured in cases where foreign equity was used or within limits of Rs 2 crore.[40] Foreign exchange being one of the weak links and prime drivers of the policy, managing reserves was important; hence, clearance from the Secretariat of Industrial Approvals in the Department of Industrial Development remained.[41]

Geographically, the policy defined industries that could be set up in specific areas. In cities with populations of more than 1 million, for instance, there was no approval required. Polluting industries would have to be located at least 25 km away from the city.[42] On the procedural front, the policy abolished all existing registration schemes such as delicensed registration or exempted industries registration. All entrepreneurs needed to do was file an 'information memorandum on new projects and substantial expansions'.[43]

2. Foreign Investment, or Partial Opening to Global Capital

Keeping control of the past in one hand and freeing the market selectively with the other, the 1991 policy approved foreign direct investment in 'high priority industries, requiring large investments and advanced technology',[44] by allowing up to 51 per cent foreign equity in such industries. By this clause, the policy shifted its stance from case by case to greater transparency. Apart from defining what high priority industries were, the policy specified that the clearance would be given 'if foreign equity covers the foreign exchange requirement for imported capital goods'.[45] And while it announced that the Foreign Exchange Regulation Act (1973) would be amended to fall in line,[46] payment of dividends would be monitored by the Reserve Bank of India 'so as to ensure that outflows on account of dividend payments are balanced by export earnings over a period of time'.[47] Finally, it disaggregated foreign equity proposals from foreign technology agreements,[48] and allowed 51 per cent foreign equity in trading companies 'primarily engaged in export activities'.[49]

3. Foreign Technology Agreements, or Limited Ease of Approval to High Priority Industries

As with foreign equity, the policy expanded the scope of foreign technology. Here, we see a fundamental understanding of the ways in which technologies work, and the limitations of regulating them:[50]

> In the fast changing world of technology the relationship between the suppliers and users of technology must be a continuous one. Such a relationship becomes difficult to achieve when the approval process includes unnecessary governmental interference on a case to case basis involving endemic delays and fostering uncertainty. The Indian entrepreneur has now come of age so that he no longer needs such bureaucratic clearances of his commercial technology relationships with foreign technology suppliers. Indian industry can scarcely be competitive with the rest of the world if it is to operate within such a regulatory environment.

The change in foreign technology policy was in harmony with and mirrored the foreign equity policy. That is, within the definition of 'high priority industries', the government allowed automatic approval for technology agreements. 'Indian companies will be free to negotiate the terms of technology transfer with their foreign counterparts according to their own commercial judgement,' the policy said in its grand statement,[51] but qualified it with the predictable bureaucratic fine print in its details:[52]

> Automatic permission will be given for foreign technology agreements in high priority industries (Annex III) up to a lumpsum payment of Rs 1 crore, 5 per cent royalty for domestic sales and 8 per cent for exports, subject to total payments of 8 per cent of sales over a 10 year period from date of agreement or 7 years from commencement of production.

4. Public Sector Policy, or Portfolio Review of State-Owned Enterprises

Although the fall of the public sector from the 'commanding role in the economy' to one where it became a symbol of inefficiency, low productivity, poor project management, and overmanning on the one side and low, often negative return on capital, extracted from taxpayers' monies on the other, was long visible, it took the 1991 policy to call it out and announce changes. The policy first encapsulated the malaise ...:[53]

> ... many of the public enterprises have become a burden rather than being an asset to the Government. The original concept of the public sector has also undergone considerable dilution. The most striking example is the takeover of sick units from the private sector. This category of public sector units accounts for almost one third of the total losses of central public enterprises. Another category of public enterprises, which does not fit into

> the original idea of the public sector being at the commanding heights of the economy, is the plethora of public enterprises which are in the consumer goods and services sectors.

... and then designed a new approach, that made these enterprises more growth oriented and technically dynamic. It identified four areas for future growth—essential infrastructure goods and services; exploration and exploitation of oil and mineral resources; technology development and building of manufacturing capabilities in areas which are crucial in the long-term development of the economy and where private sector investment is inadequate; and manufacture of products where strategic considerations predominate such as defence equipment.[54] That said, the policy did not bar the public sector from entering into any other area. Again, keeping the political economy in mind, it made a loud statement on reforms but retained a cautious tone.

While this may give the impression that the government was engaging in rhetoric rather than reality, the fact is a start was made in 1991–92 by disinvesting Rs 3,038 crore worth of shares in various companies to public sector mutual funds in a restricted manner, by bundling profit-making and loss-making enterprises into batches of stake sales.[55] The process gathered steam through the setting up of a Disinvestment Commission in 1996, which recommended divesting stakes in 58 out of 72 public sector enterprises, including 31 through strategic sales.[56] The policy simultaneously pitched for competition through private sector participation in non-strategic areas.[57] Whatever its final expression, the fact is that the 1991 policy brought the idea of public sector disinvestment into public discourse, and remains a work-in-progress even today.

5. Monopolies and Restrictive Trade Practices Act, or Ease of Entry or Expansion

Finally, the 1991 policy eased the provisions of the Monopolies and Restrictive Trade Practices (MRTP) Act, 1969,[58] a law that, while attempting to prevent restrictive practices restricted trade. This law came into force on 1 June 1970 and had five objectives—prevention of concentration of economic power to the common detriment, control of monopolies, and prohibition of monopolistic practices, of restrictive trade practices, and of unfair trade practices. While the law had been successful in keeping its mandate of preventing the concentration of economic power, its fallout was that Indian companies could not compete globally, neither in products nor in scale.[59] That has begun to change in the past few years.

The heartening part of this change was the acceptance of its failure and the ability to change course. It understood the 'complexity of industrial structure and the need for achieving economies of scale for ensuring higher productivity' to engage with the international markets. It squarely pointed out how 'interference of the Government through the MRTP Act in investment decisions of large companies has become deleterious in its effects on Indian industrial growth'.[60]

Operationally, the policy ended the 'pre-entry scrutiny of investment decisions by so called MRTP companies'. The underlining of the expression 'so called MRTP companies' clearly shows that while releasing the document, the government was talking to past policymakers and current adherents to yesterday's business as usual. What this meant was the focus of the government would shift to the objectives of the law—controlling and regulating monopolistic, restrictive and unfair trade practices—rather than making it an office of prior approval for entrepreneurs and businesses to create new companies; expand capacities; merge, amalgamate and take over firms; and more freedom to appoint directors. To ensure the spirit of the law did not get smothered under the rush for freedom, the policy enabled the new MRTP Commission to investigate suo motu or attend to complaints from consumers on the abuse of law.[61]

The policy promised to amend some provisions of the law to bring it in tune with the policy. But these proved inadequate to balance the prevention of firms from becoming large and India's multilateral commitments. This was the time around which the World Trade Organization (WTO) was being formed, and the law lacked the provisions to deal with anti-competitive practices that would accompany WTO agreements.[62]

Recommendations of the S.V.S. Raghavan Committee were clear: the MRTP Act lacked the provisions to deal with anti- competitive practices that may accompany the implementation of WTO agreements. 'In the absence of a proper competitive environment, we may find ourselves with a first class competition law but no competition. We may also end up by protecting the competitor and not the competitive system,' the committee stated.[63] The law was repealed and the committee wound up to give way to the Competition Act in 2002.[64]

The Statement on Industrial Policy 1991 is the R-Document of India's economic reforms. It is the underlying change in approach to the economy that has powered all reforms that have followed over the past thirty years. It is an introspective treatise that despite all the false celebrations of the past acknowledges the failures of the povertarian model India had adopted and shifts gears to be in tune with the rest of the world. Above all, it is a manuscript overseen by Prime Minister P.V. Narasimha Rao that has given courage to successive prime ministers to engage with and deliver prosperity to India, making it one of the fastest-growing economies of the world and moving towards attaining a size worthy of its potential. And like the evolving India story, it is a work in progress.

Union Budget 1991

The 18,425-word budget speech of Finance Minister Manmohan Singh reverberated with the economic agents on 24 July 1991; its essence and ethos continues to give confidence to reformers today, thirty years later. His speech followed four hours after his colleague P.J. Kurien had tabled the Statement on Industrial Policy 1991. While the statement may have been underplayed, the budget speech was not. Read together, and the contents and contours of the economic policy aside, they were a well-timed, well-planned communications strategy. Although Manmohan Singh had 'directly helped prepare seven budgets in the 1970s', this was the first he had conceived, written and delivered.[65] It was his public debut, his moment in history, his magnificent contribution to reshaping India's economic policy.

But even an economist of Manmohan Singh's stature could not stand on his own feet. Like the Statement on Industrial Policy 1991, Budget 1991, in its very first paragraph, paid a cringing obeisance to the Family. 'As I rise, I am overpowered by a strange feeling of loneliness,' this historic Budget speech's second sentence reads. 'I miss a handsome, smiling, face listening intently to the Budget Speech. Shri Rajiv Gandhi is no more. But his dream lives on; his dream of ushering India into the twenty-first century; his dream of a strong, united, technologically sophisticated but humane India. I dedicate this budget to his inspiring memory.' But that would have pleased only one part of the Family. Hence Para 10: 'Thanks to the efforts of Pandit Jawaharlal Nehru, Indira Gandhi and Rajiv Gandhi, we have developed a well-diversified industrial structure.'[66] Altogether, there are three credits offered to Jawaharlal Nehru (Paras 10, 21 and 150); eight to Rajiv Gandhi (Paras 1, 10, 16, twice in 47 and 57 each, and 110); and two to Indira Gandhi (Paras 10 and 150).

My sense is that these paragraphs were placed in the statement by the political side of economic policy. This could possibly be the interventions of Prime Minister P.V. Narasimha Rao or some political advisers down the line.

But despite the thirteen-part obeisance paid to the Nehru–Gandhi Family, Manmohan Singh was castigated by the Congress party. It is a tribute to him that he stood his ground. These preambles may have been a tactic to pre-empt adverse reactions from 24 Akbar Road, the office of the Indian National Congress, the source of past policies, and where a lonely Manmohan Singh would face flak at a meeting of the Congress Parliamentary Party, eight days later, on 1 August 1991. In that meeting he would get no support, neither from P.V. Narasimha Rao nor his colleagues (other than Mani Shankar Aiyar and Nathuram Mirdha), writes Jairam Ramesh,[67] capturing elegantly and dispassionately the

Congress opposition from within to what is now the party's greatest economic achievement. Ever.

In five packed paragraphs, Manmohan Singh recorded the economy he inherited and identified the eleven major problems it faced. First, large and persistent macroeconomic imbalances and the low productivity of investment. Second, unsustainable increases in government expenditure. Third, budgetary subsidies, with questionable social and economic impact, have been allowed to grow to an alarming extent. Fourth, loopholes in and opacity of the tax system. Fifth, poor management of the public sector. Sixth, excessive and indiscriminate protection to industry. Seventh, on the fiscal side, the finances were in crisis, with a fiscal deficit of more than 8 per cent. Eighth, to fix the deficit, huge borrowings resulted in internal public debt of about 55 per cent of GDP. Ninth, as a result, interest payments had risen to 4 per cent of GDP and almost 20 per cent of the total expenditure of the Union government. Tenth, there was a balance of payments crisis looming, with the current level of foreign exchange reserves standing at around Rs 2,500 crore—enough to finance imports for just a fortnight. And finally, inflation had begun to raise its head, standing at 12.1 per cent at the wholesale level and 13.6 per cent at retail.[68]

Essentially, from government finances to personal finances, public debt to foreign reserves, and taxes to potential debt default, macroeconomic crisis to microeconomic impact ... all the problems that could make an economy reel under and tip over, were there as a clear and present danger to India.

The first pillar of Budget 1991 was to enable Indian companies, thus far inefficiently and indiscriminately protected, to face global competition:[69]

> ... the Government has introduced changes in [the] import-export policy, aimed at a reduction of import licencing, vigorous export promotion and optimal import compression. The exchange rate adjustments on 1st and 3rd July 1991 and the enlargement

> and liberalization of the replenishment licence system constitute the two major initial steps in the direction of trade policy reform. They represent the beginning of a transition from a regime of quantitative restrictions to a price based mechanism.

The second pillar was exposing Indian companies to foreign investment. In other words, Indian industry would not merely face competition on the products side through a freer trade regime, it would have to fight global firms that set up industries within India as well.[70] This was a repeat and a reaffirmation of the points made in the Statement on Industrial Policy 1991:[71]

> After four decades of planning for industrialization, we have now reached a stage of development where we should welcome, rather than fear, foreign investment. Our entrepreneurs are second to none. Our industry has come of age. Direct foreign investment would provide access to capital, technology and markets. It would expose our industrial sector to competition from abroad in a phased manner. Cost, efficiency, and quality would begin to receive the attention they deserve. We have, therefore, decided to liberalize the policy regime for direct foreign investment in the following manner. First, direct foreign investment in specified high priority industries, with a raised limit for foreign equity at 51 per cent, would be given prompt approval, if equity inflows are sufficient to finance the import of capital goods at the stage of investment and if dividends are balanced by export earnings over a period of time. Second, foreign equity up to 51 per cent would be allowed for trading companies primarily engaged in export activities. Third, a special board would be constituted to negotiate with a number of large international firms and approve direct foreign investment in selected areas; this would be a special regime to attract substantial investment that would provide access to high technology and to world markets.

The third pillar of Budget 1991 rephrased the Statement on Industrial Policy 1991,[72] this time on disinvestment of shares in public sector enterprises:[73]

> In order to raise resources, encourage wider public participation and promote greater accountability, up to 20 per cent of government equity in selected public sector undertakings would be offered to mutual funds and investment institutions in the public sector, as also to workers in these firms. Public enterprises which are chronically sick and which cannot be turned around, will be referred to the Board for Industrial and Financial Reconstruction (BIFR), or to a similar high-powered body to be set up, for the formulation of revival or rehabilitation schemes; a social security mechanism will be created to fully protect the interests of the workers likely to be affected by the rehabilitation packages of the BIFR. Autonomy in management, and corresponding accountability, would be provided through a system of memorandums of understanding between the Government and public sector enterprises.

The other smaller policies announced in Budget 1991 were support structures to the overall direction of change. They included: a committee to consider all relevant aspects of the structure, organization, functions and procedures of the financial system; reduced intervention in the structure of interest rates; statutory powers to the capital markets regulator, Securities and Exchange Board of India; reforms around stock exchanges, clearing and settlement, and a central depository; private sector entry into mutual funds; ease of entry to non-resident Indian businesses; and a more transparent tariff policy by transforming the Bureau of Industrial Costs and Prices into a Tariff Commission.

Throughout this reformist stance, the burden of ideology continued to bog Manmohan Singh. So the push towards wealth creation was tempered with wealth redistribution. The entire policy edifice was formed around the latter; and in his budget, even as some focus was being placed on the former, it came on a platter called 'conditions apply' that castigated it and celebrated Prime Minister Jawaharlal Nehru's failed mixed economy model. Completely out of tune with the larger economy symphony being played by the Statement on Industrial Policy 1991 and Budget 1991, this was perhaps another political armour to protect the underlying message, which was far more optimistic and profound:[74]

> At the same time, we must restore to the creation of wealth its proper place in the development process. For, without it, we cannot remove the stigma of abject poverty, ignorance and disease. For the creation of wealth, we must encourage accumulation of capital. This will inevitably mean a regime of austerity. We have also to remove the stumbling blocks from the path of those who are creating wealth.

The corollary to wealth creation is wealth consumption. Again, in an economy that had been dwarfed by Nehruvian-povertarian policies, Manmohan Singh attacked consumption, even though it is a legitimate tool of individual expression and economic activity. The words he used are noble, the rhetoric emotional but the direction political and completely off-tune:[75]

> In highlighting the significance of reform, my purpose is not to give a fillip to mindless and heartless consumerism we have borrowed from the affluent societies of the West. My objection to the consumerist phenomenon is two-fold. First, we cannot afford it. In a society where we lack drinking water, education, health, shelter and other basic necessities, it would be tragic if our productive resources were to be devoted largely to the satisfaction of the needs of a small minority. The country's needs for water, for drinking and for irrigation, rural roads, good urban infrastructure, and massive investments in primary education and basic health services for the poor are so great as to effectively

> preclude encouragement to consumerist behaviour imitative of advanced industrial societies. Our approach to development has to combine efficiency with austerity. Austerity not in the sense of negation of life or a dry, arid creed that casts a baleful eye on joy and laughter. To my mind, austerity is a way of holding our society together in pursuit of the noble goal of banishing poverty, hunger and disease from this ancient land of ours.

The resultant tax changes were in harmony with the stance: 'One of the promises made in our election manifesto is to evolve policies and measures to curb conspicuous consumption. In pursuance of this, I propose to increase the excise duty rates on refrigerators, air-conditioners including compressors, motor cars, audio and video cassette tapes, video cassettes, picture tubes, colour television sets, VCRs and VCPs.' Accordingly, the excise duty on refrigerators was increased by Rs 200 to Rs 800;[76] for air conditioners by Rs 2,000, making the price go up to Rs 30,000;[77] on motor cars from 50 per cent to 60 per cent;[78] on audio cassette tapes from Rs 3 to Rs 5 per square metre; on video cassette tapes from Rs 10.50 to Rs 15 per square metre;[79] and on colour TVs by Rs 500 to Rs 750.[80]

But while delivering a reformist budget, Manmohan Singh could not get off the entitlement raj of the Congress model—to deliver policy while remaining rooted in granting entitlements in the name of, and managed by, the Family. In Budget 1991, he allocated Rs 100 crore of taxpayers' monies to the Rajiv Gandhi Foundation, a private charitable institution, set up just three days before Budget 1991[81] was announced.[82]

> The Rajiv Gandhi Foundation has been established to perpetuate the memory of the great leader and to promote the ideals and objectives for which he lived and laid down his life. This Foundation, among other things, will lay particular emphasis on research and action programmes relating to the application of science and technology for development, propagation of literacy,

> the protection of the environment, the promotion of communal harmony and national integration, the uplift of the under-privileged, women and handicapped persons, administrative reforms and India's role in the global economy. As a homage to the late Shri Rajiv Gandhi and in support of the laudable objectives of the Foundation, Government has decided to contribute Rs 100 crores to the Foundation at the rate of Rs 20 crores per annum for a period of five years beginning from the current year.

Predictably, this proposal was rightly criticized by the Opposition. But curiously, even the Congress members of Parliament were not in favour of it—whether theirs was a post-facto change of mind or a principled stance, we will never know. 'The foundation's trustees led by Sonia Gandhi had not even asked for it and, in fact, wanted its withdrawal. Wisely, the finance minister scrapped the idea on 6 August in the Lok Sabha,' writes Jairam Ramesh.[83] Thirty years later, three out of the nine-member board of the Foundation comprise the Family: Rajiv Gandhi's wife Sonia Gandhi, his son Rahul Gandhi and daughter Priyanka Gandhi Vadra. It also includes Manmohan Singh as trustee.[84]

Policy Measures for Promoting and Strengthening Small, Tiny and Village Enterprises

The final leg of the reforms troika was an economically needless distraction but perhaps politically heedful cushion—a focus on small. Thirteen days after tabling the Statement on Industrial Policy 1991 and presenting Budget 1991, the Parliament found itself reading through another document. 'The Policy Measures for Promoting & Strengthening Small, Tiny and Village Enterprises August 6, 1991' (henceforth STV Policy) attempted to show that small but inefficient firms would continue to be protected, their products secured, their financing increased, their compliances reduced. Reforms, in other words, would be limited to large firms. Instead of abolishing all reservations for the small-scale sector and encouraging them to become large or allowing larger firms to use economies of scale to create better products at a cheaper price, the policy turned out to be more political than economic.

Again, as with the Statement on Industrial Policy 1991, this policy was tabled in Parliament with an underlying statement that belied the politics. Here was a chance for the reforming government to show that parts of the economy would continue to revel in business as usual, talk about the 'weaker sections' of business society that create jobs and other such related rhetoric. But what finally happened on 6 August 1991 was as exciting as a cold potato. 'I beg to lay on the Table a copy of the Policy measures for promoting and strengthening small, tiny and village enterprises (Hindi and English versions),'[85] the Minister of State in the Ministry of Industry P.K. Thungon said and silently placed the thirteen-page document in Parliament.

Filled with a series of incentives that ensured the primacy of being small, the STV Policy was a ten-part document that focused on small, tiny and village industries. The rhetoric was strong—efforts to deregulate and de-bureaucratize the sector, remove all fetters on its growth potential, repose greater faith in small and young entrepreneurs, and review statutes, regulations and procedures, and modify them if necessary. And, of course, turn these enterprises that did not need to either pay a minimum wage or conform to laws that protect workers into symbols of job creation and economic nobility. Broadly, the policy focused on two sub-sections—the first seven parts apply to small and tiny enterprises, and the remaining three to village industries.

1. **Tiny Enterprises.** The policy first granted a hike in investment limits, from Rs 2 lakh to Rs 5 lakh for tiny enterprises.[86] This was similar to Prime Minister V.P. Singh's 1990 industrial policy, the Policy Measure for the Promotion of Small-Scale and Agro-Based Industries and Changes in Procedures for Industrial Approvals,[87] which had raised investment limits for small-scale industry. It followed this by expanding benefits given to small-scale enterprises to tiny enterprises. These included preference

in land allocation or power connection, access to facilities for skills and technology upgradation.[88]

2. **Financial Support Measures.** Recognizing that a lack of credit, or its inadequate scale, to small businesses was a problem, the STV Policy changed tack, from subsidized or cheap credit to ensuring an 'adequate flow of credit on a normative basis, and the quality of its delivery, for viable operations of this sector'.[89] To enable small and unorganized units to embed themselves into larger organized firms as subcontractors, the policy allowed 'equity participation by other industrial undertakings in the SSI, not exceeding 24 per cent of the total shareholding'.[90] It promised to liberalize regulatory provisions for small enterprises, including through the creation of a Limited Partnership Act, a law that has become the Limited Liabilities Partnership Act, 2008 and one that was last amended in July 2021.[91]
3. **Infrastructural Facilities.** The policy proposed the launch of a new scheme that would facilitate geographical linkages between rural and urban areas,[92] the setting up of a technology development cell to provide inputs to the small-scale sector,[93] provision of raw materials allocation to the sector (this was a clear return to or extension of the past),[94] and a district-level administrative structure to ensure delivery of these incentives.[95]
4. **Marketing and Exports.** Looking beyond production, investments and finance, the STV Policy continued with the micro-control measures of the past by pushing state infiltration into the marketing of small commercial enterprises by enabling the latter to 'have a significant share of such markets' by using cooperative or public sector institutions.[96] This included using the National Small Industries Corporation to brand and market the products,[97] pushing large public and private firms to source from small enterprises,[98] and the setting up of an Export Development Centre to support small-scale exports.[99]

5. **Modernization, Technological and Quality Upgradation.** This section was a little more than a filler. It has zero consequences. Other than encouraging industry associations to establish quality counselling,[100] clearly displaying the arrogance of the state machinery that knows nothing about doing business, the policy also pushed for enforcing 'compulsory quality control' where risks to human life and public health were concerned.[101] Undertaking studies for commercial viability and financial support,[102] another insipid idea, the policy sought top engineering colleges to serve as 'Technological Information, Design and Development Centres' in their respective command areas,[103] again displaying a hardened reluctance to let go of control.
6. **Promotion of Entrepreneurship.** This, again, shows how far the country's economic policymaking was from wealth creators. The policy said it would teach first-generation entrepreneurs, for whom Entrepreneurship Development Programmes (EDPs) would be expanded by training EDP trainers and motivators.[104] In turn, EDP would be embedded into the curriculum of vocational and degree-level courses.[105] Not to be left un-woke, the policy focused on gender issues by simplifying the definition of 'Women Enterprises', from one that leaned on the number of women workers to one where women had a majority shareholding and management control. Seriously?
7. **Simplification of Rules and Procedures.** If there's one aspect of this policy that had its mind in the right place, it was the excessive regulatory burden on businesses in general. Within the ambit of all businesses, small-scale enterprises face a more daunting battle due to the lack of scale and the accompanying paucity of talent or its funding. 'The persistent complaint of small scale units of being subjected to a large number of Acts and Laws, being required to maintain a number of registers and submit returns, and face an army of inspectors,

would be attended to within a specified time frame of three months,' the policy stated.[106] Further, it said procedures would be simplified, bureaucratic controls effectively reduced, unnecessary interference eliminated and paperwork cut down to the minimum, to enable the entrepreneurs to concentrate on production and marketing functions.[107]

Anecdotal and informal conversations with business persons tell me that the regulatory burden remains strong and is one of the biggest barriers to doing business in India. To give perspective, the regulatory burden Indian businesses face at an aggregate is a universe of 1,536 laws, 69,233 compliances and 6,618 filings. The moment an entrepreneur grows and formalizes her business, it can lead to more than 400 compliances a year that become applicable—overnight. As a result, there are only 1 million formal employers out of 63 million Indian enterprises.[108] Sadly, despite identifying the problem three decades ago, it persists even today.

8. **Handloom Sector.** Other than empty words, political rhetoric and repackaging, there is nothing in this part of the policy. It redesigned schemes keeping local and regional needs,[109] while redrawing extant schemes under three heads—the Project Package Scheme for area-based projects for product development, upgradation of technology, improvement of marketing facilities;[110] the Welfare Package Scheme, which would increase the number of welfare schemes and quantum of funds earmarked for them;[111] and the Organization Development Package, under which share capital would be redrawn for imparting a better management system in the existing state agencies.[112] All bureaucratese for doing nothing. It further expanded the role of the National Handloom Development Corporation to make it the nodal agency for increasing the supply of hank yarn and of dyes and chemicals.[113] Finally, it would undertake 'a more intensive implementation of

schemes for design and product improvement by national level publicity, exhibitions, and design'.[114] In other words, more of the failed same.

9. **Handicrafts Sector.** From encouraging production and marketing[115] to enlarging the production base,[116] this part offered words but little else. It also seems that ideas of reforms had lived their shelf life, with more of the same being doled out. These included extending raw material supply, design and technical guidance; market development by expansion of marketing infrastructure, exhibitions and publicity; and using new channels such as trading companies and departmental stores.[117]
10. **Other Village Industries.** In an attempt to step up non-farm employment in villages, the policy planned to expand the activities of the Khadi and Village Industries Commission and the State Khadi and Village Industries Boards 'to discharge their responsibilities more effectively';[118] instead of fixing itself, the government threw good money after bad. It laid emphasis on improving quality;[119] and among other things, promised to take steps to ensure better flow of credit from financial institutions. (Which large institution would lend to such tiny enterprises and at what cost is left to the imagination.)[120]

In the changing global economic environment, India's small business policies should have taken a different turn. 'In a context where an unprecedented expansion in market size is taking place, the guiding principle of support institutions for small industry should arguably be to reinforce the impulse for accelerated expansion,' the Abid Hussain chaired Report of the Expert Committee on Small Enterprises[121] stated six years later, keeping a sharp eye on growth. 'The social benefits of the enormous public expenditure in nurturing new enterprise can be realized if small scale companies grow rapidly.' Among other things, the expert group concluded that 'the changed economic circumstances suggest that the obsolete policies of small scale reservations should now be abolished'.

Stepping back, this intrusion of politics into economics was not needed; rather, P.V. Narasimha Rao had the opportunity to do the exact opposite. The administrative purchase of political lubricants such that they did not create friction in the larger economic discourse of liberalization, globalization and privatization did not help anyone. Not business. Not GDP. Not the country. Not jobs. Not wealth. Not exports. And certainly not the small-scale industry that has been overtaken by cheaper imports from China, whose landed prices are cheaper than those in India.

This is primarily because scale creates economies, protectionist incentives stunt it. If products made in India and made by small businesses were going to be substantially more expensive and less sophisticated than those made in China, the Indian consumer, freed from the tyranny of high customs duties, would switch. And switch she did. The result: a strategic and economic advantage handed over to China by India on a platter. I can see the policy mandarins of China's India desk laughing at us till today.

This lost opportunity aside, the other two pillars have held together the Indian economic reforms narrative and served the resultant actions well. As the next chapters shows, Prime Minister P.V. Narasimha Rao's 1991 reforms were not merely an economic event to be applauded in isolation; they were the deregulatory highways that changed the course of India's economic destiny, created new pathways for poverty reduction, new avenues for high growth, and an overall rise in prosperity. So strong was this surge of change that subsequent prime ministers have continued to ride it, power it, deepen it. We can visualize 1991 reforms as the laying of tracks on which several engines of growth have travelled, gathered velocity and brought India to where it stands. In the three decades of reforms, constructing these tracks was a paradigm shift. Once built, the diverse leaderships took charge with greater confidence. And each has added, accelerated and permanently altered the course of India's economic journey.

PART III

The Journey of Reforms

13

The Journey of Reforms

The big picture of reforms having been clearly sketched out in the Statement on Industrial Policy 1991 and the Union Budget 1991, this chapter explores the nitty-gritty of India's economic reforms. The sixty-nine reforms examined here tell us that opening the floodgates to prosperity is a necessary condition for reforms. But unless specific policies continuously pass through these gates it will be meaningless.

On that front, across ideologically and politically varying stances, the past three decades have seen India as a consistently reforming nation. Be it P.V. Narasimha Rao or Atal Bihari Vajpayee, H.D. Deve Gowda or Inder Kumar Gujral, Manmohan Singh or Narendra Modi, all prime ministers have done their bit, within the coalition constraints they had, to open the economy, reduce frictions to business and deliver reforms.

This chapter explores India's reforms chronology across leaderships, sectors and policies.

Reform 1: Abolition of Licensing

If an entrepreneur wants to set up an automotive plant today or a robotics plant tomorrow, the one thing she will not need is an industrial licence, a dreaded hurdle of the past. All that companies need to do is file Part A of an Industrial Entrepreneur Memorandum at the time of initiating the project and Part B after commencing commercial production. This is not to seek any permission but for data collection and 'post facto scrutiny of the unit, mainly to preclude them from manufacturing a compulsory licensable item'.

This may sound like a simple, straightforward procedure. But neither simplicity nor economic growth was the focus of India's policymakers till 24 July 1991, when the Statement on Industrial Policy 1991 broke out of the vice-like grip of state control on economic matters and began the process of delicensing. Go back to 1956 and every unit needed a licence that would be granted by the government keeping social objectives in mind. Further, there were seventeen industries, including air transport, telephones and steel, where the private sector could not enter,[1] and another twelve where the state would establish new undertakings.[2] Only the balance was left to the private sector, where licensing became a tool of state control.

The 1991 policy reduced the number of industries under compulsory licensing from eighteen to fourteen by delicensing motor cars, entertainment electronics, white goods and leather. The delicensing of five more industries followed six years later, in 1997.[3] Sugar was delicensed in 1998,[4] drugs and pharmaceuticals in 2005.[5] Today, there are just five industries that need a licence.[6]

Reform 2: Automatic Equity Clearances Expanded

Apart from delicensing, the other important step the Statement on Industrial Policy 1991 initiated was foreign investment. It opened up an automatic route for foreign direct investments (FDI).[7] The new policy allowed automatic approval of FDI of up to 51 per cent of equity in 34 specified high-priority, capital intensive, hi-tech industries, provided the foreign equity covered the foreign exchange involved in importing capital goods and outflows on account of dividend payments were balanced by export earnings over a period of five years from the commencement of production. These included not merely trading companies and tourism but also critical sectors such as hydrocarbons, refiners and marketers of petroleum products. Unable to free itself of the shackles of controls, this route came loaded with eight conditionalities, from geographical location[8] and financial limits,[9] to foreign technology restrictions[10] and projected minimum export turnover.[11]

Further, a Foreign Investment Promotion Board (FIPB) was created to invite, negotiate and facilitate investments by foreign companies with access to high technology and global markets. Non-resident Indians and overseas corporate bodies owned by them were allowed to invest 100 per cent foreign equity in high priority areas.[12] To ensure a level playing field, 'FERA companies' or firms that had more than 40 per cent foreign equity, were allowed to increase their stake to 51 per cent. The result was almost instantaneous: approvals of foreign collaborations in August to June 1992 tripled to 1,430, from 474 for the same period in 1991, while the value of equity inflow jumped more than 100-fold to Rs 1,889 crore.[13]

Reform 3: Foreign Technology Agreements Eased

Along with finance and markets, the lack of access to technology in the pre-1991 regime was a major hurdle to India's growth. Understandable, given the political economy choices of the first four decades that focused on state control, dominance of the public sector and restraints on global money transfers, through overarching economic signals such as the oppressive industrial policies of 1948 and 1956 introduced by Prime Ministers Jawaharlal Nehru and Indira Gandhi, or the Foreign Exchange Regulation Act, 1973.[14]

In 1991, Prime Minister P.V. Narasimha Rao allowed the automatic approval for technologies in high-priority industries[15] for lump sum payment of Rs 1 crore, royalty payments for 5 per cent in the case of domestic sales and 8 per cent for exports, subject to total payments of 8 per cent of sales.[16] He also opened the automatic route for other industries if no free foreign exchange was needed for payments, and removed separate permissions to hire foreign workers or testing indigenously developed technologies and raw materials.[17] These changes catalysed higher FDI into India, while simultaneously providing Indian companies access to modern technologies. However, a large number of MNCs preferred to package foreign technology agreements with equity—the share of companies looking to package equity within a technology agreement increased from 27.2 per cent in 1988–90 to 42.2 per cent in 1991–93, while those preferring to make lump sum payments fell from 74 per cent to 57.6 per cent.[18]

This trend continued. Prime Minister H.D. Deve Gowda raised the ceiling for lump sum payments for technology transfer to $2 million in 1996.[19] Prime Minister Atal Bihari Vajpayee lifted the time restrictions on royalty payments in 2003.[20] And Prime Minister Manmohan Singh permitted these payments without government approval in 2009.[21]

Reform 4: Disinvestment

India's disinvestment journey has been party neutral. The process, initiated by Prime Minister Chandra Shekhar,[22] fine-tuned under P.V. Narasimha Rao[23] and since then, all the way to Narendra Modi,[24] has been on an upward trajectory. In the first flush of disinvestment, the governments chose to replace direct government ownership with an indirect one through government-owned financial institutions such as UTI and public sector mutual funds, under a bundled format of profit- and loss-making enterprises.[25]

This journey of monetizing non-performing assets started in 1991 when 47 public sector enterprises came up for disinvestment as shares in bundles of 'very good', 'good' and 'average' companies.[26] As the gradualism expanded to include 'strategic sales', the eleven years, from 1991 to 2002, saw disinvestment in 68 companies (39 through sale of shares, and 36 through strategic sales) garner Rs 30,917 crore.[27]

Since then, the rate of disinvestment has accelerated. During Modi's tenure so far (from 2014 to 2022), the disinvestment receipts stand at Rs 3,62,765 crore,[28] while another Rs 1,75,000 crore is estimated to be raised in 2020–21.[29] The most difficult disinvestment that Modi has taken so far is of Air India that, after a series of failures in earlier dispensations and through the process of a public auction, has returned to the Tata Group for an enterprise value of Rs 18,000 crore.[30]

The future disinvestment road map will have just four strategic sectors—atomic energy, space and defence; transport and telecommunications; power, petroleum, coal and other minerals; and banking, insurance and financial services. These confirm the contours of India's disinvestment story, launched with the Statement on Industrial Policy 1991, as being one of increasing gradualism, in tune with global norms.[31]

The 17 May 2022 listing of LIC,[32] one of the most looked-forward to Initial Public Offerings (IPOs) was another big disinvestment. More lie ahead.

Reform 5: Abolition of MRTP Houses

When Prime Minister Indira Gandhi pushed through the Monopolies and Restrictive Trade Practices (MRTP) Act in 1969,[33] the policy consolidated the misplaced politics of an economy driven by the socialist ideology that included the government command and control regime, all drafted to ensure that companies did not become large—companies with assets of more than Rs 100 crore required government permissions to set up new undertakings or expand existing ones.[34] Under Prime Minister P.V. Narasimha Rao, the law was amended in 1992.[35] One of the biggest amendments was the removal of these pre-entry restrictions on new undertakings, expansions, amalgamations, mergers, takeovers or appointing directors. It also brought government-owned companies such as nationalized airlines, banks and railways under the law.

The journey from 1970, when the MRTP law came into force, to the mid-2000s, has seen three major policy regimes—a control regime till 1985, a partially liberalized regime till 1991, and a liberalized regime from 1991 to 2003.[36] The MRTP law prevented companies from scaling up and delivering higher productivity on the capital side and offering lower prices on the consumer side through economies of scale. The biggest problem in the MRTP law was that it leaned on the size of enterprises to take a view on restrictive trade practice or unfair competition—big was necessarily bad.

On the recommendations of the S.V.S. Raghavan Committee,[37] which noted that the law lacked provisions to deal with anti-competitive practices and was out of tune with World Trade Organization agreements, it was repealed when Prime Minister Atal Bihari Vajpayee ushered in the Competition Act, 2002, that came into force under Prime Minister Manmohan Singh in 2007.[38] Effectively, Prime Minister Manmohan Singh completed the task that Finance Minister Manmohan Singh had begun.

Reform 6: Securities and Exchange Board of India

Formed as an interim body with a 12 April 1988 government resolution[39] under Prime Minister Rajiv Gandhi with S.A. Dave as chairman, and powered by a 4 April 1992 law[40] under Prime Minister P.V. Narasimha Rao, the Securities and Exchange Board of India (SEBI) is the one financial sector regulator that has evolved with time, learnt from and effectively regulated market failures. It has kept pace with the needs of a changing economy, and has initiated reforms that have enabled the creation of a well-regulated capital market. From companies to exchanges, primary markets to secondary, commodities to mutual funds, and intermediaries to foreign portfolio investments, SEBI has evolved from being a late starter[41] to one that is setting consumer-first standards.

The weak spots in SEBI are intrusions from the government or other regulators. The institution of independent directors, for instance, remains contested and conflicted,[42] around which SEBI has initiated debate.[43] Or its internal lack of credibility when it enforces a 25 per cent public shareholding in private firms but exempts public sector companies because of a government mandate.[44] Or, when attempting to serve investors being cheated by insurance companies under the benign cover provided by the Insurance Regulatory and Development Authority of India; in this, SEBI lost the battle[45] but won the war.[46]

Among all the four financial sector regulators, SEBI stands ahead on every front, from technology adaption to consumer protection. As far as retail investors go, SEBI's framework for regulating mutual funds is arguably the best in the world in terms of low costs and high disclosures. But because of the inbuilt operational transparency, in tune with twenty-first century regulatory practices, SEBI, along with the agencies it regulates, remains the most critiqued, while anti-consumer excesses of other regulators stay hidden in plain sight.

Reform 7: Foreign Exchange Reserves, 1991 to 2021

Inward-looking policies since Independence and a high import bill accentuated by two oil shocks and the resultant heavy debt-servicing pushed India to the edge of a balance of payments crisis, with gross official foreign reserves at 1.3 months of imports by the end of March 1991.[47] With the opening up of the economy in July 1991, FDI inflows into the country started to increase. The relaxed norms for non-resident Indians led to larger outstanding deposits, and the entry of foreign institutional investments that began in 1993 also aided the increase in the foreign exchange reserves in India.

By end March 2005, they had risen to $141.5 billion, a twenty-four-fold rise in fourteen years.[48] The opening up of the economy, the ending of a large part of the licensing regime, a burst of entrepreneurship and the resultant rise in global engagements, saw exports rise from $17.9 billion in 1991–92 to $79.2 billion in 2004–05. Private remittances added their weight and contributed to strengthening the current account.[49]

Since the balance of payments crisis of 1991, it took India more than twelve years and four prime ministers, from P.V. Narasimha Rao to Atal Bihari Vajpayee, to build up its foreign exchange reserves and cross the $100 billion mark by December 2003.[50] Subsequent reforms undertaken by prime ministers Manmohan Singh and Narendra Modi have been accelerating this rise, and as of 23 July 2021, exactly thirty years after the crisis began, India's foreign exchange reserves stood at more than $632 billion,[51] and among the world's top four.[52] They are 45 per cent of Japan's,[53] 58 per cent of Switzerland's,[54] and more than the reserves of Germany[55] and the US[56] combined. A successful virtuous cycle of economic policy powering financial strength.

Reform 8: Deregulating Interest Rates

Opening up the economy but keeping interest rates under control makes for an incomplete policy weave. Here, markets are often the best judge of actions undertaken by economic actors—depositors, intermediaries and borrowers. It enables competition, brings financial efficiencies, and manages rather than controls risk. By regulating interest rates, particularly for consumers, what the government and the Reserve Bank of India were doing till the early 1990s was 'financial repression', one of whose expressions was administered interest rates.[57]

Although the process of deregulation of deposit interest rates began in the 1980s, the initial experiments with freedom were short-lived. The April 1985 policy under Prime Minister Rajiv Gandhi to allow banks to set interest rates for maturities of fifteen days to one year was withdrawn the next month,[58] showing the immaturity of banks and the insecurity of the RBI with markets. It wasn't until April 1992, when deregulation resumed under Prime Minister P.V. Narasimha Rao, that banks were allowed to set interest rates on two-year deposits in October 1995, one-year deposits in July 1996, thirty days to one year linked to the bank rate in April 1997.[59] In October 1997, under Prime Minister Inder Kumar Gujral, the RBI granted banks the freedom to fix their deposit rates.[60]

The stickiest and longest-serving anti-consumer interest rate policy of the RBI has been around the savings deposit rates, which were deregulated in October 2011[61] under Prime Minister Manmohan Singh two decades after the deregulation process began. This finally got the RBI and commercial banks to look at the Indian citizen as a consumer rather than merely a 'human shield to protect bank profits',[62] and completed the circle of India's interest rate reforms.

Reform 9: Liberalizing Exchange Rate Management

Globalization on the investment side needed liberalization on the currency side. As a result, following the direction of the Statement of Industrial Policy 1991, and the economic focus on macroeconomic stabilization, the C. Rangarajan–chaired High Level Committee on Balance of Payments recommended that foreign exchange rates be determined through the market rather than the state. This followed a two-step devaluation of the rupee by 18 per cent, on 1 and 3 June 1991.[63] Introduced in 1992, the Liberalized Exchange Rate Management System (LERMS) was a transitional system with dual rates, balancing full convertibility of the current account with macroeconomic developments in the global economy. On 1 March 1993, a unified exchange rate was introduced, wherein the exchange rate was determined by demand and supply in the Indian foreign exchange market.[64]

Under LERMS, a dual exchange rate arrangement would come into force that would allow higher benefits for exporters, whose prices would become more competitive. This system, which was also applied to the tourism industry in July 1992,[65] allowed businesses to surrender only 40 per cent at an official rate determined by the Reserve Bank of India, with the remaining 60 per cent converted at market-determined rates. The 40 per cent, which was to be surrendered at official rates, would then be used for the procurement of essential imports such as oil, fertilizer and life-saving drugs besides the government's debt servicing, at lower costs.[66] A temporary measure, LERMS began as a tool that taxed exporters to subsidize government imports; but with reserves rising, India shifted to a unified, market-determined exchange rate,[67] an experience that is seen to be 'satisfactory'.[68]

Reform 10: Debt Recovery Tribunals

On 30 September 1990 more than 1.5 million cases filed by public sector banks and financial institutions involving the debt recovery of more than Rs 6,000 crore were pending in various courts.[69] As a result, during Prime Minister P.V. Narasimha Rao's tenure, Parliament enacted the Recovery of Debts Due to Banks and Financial Institutions Act, 1993. More than a quarter of a century later, by May 2016, outstanding debt stood at Rs 4,50,000 crore,[70] a jump of 75 times, or rising at the rate of 18 per cent per annum for 26 years. Other than creating jobs, this 'reform' enacted with the right intentions but loose closures has failed to deliver across all political leaderships.

Part of the failure can be laid on the shoulders of the Executive and the Legislature—the law was declared 'unconstitutional' as it compromised the independence of the Judiciary and lacked provisions for counterclaims by defendants and made it biased towards creditors.[71] Two amendments to the law in 2000[72] cleared the path. But the results since then do not inspire confidence. The other reason for the delays in deciding cases is the economic-judicial actors—more than 40 per cent of the delays are because of the plaintiffs, more than 20 per cent because of defendants, and more than 15 per cent by the Tribunals.[73] This has eroded the edifice of the problem and, like several laws, has been hijacked into irrelevance by the participating actors. Addressing these judicial delays could help revive this institution. Among all changes, this is the last-mile reform needed going forward. Otherwise, it's time to repeal these laws, close this exchequer-funded chapter and confine it to the dustbin of failed policies, to be replaced by a technologically sound and time-bound system.

Reform 11: National Telecom Policy

The first step to realize the full potential of the telecom sector was taken by Prime Minister P.V. Narasimha Rao, with the National Telecom Policy (NTP) of 1994.[74] The NTP was initially announced as a means to provide basic telecommunication services. The policy set a three-year target: telephones should be available on demand, all villages should be covered, and in urban areas a PCO (public call office) should be provided for every 500 persons.[75]

Because the targets were steep and resources few, private companies were allowed into the sector. This was a licensed sector, of which the government had next to zero understanding, while the private sector was on a steep learning curve. The result: defaults on licence fees due to non-viability of projects in eleven out of fourteen telecom circles, and a default rate of almost 80 per cent.[76] Further, there was no mechanism, either with the licensor or the regulator, to ensure optimal utilization of the spectrum by the service providers.[77]

The answer was Prime Minister Atal Bihari Vajpayee's National Telecom Policy 1999,[78] which identified information technology and telecom sectors as major contributors for national growth. The targets of NTP 1994 remained unfulfilled, but NTP 1999 set new ones.[79] It also corporatized the Department of Telecommunications, VSNL and MTNL. A series of policy measures later, India's teledensity has jumped from less than 3 per cent in 1999 to more than 85 per cent in 2020.[80] The big jump in teledensity has come under Prime Minister Narendra Modi and has resulted in India having the world's lowest tariffs, led and nudged by Reliance Jio. And landlines, for which citizens had to go to members of Parliament for recommendations, have now become irrelevant. What remains to be done is for the government to privatize BSNL and MTNL.

Reform 12: India Joins WTO

As one of the twenty-three founding contracting parties of the General Agreement on Tariffs and Trade in 1947,[81] under Prime Minister Jawaharlal Nehru, India expanded its footprint to become one of the 128 members[82] as it got subsumed into the World Trade Organization (WTO) in 1995[83] during Prime Minister P.V. Narasimha Rao's tenure. The two—formation of WTO with India as a founding member[84] and India's reforms journey—not only coincided but established a new global trade equilibrium and a virtual cycle of trade growth by rebalancing asymmetries.[85]

Post 1991, India's liberalization drive for freeing up the industrial sector and boosting its economy were welcomed by WTO members.[86] But during trade negotiations the perception that India was a reluctant participant in making trade deals, bilaterally or in the WTO, arose.[87] India's tone and tenor of trade negotiations was seen as seeking moral victories rather than closing trade deals,[88] a tactic that seems to relish 'getting to no'.[89]

On its part, India has consistently reduced barriers to trade, with successive leaders having greater confidence in taking such strides towards global trade integration.[90] Besides, being seen as a country that places hurdles in the path of doing business rather than one that confidently rides with them is not in tune with the image of a nation that is the world's fifth-largest economy, which is going to be the third largest within this decade.[91] This too is changing; between 2015 and 2019, for instance, India's performance has given the world a 'mixed picture'.[92] In other words, under Prime Minister Narendra Modi, India is negotiating its way through the WTO with greater self-assurance today than ever before. It is also becoming a rule-maker than merely a rule-taker. As world trade goes digital, India must, and likely will, participate and influence that course from within,[93] while staying true to its ancient ethos of negotiating with principles while embracing pragmatism.[94]

Reform 13: Affordable Housing

Affordable housing has been a political economy issue since Independence but it took a quarter of a century before legislative introspection in a 1972 Lok Sabha Estimates Committee resulted in the launch of the House Site-cum-Construction Assistance Scheme in 1974. In June 1985, Prime Minister Rajiv Gandhi rolled out the Indira Awaas Yojana in his mother's name as an extension of the Jawahar Rozgar Yojana (which in turn was after her father), with no cohesive policy direction other than focusing on building houses for Scheduled Castes, Scheduled Tribes and freed bonded labourers. In 1992–93, the scheme was extended to other poor and families of servicemen of the armed and paramilitary forces killed in action.[95]

Other than the branding, the scheme remained ineffective, with rural housing shortage standing at 13.7 million units by 1991. Factoring in population growth, there were an estimated 22.7 million houses that needed to be built to meet the government's target of housing for all. Till 1996, however, only 5.68 million houses had been added.

Under Prime Minister P.V. Narasimha Rao, the scheme was turned into an independent programme in January 1996, with costs shared between the Union and the states in an 80:20 ratio,[96] and revised to 75:25.[97] A 2014 Comptroller and Auditor General report that audited the scheme for the 2008–13 period found several discrepancies with regard to implementation, funding, assessment and selection of beneficiaries.[98]

In 2016, Prime Minister Narendra Modi revamped the scheme and renamed it the Pradhan Mantri Awaas Yojana, under which 13.6 million houses were completed between financial years 2016–17 and 2018–19 in rural areas,[99] and 5.3 million houses in urban areas.[100] With the target to deliver 'housing for all in urban areas' shifted to 2022, the scheme includes rehabilitation of slum dwellers, promoting affordable housing for weaker sections, subsidies for beneficiary-led house construction or enhancement, keeping private developers as a bridge.[101]

Reform 14: Convertibility of the Rupee

Technically, the Indian rupee is not fully convertible. But in areas such as investments or for a group of economic actors such as households it is reasonably so. The time when regulations in the form of walls could prevent the free flow of currencies into and out of India is behind us. Barring a few restrictions, businesses can move money freely. Further, demands for services such as education has enabled households to use this effective convertibility. In 2020–21, Indians spent $6.5 billion on education and upkeep of their wards abroad,[102] or 55 per cent of all outward remittances, almost a 20-fold increase over the past decade, or about 34 per cent per annum.

This is the result of a series of steps by successive prime ministers and the Reserve Bank of India (RBI), to gradually make the rupee more convertible.[103] The Indian rupee cannot be seen to be fully convertible, but the benefits of full convertibility exist within restrictions. The one big hurdle that remains is the ability of households to buy assets abroad beyond $2,50,000 a year.[104] But how many Indians can and will make those investments in houses, restaurants or yachts? This sort of money movement between nations follows trade flows and soon, investments.

The pre-1991 currency hurdles placed before India Inc. and Indian citizens have run their course. India 2022 is wealthier, stronger and more robust on both fiscal and foreign reserves fronts. The risks of a run on the rupee are a figment of the imagination of an RBI still living in that past. This is a reform that has already happened for most: all that remains is an announcement for households. Further, while the 'internationalization of the Indian rupee'[105] cannot come without full convertibility, even though Tarapore argues that 'it can coexist with capital controls',[106] India in the 2020s, and as an economy headed towards becoming $5 trillion strong, should be ready to debate this issue afresh. The only risk to the rupee is geopolitical; that is, being ejected out of SWIFT, the international payments system, the recent instance of Russia being a case in point.

Reform 15: Telecom Regulatory Authority of India

Under Prime Minister P.V. Narasimha Rao, a 27 January 1996 Ordinance was promulgated to constitute the Telecom Regulatory Authority of India (TRAI),[107] a body that would to play the role of a 'watch-dog for the telecom sector'. The government changed and the baton shifted to Prime Minister H.D. Deve Gowda, who established TRAI[108] in February 1997; the next month Parliament enacted the TRAI law.[109]

Since its inception, TRAI has adopted a consultative approach to regulation. Given the rapid and large strides in technology, provision of service-specific licences was next to impossible and would often lead to litigation. TRAI's recommendations for a unified licensing regime[110] were adopted and given the shape of a revenue sharing arrangement in the NTP 1999.

Beginning with the Telecommunication Tariff Order[111] under Prime Minister Atal Bihari Vajpayee, TRAI has ensured fair competition and protection of consumer interest by consultative regulation of tariffs across the country. In 2004, under Prime Minister Manmohan Singh, the broadcasting and cable services sector, another result of rapid technological growth, was placed under the purview of TRAI,[112] resulting in the creation of a regulatory support structure for competition in this emerging market of FM radio and direct-to-home TV.

Over the years TRAI also created the framework for various consumer-centric reforms such as mobile portability[113] and the do-not-disturb register[114] to avoid harassment of consumers by telemarketers (the latter is an abject policy failure). In 2012, in the interest of providing unified licences with even rapidly evolving technology, the government announced the delinking of spectrum allocation from telecom licences.[115] This robust framework paved the way for the implementation of Prime Minister Narendra Modi's JAM (Jan Dhan–Aadhar–Mobile) trinity,[116] thereby making a telecom regulator a catalyst for delivering financial inclusion, the mandate of Reserve Bank of India.

Reform 16: New Normal for Personal Income Tax Rates

The constant changes in personal income tax rates and the slabs they apply to has been a taxing affair for taxpayers. A moderation in rates and a fixity of processes is what taxpayers need, more so in a country where changes in tax rates and their applicability on slabs is a constant, and where only 15 million out of 1.3 billion people pay taxes. Under Prime Minister H.D. Deve Gowda, Finance Minister P. Chidambaram created a three-part tax structure (10 per cent, 20 per cent and 30 per cent)[117] that remained unchanged until recently. This elegant structure continued till under Prime Minister Narendra Modi, Finance Minister

Nirmala Sitharaman brought seven slabs and four surcharges, reversing the gains of simplicity created after decades of harassment.[118]

This distortion aside, the journey of India and its 80.4 million individual taxpayers (as of 2018–19),[119] up from 49.6 million six years earlier, has been in the overall scheme of things, bright. Go back to the 1970s and the marginal rate of taxation was extortionist. Under Prime Minister Indira Gandhi, Finance Minister Y.B. Chavan brought it down to 70 per cent in Budget 1974–75 from 97.75 per cent,[120] Finance Minister R. Venkataraman reduced it to 66 per cent in Budget 1980–81,[121] and Finance Minister Pranab Mukherjee followed through to 55 per cent in Budget 1984–85.[122] Under Prime Minister Rajiv Gandhi, Finance Minister V.P. Singh lowered it to 50 per cent in Budget 1985–86,[123] and under Prime Minister P.V. Narasimha Rao, Finance Minister Manmohan Singh cut it down to 40 per cent in Budget 1991–92.[124] With the effective highest marginal rate of tax being 42.7 per cent,[125] India is back to where it was thirty years ago, higher than Norway and Switzerland but lower than the US and the UK.[126]

Reform 17: Tariff Authority for Major Ports

Despite the spectacular success of Indian ports in reducing the average turnaround time to 2.12 days in 2020 from 8.1 days in 1991,[127] India lags the world averages on every kind of carrier—from liquid bulk to container ships to liquefied natural gas.[128] The big fall came in 2001, when the average turnaround time fell to 4.24 days. This followed the setting up of the Tariff Authority for Major Ports in 1997,[129] under Prime Minister H.D. Deve Gowda, by amending the Major Port Trusts Act, 1963.[130] The objective was to support the entry of private ports with an independent authority that ensured a level playing field by regulating tariffs and rates for lease of properties for eleven major ports.[131]

Two problems arose—first, private firms challenging the tariffs in courts leading to delays; and second, reducing capacities to bare minimum. The result: ports tariff rates working at ceiling rates rather than competition reducing them on the one side, and users migrating to smaller, unregulated ports on the other.[132] As a result of this regulatory shopping, the share of minor ports in total cargo handled in India rose to 45 per cent in 2019 from 39 per cent in 2012.[133]

In February 2021, under Prime Minister Narendra Modi, the Major Ports Trust Act, 1963 was repealed and the Major Ports Authority Act, 2021 enacted.[134] The law enabled the setting up of separate authorities in major ports, with an adjudicating board to resolve disputes. As a decentralization mechanism, with the Union–state representatives on the boards, this is a step in the right direction. But outcomes remain to be seen, more so in the context of an upcoming Indian Ports Bill 2021[135] that proposes to leave the management and administration of the major ports to the board of each port.[136] Because of the Union–states politics,[137] this is likely to remain a work-in-progress going forward.

Reform 18: New Exploration Licensing Policy

As the policy focus of India's leaders shifted from maintaining poverty to seeking prosperity and economic growth became the engine for that transformation, the weak link in this chain—energy—began to show up. A nationalized sector with just two public sector companies in oil and gas exploration and production[138] was found inadequate to feed the energy demands of a growing economy.

Approved by Prime Minister I.K. Gujral in 1997, and executed by Prime Minister Atal Bihari Vajpayee in February 1999,[139] the New Exploration Licensing Policy (NELP) filled the gap. It allowed private companies into the sector with production sharing contracts, 100 per cent foreign direct investment and no mandatory state participation. It also appointed the Directorate General of Hydrocarbons as a nodal agency for its implementation.

Under the NELP, acreages were offered to the participating companies through the process of open competitive bidding, with the government having signed 254 contracts, with a total area of 1.5 million square kilometres awarded.[140] The companies working in the sector also increased from 35 before the NELP to 117 (including 11 PSUs, 58 domestic private companies and 48 foreign companies).[141] Over the past thirty-five years, from financial years 1984–85 to 2019–20, while crude oil production has remained stagnant at around 32 million tonnes, petroleum products have risen by 6.7 times, or 5.6 per cent per annum. But crude oil imports have jumped by more than fifteen times.[142] Lack of oil and gas reserves is one reason;[143] control over those reserves by ONGC and not the private sector is another.[144] But the most important reason lay beyond regulation or supplies. It was the demand side—a fast-growing economy required more energy, and it is clear that the need for energy to drive growth has outstripped capacity or reforms.

Reform 19: Voluntary Disclosure of Income Scheme

'It is inexplicable that in a country of over 900 million people, only 12 million people are assessed to income-tax and, what is worse, only about 12,000 assessees are in the tax bracket of income above Rs 10 lakhs.' Under Prime Minister H.D. Deve Gowda, this statement by Finance Minister P. Chidambaram in the Budget 1997–98 speech[145] was an attempt to contextualize tax evasion. He proposed and launched a Voluntary Disclosure of Income Scheme (VDIS),[146] under which 'irrespective of the year or the nature or the source of the funds, the amount disclosed, either as cash, securities or assets, whether held in India or abroad, would be charged at the revised highest rate of tax', with a waiver on interest and penalties, immunity granted, and a six-month window given. The rate of tax was 35 per cent for firms and 30 per cent for individuals. Of the taxes thus collected, 77.5 per cent would accrue to state governments.

The scheme saw 4,60,031 declarations being made that resulted in tax collections of Rs 10,050 crore.[147] From a justice point of view, such schemes present a moral hazard—they provide amnesty to tax evaders, who end up paying less tax than they should, while honest taxpayers pay their dues. 'This shatters the faith of the common man in the dignity of honest labour and virtuous living and has pernicious effect on the general moral fibre of society,'[148] a Lok Sabha report stated. From a public policy point of view, it was possibly Chidambaram's low tax rate of 30 per cent that turned the tables. This was the eleventh such scheme since Independence (the first one was launched in 1946–47), but the tax collected was more than ten times larger[149] than the next highest collected under the Voluntary Deposits (immunities and exemptions)[150] launched in 1991.

Reform 20: Autonomy to Public Sector Enterprises

From just five Central Public Sector Enterprises (CPSEs) in 1951, under Prime Minister Jawaharlal Nehru, the number had grown to 246 by 1992 under Prime Minister P.V. Narasimha Rao.[151] In other words, driven by a series of industrial policies that ensured the primacy of the state in commercial activities, Indian taxpayers were creating almost six new CPSEs every year, from steel and power to tourism and consumer goods.[152] Following Narasimha Rao's agenda-setting 1991 reforms, Prime Minister I.K. Gujral introduced Navratna[153] and Miniratna[154] CPSEs in 1997, and granted more financial and strategic autonomy to profit-making CPSEs and empowered their boards. Nine CPSEs[155] were given the Navratna status. For a company to be awarded the status of a Navratna, it had to meet financial and operational requirements such as profits in the previous three years continuously, a pre-tax profit of Rs 30 crore or more in at least one of the three years, and a positive net worth.

The outcomes were surprising: Soon after the implementation of this freedom, all CPSEs with negative profits started a positive trend, there was an increase in value addition with more sales being made per employee, and considerable growth in capital assets.[156] Some of these CPSEs started performing effectively relative to the private sector.[157] In 2010, Prime Minister Manmohan Singh introduced another category, called the Maharatna scheme. Offering greater autonomy,[158] the scheme gave their boards the powers to incur capital expenditure without any monetary ceiling, establish profit centres, and go for mergers and acquisitions in core areas.

Today, the list of CPSEs has grown to 348, of which 249 are operational. Eighty-six of these are under construction and thirteen under closure or liquidation.[159] Of them, ten are Maharatna enterprises, fourteen Navratna, sixty-one Category-I Miniratna, and twelve Category-II Miniratna CPSE.[160]

Reform 21: Electricity Regulatory Commissions

The policymakers of India had made the simple business of generating and distributing electricity so entangled that, unlike another critical infrastructure such as telecom, it has lagged the demand and the aspirations of consumers and been unable to deliver the enabling mechanism for GDP growth. The correlation as well as the causality seems to be the policy thrust on restricting the sector to the public sector.[161] Among the several attempts to fix this, one was initiated by Prime Minister I.K. Gujral.[162] It was finally brought to life by Prime Minister Atal Bihari Vajpayee through the enactment of the Electricity Regulatory Commissions Act, 1998.[163]

The law attempted to rationalize retail tariffs, reduce the high level of cross-subsidies, fix the poor planning and operation in the sector, remedy customer neglect, and increase the involvement of the private sector. All this by filling the vacuum of independent regulatory authorities in the Union and states—electricity is in the Concurrent List of the Seventh Schedule of the Constitution,[164] under which legislative powers lie with the Union and state governments—to regulate and determine tariffs of central- and state-controlled power generating companies respectively, for wholesale, bulk, grid and retail.[165]

The commissions were set up within the year and were tasked with increasing the efficiency, quality and quantity of power markets. But despite this reform, on-ground execution remained poor, thereby not only questioning the efficacy of the change but the credibility of the commissions.[166] Besides, turf conflicts between bureaucracies[167] prevented any visible outcomes of the reform, and which needed another reform, only five years later, in the form of the Electricity Act, 2003,[168] which created an enabling framework to introduce competition in the sector.

Reform 22: Internet Policies

From communication and social media to financial transactions and direct benefit transfers, India 2022 has seamlessly shifted to the digital economy. Underlying this shift was a series of policy initiatives and visionary firms. The first internet service was launched under Prime Minister P.V. Narasimha Rao on 15 August 1995 by Videsh Sanchar Nigam Ltd (VSNL), then a government-owned company.[169]

The two New Telecom Policies (NTP), in 1994 and 1999, opened up the sector to private entities, and with Telecom Regulatory Authority of India as an independent regulatory body, paved the way for unimagined growth and intense competition with an aim to add almost 2 million subscribers from a base of 40,000 within three years,[170] starting from 1997. By removing limits on the number of Internet Service Providers (ISPs) and allowing the use of any excess capacity for transmission available with the Railways and the Power Grid Corporation by private players, the virtual opening up of the sector was set in motion,[171] with licence guidelines finalized in 1998 under Prime Minister I.K. Gujral.[172] Following the entry of private players and the disinvestment of VSNL, the government under Prime Minister Manmohan Singh announced the Broadband Policy[173] in 2004, with futuristic objectives.[174]

From 4.6 million subscribers and public sector enterprises dominating with a 57 per cent market share[175] on a subscriber base of 4.55 million in March 2004,[176] the situation has reversed significantly since then. There were 776.45 million subscribers (mobile, broadband and narrowband) in September 2020,[177] with private firms leading the market share.[178] Clearly, private enterprises have expanded the market exponentially, speeding up Prime Minister Narendra Modi's idea of a Digital India. In the coming digital age, this will now deepen into delivering services based on 5G/6G networks, the reforms for which will be enabled by the government[179] but delivered by the private sector.

Reform 23: Kisan Credit Cards

Although the reforms initiated by the Statement on Industrial Policy 1991 excluded the agrarian sector and focused on industry and macroeconomics, the trickle down of financial sector reforms reached farmers too. Until 1991–92, formalized institutional credit was not of any consequence in the agricultural sector, with credit flow at Rs 11,202 crore in 1991–92.[180] Formalizing the sector was key, and in the first budget in June 1998 under Prime Minister Atal Bihari Vajpayee, Finance Minister Yashwant Sinha attempted it with Kisan Credit Cards (KCCs)[181] by getting the National Bank for Agriculture and Rural Development (NABARD) to formulate a 'model scheme for issue of Kisan Credit Cards' to farmers on the basis of their holdings for uniform adoption by commercial banks, which would enable them to buy agricultural inputs such as seeds, fertilizers and pesticides.

Two months later, the government introduced the Kisan Credit Card scheme, which enabled farmers to purchase agriculture inputs and draw cash for their production needs. The scheme was based on the size of landholdings. By December 2001, an additional 6.3 million KCCs had been issued, taking the total to 20.7 million.[182] Within six years, in 2004, the scheme was further extended for allied and non-farm activities.[183]

The scheme was and remains a success—the average farm income per household for KCC farmers was double that of non-KCC farmers: Rs 1,49,060 versus Rs 69,850.[184] By March 2019, the total operative accounts stood at 66.2 million, with 46 per cent of them held by cooperative banks, though in terms of value, commercial banks, at 64 per cent, were ahead.[185] Prime Minister Narendra Modi now proposes to expand the coverage of KCCs to 15 million dairy farmers, as part of the Atma Nirbhar Package.[186] To scale up this scheme, digitization of land records will be an essential policy action.

Reform 24: Insurance Regulatory and Development Authority of India

Envisioning the need for long-term investments to fund large-gestation infrastructure projects, Prime Minister P.V. Narasimha Rao set up a Committee to reform the insurance sector. In its 1994 report, the Committee recommended, among other things, the establishment of an independent regulatory authority,[187] on the lines of Securities and Exchange Board of India, to enable private sector firms to enter the sector. But converting those recommendations into law took five years and four prime ministers, finally coming into existence only under Atal Bihari Vajpayee.[188] The Insurance Regulatory and Development Authority of India (IRDAI) Act, 1999 also amended three existing laws that governed India's insurance sector.[189]

Constituted in April 2000,[190] although the first few words of IRDAI's mission are to protect 'interests of policyholders', this regulator has enabled companies and intermediaries at the cost of consumers, leading to an estimated policyholder loss of Rs 1,50,000 crore between 2005 and 2012 alone.[191] All this while, growth in the private sector has increased from 2 per cent in 2003 to 31.3 per cent in 2020 in the life segment, and from 15 to 55.8 per cent in non-life.

Governments have come and gone but the consumer has remained a bystander in the larger regulatory discourse. The lazy reforms that have happened in insurance are around increasing FDI—Prime Minister Narendra Modi increased it to 49 per cent in 2015 with the Insurance Laws (Amendment) Act, 2015[192]—but across leaderships, governments and IRDAI chairmen, consumer-facing reforms have been, and continue to be, invisible. All this has been done with the objective of increasing penetration. Here too, the regulator–government combine has failed: from 2.7 per cent in 2001 penetration has merely crawled ahead to 3.7 per cent in 2019.[193] Compare this with banking (53.9 per cent inclusion)[194] or broadband (53.5 per cent)[195] and you will know how far behind IRDAI lags the country, even on its statistic of choice. Modi needs to give more consumer-focused reforms attention here.

Reform 25: Foreign Exchange Management Act

Enacted twice—first in 1947 under Prime Minister Jawaharlal Nehru as an extension of the Defence of India Act, 1939,[196] with a ten-year time horizon;[197] and again in 1973[198] under Prime Minister Indira Gandhi to consolidate India's povertarian ideological policies and expel foreign companies from the country[199]—the Foreign Exchange Regulation Act (FERA) had no place in Prime Minister P.V. Narasimha Rao's post-1991 India, which laid the foundations of foreign exchange management reforms.[200] But it took eight years and four governments before the law was repealed and replaced by the Foreign Exchange Management Act (FEMA), 1999,[201] under Prime Minister Atal Bihari Vajpayee.

The differences between FERA and FEMA were wide, both in law as well as in policy. Business-wise, FERA regulated foreign exchange, FEMA facilitated and managed it; legally, FERA carried criminal offences, FEMA civil; economically, FERA functioned in an era of low foreign-exchange reserves, FEMA under stable reserves; administratively, under FERA everything was prohibited unless permitted, under FEMA, everything was permitted unless restricted or regulated.[202] Following the recommendations of the Tarapore Committee's Report on Capital Account Convertibility,[203] the law clearly stated that its objective was 'facilitating external trade or payments and for promoting the orderly development and maintenance of the foreign exchange market in India'.

Curiously, at a time when the government is trying to decriminalize provisions in law, there are voices being raised to make some FEMA offences criminal,[204] like a blast from the regressive past—Prime Minister Narendra Modi must prevent this. FEMA must not become a dark shadow of its past life (FERA), more so when there is a global regulatory convergence happening and the rupee is ready to become fully convertible. Exceptions, if any, must fall within the domain of national security, such as Chinese investments in critical infrastructure.[205]

Reform 26: Pradhan Mantri Gram Sadak Yojana

For the Statement on Industrial Policy 1991 to express itself throughout India, particularly in villages, it was necessary to connect markets in diverse and far-flung rural geographies. A start was made in 1999, when then President K.R. Narayanan raised the issue in a joint session of Parliament, talking about rural connectivity with half of the diesel cess earmarked for the scheme.[206]

Following the conclusions of a Consultative Committee on rural roads, which aimed at constructing 1 million kilometres of roads to connect 2,50,000 villages in seven years,[207] four months later, Prime Minister Atal Bihari Vajpayee launched the Pradhan Mantri Gram Sadak Yojana, on 25 December 2000, at an estimated cost of Rs 60,000 crore.[208] The legal provisions to create a fund that would finance national highways, railway projects and rural roads were enacted by Parliament two days later through the Central Road and Infrastructure Fund Act, 2000.[209]

In 1991, more than half of India's villages (53 per cent) or about 3,00,000 villages were unconnected by all-weather roads.[210] The lack of funds was limiting village road construction to states and villages that were below the national average.[211] With the scheme launched and the financing in place, road building to connect the villages began with a new zeal. Following the success of the scheme,[212] the second phase was launched in 2013 to upgrade existing rural road networks and the third phase in 2019 to consolidate the network and connect habitations to agricultural markets, and educational and medical facilities. So far, more than 7,52,000 kilometres of roads have been sanctioned, while almost 6,71,000 kilometres have been completed,[213] from 30,423 in 2000, a growth of 22 times or at an annualized growth rate of 16.7 per cent.

Reform 27: Information Technology Act, 2000

In 2000, nobody knew where technology would take us two decade later, or how deeply it would impact us. But when Prime Minister Atal Bihari

Vajpayee ushered in the Information Technology (IT) Act, 2000 to enable e-commerce in India, in tune with the rest of the world through the UNCITRAL Model Law on Electronic Commerce (1996),[214] it enabled not merely e-commerce but a stream of entrepreneurs in the tech space. Supporting the policy action was data—India's IT industry had mushroomed, with annual growth rates of more than 40 per cent, from less than $1 billion in financial year 1994–95 to more than $8 billion in 2000–01.[215]

The law created a regulatory framework for IT, with penalties for illicit activities such as unauthorized access to information, illegal downloads, publishing of obscene material and breach of privacy. Keeping pace with the newly enacted legislation, some other laws such as the Indian Evidence Act, 1872,[216] the Indian Penal Code, 1860[217] and the RBI Act, 1934[218] were also amended. In essence, the IT Act provided for the authentication of online transactions with digital signatures, so that barriers in the way of electronic commerce were effectively eliminated.

As the pace of technology adoption by households increased exponentially, the law was amended under Prime Minister Manmohan Singh in 2009.[219] Among other things, the amendment inserted Section 66A that made the posting of messages 'causing annoyance or inconvenience' an offence, carrying imprisonment of up to three years.[220] Six years later, the Supreme Court struck it down[221] saying it 'arbitrarily, excessively and disproportionately invades the right of free speech'.[222] Now, with the ongoing weaponization of social media,[223] the law may need additional tweaks.

Reform 28: Sarva Shiksha Abhiyan

Launched by Prime Minister Atal Bihari Vajpayee in 2000 as the Sarva Shiksha Abhiyan (SSA),[224] preceded by Prime Minister P.V. Narasimha Rao's District Primary Education Programme in 1994,[225] succeeded by Prime Minister Manmohan Singh's Right to Education Act in 2010,[226] and sublimated into a unified scheme by Prime Minister Narendra

Modi, the evolution of policy around delivering free education to children has been a political constant.

The SSA aimed to deliver free education to every child till Class 8, by 2010. Two years later, Atal Bihari Vajpayee ushered in the Constitution (Eighty-Sixth Amendment) Act, 2002.[227] In its initial phase, the scheme aimed to provide free education to all children in the 6–14 age by 2010. This became a 'National Mission', in 2001,[228] and was clubbed with the Mid Day Meal scheme that provided hot cooked meals for schoolchildren, already in operation since 1995.[229]

Legislating education has been a challenge, across governments. Manmohan Singh dropped Atal Bihari Vajpayee's draft Free and Compulsory Education for Children Bill, 2003,[230] and replaced it with the Free and Compulsory Education Bill, 2004.[231]

When that couldn't get enacted, he constituted a committee[232] that drafted the Right to Education Bill, 2005, which could not find consensus. He then took more than three years to draft a law, the Right of Children to Free and Compulsory Education Act, 2009[233] (RTE) that would be convenient for the neo-liberal framework.[234] In 2018, Prime Minister Narendra Modi expanded the scope of the scheme, from pre-nursery to Class 12, under the Samagra Shiksha scheme,[235] which has subsumed three schemes—Sarva Shiksha Abhiyan, Rashtriya Madhyamik Shiksha Abhiyan,[236] and Teacher Education. All through, outcomes on all parameters, such as literacy rates and enrolment ratios, have risen.

Reform 29: Prevention of Money Laundering Act

The process of converting money generated through illegal means such as drugs, trafficking,[237] illegal arms sale, or terrorist funding to appear as though it has been created from legitimate sources is called money laundering.[238] Simply put, the proceeds are washed—or laundered—and turned lawful from criminal. At scale, though the problem is as old as World War II and particularly the role of countries such as Switzerland in it,[239] the problem has multiplied to include terror-financing states such as Pakistan, with the world unsuccessfully trying to end it.[240]

In India, following the Political Declaration adopted by the Special Session of the United Nations General Assembly in June 1998,[241] the fight against money laundering was given a legal framework through the Prevention of Money Laundering Act (PMLA), 2002.[242] Ushered in by Prime Minister Atal Bihari Vajpayee, the term was defined,[243] and the Enforcement Directorate made the administrative authority.[244] Like several legislations to regulate previously non-litigated territory, the 2002 law had loopholes that could be used to escape its purview.

Under Prime Minister Manmohan Singh, the law was strengthened with two amendments, one each in 2009[245] and 2012.[246] Prime Minister Narendra Modi proposed and Parliament enacted four more amendments, in 2015,[247] 2016,[248] 2018[249] and 2019,[250] to expand the reach, plug the loopholes, and tighten gaps around definitions and administrative procedures under the law.

But despite the fact that there are sixty-six PMLA Special Courts, the track record of conviction has been poor—only thirteen people have been convicted in nine out of 757 cases between 2015–16 and October 2019.[251] Whether it is the inability of the Enforcement Directorate to convert a case into a conviction or weakness in the law, this needs to end—otherwise, the law can easily be perceived to be a harassment tool.[252]

Reform 30: Securitization and Reconstruction of Financial Assets and Enforcement of Security Interest Act

The essence underlying the sanctity of lending is: if an asset is pledged as collateral, and a loan is taken against it, then, in case the borrower fails to make payments on the principal and/or interest, the lender should be able to take away the asset. This simple market mechanism took fifty-five years to develop; it only went public before Prime Minister Atal Bihari Vajpayee legalized the idea with the Securitization and

Reconstruction of Financial Assets and Enforcement of Security Interest (SARFAESI) Act, 2002.[253] The law gave powers to banks to auction commercial as well as residential properties pledged as securities in order to recover loans in case of default by borrowers. Upon serving a notice of sixty days, the bank and/or financial institution can take possession of the pledged assets and manage them as per their capabilities. A 28 January 2003 notification expanded the law to include cooperative banks.[254]

Although SARFAESI is not the only cause, the percentage of non-performing assets had seen an impressive fall, from 10.4 per cent in 2001–02 to 2.3 per cent in 2007–08.[255] They rose steadily till 2014 (3.8 per cent) and sharply since then (9.1 per cent in 2019).[256] The rise has been the highest among public sector banks (11.6 per cent) followed by new private banks (5.3 per cent).[257] In 2011–12, SARFAESI contributed 70 per cent of the total recovered amount and was the most effective way to recover NPAs.[258] The journey to cleaning up balance sheets of banks, despite several amendments to the law and accompanying rules, has not been easy—entrepreneurs have been finding ways to misuse the court system to their advantage,[259] leaving the final leg of this crucial reform, again, in the court of the Judiciary. A two-month closure, as prescribed by the Bombay High Court, could be one way out.[260]

Reform 31: Competition Commission of India

Despite it being among the very first reforms initiated by Prime Minister P.V. Narasimha Rao in 1991,[261] the amendments[262] to the Monopolies and Restrictive Trade Practices (MRTP) Act failed to keep pace with the needs of a liberalized and fast-growing economy. In tune with the recommendations of the S.V.S. Raghavan Committee,[263] therefore, Prime Minister Atal Bihari Vajpayee ushered in the Competition Act, 2002.[264] The aim was 'to promote and sustain competition in markets, to protect the interests of consumers' rather than the MRTP Act's focus on controlling monopolies and restrictive trade practices.

However, the overarching legal and adjudicatory function of the Competition Commission faced a legal challenge. Following the Supreme Court judgement in 2005[265] that separated the regulatory and the adjudicatory functions under the doctrine of separation of powers under the Constitution,[266] Prime Minister Manmohan Singh ushered in a 2007 amendment,[267] and notified it in 2009,[268] with a Competition Appellate Tribunal established under Section 53A.

Over the years, the CCI has reviewed more than 1,000 antitrust cases and 700 merger filings[269] around cartelization, unfair or discriminatory practices. In 2017, Prime Minister Narendra Modi ushered in another amendment to the law that conferred the appellate function to the National Company Law Appellate Tribunal (NCLAT).[270] By 2018, in view of the changing economic and market scenarios, the government constituted a Competition Law Review Committee, which in its 2019 report[271] made several recommendations around the organizational structure and functionality of the CCI. One of the key recommendations was to have separate governing boards for different functions, an amalgamated investigative unit and regional offices of the CCI.[272] Based on these recommendations, a new Competition (Amendment) Bill, 2020 has been proposed.[273] The creation and maturing of this regulatory bill has been satisfactory; how it evolves to serve the digital economy of the future remains to be seen.

Reform 32: Tariff Reduction

In an increasing trajectory over four decades, customs duties in India had become among the highest in the world by 1991, with 80 per cent of industry groups having tariff levels of more than 100 per cent,[274] and in several cases more than 300 per cent.[275] Under Prime Minister P.V. Narasimha Rao, a major set of reforms made their way through the reduction of these duties, whose 'peak' rate fell to 40 per cent by 1997–98,[276] but remained among the highest in the world.

In the first two decades of trade reforms, under Prime Ministers H.D. Deve Gowda, I.K. Gujral, Atal Bihari Vajpayee and Manmohan

Singh, tariff rates have been falling consistently—in 2000–01, the percentage of industries in the 30–40 per cent tariff band rose from 23 per cent to 65 per cent, with almost 90 per cent of industries in the 20–30 per cent band. By 2009–10, the majority of industry groups were functioning in the 0–10 per cent tariff band.[277]

Under Prime Minister Narendra Modi, these reforms have continued, but in a different direction. First, tariffs on some industry segments such as renewable energy, capital equipment, some MSME and agricultural products, have been raised. Second, depending on how you view it, a dynamic—or uncertain—rationalization of exemptions on tariff structures, and on some products such as gold and silver, with a two-year shelf life has been introduced.[278]

Rationalizing exemptions is not an easy task, as Budget 2021 shows. While it has withdrawn exemptions on transformers, it has on the same page extended exemptions to products such as medical devices,[279] possibly as a reaction to COVID. Tariffs, therefore, remain a work in progress. The biggest challenge is looking at tariff policies in isolation—tariff cuts need to go hand in hand with greater ease of doing business, and making Indian businesses more competitive; the latter has lagged the former.

Reform 33: Pension Fund Regulatory and Development Authority

Drawing on the recommendations of the S.A. Dave-led Old Age Social and Income Security project report,[280] Prime Minister Atal Bihari Vajpayee decided to constitute an independent body called the Pension Fund Regulatory and Development Authority (PFRDA) in 2003. The policy idea was to deliver old age income security and reduce the fiscal burden of government pensions by establishing, developing and regulating pension funds for all government employees, except the armed forces. The PFRDA was first created as an interim body in October 2003.[281]

When Prime Minister Manmohan Singh took charge, he formalized the body in November 2008,[282] steered it through Parliament into a law in September 2013,[283] and notified it in 2014.[284] While this legal exercise was under way, the National Pension System (NPS) was rolled out in 2003 and all new government servants were placed under it from 1 January 2004, with a voluntary subscription offered to the general public—a clear, consistent and trans-governmental public policy continuity.

The management of the NPS was based on a bidding structure where all bidders would match lowest costs. When UTI (formerly, Unit Trust of India) bid to manage the funds at 0.0009 per cent of assets under management, there was no surplus left to distribute, either to fund managers or to distributors—those selling insurance were getting commissions of 40 per cent on the first-year premium and mutual funds 2 per cent. Making matters worse, at the time of exit, 40 per cent of the total amount would be invested in an annuity, the management of which is under the Insurance Regulatory and Development Authority of India that has done little for either consumers or annuities. Adopted by all state governments except West Bengal, Tripura and Telangana,[285] the NPS had 14.7 million subscribers and almost Rs 6 lakh crore of assets under management in July 2021.[286] This is a badly executed good reform—and needs a rethink.

Reform 34: PPP in Railways

From Schedule A in 1956 under which Railways would be developed as part of 'Central Government monopolies',[287] to a well-directed but hesitantly executed private–public partnership (PPP) model in 2021, the journey of rail transport has been as much ideological and political as it has been an economic series of small reforms. The first to unshackle the chains of 1956 was Prime Minister Atal Bihari Vajpayee, who in 2002 initiated the Build, Own and Maintain Agreement with Gujarat Adani Port.[288]

Four years later, Prime Minister Manmohan Singh followed through, when the Railways allowed private players to operate container traffic trains on select networks.[289] In the fourteen years since, the number of companies operating container traffic has risen to nineteen.[290] In May 2010, Manmohan Singh invited companies to develop private freight terminals[291] and increase the share of Railways in India's freight transport sector; the scheme has undergone several amendments over the years.[292]

The other successes have been Prime Minister I.K. Gujral's Own Your Wagon scheme in 1996[293] that allowed more freedom to transport companies to design and operate wagons, and the 'Roll On Roll Off' service, launched by Atal Bihari Vajpayee in 1999 to aid road transport by loading trucks directly on to wagons and offloading them at the destinations.[294] This service was also one of the major contributors for shipping liquid medical oxygen (LMO, popularly known as Oxygen Express) across India during a surge of requirement following the COVID-19 cases in April–June 2021, transporting over 32,000 metric tonnes of LMO across the country.[295] PPP in Railways remains a work in progress and includes recent reforms, such as 151 additional trains being run by private operators[296] or the redevelopment of railway stations such as in Gandhinagar.[297] The reforms destination is a long way off.

Reform 35: Fiscal Responsibility and Budgetary Management

With the revenue deficit[298] at more than 4 per cent of GDP and gross fiscal deficit[299] nearing 6 per cent in 2002,[300] Prime Minister Atal Bihari Vajpayee clearly saw the urgency to bring government finances under control. He argued for and ushered in the Fiscal Responsibility and Budgetary Management (FRBM) Act, 2003.[301] The objective of this law[302] was to provide a legal and institutional framework to bring down the fiscal deficit, contain the growth of public debt and stabilize debt as a proportion of GDP over the medium term and bind future Union governments to a pre-specified path of fiscal consolidation.[303]

The law, which envisioned a fiscal deficit of 3 per cent and zero revenue deficit by 2015, was notified by Prime Minister Manmohan

Singh in 2004.[304] This meant an increase in taxes on the one side and cutting expenditure on the other—both tricky for India's political economy. Just as the gross fiscal deficit for states and Union fell from 9.5 per cent in 2000–01 to 4 per cent in 2007–08,[305] the Trans-Atlantic Economic Crisis[306] of 2008 struck and the subsequent economic recession prevented further consolidation.

On the recommendations of the Thirteenth Finance Commission,[307] Prime Minister Narendra Modi brought the focus back on controlling public finances and achieving targets. The 2017 FRBM Review Committee's recommended glide path to 2023 was a debt to GDP ratio of 38.7 per cent (from 49.4 per cent in 2017), a fiscal deficit of 2.5 per cent (3.5 per cent), and a revenue deficit of 0.8 per cent (2.3 per cent).[308]

Although the ongoing COVID-19 pandemic has put a pause to discussions around deficits, in India[309] as well as the world,[310] the FRBM is a landmark event in India's fiscal reforms.[311] In an era of serial crises, the law may be known more for its breach, but has put a moral pressure on governments to keep expenses under check.

Reform 36: PPP in Infrastructure

Across parties, every leader has understood the importance of infrastructure and the role of the private sector in building it. Everyone knows what a PPP (public–private partnership) is, but there is no common definition[312] binding it globally.[313] The term made its way into India's public policy lexicon in the early 2000s.[314] From one PPP in 1991 under Prime Minister P.V. Narasimha Rao, the number had jumped to sixty by 2006 under Prime Minister Manmohan Singh.[315]

In 1996, an expert group under Prime Minister H.D. Deve Gowda recommended that the investment in infrastructure development should go from 5.5 per cent of GDP to 8 per cent in ten years.[316] By 2007, under Manmohan Singh, the requirement had risen to $475 billion in order to sustain a GDP growth of 9 per cent.[317] The demand context in place, the Cabinet Committee on Economic Affairs set up a framework[318] that led to the procedures for PPP projects in January 2006.[319]

Since then, this framework has recommended 333 PPP projects worth Rs 4.6 lakh crore.[320] Nine of out ten projects have been in roads, railways and ports, two-thirds of them in roads alone.[321] Prime Minister Narendra Modi has powered this private sector driven PPP infrastructure momentum, in speech[322] as well as in deeds with an ambitious Rs 100 lakh crore National Infrastructure Pipeline.[323] From this, 40 per cent of the projects will see a 21 per cent contribution from the private sector in tandem with contributions from the state (40 per cent) and Union governments (39 per cent).[324] Despite the political push, India's PPP policies have failed to deal with its political economy, resulting in stalled projects and increased risk, which leads to 'adverse selection, moral hazard, opportunism and holdup of the PPP projects'.[325] Fixing these needs a legislative intervention.

Reform 37: Airports

At 167.5 million, India was the world's fourth-largest carrier of air passengers in 2019, after the US, China and Ireland.[326] A series of policies, that pushed economic growth in general and airports in particular, have led to this rising trend—in the past two decades alone, traffic growth has seen a tenfold rise.[327] The flight to growth has its foundations in 2003, when based on the recommendations of the Naresh Chandra Committee,[328] Prime Minister Atal Bihari Vajpayee ushered in the Airports Authority of India (Amendment) Act, 2003.[329] Through this, the Airports Authority of India (AAI) was permitted to transfer operations and management of existing airports on long-term leases to private companies.

There are now five airports functioning under a successful PPP model—one each in Bengaluru, Kochi, Delhi, Hyderabad and Mumbai;[330] in 2018, Prime Minister Narendra Modi gave in-principle approval to an additional six airports to be operated on a PPP model in Ahmedabad, Jaipur, Lucknow, Guwahati, Thiruvananthapuram, and Mangaluru.[331]

The next step was to regulate them, for which Prime Minister Manmohan Singh ushered in the Airports Economic Regulatory Authority Act, 2008,[332] for all airports, state-owned or under PPP, to determine tariffs and fees, and monitor performance standards. Finally, with the National Civil Aviation Policy of 2016,[333] Narendra Modi further reformed the sector to enable more people to fly by examining twenty-two areas, and placing a renewed focus on airports. Next year, he announced UDAN as a regional connectivity scheme to operate flights with regulated airfares (Rs 2,500 per hour of flying),[334] under which regional airports would be connected to major airports/hubs across the country. A high-flying sector, with most reforms in place, now India needs more PPP airports: among other things, they are more efficient,[335] and important catalysts for trade and commerce—a virtuous cycle of good economics and good politics.

Reform 38: Free Trade Agreements

Study the outcomes of India's trade agreements,[336] from the first with Sri Lanka in 1998[337] to the last two with Mauritius in 2021[338] and Australia in 2022,[339] and it is clear that the opening up of the Indian economy within has had repercussions outside. Trade as a percentage of GDP had jumped from 14.1 per cent in 1991 to 28.2 per cent in 2019, rising in tune with growth in global averages of 29.5 per cent and 43.9 per cent, but lagging both.[340] But while trade has grown, imports into India have increased more than exports to the trading partners, as examples of ASEAN, Japan, Sri Lanka and South Korea illustrate.[341]

The economic policy lessons from India's experience with FTAs are, therefore, clear: India needs to up its game, not only in the way it negotiates[342] and signs these deals, but how it overcomes the greatest challenge to the development of a strong trade policy and catalyses manufacturing[343] by enabling and freeing its entrepreneurs from the constraints of corruption, red tape and rent seeking, who faced and continue to face 'myriad microeconomic distortions and heavy state interventions'[344] that straitjacket them.

Trade agreements calibrate mutually beneficial tariffs between nations (bilateral) and groups of nations (multilateral), to help ease the flow of goods and services. Of the 350 regional trade agreements in force globally,[345] India has seventeen,[346] while announcements for four—with the Bay of Bengal Initiative on Multi-Sectoral Technical and Economic Cooperation;[347] European Free Trade Association;[348] European Union;[349] and South African Customs Union[350]—have been made. If trade policy agreements have to deliver returns to India, it must work with dynamic and transactive reciprocity of policies across a wide range of geographies, notably the US and the EU, and thereby reduce its financially harmful overexposure to China.

Reform 39: Mahatma Gandhi National Rural Employment Guarantee Act

One of India's most high-profile and outcomes-impacting laws, the National Rural Employment Guarantee Act, 2005[351] ushered in by Prime Minister Manmohan Singh, is the culmination of several such attempts in the past. While the law came into force in 2006, the words 'Mahatma Gandhi' were inserted through a 2 October 2009 amendment. It provisions 100 days of guaranteed employment for every rural household, making it the world's largest social welfare scheme.[352]

The scheme has been a spectacular success on all fronts, particularly the Union–state relations under which state governments deliver the MGNREG Scheme.[353] In five years, the number of households being offered employment were more than 55 million—48 per cent of them women—delivering 2.5 billion person-days of work on a budgetary allocation of Rs 40,100 crore. By 2020–21, the number of person-days had risen to 3.9 billion, showing a continuity across leaderships. Above all, MGNREGA set and achieved high standards of transparency and accountability with designated ombudsmen and regular audits. And with payments transferred directly through financial institutions, it ended systemic leakages.

MGNREGA is the perfection attained after decades of policy experiments, the first going as far back as 1952, with the Community Development Programme,[354] followed by the Food for Work Programme in 1977,[355] later rebranded as the National Rural Employment Programme in 1980[356] to create additional opportunities for employment and deploying surplus foodgrains as wages. In 1983, the Rural Landless Employment Guarantee Programme[357] was launched to focus on landless rural families, which was subsequently widened into the Jawahar Rozgar Yojana.[358] Until poverty ends, hopefully within the next decade, this will be the one scheme that will provide an economic anchor to India's poor.

Reform 40: National Rural Health Mission

As in rural roads, reforms in rural health began late, with the launch of the National Rural Health Mission (NRHM) under Prime Minister Manmohan Singh on 12 April 2005. Their arrival was meant to deliver what the state had failed to do for almost six decades: public health and preventive medicine.[359] The scheme introduced the idea of ASHA (Accredited Social Health Activists) as a 'change agent' for health, to be governed by Panchayati Raj institutions.[360] It focused on eighteen states with weak public health indicators and infrastructure.[361] It also aimed to strengthen 3,222 existing community health centres of 30–50 beds as 24-hour first referral units.[362] It was a shift away from more traditional vertical programmes such as family planning in the 1960s and early 1970s, and diarrhoeal disease in the late 1980s and early 1990s to more integrated and comprehensive interventions.[363]

Four years later, in December 2009, the Manmohan Singh government launched the Mother and Child Tracking system, arguably the first intrusion of technology into rural governance, to streamline the delivery of essential healthcare to vulnerable groups in remote areas by mapping information such as a unique ID, address and even caste, for pregnant women and children till the age of 5.[364] On 1 May 2013, the scheme was subsumed under the National Health Mission.[365]

Over the years, these changes and additions to India's healthcare system have delivered healthy outcomes that have helped India converge with the world. The infant mortality rate has decreased from 55.7 in 2005 (the world average was 44.3) to 28.3 (28.2) in 2019,[366] showing policy effectivity in controlling such a humongous problem. Under Prime Minister Narendra Modi, it remains a trans-government policy continuum[367] that has a long way to go before we reach 'health for all'.

Reform 41: Bharat Nirman

In tune with the 74th Constitutional Amendment,[368] and recognizing the importance of cities in the country's economic development in general and providing basic amenities to urban poor in particular, Prime Minister Manmohan Singh launched the Jawaharlal Nehru National Urban Renewal Mission (JNNURM) on 3 December 2005.[369] The scheme was initially launched for a seven-year period but was extended by two years to March 2014[370] to facilitate the completion of a large number of unfinished projects, thereby covering almost the entire tenure of the Manmohan Singh government.

The JNNURM had two sub-missions—Basic Services to the Urban Poor (BSUP) and Urban Infrastructure and Governance (UIG)—both of which aimed to encourage reforms and fast-track planned development of identified cities by facilitating infrastructure creation and service delivery mechanisms.[371] Administratively, the execution of both the sub-missions was thought through.[372] It focused on a primary selection of sixty-three cities across India (seven megacities, twenty-eight with population in excess of 1 million, and twenty-eight with less than 1 million residents) by launching a fund-sharing arrangement with states and achieving implementation through urban and local bodies.[373]

But sixteen years after its launch, the outcomes are dismal. An idea with huge transformative potential, the Union–states financial and administrative incentives failed to achieve targets. Out of a total of 1,507 approved projects across 939 cities, only 348 were completed, even with additional central assistance.[374] In the stipulated time frame (March 2011) only 8.9 per cent of the approved projects were completed.[375] That said, the scheme mainstreamed the idea of urban development, a theme that has gathered traction, even if as a major reform it has not.[376] State governments need to up their game.

Reform 42: Benami Amendment

In the three years to May 2019, the fight against unaccounted-for money being invested in assets, mostly properties, under other people's names—benami—got a new lease of life. 'Show cause notices' were issued in more than 2,100 cases involving benami properties worth Rs 9,600 crore.[377] While we wait to see the results of this clampdown, as we do for demonetization, what seems to be clear is that the government has finally got a strong law to fix this long-ailing problem.

Ushered in by Prime Minister Narendra Modi, the Benami Transactions (Prohibition) Amendment Act of 2016[378] amended the original law that was promulgated in 1988 during Prime Minister Rajiv Gandhi's tenure.[379] Among other things, the 1988 law had four core infirmities.[380] First, powers of a civil court had to be conferred. Second, specific provisions were needed for vesting confiscated property with the government. Third, an appellate structure had to be defined, while barring jurisdiction of a civil court against an action taken by the authorities under the Act. And fourth, procedural matters around the law's administration had to be provided. The fact that there was no law till 1988 was a 'fraud on creditors' and was done to 'avoid political and social risks'.[381]

With the law now having teeth, the government has begun to get down to business. Under the Benami Transactions Informants Reward Scheme, 2018,[382] a person can get a reward of up to Rs 1 crore for giving specific information about benami transactions to authorities. Concurrently, with a general sense of transparency and digitization under way in the economy, this old problem may have been fairly resolved, through a series of new legislative and executive reforms. This, then, needs to be seen in a wider perspective of bringing in greater curbs on unaccounted-for money.

Reform 43: Value Added Tax

Paying taxes on the value added in the production cycle of a product or service is called a value added tax (VAT). Till Prime Minister Narendra Modi introduced and set in motion the goods and services tax (GST) in 2017, there were seventeen indirect taxes that Indians had to pay, eight levied by the Union government,[383] and nine by state governments.[384] But the path to GST was paved with other attempts at simplifying the rate, the procedures and the logic of tax. The first instance of such a system in India was made under Prime Minister Rajiv Gandhi through the introduction of a Modified Value Added Tax.[385]

Under Prime Minister Vajpayee, MODVAT was streamlined as central value added tax (CENVAT) in 2000,[386] with the idea to converge the three excise duty rates of 8, 16 and 24 per cent into a single 16 per cent CENVAT.[387] Prime Minister Manmohan Singh then introduced the VAT system in 2005.[388] He also announced the provision of compensation that was to be paid to states for the drop of revenue generation from implementation of VAT. The compensation would continue for three years at the rate of 100, 75 and 50 per cent for the first, second and third years respectively.[389]

From several individual taxes to a VAT system was a crucial point in the evolution of India's indirect taxes into the GST system. It, therefore, needs to be seen as a bridge reform, that is, a path to a greater reform. For this, Manmohan Singh created an Empowered Committee of State Finance Ministers[390] to iron out the differences between the Union and the states and between states around subsuming the several taxes under the new system, which Narendra Modi delivered as the GST.

Reform 44: Foreign Contribution (Regulation) Act

With every aspect of money flows in the economy regulated, protests over the regulation of non-governmental organizations (NGOs) are out of sync and seem motivated, but are part of the same philosophy—reforms are for others, not us. The option to be a not-for-profit society or trust does not make any organization more virtuous or law-abiding than a profit-making, tax-paying entity. Instead of directors upon whom huge responsibilities have been placed through several laws, the focus of the Foreign Contribution (Regulation) Act of 2010,[391] ushered in by Prime Minister Manmohan Singh, is on public servants, judges, politicians, editors, NGOs. The 2010 law replaced and tightened some provisions of the 1976 law,[392] enacted during Prime Minister Indira Gandhi's Emergency years, and the subsequent 1984 amendment, which included the erstwhile state of Jammu and Kashmir in its ambit.

While the 1976 law regulated foreign contribution and hospitality by persons or associations, the 1984 amendment expanded the scope of the law to include judges, government servants, and employees of corporations. When the 2010 law was being enacted, a Parliamentary Standing Committee was constituted to gather inputs. Here the views of NGOs on the Standing Committee revealed a sublime sense of entitlement, from freedom[393] to conversions,[394] to finances.[395]

With annual foreign contributions crossing Rs 20,000 crore in 2018–19,[396] and glaring cases where NGOs misappropriated the funding by routing them through FDI channels, as in the case of Amnesty International,[397] the FCRA guidelines were further tightened in 2020 by an amendment,[398] which among other things, reduced the administrative expenditure to be allocated to foreign contributions to 20 per cent from 50 per cent.[399] As of September 2021, the number of FCRA-registered NGOs rose to 50,032 of which 22,743 are active, 20,673 have been cancelled and 6,616 are deemed expired.[400] The message is clear: follow the law.

Reform 45: FDI in Retail

Even when the liberalization drive of 1991 was aimed towards opening up the Indian economy to foreign direct investment (FDI), politics ensured that retail and agriculture sectors remained out of bounds for a market that's worth more than $800 billion, and estimated to cross $1.5 trillion by 2030.[401] More than the economic size, it is the human factor that has raised hurdles—the sector employs 8 per cent of India's workforce.[402] The chronology below tells the story of the reluctance to and the evolution of opening up FDI in retail.

Under Prime Minister P.V. Narasimha Rao, 51 per cent FDI in trading was allowed for exports in April 1991.[403] In May 1997, Prime Minister H.D. Deve Gowda permitted 100 per cent FDI for exports, and 'cash and carry' wholesale trading.[404] Five years later, Prime Minister Manmohan Singh allowed 100 per cent FDI in single-brand retail,[405] provided the company sourced 30 per cent of its produce from small Indian firms, self-certified by the company and certified by statutory auditors.[406] But quality issues prevented large-scale FDI inflows,[407] and the mandatory 30 per cent clause was changed to 'preferably'.[408]

The next year, in August 2013, Manmohan Singh increased FDI in multi-brand retail to 51 per cent,[409] if half of it was invested in back-end infrastructure,[410] at least 30 per cent of procurement was sourced from Indian 'small industries',[411] and outlets set up only in cities with a population of more than 1 million.[412] Finally, in January 2018, Prime Minister Narendra Modi approved 100 per cent FDI in single-brand retail under the automatic route.[413] Going forward, the big reform challenge lies in opening up multi-brand retail to FDI, within the confines of Modi's Aatmanirbhar Bharat initiative.[414]

Reform 46: Fuel Price Deregulation, 2014

What sixteen governments could not do, the last two did. On 25 June 2010, Prime Minister Manmohan Singh deregulated petrol prices,[415] while on 19 October 2014, Prime Minister Narendra Modi completed the exercise by deregulating diesel prices.[416] But the one expression in both the announcements—prices being market determined—is misleading. Even if the prices have been deregulated, they have not been decontrolled. The government through oil marketing companies (OMCs) continues to influence price decisions. On their part, OMCs act in tandem and it is surprising that the Competition Commission of India has not yet raised the issue, even as private sector firms remain invisible.

The complex political economy of the key enabler of India's GDP growth, fuel, has been enmeshed in political morals and economic conflicts, pivoting around how much of fuel prices should be passed on to the people directly and how much supported by their taxes indirectly. This has resulted in a situation where all actors—the politician, the government, the bureaucrat, the oil company boards, and the consumer—know what's needed but don't act.[417]

This conflict shows up in the politics of low fuel prices that keeps inflation under control,[418] a paramount electoral issue,[419] while the fiscal burden rises. The economic issue here is to protect the poor while allowing market-based fuel prices in a country that imports more than four-fifths of its oil requirements.[420] It is the world's third-largest energy consuming nation[421] and with fast growth driving it, energy demands will rise further and faster. This will continue to place additional financial burden on the economy. The high crude prices in 2018, for instance, saw the oil subsidy burden more than double to Rs 53,000 crore.[422] This burden needs to end, alongside India's transiting to a green economy. Not an easy task.

Reform 47: Companies Act, 2013

Thirty days before Prime Minister Jawaharlal Nehru's anti-business and povertarian Industrial Policy Resolution 1956 was announced, he ushered in the Companies Act, 1956. Despite being amended twenty-five times, with eight major amendments[423]—in 1988 under Prime

Minister Rajiv Gandhi; in 1999, 2000, 2001, and twice in 2002 under Atal Bihari Vajpayee; and 2006 under Prime Minister Manmohan Singh—the law remained behind times as a caricature of a past that continues, till date. This caricature looks at businessmen as crooks and businesses as exploitative agencies.

In 2013, Manmohan Singh steered the Companies Act, 2013[424] in Parliament; the law came into force on 1 April 2014, a little over a month before Prime Minister Narendra Modi took charge, twenty-three years after India had liberalized. A law so large came into force in a time so short that the government had to introduce it in a 'phased manner', creating confusion for companies that had to refer to both, the 1956 as well as the 2013 laws, for some time.[425] Compared to thirteen parts and 658 sections in the 1956 law, the 2013 law has 29 chapters and 470 sections. While most of the changes deal with governance, the 2013 law added a section on corporate social responsibility and created another burden on companies without calling it a tax,[426] with a three-year jail term for non-compliance.[427]

The next step in the law would be to make it a catalyst for doing business rather than creating a series of regulatory hurdles, which need to be ironed out to attract twenty-first century entrepreneurs from across the world to India at a time when they are looking to exit from China.[428] With most of the groundwork done, it needs very little tinkering to bring it up to the mark.

Reform 48: Land Acquisition

Jobs need industry, industry needs land. In between stands a complex politics and the insecurities of landowners who, after being consistently denied their dues by successive governments, have now reached a point of no sale. Between 1947 and 2004, for instance, estimates suggest that 60 million people (around the total population of Italy) were displaced from 25 million hectares of land (around the area of the UK)[429] to construct dams in India. Most of the land acquired has its roots in the Land Acquisition Act, 1894,[430] which are expressed through thirteen subsequently legislated laws.[431] The missing link in land acquisition debates was rehabilitation of affected families. Prime Minister Atal Bihari Vajpayee initiated a resettlement policy in 2003,[432] which Prime Minister Manmohan Singh took forward in 2007.[433] Both attempted to provide rehabilitation for displaced persons when governments acquired land.

Six years later, in 2013, Manmohan Singh ushered in the Right to Fair Compensation and Transparency in Land Acquisition, Rehabilitation and Resettlement (LARR) Act, 2013.[434] The law defines projects that have a 'public purpose'[435] for which land may be acquired by government or associated entities. It clearly states that before any acquisition, 80 per cent of the affected families must provide their consent for private projects[436] and 70 per cent for PPP projects.[437] It also ensures proper compensation for acquired land at higher than market rates,[438] and mandates a three-option compensation—employment, cash or annuity.[439] While this law has given protection to landowners, it has made it impossible to acquire land. An attempt to fix this was made by Prime Minister Narendra Modi through a bill,[440] which lapsed and has not been revived so far. An essential component for growth, this reform needs a dynamic political push and creative legislative equilibrium that balances the interests of the country's growth requirements with the interests of landowners and related stakeholders.

Reform 49: Jan Dhan Yojana

As far as financial inclusion goes, India's Pradhan Mantri Jan Dhan Yojana (PMJDY) is arguably the most efficient scheme for scaling up a country's non-banked population. Less than 100 days in office, the PMJDY was one of the first schemes launched by Prime Minister Narendra Modi on 28 August 2014,[441] with the objective of ending what he called 'financial untouchability'.[442] Administratively, the launch was a record-creating event—in one instant, banks opened 15 million accounts and insurance companies issued 15 million policies, across more than 77,000 locations.[443]

Outcomes of the scheme have been spectacular: from 40.1 per cent Indians having access to banking services in 2011,[444] the number rose to 58 per cent by 2016,[445] and to more than 80 per cent by 2017,[446] doubling within three years of launch. This has taken India's financial inclusion rate equal to China's and higher than all other BRICS nations, but lower than developed economies such as the US, Japan, or the EU.[447]

But the real benefits started pouring in when these Jan Dhan accounts were linked with Aadhaar cards and mobile phones, as part of the 'JAM' trinity. This has become a robust pillar of India's public distribution system and welfare schemes. A recent example of this system was seen during the COVID-19 crisis when financial transfers and digital payments became necessary. The Pradhan Mantri Garib Kalyan Yojana,[448] announced to alleviate the economic impact of the pandemic, saw 317.7 million people, 63 per cent of them women, receive Rs 28,256 crore of financial aid directly into their bank accounts.[449] A successful reform, the government must not drop the ball and continue to work towards delivering 100 per cent financial inclusion base, upon which to build other financial products. This reform also illustrates how despite independent regulators (in this case the RBI) sometimes the government needs to weigh in and push reforms.

Reform 50: Arbitration

The struggle by the executive to resolve judicial inertia in delivering a faster disputes mechanism is more than a century old—it began with the Indian Arbitration Act, 1899,[450] followed through with the Arbitration (Protocol and Convention) Act, 1937[451] and the Arbitration Act, 1940.[452] With the economy opening up in 1991 and embracing globalization, inter-country disputes needed to be resolved. For this Prime Minister P.V. Narasimha Rao ushered in the Arbitration and Conciliation Act, 1996,[453] based on a United Nations' UNCITRAL Model Law on International Commercial Arbitration of 1985.[454] This proved inadequate to revolve intra-country disputes, which had increased.

Following the recommendations of the 176th Law Commission[455] and the Justice Saraf Committee,[456] Prime Minister Atal Bihari Vajpayee proposed amendments to the 1996 law with the Arbitration and Conciliation (Amendment) Bill, 2003.[457] Given that the amendment would invite substantial intervention by courts in the arbitration process, 'have the courts sitting in judgement over the arbitrators before arbitration, during arbitration and after arbitration',[458] and can cause delays,[459] Prime Minister Manmohan Singh withdrew the bill.[460]

In December 2015, Prime Minister Narendra Modi ushered in the Arbitration and Conciliation (Amendment) Act, 2015,[461] an important amendment that specified a twelve-month time frame[462] on arbitration proceedings, disclosures by arbitrators[463] and model fees.[464] The Arbitration and Conciliation (Amendment) Act, 2019 laid the framework to set up independent bodies for arbitration through the Arbitration Council of India,[465] empower the Supreme Court and high courts to designate arbitral institutions,[466] and further reduce the time frame to six months.[467] Finally, the Arbitration and Conciliation (Amendment) Act, 2021[468] ensured that arbitration remains corruption free. As a reform this is a much-needed law. But how far this evolution towards outcomes of quick disputes resolution goes, remains to be seen.

Reform 51: Skills Development

Between workers who want jobs and companies that need workers lies a creaking bridge called 'skills'. The problem of employability—workers with degrees but not skills—remains a challenge: employability rose from 37.2 per cent in 2015 to 45.9 per cent in 2021,[469] but remains below what both the employer and the employee want. The demand for talent created by the winds of growth is high but the talent's ability to join this growth continues to lag.

The problem needed a policy intervention, and Prime Minister Manmohan Singh provided it by launching a Mission on Vocational Education and Skill Development in March 2005 with an aim to set up 1,600 industrial training institutes and polytechnics, 10,000 new vocational education schools and 50,000 skill development centres under the PPP model to upskill an estimated 10 million annually.[470] In July 2008, he constituted the National Skill Development Corporation as a not-for-profit public limited company, under a PPP model with the government holding 49 per cent of the equity and private sector organizations the rest.[471]

In July 2015, Prime Minister Narendra Modi expanded the ambit and the scale of skills by launching the National Skill Development Mission (NDSM) [472] and the National Policy for Skill Development and Entrepreneurship, 2015.[473] The objective was to create convergence around skills and standards through four programmes.[474] Since then, a network of 574 training partners[475] and thirty-six sector skill councils[476] have brought industry and job-seekers together, trained more than 2 million and placed 1,86,000,[477] while the number of beneficiaries of the NSDM have jumped to more than 9 million in 2020 from less than 4 million in 2017.[478] Now that the skills bridge between workers and industry has been constructed, it's time for this partnership to reduce poverty, increase productivity and create growth.

Reform 52: Hydrocarbons Exploration and Licensing Policy

In 1999, Prime Minister Atal Bihari Vajpayee notified the New Exploration Licensing Policy (NELP) with 100 per cent foreign direct investment,[479] for the exploration and production (E&P) of hydrocarbon resources, notably oil and gas. In the subsequent seventeen years, the unanticipated complexities of the E&P sector increased. These were particularly stark in the differential contractual treatments accorded to different fuels on the one side and the system of sharing profits, which meant the government needed to audit and evaluate costs of companies, often leading to disputes and delays.

Prime Minister Narendra Modi's Hydrocarbons Exploration and Licensing Policy (HELP),[480] launched in March 2016, attempted to clear the cobwebs of stalemate between the government and private companies, and generate new interest in a sector that is dominated by geopolitical implications and the resultant imports on the one hand and the transition to new energy sources and their disruptive applications on the other.[481] This followed a series of recommendations[482] including a thoughtful debate between profit-share and revenue-share models. When HELP was finally adopted, it had five key aspects—a uniform licence for all hydrocarbons (oil, gas, coal bed methane); open acreages that can be bid for throughout the year; a revenue sharing model from profit share; marketing and pricing freedom; and a graded system of royalty rates.[483]

Since launch, five rounds of bidding have been completed with an award of 105 blocks spanning an area of over 1,50,580 square kilometres, with a total committed investment of more than $2.3 billion. The next (Round 6) is expected to add an additional 35,000 square kilometres to the mix with an investment commitment of $300–400 million.[484] HELP is part of a policy evolution reform (from nomination era to pre-NELP to NELP)[485] to deliver energy security, a core component for economic growth.

Reform 53: Aadhaar

If there is one idea that binds everything, from welfare to wealth, it is a unique identification (UID). For the first five decades, India did not have a one-citizen-one-ID structure. In 2006, Prime Minister Manmohan Singh began the process, by setting up an Empowered Group of Ministers,[486] to collate two schemes—the National Population Register and the UID.[487] Four meetings later,[488] he formed the Unique Identification Authority of India (UIDAI), through a notification,[489] an executive order, as an attached office of the Planning Commission, which itself was formed by a similar resolution.[490] Tech entrepreneur Nandan M. Nilekani was appointed chairman.[491] Without statutory support, however, the UIDAI failed to turn this idea of the time into a tide of action. A 'Council' constituted by Manmohan Singh in August 2009[492] proved inadequate. A December 2010 bill[493] attempted to change the status quo but failed in Parliament following objections regarding legitimization of unregistered immigrants and potential safety concerns with data.[494]

In 2016, Prime Minister Narendra Modi introduced the Aadhaar (Targeted Delivery of Financial and Other Subsidies, Benefits and Services) Act, 2016;[495] Parliament enacted it. Activists challenged it in the Supreme Court alleging breach of privacy; the court overruled the objections and cleared the law.[496] The result was the beginning of what today has become the world's largest identity platform.[497] On the citizens' side, the number of Aadhaar cards getting approved and generated annually started rising—from 4.2 million 2010–11, it peaked to 298.3 million in 2013–14,[498] and cumulatively stood at 1.26 billion by 2019–20.[499] From property papers to the JAM trinity to KYC norms, these numbers underline the beneficiaries of identity on the citizens' side, efficiency of governance on the governments' side, and a potential soft export for the rest of the world. This is a major reform.

Reform 54: Insolvency and Bankruptcy Code

For a crucial five-year-young law to see six amendments in three years shows either the lack of application of mind by those drafting it, ignorance of complexities in its execution, or those to whom it applies finding loopholes. Ushered in by Prime Minister Narendra Modi, the Insolvency and Bankruptcy Code (IBC), 2016[500] was a landmark reform that attempted to fill a void in resolving bankruptcies, but has been and continues to be a constant work in progress. The IBC attempts to consolidate laws relating to reorganization and insolvency resolution of companies, partnership firms and individuals in a time-bound manner to manage and balance the rights of all stakeholders, end the malaise of 'rich promoters of poor companies',[501] and through it institutionalize the process of business failures. The law, and its execution, stands on four pillars—regulatory oversight,[502] insolvency professionals and agencies,[503] information utilities,[504] and adjudicating authority.[505]

The lack of policy experience with insolvencies combined with entrenched interests have ensured six amendments. The first amendment facilitated a phased implementation and provided clarity about who can submit a resolution plan.[506] The second amendment was enacted mainly to serve the interests of wealthy homebuyers.[507] The third amendment made the Committee of Creditors the decision-maker to liquidate a corporate debtor.[508] The fourth amendment removed difficulties during the corporate insolvency resolution process by protecting the last mile funding.[509] The fifth amendment provided COVID-19-specific relief to companies, allowing them to recover without the threat of insolvency.[510] And the sixth amendment provided a pre-packaged insolvency resolution process framework for MSMEs to ensure job preservation.[511] Together, these have led India towards outcomes that are laudatory: the average time taken for resolution fell from 4.3 years in 2017 (world average: 2.496) to 1.6 years in 2020, below the world average of 2.5 years.[512]

Reform 55: Demonetization

Demonetization has been Prime Minister Narendra Modi's most controversial and most transiently disruptive economic policy,[513] with several opposers and few supporters. But this is in tune with and part of the larger family of policies undertaken by him to clamp down on unaccounted-for money and wealth.

It is ironical that a country that bemoans people not paying taxes opposes almost every reform that seeks to end it. This plays out in many ways—from two-by-four tax filing criteria under Prime Minister H.D. Deve Gowda[514] to its expansion to one-by-six under Prime Minister Atal Bihari Vajpayee,[515] and from demonetization 1.0 under Prime Minister Morarji Desai[516] (when Rs 1,000, Rs 5,000 and Rs 10,000 notes ceased to be legal tender) to demonetization 2.0 under Modi (when Rs 500 and Rs 1,000 notes got extinguished).[517] This is in addition to the Voluntary Disclosure of Income Scheme under Gowda[518] and the Rs 1,400 presumptive tax scheme under Prime Minister P.V. Narasimha Rao.[519]

Modi's demonetization 2.0 came prefixed with dollops of rhetoric, political and economic, from corruption to curbing fake currency to controlling terror financing from across the border.[520] But with 98.96 per cent of the notes returning to the banking system,[521] the public debate around demonetization shifted to acute individual distress, hard-hit sectors such as real estate, supply chains disruption, and increased economic uncertainty.[522]

Despite back-end technologies linked to bank accounts in place, there is no data on how much of the cash entering the banking system through the 'know your customer' route was unaccounted for; this is the incomplete part of this reform. In terms of outcomes, we can see demonetization as a trigger for a less-cash economy that also led to a sharp 39 per cent increase in the number of 'taxpayers',[523] from 61 million in 2015–16 to 85 million in two years.[524]

Reform 56: Real Estate Regulator

Unlike in the case of capital markets or banking, the lack of a regulator in the real estate sector was hurting consumers until 2016. From problems with delivery to the absence of a grievance redressal system, housing was a story of tragic contradictions.[525]

Prime Minister Manmohan Singh sought to fix this through the Real Estate (Regulation and Development) Bill, 2013,[526] which lapsed. When Prime Minister Narendra Modi took it up and ushered in the Real Estate (Regulation and Development) Act, 2016,[527] it changed the texture of the sector. Apart from bringing transactions around sale of plots, apartments or buildings under the Real Estate Regulatory Authority (RERA),[528] the law embeds transparency into real estate with an adjudicating mechanism and an appellate authority.[529] Being a subject that comes under the State List under the Constitution,[530] the onus of notifying and executing the law vests with state governments.

Under the law, every real estate project has to be registered with RERA if the area is 500 square metres and more or the number of apartments is eight or more.[531] Further, real estate agents need to register with RERA before any sale.[532] The law mandates that no promoter can accept more than 10 per cent as advance payment without written agreements for sale.[533] It also mandates the maintenance of separate accounts for each project with 70 per cent of the funds received deposited in it.[534]

Since its enactment in 2016, the law has now been notified by 35 of 36 states and Union Territories in India (Nagaland being the sole exception), with Adjudicating Officers appointed in 22 states and functional Appellate Tribunals in 28 of the 35 states. In terms of outcomes, 68,012 projects and 52,739 agents have registered under RERA, and 71,068 cases have been disposed of.[535] A much-needed reform has been enacted; but its effectivity needs greater study in the states.

Reform 57: GST

Ushered in by Prime Minister Narendra Modi,[536] the Goods and Services Tax (GST) is India's most complex law and most impactful reform. It took ten governments under eight prime ministers and more than three decades for it to come to life. Administratively, it has simplified indirect taxes and brought seventeen different taxes, eight levied by the Union government[537] and nine by state governments,[538] into a single tax. Legislatively, it has been done by one Constitutional Amendment,[539] five Union laws,[540] twenty-eight state legislations,[541] and one notification for eight Union Territories.[542] The rates and administration of GST are decided by the GST Council, a mix of Union and state government representatives, chaired by the Union finance minister. Currently, there are seven rates for goods (from nil to 28 per cent)[543] and five for services (nil to 28 per cent).[544]

The idea was floated under Prime Minister Rajiv Gandhi in Budget 1986–87 as MODVAT.[545] Several committee reports and various attempts to fix the fiscal power of the Union and the states such that taxpayers can deal with fewer types of tax, including an attempt in 2000 through CENVAT, came and went. In many ways, therefore, the passage of GST into law and its execution since July 2017, is a major step in the political economy of India. In the evolution of indirect tax and Union–state tussles, the idea of a single 'primary rate'[546] on value added tax has been forgotten and should be revived. Finally, three items that are out of the purview of GST—alcohol for human consumption, petroleum products and electricity—need to be brought under it. Every policy goes through a fine-tuning. A complex law like GST more so. But if the number of taxpayers and the amount of taxes collected (Rs 1,42,095 crore in March 2022)[547] is any indication, GST is doing fine and is one of India's most difficult, important and successful reforms.

Reform 58: Ayushman Bharat

Despite health being a subject under the legislative domain of state governments under the Constitution of India,[548] there have been several schemes devised by the Union government to fix it. Constitution aside, this is part of providing health coverage to Indian citizens as a desired policy goal since Independence, from Prime Minister Jawaharlal Nehru's Employees' State Insurance, 1948,[549] to Prime Minister Manmohan Singh's Rashtriya Swasthya Bima Yojana, 2008.[550] As the lexicon of universal health coverage (UHC) entered the economic discourse in 2012 with the United Nations Resolution 72/138,[551] India's health policies gathered momentum.

In 2018, Prime Minister Narendra Modi announced the ambitious Ayushman Bharat Programme.[552] This is a three-pronged approach. First, to provide comprehensive primary healthcare through Health and Wellness Centres (HWC)[553] mainly in rural areas. Second, to ensure that additional medical expenses were reduced through health insurance availed of under the Pradhan Mantri Jan Arogya Yojana (PMJAY), which entitles a Rs 5 lakh cover for secondary and tertiary care to more than 100 million poor families.[554] And third, to give flexibility to state governments through 'co-operative federalism'.[555]

Under the first component of the scheme, the target is to set up 1,50,000 HWCs of which 77,899 HWCs have so far been made operational with more than 300 million people screened for various ailments like hypertension, diabetes and different types of cancers.[556]

The second component pertaining to insurance has been an area of major focus as it aims to reduce the out-of-pocket expenditures for India's poorest households. Finally, the Union-to-states ratio of funding the schemes is placed at 60:40, with 90:10 for the Northeastern and Himalayan states. Going forward, the administrative oversight of the PMJAY should be extended as a base insurance cover for all non-poor citizens, who can pay for it.[557] Like the Jan Dhan scheme, this reform can push the somnolent insurance regulator IRDAI to wake up and serve consumers.

Reform 59: Repeal of Obsolete Laws

Philosophically, laws have to keep pace with society; politically, leaders in democracies have to gauge and aggregate societal aspirations to bring changes in law. The process of change, therefore, has to not merely reflect but pre-empt and support societal aspirations. Today's laws could be tomorrow's chains. The process of discarding obsolete laws, however, requires legislative agility. In the first sixty-six years of independent India, 1,301 obsolete laws were removed.[558]

Within three months of taking charge, Prime Minister Narendra Modi set up a committee to identify obsolete laws,[559] based on four reports of the Law Commission. The process was intense. Taking the recommendations submitted by the Law Commission—Report Nos. 248,[560] 249,[561] 250,[562] and 251[563] recommended repealing seventy-two, 113, seventy-three, and thirty laws, respectively, taking the total to 288 laws—the Commission recommended repealing 1,741 laws (777 Union Acts; 83 Union Acts relating to state subjects identified for repeal by the State Legislatures; 624 Union Appropriation Acts; and 257 Union Appropriation Acts in respect of states identified for repeal by State Legislatures).[564] Following these recommendations, the government then repealed the laws in two parts during 2015[565] and 2018,[566] and once in 2019.[567]

Some of the laws that have been repealed are those that were enacted by the current government and range from those pertaining to regional rural banks, companies, and telecom. Many of them have been from pre-Independence era (Transfer of Property [Amendment] Supplementary Act, 1929), while some were born in the nineteenth century (Calcutta Pilots Act, 1859). With the success of these repeals behind, we can expect a wider sweep of archaic laws. The next step would be to reform compliances. Stepping back, in a dynamic world as today's it may not be a bad idea for every law, rule and regulation to have a sunset clause.

Reform 60: Asset Monetization

The process of leveraging assets created by taxpayers' funds, making them more productive, redesigning incentives and raising revenues is called asset monetization. It is a limited period licence or lease of an asset owned by the government to a private sector entity for a one-time fee or a periodic consideration.[568]

If disinvestment was the currency of the government getting out of business through the 1990s, asset monetization will possibly be the political economy reform experiment during the 2020s. Between 2022 and 2025, around Rs 6 lakh crore worth of assets will be monetized from thirteen ministries across twenty asset classes.[569] Roads, railways and power transmission and generation are expected to contribute almost Rs 4,00,000 crore, while stadiums, ports and aviation will add Rs 45,000 crore.[570] In addition, the scheme also talks about monetizing immovable enemy properties under the custody of the government.

With the procedure for monetizing laid out in a March 2019 circular, this scheme has the potential to turn dead assets into income streams without losing ownership. In the way that the scheme has been envisaged, asset monetization balances the risks and the returns between public properties and private entrepreneurs—the latter gets to use the asset more efficiently, the former gets money upfront or as an annuity with which to fund other infrastructure projects. While the idea is new to India, it has had a fair play outside. In Australia, for instance, the Port of Melbourne has been leased out for fifty years under a similar scheme.[571] How this will play out, given the constraints of

India's political economy, remains to be seen. But as a conceptual idea, this is the start of an interesting reforms experiment, with the success of the Delhi[572] and Mumbai[573] airports as benchmarks.

Reform 61: Labour Reforms

When Prime Minister V.P. Singh talked about labour in 1990, the focus was on inclusion, safety, 'meaningful cooperation' and the 'right to work'.[574] Next year, when Prime Minister Manmohan Singh initiated India's boldest economic reforms, he left labour out of their purview.[575] This is not surprising: under the Constitution, labour falls under the 'Concurrent List',[576] where the Union and the states have joint jurisdiction. In fact, the Manmohan Singh government stated that liberalization will not happen at the 'cost of the workers'.[577] This inertia has led to a state of affairs where the tyranny of excesses in labour laws is preventing entrepreneurs from investing and hiring—out of 63 million Indian enterprises, there are only 1 million formal employers; more than 98 per cent of Indian employers prefer to stay small.[578]

It has taken thirty years post-liberalization for legislative conversations around labour reforms to restart and attempt to restore the balance between growth through new industries and protections accorded to workers. In March 2021, Prime Minister Narendra Modi steered labour reforms that attempt change through four laws—The Code on Wages,[579] The Occupational Safety, Health and Working Conditions Code, 2020,[580] The Code on Social Security,[581] and The Industrial Relations Code, 2020.[582] These four laws have amalgamated 29 Union laws into four Codes, the related rules for which, on wage laws for instance,[583] are under way.

The paradigm of labour reforms has expanded to the states too. Some, like Chief Minister Shivraj Singh Chouhan in Madhya Pradesh, are going in the right direction,[584] while others, such as Chief Minister Yogi Adityanath in Uttar Pradesh, veered off course.[585] As they work themselves out over the next few years, one thing is clear: you need political courage to address and bring in labour reforms, which Modi has initiated.

Reform 62: Agricultural Reforms

Like labour reforms, agricultural reforms have been hibernating in the cold storage of inertia, intensely political, unwilling for change, and living off tax-funded subsidies. In September 2020, when Prime Minister Narendra Modi ushered in three laws that attempted to change the status of small and marginal farmers by giving them flexibility to sell their produce outside monopsonies controlled by rich farmers and middlemen, it became a political issue where farmers were invisible,[586] a judicial issue for no reason,[587] and resulted in a needless executive decision to keep the laws in abeyance for eighteen months,[588] before being repealed.[589]

The reform may have been unsuccessful, but it showed Modi's courage to do the right thing. Of the three laws, the first gave farmers flexibility to sell outside designated mandis.[590] The second deregulated government control over cereals, pulses, potatoes, onions, edible oilseeds and oil,[591] and enabled storage infrastructure by amending a restrictive and outdated law. And the third protected small farmers when they negotiated contracts with companies and wholesalers.[592] Like industrial reforms of Prime Minister Manmohan Singh in 1991, these laws had the potential to change the face of India's agriculture and cart prosperity to small and marginal farmers by freeing them from the tyranny of Agriculture Produce Marketing Committees (APMCs), called out as a 'hotbed of politics, corruption and monopoly of traders and middleman'.[593]

The three laws were enacted after more than two decades of debate. Sadly, fake political narratives such as APMCs will shut down, and misinformation like minimum support price will be withdrawn, manipulated opposition to them.[594] It is surprising that yesterday's proponents of these reform ideas, across political parties, have become today's opponents of its laws.[595] This is a much-needed economic reform in the interest of small and marginal farmers, which unfortunately has been pushed back.

Reform 63: Decriminalization of Economic Offences

The manner in which economic laws have been enacted, even after liberalization in 1991, continue to cart the legislative history of repressing capital. By putting penal provisions in every new law, even when they are procedural, it looks as though the legal mechanism underlying doing business remains shackled to the past. From the Factories Act, 1948[596] to the Contract Labour (Regulation and Abolition) Act, 1970,[597] to the Food Safety and Standards Act, 2006,[598] every business law has penal provisions embedded in it, some necessary,[599] some needless,[600] but all of it feeds the Inspector Raj.[601] Without exception, all leaderships are guilty of this mindless law-making.

Under Prime Minister Narendra Modi, the green shoots of change are slowly emerging. It has begun with enacting amendments that decriminalize select clauses in the Companies Act, 2013—first by the Companies (Amendment) Act, 2019,[602] and next by the Companies (Amendment) Act, 2020,[603] notified in December 2020,[604] January 2021[605] and February 2021.[606] The laws eased penalties and converted sixteen criminal offences into civil wrongs, under which adjudicating officials would levy fines only.[607] This followed the recommendations of the 2019 Company Law Committee to 'facilitate and promote ease of doing business and ease of living'.[608] Given that the committee delivered the report in less than two months, it shows the conviction of the government to resolve such issues. It also tells us that executive solutions reside within the problems.

But these changes barely skim the surface of the 69,233 compliances that apply to businesses, of which 26,134 contain imprisonment clauses.[609] Now, Narendra Modi needs to ride the success of this legislative experiment and expand the ambit of decriminalization of business compliances to the remaining 1,535 laws. His conviction for economic growth and trust in entrepreneurs must turn into completion to hand to state governments for executive closure.

Reform 64: Atmanirbhar Bharat—Crisis Reforms

From P.V. Narasimha Rao to Narendra Modi, nothing binds leaderships like a good crisis—nothing gets the policy and the execution going better than an economic catastrophe. If the macroeconomic balance of payments crisis was the fulcrum on which the 1991 reforms were unveiled, the time since the Made in China COVID-19 pandemic[610] in 2019 has seen three sets of policy reforms that, when viewed together, weave themselves into a net of security and growth. The lexicon of Atmanirbhar Bharat is rooted in the 'self-reliance' narrative of the past as articulated by prime ministers Jawaharlal Nehru[611] and Indira Gandhi,[612] but their grammar is infused with a future being reimagined by Narendra Modi, within an economic context of a shrinking globalization.[613]

The Atmanirbhar Bharat is a five-part package, comprising economy, infrastructure, technology, demography and demand.[614] Released across three months—May 2020,[615] September 2020[616] and November 2020[617]—the package aims to push local manufacturing and local supply chains, make doing business easier. Superficially, there seems to be a conflict between attracting FDI, while empowering SMEs, but in fact, the package leverages the Indian market to attract foreign investors, while ensuring Indian businesses are able to up their game.

Another way to look at this scheme is to see a policy thrust that stands on two feet—short-term crisis management and medium-term business catalysation. Taken together, the Atmanirbhar Bharat package adds up to Rs 20 lakh crore, or 10 per cent of GDP[618]—one of the highest in the world.[619] While these would help tide over the ongoing health-economy crisis with a short spurt in the fiscal deficit, the impact of policy initiatives such as decriminalization of clauses in the Companies Act or the government limiting its presence in public sector enterprises will go a long way.

Reform 65: Payments System

In March 2022, 313 banks made 5.4 billion transactions worth Rs 9.6 lakh crore ($125.4 billion),[620] an exponential rise, almost doubling over the past twelve months and rising more than sixfold over two years. Launched in April 2016, a reform that was waiting to get executed, this less-cash achievement is a financial transit point in India's longer journey towards becoming an e-money-dominated economy. Apart from catalysing the shift from the pre-demonetization years of cash to post-demonetization years trends towards non-cash and cheques to digital,[621] India's payments system infrastructure has morphed into a world leader. A legal framework, created by Prime Minister Manmohan Singh in 2007[622] and 2008,[623] and powered by Prime Minister Narendra Modi since 2014, has consolidated this shift.

While there are several aspects of this reform, from immediate payment service[624] to Bharat Interface for Money[625] and RuPay[626] to cheque truncation system,[627] thc gamechanger has been the Unified Payments Interface (UPI)[628] that has enabled money transfer on mobile phones round the clock, across all accounts, with security authentication. All these measures come at zero cost to consumers,[629] through a series of policy measures undertaken by the Reserve Bank of India and the Ministry of Finance.

Emerging markets in general and India in particular are leading the global fintech adoption.[630] The establishment of the National Payments Corporation of India Ltd (NPCIL), a fintech policy incubator, in 2009, has not only created products but delivered never-seen-before outcomes: between 2010–11 and 2019–20, the share of electronic payments has jumped from 18 per cent to 61 per cent in terms of volume and from 10 per cent to 75 per cent in terms of value.[631] Fintech remains a fast-paced and constantly disrupting mechanism and so far India has been leading the curve that has the potential to become one of the tendrils of India's diplomacy and soft power.

Reform 66: Direct Benefit Transfer

From Prime Minister Rajiv Gandhi's 1985 estimate of 15 paise out of every rupee reaching beneficiaries of welfare schemes,[632] to Prime Minister Manmohan Singh's 2013 reform that initiated Direct Benefit Transfer (DBT) in 43 districts,[633] to Prime Minister Narendra Modi's expectations of a better delivery mechanism through Aadhaar in 2017,[634] to the entire financial entitlements actually reaching bank accounts of beneficiaries, this is the thirty-seven-year-long policy story of direct benefit transfers in India. This journey has not only been arduous but an exercise in using technology in financial governance, notably in subsidies, pensions, and food distribution. The system enabled the smooth transfer of Rs 36,659 crore to more than 160 million during the 2019 lockdown.[635]

When the first steps were taken to implement DBT, three important digital enablers were missing—a bank account, an identity, and both linked by communications technology. Under Modi, DBT got a shot in the arm by what is now known as the JAM Trinity, the virtuous cycle of a Jan Dhan account,[636] a unique Aadhaar identity[637] and a mobile phone number,[638] that connects the two with a person and enables the state to deliver direct benefits.

Since September 2015, the scheme has been shifted to the Cabinet Secretariat from the Ministry of Finance.[639] Growth in DBT has been exponential: in FY 2021–22, total DBT transfers were more than Rs 1,16,000 crore, through 141 crore transactions,[640] across 312 schemes in 54 ministries,[641] resulting in gains from the end of duplicate or fake beneficiaries of more than Rs 1,78,000 crore.[642] Outcomes of the scheme are not merely economic, they are social as well, and empower the last person standing. By June 2021, the government had procured close to Rs 50,000 crore worth of crop directly from farmers with the money going into their bank accounts, bypassing the middlemen.[643]

Reform 67: National Highways

Introduced by Prime Minister Rajiv Gandhi as he ushered in the National Highways Authority of India Act, 1988,[644] enabled by Prime Minister P.V. Narasimha Rao in 1995 with the National Highways (Amendment) Act, 1995,[645] reimagined by Prime Minister Atal Bihari Vajpayee in 2000 with the National Highways Development Project,[646] and scaled up by Prime Minister Narendra Modi in terms of expanding the span, the highways of India have magnified the reforms of India and expressed a unity of political intent. Between 1951 and 1991, national highways grew at a compounded annual growth rate of 1.3 per cent,[647] and over the next twenty-eight years by more than 5 per cent.[648] India's highway policies have worked. But they can go faster.

The NHAI was established to develop, maintain and manage the highways. What was needed following the 1991 reforms was a legal mechanism that enabled the entry of the private sector into roadmaking. That came with a 1995 amendment, which allowed the government to enter into partnerships with private entities and to also allow the collection of tolls. In 1998–2000, the Vajpayee government budgeted Rs 54,000 crore,[649] and introduced the Golden Quadrilateral project and the North-South East-West Corridor project, which not merely connected destinations but enabled the shift from farm to non-farm employment.[650]

Building highways was one thing, ease of drive another. In September 2017, Narendra Modi introduced FASTag—an electronic toll collection method based on RFID chips installed on all vehicles;[651] from February 2021, they were made mandatory for all vehicles across the country with daily collections hitting Rs 103.54 crore in July 2021,[652] and a 96 per cent penetration.[653] This is clearly a success story that all governments have built and driven on.

Reform 68: Railways Dedicated Freight Corridors

In the political economy of India, not only are railway passenger fares lower than freight rates, passenger trains get precedence over freight trains on tracks. Business priority, in other words, continues to lag passenger movement on the Railways' 1,26,366 kilometres of tracks.[654] To fix the problem of slow speeds, in 2005 Prime Minister Manmohan Singh announced a dedicated network of freight corridors,[655] between Delhi–Kolkata and Delhi–Mumbai. The next year, a special purpose vehicle, Dedicated Freight Corridor Corporation of India Ltd, was established with two arms—Eastern Dedicated Freight Corridor and Western Dedicated Corridor. The dedicated corridors would not shift the freight traffic away from passenger routes; their special design would allow for increased load capacity, from 5,400 tonners to 13,000 tonnes, making it possible to run double stacked trains up to 1.5 km in length (up from 0.7 km) with speeds reaching 100 kmph (up from 75 kmph).[656]

In 2018, Prime Minister Narendra Modi expanded the project to a 3,360 kilometre long network at a cost of Rs 81,459 crore.[657] Moreover, there would be fewer signals and level crossing, reducing operational delays even further.[658] As of April 2021, 3,452 km of tracks have been constructed (more than projected) and 311 out of 540 major bridges completed. For both corridors, the financial progress is more than 70 per cent and the finalization of related works is expected to be completed by June 2022.[659] With the Indian economy growing faster than infrastructure can keep pace, it is very likely that the completion of the corridors would be a starting point for another round of expansion.[660] An economy that's $5 trillion strong needs a world-class transporter, particularly on the freight side. This reform has the ability to cart the economy at speed and deliver jobs and prosperity at scale.

Reform 69: Power Sector Revamp

Since 1991, the evolution of power sector reforms, from idea to execution, monopolies to competition, state control to privatization, generation to distribution, and low plant load factors to a power-surplus nation, continues to remain a work in progress—a work that has bound the policy objectives of all governments and a progress that has handed the baton of delivery across leaderships, from Prime Minister

P.V. Narasimha Rao onwards. This has led to a stream of policies such as independent power producers in 1991,[661] the Mega Power Policy in 1995,[662] the Electricity Regulatory Commissions in 1998,[663] and the Electricity Act in 2003.[664]

All these laws and policies focused on the supply side, that is, how to generate more power, and transmit and distribute it efficiently. In 2020, under Prime Minister Narendra Modi, a new idea that looked at power sector reforms from the consumer side was ushered in. These laid down the rights of consumers around connections, billing, reliability of supply, compensations, grievance redressal and enabled consumers to become prosumers by setting up renewable energy generation units in their homes.[665]

Further, to increase competition in and enable delicensing of electricity distribution under a regulatory structure and appellate framework, an amendment to the Electricity Act, 2003 that includes green renewable purchase obligations is under way. Finally, if the National Electricity Policy, 2021[666] comes into force, India could be looking at not merely a more efficient power sector but also a green, consumer-focused and light-touch regulatory regime. The change and predictability in regulatory processes would include central and state regulatory commissions, focusing more on market monitoring and surveillance and less on tariffs, which will be based on a predefined, algorithm-based and transparent formula.[667]

Conclusion
Beyond Compulsions and Convictions

A triple trinity faces the economic reformers of India over the next twenty-five years that leads to a century of India's independence on 15 August 2047. Irrespective of the politics of the governments in the interim, these trinities will be the new assumptions around which India will grow, feed, protect and influence. Any person ambitious of leading India in this period will have to understand and grapple with these three trinities.

First, she will have to understand and deal with the trinity of disruptions—technology, geopolitics and narratives. Second, she will have to engage with the trinity of major actors—producers, consumers and regulators—and enable them into becoming catalysts for growth, prosperity and wealth. And third, she will have to negotiate the threats and opportunities of the first two trinities to deliver the final trinity—dismantle the colonial legal infrastructure holding India back, reinstate India as one of the major fulcrums of the global economy and become an influential rules-maker, security provider and be counted among those redrafting the emerging new world order.

Each of these triple trinities will engage and influence its components. Technology as a lever for growth will impact geopolitics through trade, for instance. Or, removing outdated laws will unleash new animal spirits that have the potential to create new Indian transnational giants. Or, the way India's poor consumes will affect what India produces or imports.

Further, these trinities will intersect with one another. Geopolitics with the demands on food consumption, for instance. Or, easing tax regulation with a more conducive atmosphere for capital—Indian and foreign. Or, technology with a greater prosperity through its several revenue-catalyzing platforms.

Magnifying the challenges of engaging all these is the fact that each component of the triple trinity is a moving target that brings opportunities and challenges. A rise in income levels will impact consumption patterns and could lead to higher inflation in one good (say, food in the short term, fuel in the medium term and housing in the long term) and lower in another (say, computers or mobile phones, Wi-Fi services, or drones), for instance. A higher GDP will influence interest-driven geopolitics. A rising power will trigger new anti-India narratives.

India's current and future leaders need to manage this triple trinity, all its complexities and amoeba-like characteristics by creative approaches to governance and statecraft. In other words, they will—simultaneously—need to get India's house back in order (rethink laws, rules and regulations), engage the world creatively (reduce security threats from within and outside, particularly the terrorist-state of Pakistan and its aggressive 'iron brother' China), all the while ensuring that the journey to a $30 trillion economy with a $20,000 per capita income does not slacken.

Economic reforms, going forward, will need to look beyond economics.

They will need to accelerate and they will have to become nimble-footed.

Conviction will be the starting point for tomorrow's reformers, who will need to manage these triple trinities, with all their sub-components, together. The urgency for doing so in an increasingly competitive politics that seeks to scratch the gains from reforms and pull India back to a povertarian pre-1991 stage (See Chapters 4 to 11) needs to be firmly kept in mind. The fight between offering free goods for votes and free markets for prosperity, for instance. Or, the idea that every citizen should get everything, from food to water to Wi-Fi, at her doorstep, without making any effort, without *parishram*. Or, the constant rise in the marginal rate at which households and corporations pay income tax.

This means having deep conversations with India that creates a political support, irrespective of the party in power, for reforms. This is really a contestation between a *rajasic*-dynamic vision of the future versus a *tamasic*-indolent politics of the past. As an old civilization, India needs to embrace its past, without shunning its present or future. Equally, as a young nation, it needs a new dynamism that will clasp change and deliver hope. Maybe, reformers will create a middle ground that balances the sattvic surge of equal opportunities for wealth creation with the delivery of wealth redistribution where required.[1] It is in between these trinities and its moving parts that India's economic reforms have to situate themselves. Let us examine these trinities.

First, the three disrupters—technology, geopolitics, narratives.

It is a myopic myth to claim that the rise of the knowledge society of the twenty-first century is the first societal transformation. Technology has been a disruptor since the use of stones and bones for hunting, the discovery of agriculture for settling, the metal ages for stability and conquests, the invention of clock to organize time, the creation of the printing press for expansion of knowledge, the invention of steam power and the resultant stream of factories for manufacturing, the discovery of and mass use of electricity for convenience, and the constant stream of inventions around computing, biological sciences and robotics that began in the late twentieth century and continues till date. To imagine that computing today has, as artificial intelligence will tomorrow, changed the world like never before is living in time-freeze. Even the rate of change of the information revolution is, according to Peter Drucker, the same as in the industrial revolution.[2] So, while

India's reformers might function from a position of five-year tenures that the Indian democracy offers them, the civilizational experience is longer, with many lessons on how to steer these changes. The evolution of policy, as we have seen over the past three decades (See Chapter 13), needs to continue.

Further, even though the intrusion of geopolitics, through the Russia–Ukraine conflict for now but several before, into economics is scorching as far as economic impact to all nations is concerned, again, this is not a new dimension. There have been two European Wars (termed World Wars) earlier, three failed attempts at global unity—Concert of Europe (1815–1914), League of Nations (1919–1946) and the United Nations (1939–)[3]—even as India has been dealing with (and continues to) defending borders from aggressive neighbours, Pakistan and China, for seven decades. Overall, the extent of violence has fallen, though the weeds of warmongering and its echoes have risen. Part of India's slow rise in the past can be attributed to military and security spending, a concept Europe is just beginning to experience. India has reduced poverty and created prosperity despite these challenges. And, apart from silly statements from one immature G7 leader—Canada's virtue-signalling Prime Minister Justin Trudeau who did the opposite of what he commented on India[4] when it came to managing protests in Canada by invoking draconian measures to smother the voice of democracy[5]—the rise of India has been welcomed by every member of the developed world. Unlike in the case of China, the rise of India is good for the planet, from security to climate action.

Most leaders understand this, and want deeper economic engagements through free trade agreements (See Reform 38 in Chapter 13) and strategic ties with India. But there is a danger geopolitics brings in the twenty-first century. In a matter of days, an entire country, Russia, has been effectively cancelled by the West.[6] Restricted to left-leaning ideological vices baptized 'Woke', this cancel culture shows how technological platforms are extensions of the arms of the state. As a result, India's reforms must push Indian entrepreneurs to create and expand Made in India platforms; in turn, Indian techpreneurs must rise to the occasion and deliver world-class facilities. Simultaneously, governments must offer G2C (government to citizens) conversations on servers under their control. The rise of India-first politics needs to seep into the India-first businesses and India-first platforms—no country should be able to cancel or deplatform India, not now, not in the future. Further, the global importance of a Made in India of a digital public utility becomes ever more important in the rising geopolitical context today.

Narrative writers of the West are and will remain behind the reality curve. Trapped in the echo chambers of an extreme-left ideology, the academia and the media have lost their credibility twice over. First, with their incessant, unending and irrational rants and attacks on India they have made themselves irrelevant to most in India, other than those echoing in their chambers. That is, a tiny sliver of extreme left and Wokes who resonate with and benefit from these narrative assaults; they may be a noisy constituency, but are inconsequential to the larger political discourse. And second, even if the global media is seen to be powerful and under the influence of states, notably in the US and the UK, the G2G (government to government) engagements have been strengthening, from trade and investments to multilateral partnerships and security in the Indo-Pacific to citizen movements.

These narratives are part of a ruthless toolkit[7] that uses any and every idea and person and weaponizes it to serve its anti-India diatribe. That said, there is another view that could help understand these attacks on India. 'Attacks on India by western Left leaning liberal media are not as much on India as they are on domestic conservative constituencies. India is just a proxy,' said former Prime Minister of Canada, Stephen Harper, recently.[8]

The truth stands on both these views. When India bought energy from Russia, these narratives condemned it, while ignoring that what India buys in a month from Russia is less than what Europe buys from it in an afternoon.[9] The new narrative is that wheat prices are rising and leading to higher food inflation across the world because India put export curbs on the commodity,[10] purposefully ignoring the fact that

India figures nowhere even in the top thirty wheat exporting nations that are led by Russia (19.5 per cent of $51.4 billion worth of wheat exports), Canada (13.7 per cent), the US (13.9 per cent), France (9.3 per cent), Ukraine (8.9 per cent), Australia (5.2 per cent) and Argentina (4.2 per cent). These narrative wars, even if irrelevant for now, need to be fought because the final goal is to choke investments into, and growth of, India.

Next, the three actors—capital, citizens, governance.

Although Prime Minister Manmohan Singh's call to 'revive the animal spirit in the country's economy' hit the headlines in 2012,[11] it did so in a political-institutional climate of policy paralysis and corruption. Being the face of Prime Minister Narasimha Rao's 1991 reforms, Manmohan Singh's words may have carried conviction. But by then the political instincts of his party had degenerated to its pre-1991 anti-business stance. It took Prime Minister Narendra Modi five years before he could publicly battle for creators of value, jobs and wealth. 'Wealth creation is a great national service,' he said in a 15 August 2019 Independence Day speech.[12] 'Those who create wealth are India's wealth and we respect them.' For a serving prime minister to come out and stand by drivers of prosperity with such a strong and open conviction provides further conviction to capital itself. 'The government's bigger contribution to India's thriving start-up movement may be the Prime Minister's continuous endorsement of the role of wealth creators and entrepreneurs in investment, job creation and nation-building,' wrote Uday S. Kotak in a recent chapter.[13]

But moral pat on the back may be a necessary condition for capital to get excited; it is not a sufficient condition. Capital needs on-ground changes, particularly in the job-intensive manufacturing sector. India has not missed the manufacturing bus, as some narratives argue;[14] our leaders simply refused to board the bus. Global consumption is expected to double to $64 trillion in the fifteen years to 2027.[15] The opportunities in manufacturing for both domestic and international markets, are increasing. They are coated by technology, but the need for cars, houses, gadgets, medicines, clothes and so on, is increasing, not decreasing.

And India is well-positioned to embed itself into global supply chains. Manufacturing value added as a percentage of global GDP stands at 16 per cent, with China, South Korea and Japan at 26 per cent, 25 per cent and 20 per cent; that of India is 13 per cent.[16]

Making manufacturing grow is important, as it is more jobs intensive. But for private capital to take a risk, it needs incentives. The recent production linked incentive scheme, launched by Narendra Modi in November 2021,[17] is a major reform. One of the objectives of this scheme is to promote domestic manufacturing in the entire electronics system design and manufacturing value chain to achieve a turnover of Rs 30,00,000 crore, or $400 billion, by 2025. The scheme is now being expanded to other sectors such as automobiles and auto components.[18]

But in addition to new incentives, India also needs to remove hurdles. For instance, major compliance reforms are required in India's business laws that end or reduce the Inspector Raj and remove harsh compliances created to serve a rent-seeking political-bureaucratic system and which, in turn, has created a regulatory cholesterol. This includes the 1,536 laws that govern doing business in India, 69,233 compliances, of which 26,134 carry imprisonment clauses for breach (See Reform 63 in Chapter 13), which change at the rate of 3,500 per annum and give immense powers to bureaucrats to extract bribes. To give just one illustration, about twenty inspectors from various departments can enter a small or medium factory and demand documents, invoices, receipts, process filings and so on—at any time.[19] Surely, these cannot be the regulatory infrastructure of a twenty-first century India; they need to change. Once done, it will the equivalent of 1991 reforms at ground-zero. The other major reforms include steady power and lower electricity tariffs. The hurdle of labour laws will end with compliance reforms.[20] Capital needs respect, otherwise it will exit.

The second part of this trinity is the citizen. From the late twentieth century till date, the citizen has evolved into a complex being. She is at once a worker, an investor, a consumer—and a voter. As a worker she seeks higher wages, as an investor greater returns, as a consumer lower prices, and as a voter an efficient government. The conflict between labour and capital may be playing out in the minds of narrative builders but as an investor the same worker's small savings are financing big business in stock markets. In other words, the twenty-first century clash of capital and labour is really labour clashing against its own capital; it's time to update Karl Marx.

Never have the stakes of Indian citizens in Indian companies been as high as today, through systematic investment plans of mutual funds, insurance policies and pension products. A generation ago, in 1990–91, when economic reforms were initiated, India's household savings added up to 17.6 per cent of GDP.[21] Three decades later, in 2020–21, they stood at 21.9 per cent of gross national disposable income (GNDI).[22] Alongside this increase, there has been a greater financialization too: in 1990–91, financial assets were 8.6 per cent of GDP, in 2020–21 they are at 15.5 per cent of GNDI. The contribution of physical assets such as real estate and gold has remained more or less the same.

As a result, the third part of this trinity—governance—needs to up its game. There is no doubt that the financial benefits of the world's fastest-growing large economy are reaching its citizens. This exposure to equities needs to be strengthened further such that citizen-investors will have a greater stake in markets, citizen-workers in underlying private companies and citizen-consumers in globally competitive products. This virtuous cycle needs reforms interventions at several points and must continue. The underlying reforms need deeper thought and wider span.

For instance, consumer protection is already a problem area; in digital India, where consumers are in millions and companies are unable to support complaints with humans, technological solutions need to deliver more. Which means, algorithms need regulatory oversight. Or, privacy. With the 'I Agree' tab, citizens are giving huge amounts of information to private companies, generally for cross-selling but equally for harassment; this needs to be plugged with a utility that matches India's cutting-edge payments systems. As India shifts from citizens giving their data free so it can be monetized by large transnational corporations to one where citizens own their own data through the advent of emerging Web 3.0

and 4.0 onwards, India needs to own the entire chain of this transition. Many reforms are needed here.

And final trinity is to work with the threats and opportunities of the first two trinities present and decolonize India's legal infrastructure, make India one of the major economic fulcrums of the global economy, and transition to become an influential rules-maker and security provider that participates actively in constructing the emerging new world order.

In this trinity, the first task is to demolish nineteenth and twentieth century control-the-natives legal infrastructure and replace it with one that powers twenty-first century entrepreneurs. It means replacing human interventions with technology, subjectivity with randomized system checks and physical checks with digital disclosures. It means making life easier for business using governance technologies that create a centralized repository of all laws, rules, regulations and their changes that happen real-time. It means reaching out to entrepreneurs using governance algorithms that enable compliances. It means replacing rent-seekers with faceless and paperless compliances and filings. In other words, replacing state suspicion for entrepreneurs and the resultant bad-guy narrative with a new deal that trusts them with intelligent tools that create checks without holding them back. Given the constant state of disruption in a knowledge economy that is still to mature, this will be a long work-in-progress. The underlying policies, therefore, need to be flexible and faster—governance needs to move as fast as, if not be ahead of, economic actors; incentives need to be redrawn. The Indian Financial Code[23] that rethinks the financial regulatory architecture from the point of view of consumers but awaits legislative clearance is one of several such ideas.

Reforms in this area would mean a complete rethinking and redrafting of the governance architecture of laws and rules that re-establish India's legal design from the point of view of an independent nation, a liberal outlook, a large, open and free economy, and delivering welfare benefits at a scale unmatched despite being a $2,000 per capita income nation. This is something the Narendra Modi government has already initiated—out of 1,800 outdated or irrelevant laws identified, 1,450 have already been repealed,[24] and more are underway. The compliance reforms described above, if they go through, come in the same category. But these repeals or amendments are only the first step. The next step is to reimagine and re-enact India's legal architecture from the point of view of an independent, large, modern, technologically strong and climate-sensitive twenty-first century economy. In other words, to think like a $30 trillion great power and legislate the path to a $20,000 per capita income—simultaneously.

Which means, fewer and simpler laws that are better enforced. It also means rethinking the process of drafting policies and enacting laws. This means the end of writing laws as a knee-jerk to events or copy-pasting clauses (imprisonment clauses for instance) from extant laws. It means the government pushing for a policy documentation process, under which every law, rule or regulation must fix a market failure, go through a cost-benefit analysis, present it to the people and only after going through reactions enact a law or devise a rule. This also means that the regulators down the line must conform to the regulations they draft. Further, amend the Constitution to enable the passage of 'sunset clauses', that is a tool that terminates a law or a regulation at a predetermined time; if it is still needed, there should be a written document that tells the people why. This could apply for the entire law or for stringent clauses (say, imprisonment) within the law. The time period could be five years for a law and between one and three years for a regulation. All these requirements must reach the entrepreneur on her smartphone, real time.

The second task in this trinity is to reach out to, and be part of, global supply chains. The arrogance of Xi Jinping and the frustration and fears of the rest of the world against his capture of the Chinese Communist Party and the resultant aggression provides a large, bright and open window for India to step in. The technological decoupling of the rest of the world with China is underway. Now that the large countries have banned Chinese manufacturers, notably Huawei and ZTE, from their 5G rollouts, the last being Canada,[25] for instance, smaller countries will follow. It will then trickle down to the exclusion of China from all critical infrastructure such as roads, ports, airports and power plants.

As countries decouple with China, there will be a huge demand for a geography of all kinds of manufacturing, from clothes and toys to robots and defence. India must reform its way such that as this shift happens, capital flows here. Combined with cheap labour that is getting increasingly skilled, India needs to see itself as the world's manufacturing destination. All global supply chains must pass through India, entrepreneurs here must add value, and either make or assemble here. There is no problem with political will or entrepreneurial fire; the only hurdle is an entrenched and self-serving bureaucracy that needs to change and will need the biggest reforms, outside the scope of this book. A major hurdle that slows doing business in India is the judicial system; deep reforms are needed here but they are outside the scope of this book.

The final task before India once it becomes a prosperous nation, with businesses catering to global as well as domestic markets, both at scale, is for it to leverage its economic strength and push its values into multilateral conversations. A large economy on a low tax GDP ratio will be the way for India. Even if tax revenues touch 20 per cent of GDP in five to ten years as planned,[26] they will be more than the world average of 14.9 per cent but less than Australia's 23.4 per cent, France's 24.6 per cent and UK's 24.9 per cent.[27] But at $10 trillion they will add up to about $2 trillion, more than the current GDPs of Italy, Canada and South Korea. It will be adequate for India to engage with the world on its own terms.

India is already punching above its weight in international forums, and there are expectations of it being a security provider in the Indo-Pacific region. Unlike China, it is also clear that India will never go rogue—its deep democracy will simply not allow it. Looking outside, it is clear to everyone that global institutions, led by the United Nations, are failing to do their job. They have failed at every point, from the inability to stop violence such as the ongoing Russia–Ukraine conflict to the World Health Organization being captured by China. Energy will remain a challenge in the short term; in the medium to long term, however, India must lead the world in innovations around non-conventional energy, particularly solar. India today is food secure. Taken together, a virtuous cycle lies ahead: standing on economic and physical stability India will grow faster, while the growth will power stability. In the emerging new world order, therefore, India will have a say.

As these trinities engage and intersect with India's democracy, a mutualism of influences will arise. This is not to say that party contestations to lead India will end. They will continue, perhaps with a greater, even violent force. It is to reconfirm that victories in the ballot box will be driven by a societal change led by a young India. Technology, for instance, engages the young much faster than the old. As is the creativity of entrepreneurs to push the boundaries of innovation and enter global supply chains. Or, leaderships that will need to move with the young, at the speed of the young, who seek opportunities, freedoms, jobs—and wealth.

These three trinities will intersect with a new geography of reforms—the states. The location of future economic reforms will shift its base from the Union government to state governments. Most mega-reforms for easing doing business at the Union level have been done; it only needs a change of tracks, and a speed of execution. The heavy lifting by the Union government has been and is being done. Incremental changes, say to disinvestment or foreign direct investment, will continue.

But as far as major reforms go, the burden of reforms will shift to the states. For instance, there are five states whose regulatory artillery includes more than 1,000 imprisonment clauses for breach of compliances—Gujarat (1,469 imprisonment clauses); Punjab (1,273); Maharashtra (1,210); Karnataka (1,175); and Tamil Nadu (1,043).[28] Apart from Punjab, all are industry-heavy states. Further, Punjab with a gross state domestic product (GSDP) of $70 billion has 33 per cent more imprisonment clauses than Uttar Pradesh that has a GSDP of $222 billion, three times more than Punjab. Or, take Goa: on a GSDP of less than $10 billion, it has more imprisonment clauses than Madhya Pradesh, whose GSDP is 10 times larger.[29]

If welfare politics is to play out within the confines of fiscal politics, if the politics of jobs is a route to power, and if migration as a tool for income or its control is to be checked, each state government will need to think up and deliver reforms. The politics of serving a tiny sliver of government servants by deforming hard-fought reforms, as the case of Rajasthan with a return to defined-benefits pensions has shown,[30] will neither deliver growth nor create prosperity nor keep fiscal discipline under check. At some point, the mass that does not have a government job will hit the streets. On the other hand, the rise of Uttar Pradesh from a crime-infested and low-opportunity area to one where investors are lining up has been a complete turnaround—out of nowhere, Chief Minister Yogi Adityanath's policies and execution has made the state the second largest by GSDP, No. 2 in ease of doing business, and the state has doubled its per capita income.[31] Watch this state for reform outcomes and delivery. Effectively, reforms in this direction need to ensure that the glamour of government jobs gets replaced by cutting-edge opportunities in the private sector.

Technology, while being part of the trinities discussed above, will remain the key pillar of reforms. All reforms around manufacturing or infrastructure will, without exception, be driven by technology. The disruption that the computing prowess has unleashed is more than technical. The information revolution has created an information society, just as the industrial revolution had created a mass production society around the factory. From Web 3.0 and 4.0 onwards to 5G and 6G innovations, to agriculture and manufacturing, to the way we travel, buy and sell, there is very little that is not impacted by information today. Entire new industries have come up. Within existing industries, processes have changed—the screen has become the starting point for everything, from dating to governance.

This has had mostly a positive impact on households comprising India. Convenience the currency of transactions, chip the medium of consumption, and digital the texture of money—the information revolution combined with expanded and wireless telecommunications networks has changed for the better our healthcare, education and direct benefit transfers. The information revolution seems to dominate social conversations.

While technology has made conversations of governance instant and transparent, there will always be constituencies of discontentment against reforms. And, because the three trinities are themselves comprised of constantly moving parts, economic and political actors will often find themselves sprinting on shifting sands. Some will try and ride the wave of prosperity, as economic reforms open up markets, increase their sizes, invite investments. Others will see reforms as a threat. These threats may be economic but will express themselves politically. We are already seeing them play out—poor farmers have become proxies in the politics of rich middlemen and wealthy farmers; selling the family silver has become a proxy in the politics of entitled workers in public sector units; labour has become a proxy in the politics against technological or regulatory change; and privacy has become a proxy in the politics for entrenched not-for-profit interests. These constituents lobby and garner support from politics, which is ever ready to capitalize on such gaps. Political contestations looking to stall economic opportunities and hold back reforms are there for all to see.

Read together, these form a complex quadratic equation. The three known components in this equation are a crisis or a problem to initiate reforms; actions of embedded actors; and the politics behind them. The unknown factor is the policy action, keeping political costs-benefits in mind. Around this equation are the other influencers that support or oppose reforms, several of them from within the system, but mostly outside. Each leader, functioning in a block of time–space–action, within unique constraints, has and will deliver different reforms solutions—including not reforming.

If the past is any indicator, in India's economic journey, every step of every reform has been intensely contested. At a policy level, however, I see lesser friction going forward. While every constituency and every citizen has benefited from economic reforms that began in 1991 and continue till date, the policy fraternity that devised these reforms three decades ago is being replaced by the next generation of policymakers. Those policymakers who joined the service before 1991 will be retiring in a few years. The entire next generation of policymakers, largely the bureaucracy, are all beneficiaries—those who joined the services in 2004, for instance, are part of self-sustaining defined contribution pensions rather than exchequer-financed defined benefits. This new crop of economic bureaucrats does not carry the baggage of the past; it looks at the future. It has reasons to be hopeful, its incentives are structured in that direction. In stray conversations that are yet to gather scale, I see Narendra Modi's political conviction for reforms trickle down to a bureaucratic conviction.

Reforms are not easy to push through. From the setting up of regulators to disinvestments, and identity to farm laws (See Reforms 6, 15, 24, 31; 4; 53; and 62 in Chapter 13), every reform has had to fight to make space for itself in the mind of India's diverse, vibrant and vociferously contested democracy. Opposition to reforms has increased from the point Narendra Modi took charge as prime minister, led ironically by the same set of people who opened the economy in 1991. Yesterday's reformers, in particular, have been the loudest in their objections to today's reforms.

As a result, narratives of reforms need to be strengthened too. Building positive narratives around economic reforms, both rhetorical or real, becomes key to either supporting or opposing reforms. The pitch for reformers includes selling dreams, reimagining incentives and communicating them. The terrain for opposers includes highlighting fears, holding on to stability and creating victimhood. A polarizing narrative is stronger than a harmonious one. 'You will lose now' is easier to sell than 'these reforms will expand the market and create prosperity for all, including you in the long term'.

Democracy, the bedrock of the three trinities, demands constituencies to speak to one another, debate, disagree and, finally, reach a consensus of compromises. In politics, and therefore in policy, good cannot be the enemy of excellent. India needs to focus on definitive progress, while aspiring towards a perfect model. In any case, who defines 'perfect' has also become a political statement, with yesterday's rockstar economic policymakers becoming today's intellectual trolls, spewing out rubbish. Economists and advisors don't seem to understand this. Perfection or nothing, a gravity-free ride to a destination at the top and not a series of stairways, is their stance. Not so for the politician, who needs to do the heavy lifting, climb every step of the stairway, meet the people stumbling along, heal the losers, push the winners, and carry as many constituents with him as possible. This is the biggest service politicians provide.

Further, as you may have seen throughout the book, every reform is an evolution, with one leadership taking the change idea one step further, making it more efficient and effective, keeping current democratic needs and enablers like technology in mind. The introduction of MGNREGA (See Reform 39 in Chapter 13) by Prime Minister Manmohan Singh, for instance, is the culmination of a series of steps that began with the Community Development Programme of 1952, the Food for Work Programme of 1977, the National Rural Employment Programme of 1980, and the Rural Landless Employment Guarantee of 1983. All through, the objective was to provide an economic anchor to the poor.

It's the same evolution that has brought in the biggest indirect taxes reform, the goods and services tax (GST, See Reform 57 in Chapter 13). This tax reforms story began more than three decades ago under Prime Minister Rajiv Gandhi as MODVAT in 1986, it was polished under Prime Minister Atal Bihari Vajpayee as CENVAT in 2000, and under Prime Minister Manmohan Singh as VAT in 2005, to finally conclude under Prime Minister Narendra Modi as GST in 2017. Most policies, from opening up foreign direct investment to setting up regulators, are part of this trans-governmental evolutionary cycle. That's good news: it tells us that several reforms started by one government continue through the next.

With continuity as a backdrop, how is it that the acceptance of reforms by yesterday's reformers as a way forward have come to a halt post 2014? A sharply changed politics seems to be the sole answer. Irrespective of what whether other parties believe, or even agree, if a reform is being brought by Prime Minister Narendra Modi, it must be opposed—this seems to be the new political stance around which narratives are built. This then becomes a political stalemate that leads the Opposition nowhere.

It doesn't affect the conviction of Modi, he continues with the reforms.

But it's not just political leaders that need to have conviction for reforms. This conviction needs to trickle down the line and must reform governance itself. Much has been written about processes. But ask yourself this question: in the twenty-first century governance matrix, should there be any space for ageism, the stereotypes, prejudice and discrimination towards others or oneself based on age?[32] Why, for instance, should heads of regulatory bodies be made sinecures for retired secretaries? In the world of Web 3.0 or further, in the channels of 5G and beyond, smarter talent is found outside. Surely, understanding batch-networks and getting them to deliver on a phone call cannot be the sole skill to deliver efficiency. The revolving door that Narendra Modi has opened for lateral entry of professionals is just a start. His next move should be to break the IAS fraternity nexus and replace it with the triple nexus of education, experience and execution. As far as key positions go, the tyranny of ageism has to give way to the delivery of efficiency.

There has been a shift in our governance priorities too. Take urbanization. India's cities occupy 3 per cent of the land but contribute 60 per cent to GDP. Further, each percentage point increase in a district's urban population share is associated with a 2.7 per cent increase in district GDP. At the level of individuals, salaries are higher in cities with populations of more than 1.5 million.[33] Here, the responsibility to grow cities lies with state governments. With NITI Aayog as partner, seven states have identified twelve cities to enable them reach their economic potential.[34] But in addition to the physical change and regulatory architecture, what this endeavour needs are urban reforms that include a more accountable municipal regulatory framework, with growth incentives plugged into the architecture. This is not rocket science. If tax officials can be given targets,[35] which several of whom achieve through zero-accountability extortion, surely city officials can have targets of growth, jobs and wealth.

Of course, the baseline foundations for such reforms are political harmonies. What India needs today are not one, not two, but several pitches around economic reforms in its political discourse. But so far gone is the polarity of ideas, so wide the ideological shorelines, and so aggressive the communication, that even the space for political conversations, leave aside an expected harmony of discourse, has receded. Political contestations define and power India's democracy; political pullbacks to win such a contest hurt the nation. And yet, it is politics that must persuade.

Between the compulsions of P.V. Narasimha Rao and the convictions of Narendra Modi lies a politics of consensus. In the twentieth century politics, Narasimha Rao did not need to persuade; in the twenty-first century politics Narendra Modi does. On its part, within the democratic processes, consensus is neither a necessary nor a sufficient condition for economic reforms. As long as constitutional rights are not being violated, for which the judiciary remains a strong institutional mechanism, we should accept that it is not possible for a nation the size of India to serve every small voice or bend the aspirations of the most to serve the demands of the few.

Electoral decisions create winners and losers. The winner gets to govern, the rest oppose. The BJP has done its share of sitting in the Opposition, but even there it supported the reforms it initiated, the PFRDA (Pension Fund Regulatory and Development Authority, for instance). For now, democracy has handed the baton of governance to the BJP by a wide margin. As such, a legislative consensus may be an aspired-for ideal but remains politically immaterial. Conversations around reforms are needed but reforms themselves are not dependent on them. That said, every party worth its victory knows that political insignificance is not a permanent state of affairs. The winners of today could be the losers of tomorrow. The winners at the national level could be losers in states. Such is the nature of India's complex democracy.

What's to the advantage of the Opposition is the state of constant elections India is in. The smallest election, in municipalities for instance, is seen as a larger than life signal for general elections. As we all know, that's untrue. The Indian electorate is wiser, it doesn't allow anyone to predict any electoral outcome. Reforms, therefore, have to progress on their own steam, own conviction. On the other hand, the governing coalition has the advantage of delivering, and communicating that delivery, to the man standing in the last village. The voter needs to decide between an ideological promise and on-ground delivery of benefits. Thus far, she has voted for the latter. With no alternative governance model to offer, all that the Opposition has been doing is lamenting about reforms and attacking policy decisions of the Narendra Modi government. The voter needs a more refined Opposition, and the latter needs better advisors and ear-to-the ground leaders.

In other words, power itself has to be rethought, this time to facilitate and build India rather than control and smother aspirations. The resultant insignificance of power consensus does not mean the end of political consensus. Every reformer has, is and must continue to engage with the people directly—the people themselves have to become proponents of reforms, demand them with conviction. Technology can, and has, become an enabler of these conversations. A large part of the political discourse has shifted to these platforms. Like politics, technological platforms will come and go—they will be neutral or ideological, they will be pro or against a particular party. But the essential feedback loop they offer will continue. But these too are moving parts, and a massive creative destruction in these platforms awaits us.

The conviction of Narendra Modi is fast trickling down to governments and businesses. The enthusiasm with which he is embracing economic reforms is infectious and we can see a large start-up ecosystem emerge, small companies thinking big, and large corporations going global. For the Opposition to claim every success as cronyism is part of an outdated and factually incorrect narrative; it will not work anymore. What will work for the Opposition is to push reforms in the states where it governs, make their geographies of governance wealthier, attract more capital, create more jobs, show performance and get voters to elect them again, in states and in the Union. Some states could even lead the reforms, as the case of Uttar Pradesh, discussed above, shows.

It has been a long journey of seventy-five years since Independence. The first stretch of this journey, from 1947 through 1990, took India from hopes and aspirations to disappointments and deforms (See Chapters 3 through 11). The second, from 1991 through 2022, has been of convictions that gave India a second wind and has brought us to a $3 trillion economy brimming with a new confidence and optimism. Prime Minister P.V. Narasimha Rao ignited this flame, because of compulsions in 1991s (Chapter 12); serial leaders since have carried that flame with an increasing conviction through 2022 (Chapter 13), currently in the hands of Prime Minister Narendra Modi. If the trends of the past leaderships are studied, the next quarter century will strengthen this conviction, irrespective of short-term challenges, economic, political or global. By 2047, when India celebrates 100 years of its Independence, it will be from a position of a prosperous nation with zero poverty, all the while leveraging the fundamental force of its democracy. A reform nation today, India will evolve into an aspirational nation tomorrow. The journey to affluence that began under compulsions will become a journey to wealth through convictions.

Acknowledgements

It is on the shoulders of giants that knowledge moves forward. And I have been fortunate to have stood on several shoulders. As a book that brings together the politics and economics of reforms, I have engaged with actors from both these fields, and several others.

In the field of politics, I have had direct learnings through conversations with two prime ministers, Manmohan Singh and Narendra Modi. Through them, I have learnt not just the economics of reforms but the restraints to reforms. I thank them for the time they spent with me in personal interviews, in-flight meetings and press conferences in India and abroad. I have also learnt several aspects of a broader statecraft from former President of India, Pranab Mukherji, a practitioner of politics, a crisis manager of his party and a policymaker across several fields. Always polite, gracious and patient, there was iron in his hand but a smile on his lips. Two finance ministers, Yashwant Sinha and P. Chidambaram, showed me various aspects of policymaking from two different political spectrums; both, at different points in time, have been annoyed by my writings.

Three economists have helped me sharpen my ideas. All three were part of the 1991 reforms and I have benefited immensely from meeting them. First, Jairam Ramesh, who initially as minister with many portfolios and now as member of Parliament spent long hours explaining the nuances of policy and reforms. And even if our stances are not always in tune, Jairam has been and will remain a fellow traveller on the long intellectual road ahead. Second, former deputy chairman of the erstwhile Planning Commission of India, Montek Singh Ahluwalia, who showed me several windows with which to view economic reforms and understand political constraints. And third, Rakesh Mohan, whose impeccable credentials as an economist and policy driver brought out the nuances of reforms with insights and wit over discussions in think tanks and that delicious lunch at Yale. He is conversant with my work and has encouraged me by writing the Foreword for my earlier book, *70 Policies that Shaped India*.

Bibek Debroy, chairman of Economic Advisory Council to the Prime Minister, has walked me across several polices through personal meetings and his writings. He brings a wealth of knowledge to India's twenty-first century policymaking through an understanding of the Indian ethos like none else. He is an economist and more, a writer and more, a friend and more. Bibek is an inspiration across prolific writings and a benchmark in meticulous precision.

The other economists whose work I have leaned on for clarity of issues, again across various ideological spectrums, include, but are not restricted to, Jagdish Bhagwati, Arvind Panagariya and Amartya Sen. I am grateful to Rana Hasan and Ajay Shah for regular discussions on economic policy across decades. To Gaurav Dalmia for helping me understand the business point of view. And to Samir Saran for expanding the ambit of my analyses and getting me to interrogate economics from the standpoint of technology, geopolitics and international relations. Among political scientists, intense dinner chats at IIC with Ashutosh Varshney have sharpened my ideas. Countless other actors and thinkers have shown me trails of knowledge that I may not have travelled on; to that extent, I was lucky to be an economic journalist and get access to them.

Beyond economics, I have travelled with several thinkers on related tributaries of fields that influence economic policy in general and reforms in particular—Ram Madhav for politics, B.N. Srikrishna for law, Abhijit Iyer-Mitra for defence, Vikram Sood for intelligence, Sushant Sareen for Pakistan, Amrita Narlikar for trade negotiations, Kirit S. Parikh for energy, Reuben Abraham for urbanization, Manish Sabharwal for compliances, Parth J. Shah for education, Raghunath Anant Mashelkar for science and technology. Thinkers at Observer Research Foundation where I work added their weight to my thoughts, particularly Sunjoy Joshi and Oommen C. Kurien. Among those who have been consistent believers in economic reforms since I began my professional life, I have been lucky to have worked with editors R. Jagannathan, Shekhar Gupta and Sanjaya Baru.

For several policy contexts, thanks to Akhilesh Mishra who is an organizer par excellence with ideas that can fill a room, and Vinayak Swami who is the best research assistant I have worked with, yet. Special thanks to Sanjeev Sanyal and Amish Tripathi for their conversations, their ideas—and above all, their friendship.

Special thanks to the team at HarperCollins: you welcomed me, worked with me tirelessly, indulged me and my idiosyncrasies, and produced a book worthy of the ideas contained in it. In particular, thanks to Ananth Padmanabhan, Udayan Mitra, Sachin Sharma and Anju Christine Lingham. You are a great team.

Among family, my gratitude to Yogesh Halan and Lakshmi Chikermane for being patient with my absence from meals and chai-samosas. My extended family in the Sri Aurobindo Ashram has, as always, been a source of inspiration, as I explore and adapt to the inner pathways that the Integral Yoga Sri Aurobindo and the Mother pointed to while working in outer worlds. In particular, Manoj Dasgupta, Matriprasad, Devdip Ganguli, and Anjali and Aurofilio Schiavina. Among the young, Satya Schiavina and Meera Chikermane infused a new excitement and wonder of exploration with their enthusiasm for pursuing knowledge and its expressions in their relative fields of problem-solving inventions and neurosciences.

Finally, to my partner-in-ideas and anchor-in-chief, Monika Halan, who, apart from being one of India's greatest financial writers, is simultaneously my pillar of strength, my most stringent critic and above all, an ocean of love—words are not enough.

Notes

Preface

1. Manoj Joshi, 'Case Analysis: INFOSYS Technologies Limited', *SSRN*, 29 September 2009, https://ssrn.com/abstract=1479998 or http://dx.doi.org/10.2139/ssrn.1479998.
2. 'Students from two IIMs & ISB receive five offers of over Rs 1 crore', *The Economic Times*, 25 November 2011, http://www.ecoti.in/cTI1jb.
3. 'Indian Startup Ecosystem', Department for Promotion of Industry and Internal Trade, Ministry of Commerce and Industry, Government of India, Undated, https://www.startupindia.gov.in/content/sih/en/international/go-to-market-guide/indian-startup-ecosystem.html.
4. 'SIAM Annual Reports', Society of Indian Automobile Manufacturers, Undated, https://www.siam.in/cpage.aspx?mpgid=42&pgidtrail=89.
5. World Bank Open Data, The World Bank, https://data.worldbank.org/indicator/SI.POV.
6. Ibid., https://data.worldbank.org/indicator/SI.POV.DDAY?locations=IN.DDAY.
7. Ibid., https://data.worldbank.org/indicator/SI.POV.DDAY?locations=IN.DDAY.
8. Roy Katayama and Divyanshi Wadhwa, 'Half of the world's poor live in just 5 countries', World Bank Blogs, The World Bank, 9 January 2019, https://blogs.worldbank.org/opendata/half-world-s-poor-live-just-5-countries.
9. Surjit S. Bhalla, Karan Bhasin and Arvind Virmani, 'Pandemic, Poverty, and Inequality: Evidence from India', IMF Working Paper, International Monetary Fund, April 2022, https://www.imf.org/en/Publications/WP/Issues/2022/04/05/Pandemic-Poverty-and-Inequality-Evidence-from-India-516155?cid=em-COM-123-44567.
10. 'India National Floor Level Minimum Wage', Trading Economics, Undated, https://tradingeconomics.com/india/minimum-wages.

11. All data from BSE.

1. A Tale of Two Protests: Challenges to India's Economic Reforms

1. ANI, '#WATCH Violence continues at ITO in central Delhi, tractors being driven by protestors deliberately try to run over police personnel', Twitter, 26 January 2021, https://twitter.com/ANI/status/1353975938812317698?s=20.
2. Aditya Raj Kaul, 'CCTV footage showing how the farmer who died actually rammed his tractor with the police barricades with force upon which the tractor overturned and got crushed under it. This is so tragic and sad. Who were those leaders provoking tractors to break police cordon by force? (1/2)', Twitter, 26 January 2021, https://twitter.com/AdityaRajKaul/status/1354063886723424256?s=20.
3. Anushree Fadnavis and Zeba Siddiqui, 'Indian farmers block highway outside Delhi to mark 100th day of protest', Reuters, 6 March 2021, https://www.reuters.com/article/india-farms-protests-idUSKCN2AY07K.
4. Padmaja Joshi, 'Police attacked with lathis and rods, clearly told to hold back. Had no option but to jump in moat to escape. Many injured in process. Also attempt to charge at fleeing cops with a tractor by alleged farmers. All of this, at Red Fort', Twitter, 26 January 2021, https://twitter.com/PadmajaJoshi/status/1354094771229216768?s=20&t=LQ9d3W_kkeo113uuzL72Xw.
5. 'Farmers threaten to intensify protest, block railway tracks; govt says let's talk | 10 points', *India Today*, 10 December 2020, https://www.indiatoday.in/india/story/farmers-threaten-to-intensify-protest-block-railway-tracks-govt-says-let-s-talk-10-points-1748503-2020-12-10.
6. 'Nihang protester flashes sword as police block road to New Delhi', *India Today*, 26 January 2021, https://www.indiatoday.in/india/story/farmers-attack-police-with-swords-near-delhi-akshardham-cops-fire-tear-gas-shells-lathi-charged-1762811-2021-01-26.
7. Gautam Chikermane, 'Towards a 21st century protest playbook', Observer Research Foundation, 6 February 2021, https://www.orfonline.org/expert-speak/towards-21st-century-protest-playbook/.
8. Press Trust of India, 'Over 300 Twitter Handles Generated from Pakistan to Disrupt Farmers' Tractor Rally: Delhi Police', News 18, 24 January 2021, https://www.news18.com/news/india/over-300-twitter-handles-generated-from-pakistan-to-disrupt-farmers-tractor-rally-delhi-police-3334496.html.
9. Press Trust of India, 'Farm stir: Protesters deface Mahatma Gandhi statue in Washington; "Khalistani" flags sighted', *The Times of India*, 13 December 2020, https://timesofindia.indiatimes.com/india/farn-stir-protesters-

deface-mahatma-gandhi-statue-in-washington-khalistani-flags-sighted/articleshow/79702621.cms.

10. Rihanna, 'Why aren't we talking about this?! #FarmersProtest', Twitter, 2 February 2021, https://twitter.com/rihanna/status/1356625889602199552?s=20.
11. Greta Thunberg, 'We stand in solidarity with the #FarmersProtest in India', Twitter, 3 February 2021, https://twitter.com/GretaThunberg/status/1356694884615340037?s=20.
12. 'Who is Mia Khalifa? The former adult star extending support to farmers' protest in India', *DNA*, 4 February 2021, https://www.dnaindia.com/world/photo-gallery-who-is-mia-khalifa-the-ex-porn-star-extending-support-to-farmers-protest-in-india-2873205.
13. Mia Khalifa, 'Shoutout to the farmers', Twitter, 7 February 2021, https://twitter.com/miakhalifa/status/1358253827988750337?s=20.
14. 'Farmers desecrate Tiranga at the Red Fort; Self-pride over Nation? | The Newshour Agenda', Times Now, 26 January 2021, https://youtu.be/EOiYjaHLBOM.
15. Swati Goel Sharma, 'Warning: Graphic content …', Twitter, 18 October 2021, https://twitter.com/swati_gs/status/1450103865638998029?s=20.
16. Gautam Chikermane, 'Modi's U-turn on farm laws: A setback in the history of India's economic reforms', Observer Research Foundation, 19 November 2021, https://www.orfonline.org/expert-speak/modis-u-turn-on-farm-laws/.
17. 'Chapter 7: Agriculture & Food Management', Economic Survey 2020–21, Volume 2, Ministry of Finance, Government of India, https://www.indiabudget.gov.in/economicsurvey/doc/vol2chapter/echap07_vol2.pdf.
18. Rob Jenkins, *Democratic Politics and Economic Reform in India*, Cambridge University Press (1999), p. 115.
19. This has been discussed later.
20. World Bank Data.
21. 'External Affairs Minister's remarks at the WEF India Economic Summit 2019 on 4 October 2019', Media Centre, Ministry of External Affairs, Government of India, 9 October 2019.
22. World Bank Data.
23. Atul Kohli, 'Politics of Economic Growth in India, 1980–2005: Part II: The 1990s and Beyond', *Economic and Political Weekly* 41, No. 14 (2006), pp. 1361–1370, https://www.jstor.org/stable/4418059.
24. Sri Aurobindo, 'The Revival of Industry in India', in *The Complete Works of Sri Aurobindo, Volume 1*, ed. (Sri Aurobindo Ashram Trust, 2003), p. 712.
25. Dwijendra Tripathi, *The Oxford History of Indian Business* (Oxford University Press, 2004), p. 320.

26. Ajay Shah, 'Where did the Bombay Club go wrong?', *The Financial Express*, 14 December 2009, http://www.mayin.org/ajayshah/MEDIA/2009/p_india.html.
27. Press Note No. 18 (1998 Series), Department of Industrial Policy & Promotion, Ministry of Industry, Government of India, 14 December 1998, https://dipp.gov.in/sites/default/files/pn12.pdf.
28. Ibid.; Ajay Shah, 'Where did the Bombay Club go wrong?'
29. Gautam Chikermane, *70 Policies that Shaped India: 1947 to 2017, Independence to $2.5 Trillion*, Observer Research Foundation 2018, pp. 49–50, https://www.orfonline.org/wp-content/uploads/2018/07/70_Policies.pdf.
30. Atul Kohli, 'Politics of Economic Growth in India, 1980–2005: Part II: The 1990s and Beyond', *Economic and Political Weekly* 41, No. 14 (2006), pp. 1361–1370, https://www.jstor.org/stable/4418059.
31. The Farmers' Produce Trade and Commerce (Promotion and Facilitation) Act 2020, Ministry of Law and Justice, Government of India, The Gazette of India, 24 September 2020, http://egazette.nic.in/WriteReadData/2020/222039.pdf.
32. 'Entry 14, List II—State List', Seventh Schedule, The Constitution of India, https://www.india.gov.in/sites/upload_files/npi/files/coi-eng-schedules_1-12.pdf.
33. The Farmers (Empowerment and Protection) Agreement on Price Assurance and Farm Services Act 2020, Ministry of Law and Justice, Government of India, The Gazette of India, 24 September 2020, http://egazette.nic.in/WriteReadData/2020/222040.pdf.
34. The Essential Commodities (Amendment) Act 2020, Ministry of Law and Justice, Government of India, The Gazette of India, 26 September 2020, https://dpal.karnataka.gov.in/storage/pdf-files/The%20Essential%20Commodities%20(Amendment)%20Act,%202020%20(No%2022%20of%202020).pdf.
35. Gautam Chikermane, *70 Policies that Shaped India: 1947 to 2017, Independence to $2.5 Trillion*, Observer Research Foundation (2018), pp. 25–26.
36. Ibid., The Essential Commodities (Amendment) Act, 2020, Section 2(1A)(a).
37. Ibid., Section 2(1A)(b)(i).
38. Ibid., Section 2(1A)(b)(ii).
39. Gautam Chikermane, 'An intellectual biography of India's new farm laws', Observer Research Foundation, 11 December 2020, https://www.orfonline.org/research/intellectual-biography-india-new-farm-laws/.
40. 'Expert Committee Report', Marketing Infrastructure & Agricultural Marketing Reforms, Department of Agriculture & Cooperation, Directorate of Marketing and Inspection, Ministry of Agriculture and Farmers Welfare,

Government of India, 29 June 2001, https://dmi.gov.in/Documents/EXPERT%20COMMITTEE%20REPORT.pdf.

41. 'Report of the Task Force on Employment Opportunities', Planning Commission, NITI Aayog, Government of India, 1 July 2001, https://niti.gov.in/planningcommission.gov.in/docs/aboutus/taskforce/tk_empopp.pdf.
42. 'Inter-Ministerial Task Force to examine the recommendations of the Expert Committee on Strengthening and Developing of Agricultural Marketing', Department of Agriculture & Cooperation, Ministry of Agriculture, Government of India, 4 July 2001, https://dmi.gov.in/Documents/ReportTaskForceAMR.pdf.
43. 'The Model Act: The State Agricultural Produce Marketing (Development & Regulation) Act, 2003', Department of Agriculture & Cooperation, Ministry of Agriculture, Government of India, https://dmi.gov.in/Documents/Marketing.pdf.
44. 'Serving Farmers and Saving Farming: From Crisis to Confidence', First Report, National Commission on Farmers, Ministry of Agriculture, Government of India, December 2004, https://ruralindiaonline.org/en/library/resource/serving-farmers-and-saving-farming-first-report/.
45. Ibid.
46. 'Towards an Indian Common Market: Removal of Restrictions on Internal Trade in Agriculture Commodities', Food and Agriculture Organization, Submitted to National Commission on Farmers, December 2005, http://www.fao.org/3/ai566e/ai566e00.pdf.
47. 'Serving Farmers and Saving Farming: From Crisis to Confidence, 2006: Year of Agricultural Renewal', Third Report, National Commission on Farmers, Ministry of Agriculture, Government of India, December 2005, https://ruralindiaonline.org/en/library/resource/serving-farmers-and-saving-farming-2006-year-of-agricultural-renewal---third-report/.
48. 'Serving Farmers and Saving Farming: From Crisis to Confidence, Jai Kisan: A Draft National Policy for Farmers', Fourth Report, National Commission on Farmers, Ministry of Agriculture, Government of India, April 2006, https://ruralindiaonline.org/en/library/resource/serving-farmers-and-saving-farming-jai-kisan-a-draft-national-policy-for-farmers---fourth-report/.
49. 'Serving Farmers and Saving Farming: From Crisis to Confidence; Towards Faster and More Inclusive Growth of Farmers' Welfare', Fifth & Final Report, Volume I, National Commission on Farmers, Ministry of Agriculture, Government of India, October 2006, https://ruralindiaonline.org/en/library/resource/serving-farmers-and-saving-farming-fifth-final-report-4-october-2006---towards-faster-and-more-inclusive-growth-of-farmers-welfare/.
50. 'Serving Farmers and Saving Farming: From Crisis to Confidence; Towards Faster and More Inclusive Growth of Farmers' Welfare', Fifth & Final Report,

Volume II, National Commission on Farmers, Ministry of Agriculture, Government of India, Hosted on People's Archive of Rural India, October 2006, https://ruralindiaonline.org/en/library/resource/serving-farmers-and-saving-farming-towards-faster-and-more-inclusive-growth-of-farmers-welfare---fifth-report-volume-ii/.

51. 'The State Agricultural Produce Marketing (Development and Regulation) Rules, 2007, Directorate of Marketing & Inspection, Ministry of Agriculture and Farmers Welfare, Government of India, Undated, https://dmi.gov.in/Documents/FinalDraftRules2007.pdf.
52. Chapter 8: Agriculture and Food, Economic Survey 2011–12, Ministry of Finance, Government of India, February 2012, https://www.indiabudget.gov.in/budget2012-2013/es2011-12/echap-08.pdf.
53. 'Final Report of Committee of State Ministers, In-charge of Agriculture Marketing to Promote Reforms', Department of Agriculture and Co-operation, Ministry of Agriculture, Government of India, 22 January 2013, https://dmi.gov.in/Documents/stminprreform.pdf.
54. Chapter 8: Agriculture and Food Management, Economic Survey 2012–13, Ministry of Finance, Government of India, February 2013, https://www.indiabudget.gov.in/budget2013-2014/es2012-13/echap-08.pdf.
55. Chapter 8: Agriculture and Food Management, Economic Survey 2013–14, Ministry of Finance, Government of India, February 2013, https://www.indiabudget.gov.in/budget2014-2015/es2013-14/echap-08.pdf.
56. 'Agriculture Marketing and Role of Weekly Gramin Haats', Standing Committee on Agriculture (2018–2019), Ministry of Agriculture and Farmers Welfare (Department of Agricultural, Cooperation and Farmers Welfare), Sixteenth Lok Sabha, Sixty-Second Report, 3 January 2019, http://164.100.47.193/lsscommittee/Agriculture/16_Agriculture_62.pdf.
57. Chapter 7: Agriculture and Food Management, Economic Survey 2020-21, Volume 2, Ministry of Finance, Government of India, February 2013, https://www.indiabudget.gov.in/economicsurvey/doc/vol2chapter/echap07_vol2.pdf.
58. Ibid., Standing Committee on Agriculture (2018–2019).
59. 'Agriculture Marketing and Role of Weekly Gramin Haats', Standing Committee on Agriculture (2018–2019), Ministry of Agriculture and Farmers Welfare (Department of Agricultural, Cooperation and Farmers Welfare), Sixteenth Lok Sabha, Sixty-Second Report, 3 January 2019, p. 39.
60. Ibid., p. 46.
61. Ibid., p. 49.
62. Ibid., pp. 49–50.
63. Ibid., p. 43.
64. Ibid., p. 41.

65. The members from the BJP are 1. Bodhsingh Bhagat, 2. Sanjay Dhotre, 3. Sanganna Amarappa Karadi, 4. Nalin Kumar Kateel, 5. Raksha Tai Khadase, 6. Janardan Mishra, 7. Praveen Kumar Nishad, 8. Devji M. Patel, 9. Mukesh Rajput, 10. Virendra Singh, 11. Narayan Rane, 12. Kailash Soni, 13. Harnath Singh Yadav, 14. Hukmdev Narayan Yadav (Chairperson of the Committee). The non-BJP part of the NDA were 1. Arjun Charan Sethi from Biju Janata Dal (BJD), and 14. Ram Nath Thakur from Janata Dal (United) or JDU. The 14 members from non-NDA political parties are 1. Ravindra Vishwanath Gaikwad from Shiv Sena, 2. Md. Badaruddoza Khan from Communist Party of India (Marxist) (CPI-M), 3. C. Mahendran from All India Anna Dravida Munnetra Kazhagam (AIADMK), 4. Tapas Mandal from All India Trinamool Congress (AITC), 5. Konakalla Narayana Rao from Telugu Desam Party (TDP), 6. C.L. Ruala from Mizo National Front (MNF), 7. Dharmendra Yadav from Samajwadi Party (SP), 8. Jai Prakash Narayan Yadav from Rashtriya Janata Dal (RJD), 9. Sardar Sukhdev Singh Dhindsa from Shiromani Akali Dal (SAD), 10. Rajmani Patel from Indian National Congress (INC), 11. Mohd. Ali Khan from INC, 12. K.K. Ragesh from CPI-M, 13. R. Vaithilingam from AIADMK, and 14. Chandrapal Singh Yadav from SP.
66. See 1) Prashant Prabhakar Deshpande, 'Politics over the farmers' protest – Part 1,' *The Times of India*, 12 November 2021, https://timesofindia.indiatimes.com/blogs/truth-lies-and-politics/politics-over-the-farmers-protest-part-1/; and 2) Prashant Prabhakar Deshpande, 'Politics over the farmers' protest – Part 2,' *The Times of India*, 12 November 2021, https://timesofindia.indiatimes.com/blogs/truth-lies-and-politics/politics-over-the-farmers-protest-part-2/.
67. Gautam Chikermane, 'Farmer interests are missing in farm protest politics', Observer Research Foundation, 7 December 2020, https://www.orfonline.org/expert-speak/farmer-interests-are-missing-in-farm-protest-politics/.
68. Narendra Modi, 'PM addresses the Nation', Prime Minister's Office, Government of India, 19 November 2021, https://www.pmindia.gov.in/en/news_updates/pm-addresses-the-nation-3/.
69. Gautam Chikermane, 'Modi's U-turn on farm laws: A setback in the history of India's economic reforms', Observer Research Foundation, 19 November 2021, https://www.orfonline.org/expert-speak/modis-u-turn-on-farm-laws/.
70. Ibid.
71. 'Faceless Assessment is a Tax Assessment System designed for the 21st century', Press Information Bureau, Government of India, 26 August 2020, https://pib.gov.in/PressReleseDetailm.aspx?PRID=1648814.
72. 'Providing Ease of Tax Compliance and Opportunity to taxpayers before finalizing of Assessment Order are the core features of Faceless Assessment Scheme, a right step towards Minimum Government, Maximum

Governance: Principal Chief Commissioner – Income Tax, Mumbai', Press Information Bureau, Government of India, 27 August 2020, https://pib.gov.in/PressReleseDetailm.aspx?PRID=1649006.

73. 'Faceless E-Assessment Scheme will provide Ease of Doing Business to taxpayers: Principal Chief Commissioner (Income Tax), Mumbai; Faceless E-Assessment Scheme is a "vaccine" for direct tax administration: President, Assocham', Press Information Bureau, Government of India, 29 August 2020, https://pib.gov.in/PressReleasePage.aspx?PRID=1649504.
74. 'Implementation of Faceless Assessment Scheme, 2019', No.JCA/2020-21/Faceless Assessment/01, Joint Council of Action, Income Tax Employees Federation & Income Tax Gazetted Officers' Association, 16 August 2020, http://www.itgoawbunit.org/pdf/62800-letter-to-chairman-from-jca-on-diversion-of-posts.pdf.
75. Ibid.

2. The Philosophy of Economic Reforms

1. 'Wilson's Fourteen Points', Newspaper Pictorials: World War I Rotogravures, 1914 to 1919, Library of Congress, 8 January 1918, https://www.loc.gov/collections/world-war-i-rotogravures/articles-and-essays/events-and-statistics/wilsons-fourteen-points/.
2. 'Tariff of 1930 (Smoot-Hawley Tariff)', FRASER, 17 June 1930, https://fraser.stlouisfed.org/title/tariff-1930-smoot-hawley-tariff-5882.
3. 'Protectionism in the Interwar Period', The Historian of the US Department of State, United States government, https://history.state.gov/milestones/1921-1936/protectionism.
4. 'President Franklin Delano Roosevelt and the New Deal', US History Primary Source Timeline, Library of Congress, https://www.loc.gov/classroom-materials/united-states-history-primary-source-timeline/great-depression-and-world-war-ii-1929-1945/franklin-delano-roosevelt-and-the-new-deal/.
5. Allan M. Winkler, 'The New Deal: Accomplishments and Failures', Testimony before the US Senate Committee on Banking, Housing, and Urban Affairs, 31 March 2009, https://www.banking.senate.gov/imo/media/doc/WinklerTestimony33109TheNewDealSenateTestimony.pdf.
6. John Williamson, 'The Strange History of the Washington Consensus', *Journal of Post Keynesian Economics*, 27, No. 2 (2004–2005,), pp. 195–206, https://www.jstor.org/stable/4538920.
7. Leonardo Baccini and Johannes Urpelainen, 'International Institutions and Domestic Politics: Can Preferential Trading Agreements Help Leaders Promote Economic Reform?', *The Journal of Politics* 76, No. 1 (2014), pp. 195–214, https://www.jstor.org/stable/10.1017/s0022381613001278.

8. David H. Bearce and Daniel C. Tirone, 'Foreign Aid Effectiveness and the Strategic Goals of Donor Governments', *The Journal of Politics* 72, No. 3 (2010), pp. 837–851, https://www.jstor.org/stable/10.1017/s0022381610000204.
9. Aurelia George Mulgan, *Japan's Failed Revolution: Koizumi and the Politics of Economic Reform* (ANU Press, 2013), https://www.jstor.org/stable/j.ctt31ngnn.5.
10. Gautam Chikermane, 'As Air India flies to the Tatas, a brief history of India's biggest policy failure', Observer Research Foundation, 9 October 2021, https://www.orfonline.org/expert-speak/as-air-india-flies-to-the-tatas-a-brief-history-of-indias-biggest-policy-failure/.
11. Jos Mooij, 'The Politics of Economic Reforms in India: A Review of the Literature', in *Rethinking Indian Political Institutions,* eds. C. Bates and S. Basu (Anthem Press, 2005), pp. 1–20.
12. Leonardo Baccini and Johannes Urpelainen, 'International Institutions and Domestic Politics: Can Preferential Trading Agreements Help Leaders Promote Economic Reform?,' *The Journal of Politics* 76, No. 1, (2014), pp. 195–214, https://www.jstor.org/stable/10.1017/s0022381613001278.
13. Nancy Birdsall, Augusto de la Torre and Felipe Valencia Caicedo, 'The Washington Consensus: Assessing a Damaged Brand'. Office of the Chief Economist, Latin America and the Caribbean Region, and Center for Global Development, The World Bank, May 2010, http://documents1.worldbank.org/curated/pt/848411468156560921/pdf/WPS5316.pdf.
14. Ibid.
15. Gobind Nankani et al., 'Economic Growth in the 1990s: Learning from a Decade of Reform', World Bank, 2005, https://openknowledge.worldbank.org/bitstream/handle/10986/7370/32692.pdf?sequence=1&isAllowed=y.
16. Dani Rodrik and World Bank, 'Goodbye Washington Consensus, Hello Washington: Confusion? A Review of the World Bank's Economic Growth in the 1990s: Learning from a Decade of Reform', *Journal of Economic Literature* 44, No. 4 (2006), pp. 973–987, https://www.jstor.org/stable/30032391.
17. Ibid.
18. John Williamson, 'What Washington Means by Policy Reform', in *Latin American Adjustment: How Much Has Happened?*, ed. John Williamson (Peterson Institute for International Economics, 1990), 1 November 2002.
19. Dwight H. Perkins, 'The complex task of evaluating China's economic reforms', in *China's 40 Years of Reform and Development: 1978–2018*, eds. Ross Garnaut, Ligang Song and Cai Fang (ANU Press), p. 135, https://www.jstor.org/stable/j.ctv5cgbnk.16.
20. Gautam Chikermane, 'The spoils of World War 2 are handing World War 3 victories to China', Observer Research Foundation, 21 September 2021,

https://www.orfonline.org/expert-speak/the-spoils-of-world-war-2-are-handing-world-war-3-victories-to-china/.

21. 'World Bank Group to Discontinue Doing Business Report', The World Bank, 16 September 2021, https://www.worldbank.org/en/news/statement/2021/09/16/world-bank-group-to-discontinue-doing-business-report.
22. Yi Wen, *The Making of an Economic Superpower: Unlocking China's Secret of Rapid Industrialization*, *World Scientific* (2016), pp. 99–100.
23. L.V. Palei and K.L. Radzivanovich, 'How to Carry out Economic Reform: Points of View and Reality', *Soviet Studies*, 42, No. 1 (1990), pp. 25–37, https://www.jstor.org/stable/152161.
24. Peter Ping Li, Chapter: 'Foreword: The Deep-Level Substance of the Belt and Road Initiative', in *China's Belt and Road Initiative: Changing the Rules of Globalization*, Palgrave Studies of Internationalization in Emerging Markets, Palgrave Macmillan (2018), pp. ix and x.
25. Yiwei Wang, Chapter: 'Plenary Chapter: The Belt and Road Initiative: Mutual Connectivity of the World', in *Silk Road to Belt Road: Reinventing the Past and Shaping the Future*, eds. Wenxian Zhang, Ilan Alon and Christoph Lattemann (Springer, 2019), p. xxii.
26. Samir Saran, '#Covid19: Made in China pandemic', Observer Research Foundation, 20 March 2020, https://www.orfonline.org/expert-speak/covid19-made-in-china-pandemic-63531/.
27. Stuti Khemani, 'Political Economy of Reform', Policy Research Working Paper 8224, Development Research Group, Macroeconomics and Growth Team, World Bank Group, October 2017, http://documents1.worldbank.org/curated/en/290071508764607858/pdf/WPS8224.pdf.

3. How We Got Here: Eight Preludes to 1991

1. Made on a budget of Rs 3 crore, the film grossed more than Rs 16 crore: Box Office India, Undated, https://boxofficeindia.com/movie.php?movieid=336.
2. Nikhil Roshan, 'Small is big', *The Indian Express*, 13 January 2009, https://indianexpress.com/article/cities/lucknow/small-is-big-9/.

4. Prelude 1: The Bombay Plan: 1944–1945

1. Frank Moraes, *Sir Purshotamdas Takurdas*, Asia Publishing House (1957).
2. R.M. Lala, *Beyond the Last Blue Mountain: A Life of J.R.D. Tata*, Penguin (1992).
3. Ed. Parasnath Sinha, *The Path to Prosperity: A Collection of the Speeches and Writings of G.D. Birla*, The Leader Press (1950).

4. Jay Dubashi, "Lala Shri Ram (1884-1963): The merchant of Delhi," India Today, 31 May 1984, https://www.indiatoday.in/magazine/guest-column/story/19840531-lala-shri-ram-1884-1963-the-merchant-of-delhi-803661-1984-05-31.
5. Minoo Shroff, "AD Shroff: The Defender of Free Enterprise," in Parth J. Shah ed. *Profiles in Courage: Dissent on Indian Socialism*, Centre for Civil Society (2001), pp. 159-178, https://ccs.in/sites/all/books/com_books/profiles_in_courage.pdf.
6. Purshotamdas Thakurdas, J.R.D. Tata, Ardeshir Dalal, G.D. Birla, Shri Ram, Kasturbhai Lalbhai, A.D. Shroff and John Mathai, *Memorandum Outlining a Plan of Economic Development of India: Parts One and Two* (New Delhi: Penguin Books, 1945).
7. Gautam Chikermane, *70 Policies that Shaped India: 1947 to 2017, Independence to $2.5 Trillion*, Observer Research Foundation (2018).
8. I. INTRODUCTORY: Aim of Memorandum; Political Assumptions; Planning Organization; Objective of Plan; Industrial Development; Difficulties Anticipated; Problem of Finance; and Explanatory Remarks.

   II. REQUIREMENTS OF A MINIMUM STANDARD: Minimum Standard Defined; Balanced Diet; Cost of Nourishment; Clothing Needs; Cost of Clothing; Housing Needs; Cost of Housing; Standard of Housing; Present State of Health; Needs of Public Health; Inadequate Preventive Measures; Lack of Medical Facilities; Minimum Health Standard; Sanitation and Water Supply; Village Dispensaries; Cost of Dispensaries; General Hospitals; Maternity Hospitals; Specialized Treatment; Cost of Public Health; Minimum Educational Needs; Primary Education: Capital Cost; Primary Education: Recurring Cost; Adult Literacy; Minimum Cost of Living; and Income Below Minimum.

   III. ECONOMIC PLAN EXPLAINED: Low National Income; Aim of Plan; Increase in Per Capita Income; A Modest Goal; Balanced Economy; Agricultural Character Unchanged; Industries Classified; Basic Industries; Importance of Basic Industries; Production of Power; Consumption Goods Industries; Consumer's Choice; Scope for Small Industries; Capital for Industries; Wide Variations in the Ratio; A Low Ratio Assumed; Agricultural Development; Reforms Proposed; Rural Indebtedness; Soil Erosion; Ways of Increasing Output; Yield per Acre; Irrigation; Model Farms; Working Capital; Capital for Agriculture; Transport and Communications; Railways; Roads; Reconstruction of Existing Roads; Shipping; Cost of Transport; Co-operation of the People; Programme of Education; Adult Education; Secondary Education; University and Technical Education; Public Health; Allowance for Increase in Population; Cost of Additional Housing; Miscellaneous Capital Expenditure; Cost Classified; Total Capital Required.

IV. SOURCES OF FINANCE: External and Internal Finance; Hoarded Wealth; Sterling Securities; Balance of Trade; Foreign Borrowing; Savings in Foreign Countries; Savings in India; 'Created Money'; Sources of Finance Summarized; Method of Raising Finance; Finance, Only a Camp Follower.

V. STAGES OF DEVELOPMENT: Determination of Stages; Adequacy of Resources; Priority for Basic Industries; Needs of Consumers; Imperfections in Early Stages; Three Five-Year Plans; Plans Explained; Consideration for Consumer; Basic Industries and Consumption Goods; Progress of Basic Industries; Balanced View.

9. I. INTRODUCTORY: Preliminary; Line of Approach; Twin Foundations of Economic Structure.

II. DISTRIBUTION OF THE NATIONAL INCOME: Production and Distribution Closely Related; Disparities of Income; Equitable Distribution; Ownership of the Means of Production; Total Abolition of Inequalities Undesirable; Rewards to Factors of Production; Measures to Secure a Minimum Standard; Income Level; Full Employment; Employment in Industry; Seasonal Unemployment in Agriculture; Occupational Distribution; Temporary Unemployment; Increase in Efficiency; Urban and Rural Wages; A Minimum Wage; Agricultural Prices; Cooperative Societies; Land Tenures; Ryotwari System; Land Revenue; Income Distribution in 1962; Cost of Living; Free Social Services; Utility Services; National Relief Fund; Social Security; Taxation of Income; Regional Development; Conditions for Heavy Taxation.

III. THE STATE AND ECONOMIC ORGANIZATION: Choice of Economic Organization; State Intervention Inherent in Planning; Planning and Democracy; Basic Principles; Role of the State; Methods of Intervention; Control More Important; State Ownership; State Control; State Management; Compromise Formula; Control during Planning Period; Controls Illustrated; National Government; Future Economic Organization.

10. Purshotamdas Thakurdas, J.R.D. Tata, Ardeshir Dalal, G.D. Birla, Shri Ram, Kasturbhai Lalbhai, A.D. Shroff and John Mathai, *Memorandum Outlining a Plan of Economic Development of India: Parts One and Two* (Penguin Books (April 1945), Section 4, p. 9.
11. Ibid., Section 34, p. 26.
12. Ibid., Section 9, p. 12.
13. Ibid., Sections 29, 30 and 31, pp. 22–24.
14. Ibid., Section 32, pp. 24-25; and Section 69, pp. 45–46.
15. Ibid., Section 70, pp. 46–47.
16. Ibid., Section 71, p. 48.
17. Ibid., Section 19, p. 17.

18. Ibid., Section 41, p. 31.
19. Ibid., Section 42, p. 31.
20. Ibid., Section 45, p. 33.
21. Ibid., Section 47, pp. 33–34.
22. Ibid., Section 51, pp. 35–36.
23. Ibid., Section 56, p. 38.
24. Ibid., Section 52, pp. 36–37.
25. Ibid., Section 57, pp. 38–39.
26. Ibid., Section 58, p. 39.
27. Ibid., Sections 59 and 60, p. 40.
28. Ibid., Section 62, pp. 41–42.
29. Ibid., Sections 63 and 64, pp. 42–43.
30. Ibid., Section 65, p. 43.
31. Ibid., Section 66, p. 43.
32. Ibid., Part IV, Sections 78 to 88, pp. 51–56.
33. Ibid., Section 3, p. 66.
34. Ibid., Section 6, p. 68.
35. Ibid., Section 7, p. 69.
36. Ibid., Section 8, p. 69.
37. Ibid., Section 9, p. 70.
38. Ibid., Section 11, p. 71.
39. Ibid., Section 36, p. 91.
40. Ibid., Section 37, p. 93.
41. Ibid., Section 39, p. 94.
42. Ibid., Section 46, p. 99.
43. Ibid., Section 88, p. 56.
44. Ibid., Section 5, p. 67.
45. Ibid., Section 31, p. 86.
46. Ibid., p. 89.
47. Frank Moraes, *Sir Purshotamdas Takurdas* (Asia Publishing House, 1957), pp. 193–194.
48. G.D. Birla, 'The Bombay Plan', in *The Path to Prosperity: A Collection of the Speeches and Writings of G.D. Birla*, ed. Parasnath Sinha, The Leader Press (1950), pp. 35–57, http://ignca.gov.in/Asi_data/7528.pdf.
49. H.V.R. Iengar, 'A Look at the Bombay Plan in the Light of Today', *The Bombay Plan and Other Essays: Second A.D. Shroff Memorial Lectures Delivered under the Auspices of Forum of Free Enterprise* (Lavani Publishing House, 1968), https://indianliberals.in/forum-of-free-enterprise/the-bombay-plan-and-other-essays-a-d-shroff-1968.pdf.

50. Medha Kudaisya, 'The Promise of Partnership: Indian Business, the State, and the Bombay Plan of 1944', *The Business History Review*, Spring 2014, Vol. 88, No. 1, p. 97–131, https://www.jstor.org/stable/43299521.
51. Manmohan Singh, 'PM's address at ASSOCHAM's JRD Tata birth centenary celebration', Prime Minister's Office, 24 August 2004, https://archivepmo.nic.in/drmanmohansingh/speech-details.php?nodeid=7.
52. Amal Sanyal, 'The Curious Case of the Bombay Plan', *Contemporary Issues and Ideas in Social Sciences*, June 2010, https://citeseerx.ist.psu.edu/viewdoc/download?doi=10.1.1.680.334&rep=rep1&type=pdf.
53. Ibid.
54. Cited from the Birla Paper by Medha Kudaisya, 'The Promise of Partnership': Indian Business, the State, and the Bombay Plan of 1944, *The Business History Review* 88, No. 1 (2014), p. 27, https://www.jstor.org/stable/43299521.
55. Dietmar Rothermund, *An Economic History of India: From Pre-Colonial Times to 1991*, Second Edition, Routledge (2003), pp. 125.
56. Ibid., Amal Sanyal, 'The Curious Case of the Bombay Plan'.
57. Ibid.
58. Ibid.

5. Prelude 2: Statement of Industrial Policy 1945

1. Sharad S. Marathe, 'Appendix I: Statement of Industrial Policy, April 1954', *Regulation and Development: The Indian Policy Experience of Controls Over Industry*, SAGE Publications (1986), pp. 298–312.
2. Ibid., p. 37.
3. Raghabendra Chattopadhyay, 'The Idea of Planning in India, 1930–1951', Appendix III, pp. 394–409, Thesis submitted for the Degree of Doctor of Philosophy, The Australian National University, Canberra, April 1985, https://openresearch-repository.anu.edu.au/bitstream/1885/109360/4/b15457898-Chattopadhyay%20Raghabendra.pdf.
4. Item 27 (Trade and commerce within the Province; markets and fairs; moneylending and moneylenders) and Item 29 (Production, supply and distribution of goods; development of industries, subject to the provisions in List I with respect to the development of certain industries under Federal control), 'Government of India Act, 1935', Seventh Schedule, List II, Provincial Legislative List, The National Archives on behalf of HM Government, United Kingdom, pp. 305, https://www.legislation.gov.uk/ukpga/1935/2/pdfs/ukpga_19350002_en.pdf.
5. Ibid., Marathe, 'Statement of Industrial Policy, April 1954', Section 2, p. 299.
6. Ibid.

7. Ibid., Iron and steel; manufacture of prime movers; automobiles and tractors and transport vehicles; aircraft; ship-building and marine engineering; electrical machinery; heavy machinery, such as textiles, sugar, paper, mining, cement and chemical; machine tools; heavy chemicals and fine chemicals, chemical dyes, fertilizers and pharmaceutical drugs; electro-chemical industry; cotton and woollen textiles; cement; power; alcohol; sugar; motor and aviation fuel; rubber manufacture; non-ferrous metals industry; electric power; coal; and radio engineering.
8. Gautam Chikermane, *70 Policies that Shaped India: 1947 to 2017, Independence to $2.5 Trillion*, Observer Research Foundation (2018), p. 19, https://www.orfonline.org/wp-content/uploads/2018/07/70_Policies.pdf.
9. Ibid., p. 29.
10. Ibid., p. 45.
11. Ibid., p. 49.
12. Ibid., p. 53.
13. Ibid., p. 57.
14. Ibid., p. 69.
15. Ibid., Marathe, 'Statement of Industrial Policy, April 1954', Section 7 (i), p. 304.
16. Ibid., Section 9 (i), p. 306.
17. Ibid., Section 9 (iv), p. 307.
18. Ibid., Section 9 (vi), p. 307.
19. Ibid., Section 9 (iii), p. 307.
20. Ibid., Section 9 (vii), p. 307.
21. Ibid., Section 9 (vii), p. 307.
22. Ivan T. Berend, *An Economic History of Twentieth-Century Europe: Economic Regimes from Laissez-Faire to Globalization* (Cambridge University Press, 2006).
23. Ibid., Section 4, p. 301.
24. Ibid., Section 10, pp. 307–308.
25. Ibid., Section 11, p. 308.
26. Ibid., Section 12, p. 309.
27. Ibid., Section 14, pp. 310–311.
28. Babita Thakur, Rozika Gupta, Rajesh Singh, 'Changing Face of India's Industrial Policies: A Look', *International Journal of Scientific and Research Publications* 2, No. 12 (2012), http://www.ijsrp.org/research-paper-1212/ijsrp-p12104.pdf.

29. H.K. Paranjape, 'New Lamps for Old!: A Critique of the New Economic Policy', *Economic and Political Weekly*, 20, No. 36 (7 September 1985), pp. 1513–1522, http://www.jstor.com/stable/4374798.
30. 'Economic Survey of Asia and the Far East, 1950', Department of Economic Affairs, United Nations, 31 July 1951, pp. 171–172, https://www.unescap.org/sites/default/files/publications/Economic%20survey%20of%20Asia%20and%20the%20Far%20East%201950.pdf.
31. '37(IV). Economic Commission for Asia and the Far East', Resolution of 28 March 1947 (document E/45), United Nations, 28 March 1947, https://www.un.org/ga/search/view_doc.asp?symbol=E/RES/37(IV).
32. '1895 (LVII). Change of name from "Economic Commission for Asia and the Far East" to "Economic and Social Commission for Asia and the Pacific"'. United Nations, 1 August 1974, https://www.un.org/ga/search/view_doc.asp?symbol=E/RES/1895(LVII).

6. Prelude 3: Resolution, 1948

1. The error of labelling this policy 'Industrial Policy Resolution 1948' has several sources. First, the government. See (1) The Office of the Development Commissioner (Small Scalc Industries), Ministry of Small Scale Industries, Government of India (http://laghu-udyog.gov.in/policies/iip.htm) and (2) 'Government of India Resolution on Industrial Policy Dated the 6th April 1948', Appendix III, Report of the Fiscal Commission 1949–50, Chairman: V.T. Krishnamachari, Government of India, https://dspace.gipe.ac.in/xmlui/handle/10973/29248. Second, authors. See (1) Laura Alfaro and Anusha Chari, 'Reforms and the Competitive Environment', in *Reforms and Economic Transformation in India*, eds. Jagdish Bhagwati and Arvind Panagariya (Oxford University Press, 2013), p. 224; (2) Subrata K. Mitra, *Politics in India: Structure, Process and Policy*, Routledge (2017); and (3) Sagarika Dutt, 'Economic development: from import-substitution industrialization to economic liberalization', in *India in a Globalized World*, (Manchester University Press, 2006), https://www.jstor.org/stable/j.ctt155j8n3.11. And third, scholars. See (1) R.C. Dutt, 'Socialistic goals of the public sector', *India International Centre Quarterly*, Monsoon 1987, Vol. 14, No. 3, pp. 89–100, https://www.jstor.org/stable/23002347; (2) Pami Dua and Aneesa I. Rashid, 'Foreign Direct Investment and Economic Activity in India', *Indian Economic Review*, July–December 1998, New Series, Vol. 33, No. 2, pp. 153–168, https://www.jstor.org/stable/29794166; and (3) Ausaf Ahmad, 'Regional Pattern of Industrial Licensing', *Social Scientist*, April 1974, Vol. 2, No. 9, pp. 3–17, https://www.jstor.org/stable/3516109. Worse, what students of Class XI are taught as curriculum from the government-run, government-produced National

Council of Educational Research and Training uses the term Industrial Policy Resolution of 1948, in the textbook *Indian Economic Development*.

2. 'Resolution', Ministry of Industry and Supply, The Gazette of India, Government of India, 6 April 1948, pp. 533-538, https://archive.pib.gov.in/archive/ArchiveSecondPhase/DEVELOPMENT/1948-JAN-DEC-INDUSTRY&SUPPY/IND-1948-04-06_040.pdf.
3. G.S. Raychaudhuri, 'On Some Estimates of National Income: Indian Economy 1858-1947', *Economic and Political Weekly*, 3 December 1966, Vol. 1, No. 16, Table on p. 678, https://www.jstor.org/stable/4357298.
4. Suphan Andic and Alan T. Peacock, 'The International Distribution of Income, 1949 and 1957', *Journal of the Royal Statistical Society*, Series A (General), 1961, Vol. 124, No. 2, pp. 206–218, https://www.jstor.org/stable/2984130.
5. Ibid.
6. World Bank Data.
7. Ibid., Resolution, Section 3, p. 533.
8. Ibid., Section 4, p. 534.
9. Ibid.
10. Ibid., the list comprised salt; automobiles and tractors; prime movers; electric engineering; other heavy machinery; machine tools; heavy chemicals, fertilizers and pharmaceuticals and drugs; electro-chemical industries; non-ferrous metals; rubber manufactures; power and industrial alcohol; cotton and woollen textiles; cement; sugar; paper and newsprint; air and sea transport; minerals; and industries related to defence, Section 7, p. 535.
11. The chapters are individually available at '1st Five Year Plan', NITI Aayog, https://niti.gov.in/planningcommission.gov.in/docs/plans/planrel/fiveyr/index1.html.
12. The original resolution is not available online. A reference to it has been made by Planning Commission. 'Chapter 34: Labour', First Five Year Plan, Planning Commission [now, NITI Aayog], Government of India, Paragraph 43, https://niti.gov.in/planningcommission.gov.in/docs/plans/planrel/fiveyr/1st/1planch34.html.
13. Ibid., Resolution, Section 9, p. 536.
14. Gautam Chikermane, *70 Policies that Shaped India: 1947 to 2017, Independence to $2.5 Trillion*, Observer Research Foundation (2018), p. 3.
15. Ibid., p. 5.
16. Ibid., p. 15.
17. Ibid., p. 25.
18. Ibid., p. 19.
19. Ibid., p. 11.
20. Ibid., p. 7.

21. Speech of Nirmala Sitharaman, Minister of Finance, Ministry of Finance, Government of India, Paragraphs 45 and 46, 1 February 2021, pp. 8–9, https://www.indiabudget.gov.in/doc/budget_speech.pdf.
22. 'The Industrial Disputes Act, 1947', India Code, Government of India, 11 March 1947, https://www.indiacode.nic.in/bitstream/123456789/15191/1/AAA1947___14.pdf.
23. Shashi Tharoor, *Nehru: The Invention of India* (Penguin, 2003), p. 177.
24. Om Prakash Aggarwala and S.K. Aiyar, *The Constitution of India (with an Exhaustive, Critical and Analytical Commentary, Notifications, Rules, Orders etc.)* (Metropolitan Book Company, 1950), Article 38, p. 61.
25. 'Constitution of Ireland', Article 45, 1 July 1937, http://www.irishstatutebook.ie/eli/cons/en.
26. Ibid., Constitution of India, Article 39, p. 62.
27. Part IV of the Constitution of India, i.e., Directive Principles of State Policy.
28. Ibid., Constitution of India, Article 37, p. 61.

7. Prelude 4: Industrial Policy Resolution 1956

1. 'Industrial Policy Resolution, New Delhi, the 30 April, 1956', The Gazette of India: Extraordinary, Part I—Section I, Cabinet Secretariat, Government of India, 30 April 1956, pp. 137–144, https://ia800807.us.archive.org/24/items/in.gazette.e.1956.491/E-2182-1956-0039-99550.pdf.
2. Ibid., Section 4, p. 138.
3. Ibid., Section 6, p. 139.
4. Ibid., Section 7, pp. 139–140.
5. Ibid., Section 8, p. 140.
6. Ibid., Schedule A, p. 5. The complete list of seventeen industries is: arms and ammunition and allied items of defence equipment; atomic energy; iron and steel; heavy castings and forgings of iron and steel; heavy plant and machinery required for iron and steel production, for mining, for machine tool manufacture and for such other basic industries as may be specified by the Central government; heavy electrical plant including large hydraulic and steam turbines; coal and lignite; mineral oils; mining of iron ore, manganese ore, chrome-ore, gypsum, sulphur, gold and diamond; mining and processing of copper, lead, zinc, tin, molybdenum and wolfram; minerals specified in the Schedule to the Atomic Energy (Control of Production and Use) Order, 1953; aircraft; air transport; railway transport; shipbuilding; telephones and telephone cables, telegraph and wireless apparatus (excluding radio receiving sets); and generation and distribution of electricity.

7. Gautam Chikermane, *70 Policies that Shaped India: 1947 to 2017, Independence to $2.5 Trillion*, Observer Research Foundation (2018), pp. 19–20, https://www.orfonline.org/wp-content/uploads/2018/07/70_Policies.pdf.
8. Ibid., Schedule B. These were 1. All other minerals except 'minor minerals' as defined in Section 3 of the Minerals Concession Rules, 1949; 2. Aluminium and other non-ferrous metals not included in Schedule 'A'; 3. Machine tools; 4. Ferro alloys and tool steels; 5. Basic and intermediate products required by chemical industries such as the manufacture of drugs, dyestuffs and plastics; 6. Antibiotics and other essential drugs; 7. Fertilizers; 8. Synthetic rubber; 9. Carbonization of coal; 10. Chemical pulp; 11. Road transport; and 12. Sea transport.
9. Ibid., Section 9, p. 140.
10. Ibid., Section 10, p. 140.
11. Shashi Tharoor, *Nehru: The Invention of India* (Penguin Viking, 2003), p. 177.
12. The Industries (Development and Regulation) Act, 1951, Ministry of Law and Justice, Government of India, https://legislative.gov.in/sites/default/files/A1951-65.pdf.
13. Ibid., Chapter I, Section 2.
14. Ibid., First Schedule.
15. Ibid., Item 3.
16. Ibid., Item 9.
17. Ibid., Item 13.
18. Ibid., Item 20.
19. Ibid., Item 8.
20. Ibid., Schedule II, Section 6(4)(7).
21. Benjamin Zachariah, *Nehru* (Routledge, 2004), pp. 224–225.
22. Ibid., IPR 1956, Section 13, p. 141.
23. Ibid., Section 14, p. 141–142.
24. Ibid., Section 15, p. 142.

8. Prelude 5: Industrial Policy 1973

1. 'Industrial Policy—Government Decisions of February 2, 1973—Key Provisions', Department for Promotion of Industry and Internal Trade, Ministry of Commerce and Industry, Government of India, 2 February 1973, p. 6, https://dipp.gov.in/sites/default/files/chap001%20%2013.pdf.
2. 'The Monopolies and Restrictive Trade Practices Act, 1969', Bare Acts Live, Chawla Publications, 27 December 1969, http://www.bareactslive.com/ACA/ACT755.HTM.

3. The definition of 'public interest' had eleven points—(a) that the restriction is reasonably necessary, having regard to the character of the goods to which it applies, to protect the public against injury (whether to persons or to premises) in connection with the consumption, installation or use of those goods; (b) that the removal of the restriction would deny to the public as purchasers, consumers or users of any goods, other specific and substantial benefits or advantages enjoyed or likely to be enjoyed by them as such, whether by virtue of the restriction itself or of any arrangements or operations resulting therefrom; (c) that the restriction is reasonably necessary to counteract measures taken by any one person not party to the agreement with a view to preventing or restricting competition in or in relation to the trade or business in which the persons party thereto are engaged; (d) that the restriction is reasonably necessary to enable the persons party to the agreement to negotiate fair terms for the supply of goods to, or the acquisition of goods from, any one person not party thereto who controls a preponderant part of the trade or business of acquiring or supplying such goods, or for the supply of goods to any person not party to the agreement and not carrying on such a trade or business who, either alone or in combination with any other such persons, controls a preponderant part of the market for such goods; (e) that, having regard to the conditions actually obtaining or reasonably foreseen at the time of the application, the removal of the restriction would be likely to have a serious and persistent adverse effect on the general level of unemployment in an area, or in areas taken together, in which a substantial proportion of the trade, or industry to which the agreement relates is situated; (f) that, having regard to the conditions actually obtaining or reasonably foreseen at the time of the application, the removal of the restriction would be likely to cause a reduction in the volume or earnings of the export business which is substantial either in relation to the whole export business of India or in relation to the whole business (including export business) of the said trade or industry; (g) that the restriction is reasonably required for purposes in connection with the maintenance of any other restriction accepted by the parties, whether under the same agreement or under any other agreement between them, being a restriction which is found by the Commission not to be contrary to the public interest upon grounds other than those specified in this paragraph, or has been so found in previous proceedings before the Commission; (h) that the restriction does not directly or indirectly restrict or discourage competition to any material degree in any relevant trade or industry and is not likely to do so; [(i) that such restriction has been expressly authorized and approved by the Central Government; (j) that such restriction is necessary to meet the requirements of the defence of India or any part thereof, or for the security of the State; or (k) that the restriction is necessary to ensure the maintenance of supply of goods and services essential to the community].

4. Report of the Industrial Licensing Policy Inquiry Committee (Main Report), Department of Industrial Development, Ministry of Industrial Development, Internal Trade and Company Affairs, Government of India, July 1969, Table I, p. 45, https://ia902804.us.archive.org/30/items/dli.csl.414/414_text.pdf.
5. 'This category includes Indian subsidiaries of foreign companies and branches of foreign companies (companies which have been covered under the preceding three categories are not included here)'; Report of the Industrial Licensing Policy Inquiry Committee (Main Report), Department of Industrial Development, Ministry of Industrial Development, Internal Trade and Company Affairs, Government of India, July 1969, p. 46, https://ia902804.us.archive.org/30/items/dli.csl.414/414_text.pdf.
6. 'All Indian companies not covered by the above four categories'; Ibid.
7. 'Those who obtained licences in their own names and did not transfer their licences to some other body and whose address as given in the list of licences did not indicate their association with any business enterprise'; Ibid.
8. 'Partnership firms and proprietary concerns about which we could secure information and also licensees whom we were unable to classify under any one of the above mentioned categories because of lack of information'; Ibid.
9. 'Government companies, statutory corporations and Government departments'; Ibid.
10. 'Registered under the Co-operative Societies Acts.' Ibid.
11. Ibid., p. 78.
12. These included ACC (with 5 concerns or firms), Andrew Yule (43), Bangur (93), Bird-Heilgers (76), Birla (203), ICI (6), JK (Singhania) (47), Kilachand (24), Killick (17), Mafatlal (34), Martin Burn (24), Sahu Jain (29), Sarabhai (29), Scindia (8), Shri Ram (36), Sooraj Mull Nagar Mull (104), Tata (70), Thapar (59) and Walchand (29).
13. Ibid., p. 196.
14. R.K. Hazari, Industrial Planning and Licensing Policy, Planning Commission, Government of India, p. 9.
15. Ibid., p. 194.
16. Fourth Five Year Plan 1969–74, Planning Commission, Government of India, p. 305: 'The Industrial Licensing Policy Inquiry Committee, in its Report, had taken the view that, with all its defects, the industrial licensing system has an important role to play, though its limitations should also be borne in mind. The Committee recommended that the use of such licensing as a positive instrument should be confined to industries which come within the basic, strategic and critical sectors, for which detailed industry plans should be prepared, and where the major inputs would have to be assured and the targets implemented. These industries would be deemed to be in the "core" sector.'

17. Ibid.; Report of the Industrial Licensing Policy Inquiry Committee (Main Report), p. 191.
18. Report of the Monopolies Inquiry Commission, Volume I, Ministry of Corporate Affairs, Government of India, 28 October 1965, p. 165, http://reports.mca.gov.in/Reports/44-Report%20of%20the%20monopolies%20inquiry%20commission%201965,%20Vo1.-I-II.pdf.
19. Ibid.
20. Ibid.; Report of the Industrial Licensing Policy Inquiry Committee (Main Report), pp. 194–195.
21. Ibid., p. 9.
22. Ibid.
23. Ibid.
24. 'Industrial Policy—Government Decisions of February 2, 1973', Department of Industrial Development, Ministry of Industry, Government of India, 2 February 1973, p. 6.
25. Gautam Chikermane, *70 Policies that Shaped India: 1947 to 2017, Independence to $2.5 Trillion*, Observer Research Foundation (2018), p. 29.
26. Ibid., p. 45.
27. Ibid., p. 49.
28. Ibid., p. 51.
29. Ibid., p. 53.
30. Ibid., p. 55.
31. 'Industrial Licensing,' Estimates Committee (1971–72), Ministry of Industrial Development (Department of Industrial Development), Lok Sabha, April 1972, p. 69, https://eparlib.nic.in/bitstream/123456789/57758/1/ec_05_19_1971.pdf.
32. Ibid., pp. 70–71.
33. Ibid., p. 75.

9. Prelude 6: Industrial Policy 1977

1. 'Industrial Policy—Government Decisions of December 23, 1977—Key Provisions', Department for Promotion of Industry and Internal Trade, Ministry of Commerce and Industry, Government of India, 23 December 1977.
2. 'Purity of Means', Inaugural address at the Golden Jubilee Session of the Federation of Indian Chambers of Commerce and Industry, New Delhi, 23 April 1977, *Selected Speeches of Morarji Desai: 1977–1979*, Publications Division, Ministry of Information and Broadcasting, Government of India, August 1986, pp. 8–9.

3. R.V.R. Chandrasekhara Rao, 'The Janata Government and the Soviet Connexion', *The World Today* 34, No. 2 (February 1978), pp. 70–76, https://www.jstor.org/stable/40395035.
4. 'Speech on Soviet T.V., Moscow, 25 October 1977', in *Selected Speeches of Morarji Desai: 1977–1979,* Publications Division, Ministry of Information and Broadcasting, Government of India, 1986, p. 170.
5. Morarji Desai was India's prime minister from 24 March 1977 to 28 July 1978.
6. Charan Singh was India's prime minister from 28 July 1979 to 14 January 1980.
7. 'Broadcast to the Nation, New Delhi, 28 July 1979', *Charan Singh Selected Speeches: July 1979 to December 1979*, Publications Division, Ministry of Information and Broadcasting, Government of India, May 1992, p. 1.
8. 'Industrial Policy—Government Decisions of December 23, 1977—Key Provisions', Department for Promotion of Industry and Internal Trade, Ministry of Commerce and Industry, Government of India, 23 December 1977, p. 7, https://dipp.gov.in/sites/default/files/chap001%20%2013.pdf.
9. Ibid.
10. Ibid.
11. Ibid.
12. Myron Weiner, *India at the Polls: The Parliamentary Elections of 1977* (American Enterprise Institute for Public Policy Research, 1978), p. 139. The original document is unavailable publicly, hence we had to lean on Weiner's scholarly generosity in placing this as part of 'Appendix H: The Janata Party Manifesto'.
13. Sol W. Sanders, 'India: Ending the Permit-License Raj', *Asian Affairs: An American Review* 5, No. 2 (1977), p. 88–96, https://www.jstor.org/stable/30171608.
14. 'Speech of Shri H.M. Patel, Minister of Finance, Introducing the Budget for the Year 1977–78 (Final)', Ministry of Finance, Government of India, 17 June 1977, p. 8.
15. Y.C. Bhatnagar and Moin Shakir, 'The Seventh Lok Sabha Elections', *The Indian Journal of Political Science* 41, No. 1 (March 1980), pp. 69–78, http://www.jstor.com/stable/41854990.
16. Press Trust of India, 'Morarji, Charan waited for each other to die', *Mumbai Mirror*, 12 November 2008, https://mumbaimirror.indiatimes.com/news/india/morarji-charan-waited-for-each-other-to-die/articleshow/15868898.cms.
17. Romesh Thapar, 'A Change for the Better?' *Economic and Political Weekly* 13, No. 27 (1978), pp. 1089–1090, https://www.jstor.org/stable/4366781.

18. Jyotirindra Das Gupta, 'The Janata Phase: Reorganization and Redirection in Indian Politics', *Asian Survey*, Vol. 19, No. 4 (April 1979), pp. 390–403, https://www.jstor.org/stable/2643859.
19. The High Denomination Bank Notes (Demonetisation) Act, 1978, Ministry of Law and Justice, Government of India, 30 March 1978, https://legislative.gov.in/sites/default/files/A1978-11_0.pdf.
20. Speech of Shri H.M. Patel, Minister of Finance, Introducing the Budget for the Year 1978–79, Ministry of Finance, Government of India, 28 February 1978, p. 13.
21. Iqbal Narain, 'India 1978: Politics of Nonissues', *Asian Survey: A Survey of Asia in 1978: Part II* (February 1979), pp. 165–177, https://www.jstor.org/stable/2643783.
22. Gautam Chikermane, *70 Policies that Shaped India: 1947 to 2017, Independence to $2.5 Trillion*, Observer Research Foundation (2018), pp. 67-68, https://www.orfonline.org/wp-content/uploads/2018/07/70_Policies.pdf.
23. Iqbal Narain, 'India 1978: Politics of Nonissues', *Asian Survey: A Survey of Asia in 1978: Part II* (February 1979), pp. 165–177, University of California Press, https://www.jstor.org/stable/2643783.
24. Indira Gandhi's second term as Prime Minister was from 14 January 1980 to 31 October 1984.

10. Prelude 7: Statement on Industrial Policy 1980

1. 'Statement on Industrial Policy July 23, 1980—Key Provisions', Department for Promotion of Industry and Internal Trade, Ministry of Commerce and Industry, Government of India, 23 July 1980.
2. 'Miscellaneous Notifications including Notifications, Orders, Advertisements and Notices issued by Statutory Bodies [Part III—Section 4]', The Gazette of India, 27 December 1980, pp. 4845–4846, https://ia800600.us.archive.org/12/items/in.gazette.1980.473/O-1028-1980-0052-44948.pdf.
3. 'Unstarred Question No. 4233', Lok Sabha Debates, Seventh Series, Vol. XI, No. 22, Lok Sabha Secretariat, Parliament of India, 17 December 1980, p. 129, https://eparlib.nic.in/bitstream/123456789/2153/1/lsd_07_04_17-12-1980.pdf.
4. Ibid., Statement on Industrial Policy July 23, 1980—Key Provisions.
5. Jagdish Bhagwati, *India in Transition: Freeing the Economy*, (Clarendon Press Oxford 1993), p. 49. Cited by Sumit K. Majumdar, 'Government Policies and Industrial Performance: An Institutional Analysis of the Indian Experience', *Journal of Institutional and Theoretical Economics / Zeitschrift für die gesamte Staatswissenschaft* 152, No. 2 (June 1996), p. 387, https://www.jstor.org/stable/40752962.

6. Ibid., p. 388.
7. S.K. Goyal et al., 'Functioning of Industrial Licensing System: A Report', The Corporate Studies Group, The Indian Institute of Public Administration, 20 January 1983, p. 101, https://ia801900.us.archive.org/13/items/in.ernet.dli.2015.275049/2015.275049.Functioning-Of_text.pdf.
8. Ibid., pp. 102–111.
9. The Industries (Development and Regulation) Act, 1951, Ministry of Law and Justice, Government of India, https://legislative.gov.in/sites/default/files/A1951-65.pdf.
10. 'Industrial Policy Statement July 1980', India's Industrial Policies from 1948 to 1991, Office of the Development Commissioner (Small Scale Industries), Ministry of Small Scale Industries, Government of India, Para 9, http://laghu-udyog.gov.in/policies/iip.htm.
11. Ibid.; Goyal et al., p. 6.
12. Charles R. Hankla, *Party Linkages and Economic Policy: An Examination of Indira Gandhi's India* (Georgia State University, The Berkley Electronic Press), p. 16, https://scholarworks.gsu.edu/cgi/viewcontent.cgi?article=1071&context=political_science_facpub.
13. Ibid., p. 17.
14. Stuart Corbridge and John Harriss, *Reinventing India: Liberalization, Hindu Nationalism and Popular Democracy* (Polity Press, 2000), p. 101.
15. S.K. Dhawan, *Discovery of Indira Gandhi: A Select Chronology* (Wave Publications, 1986), pp. 266–267.
16. Ibid.
17. Neelam Sanjiva Reddy, The Parliamentary Debates: Official Report in the Hundred and Twenty-First Session of the Rajya Sabha, PRS Legislative, 18 February 1982, pp. 3–4, https://prsindia.org/files/policy/Policy_President_Speech/1982.pdf.
18. Ibid., Industrial Policy Statement July 1980, Para 23.
19. 'Statement on Industrial Policy July 23, 1980—Key Provisions', Department for Promotion of Industry and Internal Trade, Ministry of Commerce and Industry, Government of India, 23 July 1980.
20. Ibid.
21. Kalpana Kochhar, Utsav Kumar, Raghuram Rajan, Arvind Subramanian and Ioannis Tokatlidis, 'India's Pattern of Development: What Happened, What Follows?', IMF Working Paper, International Monetary Fund, January 2006, p. 17, https://www.imf.org/external/pubs/ft/wp/2006/wp0622.pdf.
22. 'The Crisis of Democratic Order', in *Politics in India Since Independence: Textbook in Political Science for Class XII*, National Council of Educational Research and Training (February 2020), p. 104.

23. 'The Maruti Limited (Acquisition and Transfer of Undertaking) Act, 1980, Advocatespedia, 27 December 1980, https://advocatespedia.com/Maruti_lime_act_1980.
24. Gautam Chikermane, 'Nationalization, then Privatization, of Maruti Udyog, 1980', in *70 Policies that Shaped India*, Observer Research Foundation (2018), pp. 69–70, https://www.orfonline.org/wp-content/uploads/2018/07/70_Policies.pdf.
25. Prosenjit Datta, '1980s: The over looked decade, the decade when India began to change', *National Herald*, 7 December 2020, https://www.nationalheraldindia.com/india/1980s-the-over-looked-decade-the-decade-when-india-began-to-change.
26. Kalpana Kochhar, Utsav Kumar, Raghuram Rajan, Arvind Subramanian and Ioannis Tokatlidis, 'India's Pattern of Development: What Happened, What Follows?', IMF Working Paper, International Monetary Fund, January 2006, p. 18, https://www.imf.org/external/pubs/ft/wp/2006/wp0622.pdf.
27. Montek Singh Ahluwalia, *Backstage: The Story Behind India's High Growth Years* (Rupa, 2020), p. 55.
28. Gautam Chikermane, 'Nationalisation of Air India', *70 Policies that Shaped India: 1947 to 2017, Independence to $2.5 Trillion*, Observer Research Foundation (2018), pp. 19–20.
29. Ibid., 'Nationalisation of Life Insurance, 1956', pp. 29–30.
30. Ibid., 'Nationalisation of General Insurance, 1972', pp. 53-54.
31. Ibid., 'Nationalisation of Coal Mines, 1971', pp. 49-50.
32. Ibid., 'Sick Textile Undertakings (Nationalisation) Act, 1974', pp. 57–58.
33. Ibid., 'Nationalisation of Banks, 1969', pp. 45–46.
34. Ibid.
35. Atul Kohli, 'Politics of Economic Growth in India, 1980–2005, Part I: The 1980s', *Economic and Political Weekly*, 1 April 2006, pp. 1255, https://www.princeton.edu/~kohli/docs/PEGI_PartI.pdf.
36. Ibid.
37. 'Address to the Congress Centenary Session, Bombay, 28 December 1985', in *Rajiv Gandhi: Selected Speeches and Writings (*New Delhi: Publications Division, Ministry of Information and Broadcasting, Government of India, 1987), pp. 79–81.
38. 'Speech at the meeting of the National Development Council, New Delhi, 8 November 1985', *Rajiv Gandhi: Selected Speeches and Writings, Volume 1: 31 October 1984–31 December 1985* (New Delhi: Publications Division, Ministry of Information and Broadcasting, Government of India, 1987), p. 134.
39. Sam Pitroda with David Chanoff, *Dreaming Big: My Journey to Connect India* (Penguin, 2015), pp. 106–107.

40. Dinsha Mistree, 'From Produce and Protect to Promoting Private Industry: The Indian State's Role in Creating a Domestic Software Industry', Working Paper 07-2018, Stanford Law School, June 2019, https://www-cdn.law.stanford.edu/wp-content/uploads/2019/12/Mistree-Making-Electonics-in-India.pdf.
41. Sujoy Dutta, 'An uneven path to accountability: A comparative study of MGNREGA in two states of India', WZB Discussion Paper, No. SP I 2015-201, Wissenschaftszentrum Berlin für Sozialforschung (WZB), Berlin, February 2015, p. 22, https://www.econstor.eu/bitstream/10419/108736/1/820319341.pdf.
42. He decreased indirect taxes on goods such as computers, TVs and VCRs.
43. Speech of Shri Vishwanath Pratap Singh, Minister of Finance, Introducing the Budget for the Year 1985–86, Ministry of Finance, Government of India, 16 March 1985.
44. Dani Rodrik and Arvind Subramanian, 'From "Hindu Growth" to Productivity Surge: The Mystery of the Indian Growth Transition', *IMF Staff Papers* 52, No. 2 (2005), pp. 193–228, https://www.jstor.org/stable/30035894.
45. Ibid., pp. 224–225.
46. T.N. Srinivasan, 'Comments on 'From "Hindu Growth" to Productivity Surge: The Mystery of the Indian Growth Transition,' *IMF Staff Papers* 52, No. 2 (2005), pp. 230–231, https://www.jstor.org/stable/30035895.

11. Prelude 8: Industrial Policy 1990

1. 'Shri Vishwanath Pratap Singh', Prime Minister's Office, https://www.pmindia.gov.in/en/former-prime-ministers/.
2. M.P. Singh, 'India's National Front and United Front Coalition Governments: A Phase in Federalized Governance', *Asian Survey*, Vol. XLI, No. 2, March–April 2001, https://library.fes.de/libalt/journals/swetsfulltext/14218787.PDF.
3. Arvind Panagariya, *India: The Emerging Giant* (Oxford University Press, 2018), pp. 455–459.
4. Ibid., p. 456.
5. Ibid.
6. Ibid., Sections 12 and 13, p. 457.
7. Ibid., Section 14, pp. 457–458.
8. Ibid., Section 15, p. 458.
9. Ibid., pp. 99–100.
10. Ibid.
11. Ibid., p. 231.
12. Ibid., p. 213.

13. Ibid., p. 270.
14. Ibid., p. 12.
15. Ibid., p. 199.
16. Ibid., p. 339.
17. Ibid., p. 362.
18. Ibid., p. 15.
19. Montek S. Ahluwalia, 'Economic Reforms in India since 1991: Has Gradualism Worked?', *The Journal of Economic Perspectives* 16, No. 3 (2002), pp. 67–88, https://www.jstor.org/stable/3216951.
20. Montek Singh Ahluwalia, *Backstage: The Story Behind India's High Growth Years*, (Rupa 2020), p. 410.
21. Baldev Raj Nayar, 'Political Structure and India's Economic Reforms of the 1990s', *Pacific Affairs* 71, No. 3 (1998), pp. 335–358, https://www.jstor.org/stable/2761414.
22. Ibid.
23. Devesh Kapur and Ravi Ramamurti, 'Privatization in India: The Imperatives and Consequences of Gradualism', Working Paper No. 142, Stanford University, 3–4 June 2002, https://kingcenter.stanford.edu/sites/default/files/publications/142wp.pdf.
24. Ibid.
25. Gautam Chikermane, 'An intellectual biography of India's new farm laws', Observer Research Foundation, 11 December 2020, https://www.orfonline.org/research/intellectual-biography-india-new-farm-laws/.
26. Ibid., Panagariya, p. 103.

12. The Beginning of India's Economic Reforms, 1991

1. Montek Singh Ahluwalia, *Backstage: The Story Behind India's High Growth Years* (Rupa Publications, 2020), p. 115.
2. 'GDP (current US$) – India', World Bank Open Data, The World Bank.
3. Ashok Gulati and Shweta Saini, '25 Years of Policy Tinkering in Agriculture', Rakesh Mohan ed., *India Transformed: Twenty-Five Years of Economic Reforms*, Brookings Institution Press, p. 275, https://www.jstor.org/stable/10.7864/j.ctt20d8754.18.
4. *The Reserve Bank of India: Volume 4, 1981–1997*, Academic Foundation (2013), p. 421.
5. Ibid., pp. 454–455.
6. Montek Singh Ahluwalia, *Backstage*, p. 122.
7. World Bank Open Data, The World Bank.

8. *The Reserve Bank of India: Volume 4, 1981–1997*, Academic Foundation (2013), p. 455.
9. Rakesh Mohan, *India Transformed: 25 Years of Economic Reforms* (Penguin Random House, 2017), p. 11–12.
10. H.K. Paranjape, 'Indian "Liberalization": Perestroika or Salaami Tactics?' *Economic and Political Weekly* 23, No. 45/47 (1988), p. 2357, https://www.jstor.org/stable/4394005.
11. Jairam Ramesh, *To the Brink and Back: India's 1991 Story* (Rupa, 2015), Annexure 1, pp. 153–173.
12. Montek Singh Ahluwalia, *Backstage.*
13. Ibid., p. 40.
14. Jairam Ramesh, *To the Brink and Back: India's 1991 Story*, Annexure 2, pp. 174–182.
15. 'Agenda for economic reform: Joint statement by P.N. Dhar, M. Narasimham, I.G. Patel and R.N. Malhotra', Observer Research Foundation, First published in July 1991, Republished on 24 July 2021, https://www.orfonline.org/expert-speak/agenda-for-economic-reform/.
16. Ibid.
17. 'Devaluation and IMF Loan: Leading Economists' Alternative View', *Mainstream*, Vol. LIV, No. 29, 9 July 2016, https://www.mainstreamweekly.net/article6531.html.
18. Ibid.
19. 'Statement on Industrial Policy 1991', p. 9, 24 July 1991.
20. Ibid.
21. Ibid.
22. Ibid.
23. Ibid.
24. Ibid.
25. Rakesh Mohan, *India Transformed: 25 Years of Economic Reforms* (Penguin Random House, 2017), p. 14.
26. 'Papers laid on the table', Parliament of India, 24 July 1991, https://parliamentofindia.nic.in/ls/lsdeb/ls10/ses1/06240791.htm.
27. Jairam Ramesh, *To the Brink and Back,* p. 98.
28. 'Statement on Industrial Policy 1991', p. 9, 24 July 1991, para 9.
29. Ibid., para 11.
30. Ibid., para 13.
31. Ibid., para 15.
32. Ibid.
33. Ibid., para 16.

34. Ibid., para 18.
35. Ibid., para 17.
36. Ibid., para 21.
37. Ibid., para 23.
38. Ibid., para 39, A, i.
39. Ibid.
40. Ibid., para 39, A, iii b.
41. Ibid., para 39, A, iii.
42. Ibid., para 39, A, iv.
43. Ibid., para 39, A, ix and x.
44. Ibid., para 25.
45. Ibid., para 39, B, i.
46. Ibid.
47. Ibid., para 39, B, ii.
48. Ibid., para 39, B, iii.
49. Ibid., para 39, B, iv.
50. Ibid., para 27.
51. Ibid., para 28.
52. Ibid., para 39, C, i.
53. Ibid., para 31.
54. Ibid., para 32.
55. Gautam Chikermane, *70 Policies that Shaped India: 1947 to 2017, Independence to $2.5 Trillion*, Observer Research Foundation (2018), pp. 85–86.
56. Ibid.
57. 'Statement on Industrial Policy 1991', 24 July 1991, para 34.
58. The Monopolies and Restrictive Trade Practices Act, 2002, Universal Law Publishing, 27 December 1969.
59. Gautam Chikermane, *70 Policies that Shaped India: 1947 to 2017, Independence to $2.5 Trillion*, Observer Research Foundation (2018), p. 48.
60. Ibid., para 37.
61. Ibid., para 38.
62. S.V.S. Raghavan Committee, para 7.1.7., http://www.ccr.org.in/uploads/2/1/9/6/21961628/report_of_high_level_committee_on_competition_policy_and_law.pdf.
63. Ibid., para 1.2.9.
64. The Competition Act, 2002, Competition Commission of India, 13 January 2003, https://www.cci.gov.in/sites/default/files/cci_pdf/competitionact2012.pdf.

65. Jairam Ramesh, *To the Brink and Back: India's 1991 Story* (Rupa, 2015), p. 104.
66. Budget Speech of Shri Manmohan Singh, Minister of Finance, Part A, Ministry of Finance, Government of India, 24 July 1991, para 10.
67. Ibid., Ramesh, p. 108–109.
68. Ibid., Budget Speech, paras 2, 3, 4, 5 and 6.
69. Ibid., para 11.
70. Ibid., para 12.
71. 'Statement on Industrial Policy 1991', p. 9, 24 July 1991, paras 24, 25, 26 and 39B.
72. 'Statement on Industrial Policy 1991', p. 9, 24 July 1991, paras 29, 30, 31, 32, 33, 24, and 39D.
73. Ibid., Budget Speech, para 13.
74. Ibid., Budget Speech, paras 22 and 23.
75. Ibid., Budget Speech, para 24.
76. Ibid., Budget Speech, para 135.
77. Ibid.
78. Ibid., Budget Speech, para 136.
79. Ibid., Budget Speech, para 137.
80. Ibid., Budget Speech, para 138.
81. About the Foundation, Rajiv Gandhi Foundation, https://rgfindia.org/about-the-foundation-rgf/.
82. Ibid., Budget Speech, para 57.
83. Ibid., Ramesh, p. 110.
84. Audited Financials 2018–2019, Annual Report 2018–2019, Rajiv Gandhi Foundation, p. 3, http://rgfindia.org/wp-content/uploads/2019/08/RGF-AR18-19.pdf.
85. 'Papers laid on the table', Parliament of India, 6 August 1991, https://parliamentofindia.nic.in/ls/lsdeb/ls10/ses1/04060891.htm.
86. 'Policy Measures for Promoting & Strengthening Small, Tiny and Village Enterprises', Department of Small Scale Industry, Agro and Rural Industry, Ministry of Industry, Government of India, 6 August 1991, para 2.1.
87. Arvind Panagariya, *India: The Emerging Giant* (Oxford University Press, 2008), Appendix I: Industrial Policy 1990, pp. 455–459. This policy had raised the investment ceiling in plant and machinery, fixed in 1985, for small-scale industries from Rs 35 lakh to Rs 60 lakh, and for ancillary units from Rs 45 lakh to Rs 75 lakh. Further, small-scale units that assured exports of 30 per cent of their annual turnover by the third year of commencement would be permitted to step up their investment in plant and machinery to Rs 75 lakh.
88. Ibid., STV Policy, para 2.4.

89. Ibid., STV Policy, para 3.1.
90. Ibid., STV Policy, para 3.2.
91. Ruchika Chitravanshi, 'Cabinet approves amendments to LLP Act; 12 offences to be decriminalized', *Business Standard*, 29 July 2021, https://www.business-standard.com/article/economy-policy/cabinet-approves-amendment-to-llp-act-12-offences-to-be-decriminalised-121072900030_1.html.
92. Ibid., STV Policy, para 4.1.
93. Ibid., STV Policy, para 4.2.
94. Ibid., STV Policy, para 4.3.
95. Ibid., STV Policy, para 4.4.
96. Ibid., STV Policy, para 5.1.
97. Ibid., STV Policy, para 5.2.
98. Ibid., STV Policy, para 5.3.
99. Ibid., STV Policy, para 5.4.
100. Ibid., STV Policy, para 6.2.
101. Ibid., STV Policy, para 6.3.
102. Ibid., STV Policy, para 6.4.
103. Ibid., STV Policy, para 6.5.
104. Ibid., STV Policy, para 7.1.
105. Ibid., STV Policy, para 7.2.
106. Ibid., STV Policy, para 8.1.
107. Ibid., STV Policy, para 8.2.
108. Gautam Chikermane and Rishi Agrawal, '8 reforms to end India's regulatory cholesterol,' Observer Research Foundation, 24 July 2021.
109. Ibid., STV Policy, para 9.2.
110. Ibid., STV Policy, para 9.3(a).
111. Ibid., STV Policy, para 9.3(b).
112. Ibid., STV Policy, para 9.3(c).
113. Ibid., STV Policy, para 9.5.
114. Ibid., STV Policy, para 9.6.
115. Ibid., STV Policy, para 10.1.
116. Ibid., STV Policy, para 10.2.
117. Ibid., STV Policy, para 10.3.
118. Ibid., STV Policy, para 11.2.
119. Ibid., STV Policy, para 11.3.
120. Ibid., STV Policy, para 11.4.
121. 'Report of the Expert Committee on Small Enterprises', Ministry of Micro, Small and Medium Enterprises, Government of India, 27 January 1997, http://www.dcmsme.gov.in/publications/comitterep/abid.htm.

13. The Journey of Reforms

1. 'Schedule A, Industrial Policy Resolution, New Delhi, the 30th April, 1956', The Gazette of India: Extraordinary, Part I—Section I, Cabinet Secretariat, Government of India, 30 April 1956, pp. 137-144, https://ia800807.us.archive.org/24/items/in.gazette.e.1956.491/E-2182-1956-0039-99550.pdf.
2. Ibid., Schedule B. These were 1. All other minerals except 'minor minerals' as defined in Section 3 of the Minerals Concession Rules, 1949; 2. Aluminium and other non-ferrous metals not included in Schedule 'A'; 3. Machine tools; 4. Ferro alloys and tool steels; 5. Basic and intermediate products required by chemical industries such as the manufacture of drugs, dyestuffs and plastics; 6. Antibiotics and other essential drugs; 7. Fertilizers; 8. Synthetic rubber; 9. Carbonization of coal; 10. Chemical pulp; 11. Road transport; and 12. Sea transport.
3. 'Five More Categories of Industries Delicensed', Press Note (11/1997), Department of Industrial Policy and Promotion, Ministry of Industry, Government of India, 21 July 1997, https://archive.pib.gov.in/archive/ArchiveSecondPhase/DEVELOPMENT/1997-JULY-DEC-INDUSTRY/IND-1997-07-21_016.pdf.
4. 'De-licensing of Sugar Industry', Press Note No. 12 (1998 Series), Department of Industrial Policy and Promotion, Ministry of Industry, Government of India, 31 August 1998, https://dipp.gov.in/sites/default/files/pn6.pdf.
5. Notification, Department of Industrial Policy and Promotion, Ministry of Industry, Government of India, The Gazette of India: Extraordinary, 23 September 2005, https://dipp.gov.in/sites/default/files/notifcation_sept_2305%20%2017_0.pdf.
6. 'An Analysis on Industrial Investment Intentions in the Licensable and Delicenced Sector During the 12th Plan Period', SIA Statistics Annual Issue 2016–2017, Department for Promotion of Industry and Internal Trade, Ministry of Commerce and Industry, Government of India, https://dipp.gov.in/sites/default/files/chapter1.2_10_0.pdf.

   These are distillation and brewing of alcoholic drinks; cigars and cigarettes of tobacco and manufactured tobacco substitutes; electronic aerospace and all types of defence equipment; industrial explosives including detonating fuses, safety fuses, gunpowder, nitrocellulose and matches; and hazardous chemicals such as hydrocyanic acid and its derivatives, phosgene and its derivatives, isocyanates and di-isocyanates of hydrocarbon.
7. Press Note No. 3 (1995 Series), Revised Policy and Procedure Governing Approval Under the Scheme for 100% EOUs and EPZs, Department for Promotion of Industry and Internal Trade, Ministry of Commerce and Industry, Government of India, 19 April 1995, https://dipp.gov.in/sites/default/files/chap007_0.pdf.

8. Ibid., C(ii).
9. Ibid., C(iv).
10. Ibid., C(v).
11. Ibid., C(viii).
12. Annual Report 1991–92, Reserve Bank of India, para 1.62, p. 21, https://rbidocs.rbi.org.in/rdocs/AnnualReport/PDFs/9032020AR1991_92.PDF.
13. Ibid., Appendix Table 1.5: Foreign Collaboration Approvals, p. 157.
14. The Foreign Exchange Regulation Act, 1973, Enforcement Directorate, Ministry of Finance, Government of India, 19 September 1973, https://enforcementdirectorate.gov.in/foreign_exchange_regulation_act_1973.pdf?p1=1188261538006400044.
15. 'List of Industries for Automatic Approval of Foreign Technology Agreements and for 51% Foreign Equity Approvals (In I.T.C. (Hs) Classification)', Press Note No.10 (1992 Series), Revised List of Annex–III Items, Department for Promotion of Industry and Internal Trade, Ministry of Commerce and Industry, Government of India, 24 June 1992, https://dpiit.gov.in/sites/default/files/chap004_0.pdf
16. Ibid.
17. 'Procedures in Respect of Foreign Technology Agreements', Press Note No. 10 (1991 Series), Department for Promotion of Industry and Internal Trade, Ministry of Commerce and Industry, Government of India, 14 August 1991, https://dpiit.gov.in/sites/default/files/chap002_0.pdf.
18. K.K. Subrahmanian, D.V.S. Sastry, Siti Kantha Pattanaik and Sujan Hajra, 'Foreign Collaboration Under Liberalization Policy Patterns of FDI and Technology-Transfer in Indian Industry Since 1991\, Department of Economic Analysis and Policy, Reserve Bank of India, Table 3.11: Proportion of Agreements in the Total with 'Packaging', 30 August 1996, p. 39, https://rbidocs.rbi.org.in/rdocs/Publications/PDFs/GR674_August301996.PDF.
19. 'Further Liberalisation in Parameters For Automatic Approval In Foreign Collaboration', Press Note No. 4 (1996 Series), Department for Promotion of Industry and Internal Trade, Ministry of Commerce and Industry, Government of India, 5 November 1996, https://dpiit.gov.in/sites/default/files/chap007_0.pdf.
20. 'Liberalization of Foreign Technology Agreement policy and procedures', Press Note No. 2 (2003 Series), Department for Promotion of Industry and Internal Trade, Ministry of Commerce and Industry, Government of India, 24 June 2003, https://dpiit.gov.in/sites/default/files/pn62.pdf.
21. 'Liberalization of Foreign Technology Agreement Policy', Press Note No. 8 (2009 Series), Department for Promotion of Industry and Internal Trade,

Ministry of Commerce and Industry, Government of India, https://dpiit.gov.in/sites/default/files/pn8_2009_0.pdf.

22. Interim Budget 1991–92, Speech of Shri Yashwant Sinha, Minister of Finance, para 20, Ministry of Finance, Government of India, 4 March 1991, https://www.indiabudget.gov.in/doc/bspeech/bs199192(I).pdf.
23. Budget 1991–92, Speech of Shri Manmohan Singh, Minister of Finance, para 13, Ministry of Finance, Government of India, 24 July 1991, http://indiabudget.nic.in/bspeech/bs199192.pdf.
24. Budget 2021–2022, Speech of Nirmala Sitharaman, Minister of Finance, paras 84 to 91, Ministry of Finance, Government of India, 1 February 2021, https://www.indiabudget.gov.in/doc/budget_speech.pdf.
25. Gautam Chikermane, 'Disinvestment, 1991', *70 Policies that Shaped India: 1947 to 2017, Independence to $2.5 Trillion*, Observer Research Foundation (2018), p. 85, https://www.orfonline.org/wp-content/uploads/2018/07/70_Policies.pdf.
26. Disinvestment: Policy, Procedures and Progress, Ministry of Disinvestment, Government of India, February 2003, p. 104, file:///Users/gautam/Downloads/Disinvestment%20-%20Policy,%20Procedures%20and%20Progress_ebook2.pdf.
27. Ibid., p. 104.
28. Aggregated from Department of Investment and Public Asset Management, Ministry of Finance, Government of India.
29. 'Policy of Strategic Disinvestment Announced; Clear Roadmap for Strategic and Non-Strategic Sectors', Press Information Bureau, Government of India, https://pib.gov.in/PressReleasePage.aspx?PRID=1693899.
30. Gautam Chikermane, 'As Air India flies to the Tatas, a brief history of India's biggest policy failure', Observer Research Foundation, 9 October 2021, https://www.orfonline.org/expert-speak/as-air-india-flies-to-the-tatas-a-brief-history-of-indias-biggest-policy-failure/.
31. Ibid.
32. Devesh Kapur and Ravi Ramamurti, 'Privatization in India: The Imperatives and Consequences of Gradualism', Working Paper No. 142, Stanford Center for International Development, 3–4 June 2002, https://kingcenter.stanford.edu/sites/default/files/publications/142wp.pdf.
33. The Monopolies and Restrictive Trade Practices Act, 1969, Ministry of Corporate Affairs, Government of India, 27 December 1969, https://www.mca.gov.in/Ministry/actsbills/pdf/The_Monopolies_and_Restrictive_Trade_Practices_Act_1969.pdf.

34. S. Chakravarthy, 'Why India Adopted a New Competition Law', CUTS International (2006), p. 14, http://www.cuts-ccier.org/pdf/Why_India_Adopted_a_new_Competition_Law.pdf.
35. The Monopolies and Restrictive Trade Practices (Amendment) Act, 1991, Press Information Bureau, Government of India, 14 April 1992, https://archive.pib.gov.in/archive/ArchiveSecondPhase/LAW/1992-JAN-DEC%20MIN%20OF%20COMPANY%20AFFAIRS/PDF/LAW-1992-04-14_039.pdf.
36. Manish Agarwal and Aditya Bhattacharjea, 'Mergers in India: A Response to Regulatory Shocks', *Emerging Markets Finance & Trade*, Vol. 42, No. 3 (May—June 2006), pp. 46–65, https://www.jstor.org/stable/27750498.
37. Altamas Kabir, 'Competition Laws and the Indian Economy', *National Law School of India Review* 23, No. 1 (2011), pp. 1–8, https://www.jstor.org/stable/44283735.
38. Gautam Chikermane, *70 Policies that Shaped India: 1947 to 2017, Independence to $2.5 Trillion*, Observer Research Foundation (2018), pp. 115—116, https://www.orfonline.org/wp-content/uploads/2018/07/70_Policies.pdf.
39. 'Resolution', Investment Division, Department of Economic Affairs, Ministry of Finance, Government of India, 12 April 1988, https://www.sebi.gov.in/sebi_data/commondocs/may-2019/Gazette%20notification%20of%20constitution%20of%20SEBI.PDF_p_p.PDF.
40. The Securities and Exchange Board of India Act, 1992, Securities and Exchange Board of India, 4 April 1992, https://www.sebi.gov.in/sebi_data/attachdocs/1456380272563.pdf.
41. For context, the US Securities and Exchange Commission was established in 1934.
42. 'Despite efforts, independent directors not entirely independent: SEBI chief', *BusinessLine*, 6 April 2021, https://www.thehindubusinessline.com/companies/despite-efforts-independent-directors-not-entirely-independent-sebi-chief/article34256886.ece.
43. 'Consultation Paper on Review of Regulatory Provisions related to Independent Directors', Securities and Exchange Board of India, 1 March 2021, https://www.sebi.gov.in/reports-and-statistics/reports/mar-2021/consultation-paper-on-review-of-regulatory-provisions-related-to-independent-directors_49336.html.
44. 'Government can exempt any listed PSU from minimum public holding', *The Economic Times*, 1 August 2021, https://economictimes.indiatimes.com/news/economy/policy/govt-can-exempt-any-listed-psu-from-min-public-holding/articleshow/84929409.cms?.

45. The Securities and Insurance Laws (Amendment and Validation) Ordinance, 2010', The Gazette of India, Ministry of Law and Justice (Legislative Department), 18 June 2010, https://thc.nic.in/Central%20Governmental%20Ordinances/2010/2010.03.pdf.
46. Guidance Notes on Recent Regulatory Changes Related to Unit Linked Insurance Products (Ulips), Insurance Regulatory and Development Authority of India, 28 June 2010, https://www.irdai.gov.in/ADMINCMS/cms/frmGeneral_Layout.aspx?page=PageNo758.
47. *The Reserve Bank of India: Volume 4, 1981–1997*, Reserve Bank of India, Academic Foundation (2013), p. 418, https://rbidocs.rbi.org.in/rdocs/content/PDFs/Chapter11_04122018.pdf.
48. Report on Foreign Exchange Reserves, Reserve Bank of India, 6 July 2005, p. 4, https://www.rbi.org.in/scripts/PublicationReportDetails.aspx?ID=444#2.
49. Ibid., p. 6.
50. Ibid.
51. Weekly Statistical Supplement: Foreign Exchange Reserves, Reserve Bank of India, 7 January 2022, https://rbidocs.rbi.org.in/rdocs/Wss/PDFs/2T_14012022D5E7D8B9829E4D7AA36C1C0A99E91531.PDF.
52. Anup Roy, 'At $605 bn, India ties with Russia as fourth largest forex reserves holder', *Business Standard*, 12 June 2021, https://www.business-standard.com/article/economy-policy/at-605-bn-india-ties-with-russia-as-fourth-largest-forex-reserves-holder-121061101316_1.html.
53. 'International Reserves/Foreign Currency Liquidity (as of December 31, 2021)', Ministry of Finance, Government of Japan, https://www.mof.go.jp/english/policy/international_policy/reference/official_reserve_assets/e0312.html.
54. 'Switzerland's reserve assets – Section 1,' Swiss National Bank, https://data.snb.ch/en/topics/snb#!/cube/snbimfra.
55. 'International Investment Position: Balance of Payments Statistics, December 2021', Deutsche Bundesbank Eurosystem, https://www.bundesbank.de/resource/blob/640884/fe26c68691221a5902fcdf9ffcecc95d/mL/sdds-auslandsvermoegen-quartal-data.pdf.
56. 'U.S. International Reserve Position – January 7, 2022', U.S. Department of the Treasury, https://home.treasury.gov/data/us-international-reserve-position/01072022.
57. Rakesh Mohan, 'Financial Sector Reforms in India: Policies and Performance Analysis', Reserve Bank of India Bulletin, Reserve Bank of India, October 2004, https://rbidocs.rbi.org.in/rdocs/Speeches/PDFs/58346.pdf.
58. *The Reserve Bank of India: Volume 4: 1981–1997*, Academic Foundation (2013), Reserve Bank of India, pp. 122–127.

59. 'Deregulation of Savings Bank Deposit Interest Rate: A Discussion Paper', Reserve Bank of India, 2011, https://rbidocs.rbi.org.in/rdocs/Content/PDFs/DPS270411F.pdf.
60. 'Master Circular on Interest Rates on Rupee Deposits held in Domestic, Ordinary Non-Resident (NRO) and Non-Resident (External) (NRE) Accounts', Reserve Bank of India, 1 July 2009, https://www.rbi.org.in/commonman/Upload/English/Notification/PDFs/67IINTB010709_F.pdf.
61. 'Deregulation of Savings Bank Deposit Interest Rate – Guidelines', Reserve Bank of India, 25 October 2011, https://rbidocs.rbi.org.in/rdocs/notification/PDFs/CAN251011FL.pdf.
62. Monika Halan, 'Of human shields. And the banks savings deposit rate', *Mint*, 2 July 2011, https://www.livemint.com/Opinion/FDhKK4sBMWB8oDz680hIRP/Of-human-shields-And-the-bank-savings-deposit-rate.html.
63. Budget 1991–92, Speech of Shri Manmohan Singh, Minister of Finance, Ministry of Finance, Government of India, para 11, 24 July 1991.
64. *The Reserve Bank of India, Volume 4, 1981–1997*, Academic Foundation (2013), pp. 29–30, https://rbidocs.rbi.org.in/rdocs/content/PDFs/RBIvol404122018_PartA.pdf.
65. 'LERMS extended to the tourism industry', Press Information Bureau, Government of India, 24 July 1992, https://archive.pib.gov.in/archive/ArchiveSecondPhase/TOURISM%20&%20CIVIL%20AVIATION/1992%20MIN%20OF%20TOURISM/TOU-1992-07-24_032.pdf
66. Report on Currency and Finance 2002-03, Reserve Bank of India, 2004, para 7.73, p. 203, https://rbidocs.rbi.org.in/rdocs//PublicationReport/Pdfs/51018.pdf.
67. Arunabha Ghosh, 'Pathways Through Financial Crisis: India', *Global Governance*, Vol. 12, No. 4, Understanding Pathways Through Financial Crises and the Impact of the IMF (2006), pp. 413–429, https://www.jstor.org/stable/27800629.
68. Pami Dua and Rajiv Rajan, 'Exchange Rate Policy and Modelling in India', Department of Economic Analysis and Policy, Reserve Bank of India, Undated, p. 25, https://rbidocs.rbi.org.in/rdocs/Publications/PDFs/DRS33250210.pdf.
69. 'Statement of Objects and Reasons', The Recovery of Debts Due to Banks and Financial Institutions Act, 1993, The Debt Recovery Appellate Tribunal, Chennai, 27 August 1993, http://www.drat.tn.nic.in/Docu/RDDBFI-Act.pdf.
70. Shayan Ghosh, 'Debt recovery tribunals fail to clear cases on time; outstanding debts stand at Rs 4,50,000 crore', *The Financial Express*, 17 May 2016, https://

www.financialexpress.com/economy/cases-pile-up-at-drts-cross-rs-450000-crore/257066/.

71. Manasi Phadnis and N. Prabhala, 'Debt Recovery Tribunals in India: A Short Note', The Centre for Advanced Financial Research and Learning, March 2015, https://www.cafral.org.in/sfControl/content/Speech/462016115856AM-Phadnis_Prabhala_Paper_Mar_2015.pdf.

72. See 'Debts Recovery Appellate Tribunals (Procedure for Appointment as Chairperson of the Appellate Tribunal Amendment Rules), 2000', https://financialservices.gov.in/sites/default/files/DRAT%20Procedure%20for%20appointment%20as%20Chairperson%20of%20the%20Appellate%20Tribunal%20Amendment%20Rules%202000.pdf, and 'Debts Recovery Tribunals (Procedure for appointment as PO of the Tribunal Amendment Rules), 2000,' https://financialservices.gov.in/sites/default/files/DRT%20Procedure%20for%20appointment%20as%20PO%20of%20the%20Tribunal%20Amendment%20Rules%202000.pdf, Ministry of Finance, Government of India, 2 August 2000.

73. Prasanth V. Regy and Shubho Roy, 'Understanding Judicial Delays in Debt Tribunals', National Institute of Public Finance and Policy, 2 May 2017, https://macrofinance.nipfp.org.in/PDF/RoyRegy2017_judicial-delay-debt-tribunals.pdf.

74. 'National Telecom Policy, 1994', Department of Telecommunications, Ministry of Communications, Undated, https://dot.gov.in/national-telecom-policy-1994.

75. Ibid., para 4.

76. 'Report: Joint Parliamentary Committee (JPC) to Examine Matters Relating to Allocation and Pricing of Telecom Licences and Spectrum', Lok Sabha Secretariat, October 2013, p. 149, http://loksabhaph.nic.in/writereaddata/investigativejpc/investigativejpc_635612535475047737.pdf.

77. Ibid., p. 189.

78. 'New Telecom Policy, 1999', Department of Telecommunications, Ministry of Communications, Undated, https://dot.gov.in/new-telecom-policy-1999.

79. Ibid., paras 2.0 and 3.0.

80. 'Annual Report 2019-20', Telecom Regulatory Authority of India, October 2020, p. 13, https://www.trai.gov.in/sites/default/files/Annaul_Report_02032021_0.pdf.

81. 'Press Brief: Fiftieth Anniversary of the Multilateral Trading System', World Trade Organization, Undated, https://www.wto.org/english/thewto_e/minist_e/min96_e/chrono.htm.

82. Craig Van Grasstek, *The History and Future of the World Trade Organization*, World Trade Organization (2013), p. 87.

83. Ibid., p. 11.
84. 'India and the WTO', World Trade Organization, Undated, https://www.wto.org/english/thewto_e/countries_e/india_e.htm.
85. Kamal Saggi, 'India at the WTO: From Uruguay to Doha and Beyond', Stanford University Working Paper No. 425, August 2010, https://kingcenter.stanford.edu/sites/default/files/publications/425wp.pdf.
86. 'Trade Policy Review of India: 19-20 October 1993', GATT Council's Evaluation, 21 October 1993, https://docs.wto.org/gattdocs/q/GG/GATT/1598.PDF.
87. Julius Sen, 'Negotiating Trade Agreements with India: The Reality Below the Water Line', SAIIA Trade Policy Briefing No. 8, November 2004, https://sarpn.org/documents/d0001065/Sen_Nov2004.pdf.
88. Amrita Narlikar and Aruna Narlikar, *Bargaining with a Rising India: Lessons from the Mahabharata* (Oxford University Press, 2014).
89. Stephen Philip Cohen, *India: Emerging Power*, Brookings Institution Press (2001), p. 87.
90. Arvind Panagariya, 'India's Trade Reform: Progress, Impact and Future Strategy', International Trade, University Library of Munich, Germany, 4 March 2004, https://ideas.repec.org/p/wpa/wuwpit/0403004.html.
91. 'External Affairs Minister's remarks at the WEF India Economic Summit 2019 on 4 October 2019', Ministry of External Affairs, Government of India, 9 October 2019, https://www.mea.gov.in/Speeches-Statements.htm?dtl/31921.
92. Vijay Singh Chauhan and Sruti Vijayakumar, 'India's Performance as Measured by Global Indicators', 'Measuring Trade Facilitation: Evidence from India', Carnegie Endowment for International Peace (2021), https://www.jstor.org/stable/resrep32138.7.
93. Mohan Kumar, 'An Indian perspective on reviving the World Trade Organization', Observer Research Foundation, 28 April 2021, https://www.orfonline.org/expert-speak/indian-perspective-reviving-world-trade-organization/.
94. Amrita Narlikar and Aruna Narlikar, *Bargaining with a Rising India: Lessons from the Mahabharata* (Oxford University Press, 2014), pp. 222–223.
95. 'Indira Awaas Yojana: Backgrounder '96', Press Information Bureau, Government of India, 23 December 1996, https://archive.pib.gov.in/archive/ArchiveSecondPhase/WORK%20AND%20HOUSING/1996-JAN%20TO%20DEC-MO%20RURAL%20ARBAS%20EMPLOMENT/WOR-1996-12-23_117.pdf.
96. 'Cost Sharing of Projects', Press Information Bureau, Government of India, 23 July 1997, https://archive.pib.gov.in/archive/ArchiveSecondPhase/WORK%20AND%20HOUSING/1997-JAN%20TO%20DEC-MO%20RURAL%20ARES%20EMPLOYMENT/WOR-1997-07-23_079.pdf.

97. 'Centrally Sponsored Schemes: Indira Awaas Yojana', Rural Development and Panchayat Raj Department, Undated, Government of Tamil Nadu, https://tnrd.gov.in/schemes/cen_iay_13.html.
98. 'Report of the Comptroller and Auditor General of India on Performance Audit of Indira Awaas Yojana', Union Government (Civil), Ministry of Rural Development, Comptroller and Auditor General of India, https://cag.gov.in/cag_old/sites/default/files/audit_report_files/Union_Performance_Indira_Awaas_Yojana%20_37_2014.pdf.
99. 'About Us', Pradhan Mantri Awaas Yojana—Gramin, Ministry of Rural Development, Government of India, http://www.iay.nic.in/netiay/about.aspx.
100. 'PMAY (U) Achievement (provisional) [as on 3rd January, 2022]', Pradhan Mantri Awaas Yojana—Urban, https://pmay-urban.gov.in/uploads/progress-pdfs/61dbf7b293d9c-National_1.pdf.
101. 'Housing for All by 2022 Mission – National Mission for Urban Housing', Prime Minister's Office, 17 June 2015, https://www.pmindia.gov.in/en/news_updates/housing-for-all-by-2022-mission-national-mission-for-urban-housing/.
102. 'Outward Remittances under the Liberalized Remittance Scheme for Resident Individuals—Yearly', Database on Indian Economy, RBI's Data Warehouse, https://dbie.rbi.org.in/DBIE/statistics.rbi?action=RL&f=365&sd=3.
103. Read the two Tarapore Committee reports, one each in 1997 and 2006, for instance. 'Report of the Committee on Fuller Capital Account Convertibility', Reserve Bank of India, 31 July 2006, https://rbidocs.rbi.org.in/rdocs/PublicationReport/Pdfs/72250.pdf; and 'Committee on Capital Account Convertibility', Press Relations Department, Reserve Bank of India, 3 June 1997, https://rbidocs.rbi.org.in/rdocs/PressRelease/PDFs/2450.pdf.
104. 'Master Direction—Liberalised Remittance Scheme (LRS) of USD 2,50,000 for resident individuals', Reserve Bank of India, 20 June 2018, https://www.rbi.org.in/Scripts/BS_ViewMasDirections.aspx?id=10192#1.
105. Rajiv Ranjan and Anand Prakash, 'Internationalisation Of Currency: The Case of the Indian Rupee and Chinese Renminbi', Reserve Bank of India, April 2010, https://rbidocs.rbi.org.in/rdocs/PublicationReport/Pdfs/RRSS180510F.pdf.
106. 'Report of the Committee on Fuller Capital Account Convertibility', Reserve Bank of India, 31 July 2006, pp. 59, https://rbidocs.rbi.org.in/rdocs/PublicationReport/Pdfs/72250.pdf.
107. 'Ordinance for Telecom Regulatory Authority of India Promulgated', Press Information Bureau, Government of India, 30 January 1996, https://archive.pib.gov.in/archive/ArchiveSecondPhase/COMMUNICATION/1996-JAN-DEC-COMMUNICATIONS/COM-1996-01-30_007.pdf. It was also tasked with promoting orderly and healthy growth of telecommunication

infrastructure in the country, promoting and protecting consumer interests, and ensuring fair competition.

108. 'Establishing the Telecom Regulatory Authority of India', Ministry of Communications (Department of Telecommunication), Gazette of India, Government of India, 20 February 1997, https://egazette.nic.in/WriteReadData/1997/E-0256-1997-0103-9091.pdf.
109. 'The Telecom Regulatory Authority of India Act, 1997', Telecom Authority of India, 28 March 1997.
110. 'Preliminary Consultation Paper on Unified Licensing Regime', Consultation Paper No. 5/2003, Telecom Regulatory Authority of India, 15 November 2003, https://www.trai.gov.in/sites/default/files/Preconsultation_paper_ULR_15_nov_2003.pdf.
111. 'The Telecommunication Tariff Order 1999', Telecom Regulatory Authority of India, 9 March 1999, https://trai.gov.in/sites/default/files/TTO_Main_Regulation_Hin_09031999.pdf.
112. 'The Telecommunication (Broadcasting and Cable Services) Interconnection Regulation 2004', Telecom Regulatory Authority of India, 10 December 2004, https://egazette.nic.in/WriteReadData/2004/E_190_2011_022.pdf.
113. A series of fifteen regulations, from 2009 to 2019, have ensured that consumers can seamlessly shift their service provider. Details here: https://www.trai.gov.in/telecom/mobile-number-portability.
114. 'The Telecom Commercial Communications Customer Preference Regulations, 2018', Telecom Regulatory Authority of India, 19 July 2018, https://trai.gov.in/sites/default/files/RegulationUcc19072018.pdf.
115. 'Delinking of Spectrum Allocation from Licences', Ministry of Communications, Press Information Bureau, Government of India, 11 May 2012, https://pib.gov.in/newsite/PrintRelease.aspx?relid=83617.
116. 'The Telecommunication Tariff (Sixty First Amendment) Order, 2016', Telecom Regulatory Authority of India, 22 November 2016, para 4, https://www.trai.gov.in/sites/default/files/TTO_on_Mobile_Banking_Nov_2016_22_11_16.pdf.
117. Budget 1997–98, Speech of Shri P. Chidambaram, Minister of Finance, Ministry of Finance, Government of India, 28 February 1997, para 90.
118. Monika Halan, 'The FM needs to go beyond just good intentions. They are not enough', *Mint*, 2 February 2020, https://www.livemint.com/opinion/columns/opinion-when-just-good-intentions-are-not-enough-11580569299015.html.
119. 'Income Tax Department Time Series Data Financial Year 2000-01 to 2018-19', Central Board of Direct Taxes, Income Tax Department, Ministry of Finance, Government of India, Table 1.9, Undated, https://www.incometaxindia.gov.in/Documents/Direct%20Tax%20Data/IT-Department-

Time-Series-Data-FY-2000-01-to-2018–19.pdf: A 'Taxpayer' is a person who either has filed a return of income for the relevant Assessment Year or in whose case tax has been deducted at source in the relevant Financial Year but the taxpayer has not filed the return of income.

120. Speech of Shri Y.B. Chavan, Minister of Finance Introducing the Budget for the Year 1974–75, Ministry of Finance, Government of India, 28 February 1974, Para 36.
121. Speech of Shri R. Venkataraman Minister of Finance, Introducing the Budget for the Year 1980–81 (Final), Ministry of Finance, Government of India, 18 June 1980, Para 65.
122. Speech of Shri Pranab Mukherjee Minister of Finance, Introducing the Budget for the Year 1984–85, Ministry of Finance, Government of India, 29 February 1984, Para 65.
123. Speech of Shri Vishwanath Pratap Singh, Minister of Finance, Introducing the Budget for the Year 1985–86, Ministry of Finance, Government of India, 16 March 1985, Para 80.
124. Budget Speech of Shri Manmohan Singh, Minister of Finance, Ministry of Finance, Government of India, 29 February 1992, Para 58.
125. ET Bureau, 'Super-rich will have to pay up to 42.7% tax; Rs 2-5 crore, Rs 5 cr+ brackets affected', *The Economic Times*, 6 June 2019, https://economictimes.indiatimes.com/wealth/personal-finance-news/super-rich-will-have-to-pay-up-to-42-7-tax-rs-2-5-crore-rs-5-cr-brackets-affected/articleshow/70099837.cms?from=mdr.
126. 'Table I.7. Top statutory personal income tax rates', Organisation for Economic Co-operation and Development data retrieved on 31 July 2021, Undated, https://stats.oecd.org/index.aspx?DataSetCode=TABLE_I7.
127. 'Average turnaround time across major ports in India from financial year 1991 to 2020 (in days)', Statista, 2021, https://www.statista.com/statistics/693742/average-turnaround-time-at-major-ports-india/.
128. 'Table 3.1: Median time spent in port in top 25 economies by number of port calls and market segment, 2018', Review of Maritime Transport 2019, United Nations (2019), pp. 66, https://unctad.org/system/files/official-document/rmt2019_en.pdf.
129. 'Establishment of the TAMP', Tariff Authority for Major Ports, Ministry of Ports, Shipping and Waterways, Government of India, Undated, http://tariffauthority.gov.in/UserView/index?mid=1200.
130. The Port Laws (Amendment) Act, 1997, Legislative Department, Ministry of Law and Justice, Government of India, 25 March 1997, https://legislative.gov.in/sites/default/files/legislative_references/1997.pdf.

131. These are: Chennai Port Trust, Cochin Port Trust, Deendayal Port Trust, Jawaharlal Nehru Port Trust, Mormugao Port Trust, Mumbai Port Trust, New Mangalore Port Trust, Paradip Port Trust, Syama Prasad Mookerjee Port Trust, V.O. Chidambaranar Port Trust, and Visakhapatnam Port Trust.
132. Rachna Gangwar, 'Tariff Regulation in Port Sector: Experiences from India,' Selected Proceedings, WCTR, 15–18 July 2013, p. 8, http://www.wctrs-society.com/wp-content/uploads/abstracts/rio/selected/2046.pdf.
133. 'Ports', India Brand Equity Foundation, March 2021, p. 11, https://www.ibef.org/download/Ports-March-2021.pdf.
134. The Major Ports Authority Act, 2021, Legislative Department, Ministry of Law and Justice, Government of India, 17 February 2021, https://egazette.nic.in/WriteReadData/2021/225265.pdf.
135. Indian Ports Bill, 2021, Ministry of Ports, Shipping and Waterways, Government of India, https://shipmin.gov.in/sites/default/files/Indianportbill2021.pdf.
136. 'Draft Indian Ports Bill 2021', Ministry of Ports, Shipping and Waterways, Press Information Bureau, 9 August 2021, https://www.pib.gov.in/PressReleasePage.aspx?PRID=1744034.
137. 'Oppose new draft Indian Ports Bill 2021, Stalin urges in letter to 9 CMs', *The Hindu*, 22 June 2021, https://www.thehindu.com/news/national/tamil-nadu/oppose-new-draft-indian-ports-bill-2021-stalin-urges-in-letter-to-9-cms/article34900574.ece.
138. Oil and Natural Gas Corporation Ltd, and Oil India Ltd.
139. 'New Exploration Licensing Policy (NELP)', Ministry of Petroleum and Natural Gas, Government of India, Undated, http://petroleum.nic.in/sites/default/files/2exp.policy.NELP2015.pdf.
140. Rose Mary K. Abraham, 'New Exploration and Licensing Policy (NELP)', Arthapedia, Ministry of Finance, Government of India, http://arthapedia.in/index.php?title=New_Exploration_and_Licensing_Policy_(NELP).
141. Ibid.
142. 'Table 34: Production and Imports of Crude Oil and Petroleum Products', Handbook of Statistics on the Indian Economy: 2019–20, Reserve Bank of India, p. 75, https://rbidocs.rbi.org.in/rdocs/Publications/PDFs/0HBS202024D4CA0CC03F4674B040F7DEDE7E5360.PDF.
143. Jean-François Seznec and Ramesh Pallakonda, 'Indian Oil Consumption's Place in the World', 'India's Energy Needs and the Arab/Persian Gulf', Atlantic Council (2017), https://www.jstor.org/stable/resrep03692.5. 'India has its own minor, domestic oil supply with reserves of just 5.7 billion barrels, a very small figure when compared to those in the Middle East. Global majors have not shown an interest in exploring India due to its lower reserve size and

regulatory uncertainty. Hence, India has been and will increasingly be an oil importer.'

144. Anupama Sen, 'Summary and Conclusions', 'Gas Pricing Reform in India, Report Subtitle: Implications for the Indian Gas Landscape Report', Oxford Institute for Energy Studies (2015), https://www.jstor.org/stable/resrep31033.10. 'A review of existing reserves shows that the decline in domestic production is unlikely to be fully reversed, although it is plausible that production could be increased (by roughly 18Bcm/year) through prices of approximately $6–7.15/MMBtu. However, this would have to come from NOC (ONGC) rather than private sector production in the absence of a significant new "giant" discovery, as ONGC appears to hold the largest proportion of gas reserves as well as Petroleum Exploration Licenses.'
145. Budget 1997–98, Speech of Shri P. Chidambaram, Minister of Finance, Ministry of Finance, Government of India, 28 February 1997, Para 87.
146. 'Voluntary Disclosure of Income Scheme, 1997: Notified Effective Date of Voluntary Disclosure of Income Scheme, 1997', Income Tax Department, Ministry of Finance, Government of India, 9 June 1997.
147. 'VDIS Tax Collections Crosses Rs 10,000 Crores', Press Information Bureau, Ministry of Finance, Government of India, 3 January 1998, https://archive.pib.gov.in/archive/ArchiveSecondPhase/FINANCE/1998-JAN-JULY-FINANCE/PDF/FIN-1998-01-03_002.pdf.
148. 'Amnesty Schemes of the Government of India since Independence', Black Money, Lok Sabha Secretariat, Parliament Library and Reference, Research, Documentation and Information Service, November 2015, p. 9, http://164.100.47.193/Refinput/New_Reference_Notes/English/BLACK_MONEY_19-11-2015.pdf.
149. Ibid.
150. Voluntary Deposits (Immunities and Exemptions) Act, 1991, Income Tax Department, Ministry of Finance, Government of India, 1991, https://www.incometaxindia.gov.in/pages/acts/voluntary-deposits-act.aspx.
151. 'Public Enterprises Survey 2004–05, Volume 1, Part 1', Department of Public Enterprises, Ministry of Finance, Government of India, Undated, p. 9, https://dpe.gov.in/sites/default/files/Volume1Part01_1.pdf.
152. Ibid., p. 5.
153. 'Turning selected public sector units into global giants—monitoring of performance towards globalization effort', Department of Public Enterprises, Ministry of Finance, Government of India, 22 July 1997, https://dpe.gov.in/sites/default/files/MaharatnaNavratnaMiniratna-Chapter-9_0_0.pdf.
154. Ibid., 'Financial and operational autonomy for profit making public sector enterprises—Mini-Ratnas', 9 October 1997.

155. Ibid. These were: Bharat Heavy Electricals Ltd, Bharat Petroleum Corporation Ltd, Hindustan Petroleum Corporation Ltd, India Oil Corporation Ltd, Indian Petrochemicals Corporation Ltd, National Thermal Power Corporation Ltd, Oil and Natural Gas Corporation Ltd, Steel Authority of India Ltd, and Videsh Sanchar Nigam Ltd.
156. Namrata Kala, 'The Impacts of Managerial Autonomy on Firm Outcomes', NBER Working Paper No. 26304, September 2019, https://www.nber.org/system/files/working_papers/w26304/w26304.pdf.
157. Ibid.
158. 'Introduction of "Maharatna" Scheme for Central Public Sector Enterprises (CPSEs),' Office Memorandum, Department of Public Enterprises, Ministry of Heavy Industries and Public Enterprises, Government of India, 4 February 2010, https://dpe.gov.in/sites/default/files/R-121.pdf.
159. 'Public Enterprises Survey 2018–19 Tabled in Parliament; Total Paid up Capital in all CPSEs as on 31.3.2019 Stood at Rs. 2,75,697 Crore Registering a Growth of 8.55%; Financial Investment in all CPSEs Stood at Rs.16,40,628 Crore Recording a Growth of 14.65%', Ministry of Heavy Industries, Press Information Bureau, Government of India, 10 February 2020, https://pib.gov.in/PressReleseDetailm.aspx?PRID=1602623.
160. 'List of Maharatna, Navratna and Miniratna CPSEs: As per available information (as on July, 2021)', Department of Public Enterprises, Ministry of Finance, Government of India, Undated, https://dpe.gov.in/sites/default/files/List_of_Maharatna_Navratna_and_miniratna_12_07_2021.pdf.
161. Harbans L. Bajaj and Deepak Sharma, 'Power Sector Reforms in India', Conference, World Energy Council, 1 July 2007, https://www.osti.gov/etdeweb/servlets/purl/21115880. Till the 1990s, the authors write, 'the public sector was the best avenue for delivering infrastructure services, and the private sector's presence in it was to be restricted, if not prohibited; public sector entities would serve the public interest the best; parliamentary democracy provided sufficient accountability to protect consumers' interest and to ensure efficiency'.
162. 'The Electricity Regulatory Commissions Act, 1998', The Gazette of India, Extraordinary, Part II, Central Electricity Regulatory Commission, Government of India, 2 July 1998, https://cercind.gov.in/electregucommiact1998.pdf. See Para 3 under Statement of Objects and Reasons: 'The Electricity Regulatory Commissions Bill, 1997 was introduced in the Lok Sabha on 14th August, 1997. However it could not be passed due to the dissolution of the Eleventh Lok Sabha'.
163. Ibid.

164. Entry 38, Seventh Schedule, Constitution of India.
165. Ibid.
166. Madhav Godbole, 'Electricity Regulatory Commissions: The Jury Is Still Out', *Economic and Political Weekly*, Vol. 37, No. 23 (8–14 June 2002), pp. 2195–2200, https://www.jstor.org/stable/4412206.
167. See: 1) V. Ranganathan, 'Electricity Act 2003: Moving to a Competitive Environment,' *Economic and Political Weekly*, Vol. 39, No. 20 (15-21 May 2004), pp. 2001–2005, https://www.jstor.org/stable/4415021.
168. Ibid.
169. 'Internet Services', Department of Telecommunications, Ministry of Communications, Government of India, Undated, https://dot.gov.in/relatedlinks/internet-services.
170. 'Expansion of Internet Services to Attract Two Million Users, Pending Issues on Internet Policy Cleared, Implementation Committee to Tackle Operational Aspects', Press Information Bureau, Government of India, 5 November 1997, p. 1, https://archive.pib.gov.in/archive/ArchiveSecondPhase/COMMUNICATION/1997-JAN-DEC-COMMUNICATIONS/COM-1997-11-05_153.pdf.
171. Ibid.
172. 'Eligibility Criteria for Internet Service Providers, Application Form and Licence Agreement Finalized, Three-Tier Licence for Internet Services', Press Information Bureau, Government of India, 15 January 1998, https://archive.pib.gov.in/archive/ArchiveSecondPhase/COMMUNICATION/1998-JAN-DEC-COMUNICATIONS/COM-1998-01-15_013.pdf.
173. 'Broadband Policy 2004', Department of Telecommunications, Ministry of Communications and Information Technology, Government of India, 13 December 2004, https://dot.gov.in/sites/default/files/broadbandpolicy2004_htm.pdf.
174. Ibid. The Preamble: 'Recognising the potential of ubiquitous Broadband service in growth of GDP and enhancement in quality of life through societal applications including tele-education, tele-medicine, e-governance, entertainment as well as employment generation by way of high speed access to information and web-based communication, Government have finalised a policy to accelerate the growth of Broadband services.' Futuristic because nobody then had foreseen how the Internet would impact education, healthcare, governance and entertainment.
175. 'The Indian Telecom Services Performance Indicators Jan-Mar'04', Table 3.1: Subscribers Base of Internet Services, Telecom Regulatory Authority of India, June 2004, p. 34, https://www.trai.gov.in/sites/default/files/indireport230604.pdf.

176. Ibid., 'Growth of Internet Services', p. 5.
177. 'The Indian Telecom Services Performance Indicators: July–September 2020', Telecom Regulatory Authority of India, 21 January, 2021, p. ii, https://www.trai.gov.in/sites/default/files/QPIR_21012021_0.pdf.
178. Ibid., p. 40. Reliance Jio has a market share of 53.73 per cent, Bharti Airtel 25.15 per cent, Vodafone 18.29 per cent, and BSNL 2.7 per cent.
179. 'Cabinet approves major Reforms in Telecom Sector', Prime Minister's Office, 15 September 2021, https://www.pmindia.gov.in/en/news_updates/cabinet-approves-major-reforms-in-telecom-sector/.
180. Report of the High-level Committee on Agricultural Credit through Commercial Banks, Reserve Bank of India, p. 1, 21 April 1998, https://rbidocs.rbi.org.in/rdocs/PublicationReport/Pdfs/CR243_19988448650447BA4E0D8A14F6DB7BFF1ED3.PDF.
181. Budget 1998–99, Speech of Shri Yashwant Sinha, Minister of Finance, Ministry of Finance, Government of India, Para 8, 1 June 1998.
182. 'Kisan Credit Cards', Reserve Bank of India, 28 February 2002, https://www.rbi.org.in/Scripts/NotificationUser.aspx?Id=592&Mode=0.
183. 'Master Circular—Kisan Credit Card (KCC) Scheme', Reserve Bank of India, 3 July 2017, https://www.rbi.org.in/commonperson/English/Scripts/Notification.aspx?Id=2311.
184. Gyanendra Mani, 'Study on Implementation of Kisan Credit Card Scheme', Department of Economic Analysis and Research, National Bank for Agriculture and Rural Development, December 2016, Para 27, p. 6, https://www.nabard.org/auth/writereaddata/tender/3103171130OP-64_Study%20on%20Implementation%20of%20KCC%20Scheme_wb.pdf.
185. 'Report of the Internal Working Group to Review Agricultural Credit', Reserve Bank of India, September 2019, p. 26, https://rbidocs.rbi.org.in/rdocs//PublicationReport/Pdfs/WGREPORT101A17FBDC144237BD114BF2D01FF9C9.PDF.
186. 'Kisan Credit Cards (KCC) campaign launched for 1.5 crore dairy farmers: Special drive part of Prime Minister's Atma Nirbhar Bharat package for Farmers', Ministry of Fisheries, Animal Husbandry & Dairying, Press Information Bureau, Government of India, 1 June 2020, https://pib.gov.in/PressReleasePage.aspx?PRID=1628393.
187. 'Consultation Paper on Revision of the Insurance Act 1938 & The Insurance Regulatory & Development Act 1999', Law Commission of India, June 2003, Para 3.3(a), and Paras 4.1 to 4.5, https://lawcommissionofindia.nic.in/consult_papers/insurance%201-27.pdf.
188. 'History of insurance in India', Insurance Regulatory and Development Authority of India, 31 July 2020, https://www.irdai.gov.in/ADMINCMS/cms/NormalData_Layout.aspx?page=PageNo4&mid=2.

189. These are the Insurance Act, 1938, the Life Insurance Corporation Act, 1956, and the General Insurance Business (Nationalisation) Act, 1972.
190. Ibid., History of Insurance in India.
191. Monika Halan, Renuka Sane and Susan Thomas, 'Estimating losses to customers on account of mis-selling life insurance policies in India', Indira Gandhi Institute of Development Research, 10 April 2013, http://www.igidr.ac.in/pdf/publication/WP-2013-007.pdf.
192. The Insurance Laws (Amendment) Act, 2015, Legislative Department, Ministry of Law and Justice, Government of India, 20 March 2015, https://financialservices.gov.in/sites/default/files/The%20Insuance%20Laws%20%28Amendment%29%20Act%202015.pdf.
193. 'Indian Insurance Market', Insurance Regulatory and Development Authority of India, Undated, https://www.policyholder.gov.in/indian_insurance_market.aspx.
194. 'Reserve Bank of India introduces the Financial Inclusion Index', Reserve Bank of India, 17 August 2021, https://rbidocs.rbi.org.in/rdocs/PressRelease/PDFs/PR7033B7A01D0DF9D459D9FF992B53A5538C1.PDF.
195. 'Recommendations on Roadmap to Promote Broadband Connectivity and Enhanced Broadband Speed', Telecom Regulatory Authority of India, 31 August 2021, p. 6, https://trai.gov.in/sites/default/files/Recommendations_31082021.pdf.
196. The Defence of India Act, 1939, XXXV of 1939, A Collection of the Acts of the Indian Legislature and of the Governor General for the Year 1939, Legislative Department, Government of India, Housed on Archive.org, 29 September 1939, https://web.archive.org/web/20131029204142/http://lawmin.nic.in/legislative/textofcentralacts/1939.pdf.
197. 'K.N. Mehta vs Director of Enforcement and Others: Court Judgment', Delhi High Court, India Kanoon, 20 May 1982, Para 22, https://indiankanoon.org/doc/919892/.
198. The Foreign Exchange Regulation Act, 1973, Enforcement Directorate, Ministry of Finance, Government of India, 19 September 1973, https://www.indiacode.nic.in/bitstream/123456789/1988/1/A1999_42.pdf.
199. Prithwiraj Choudhury and Tarun Khanna, 'Charting Dynamic Trajectories: Multinational Enterprises in India', *The Business History Review*, Vol. 88, No. 1 Business, Networks, and the State in India (Spring 2014), p. 133–169, https://www.jstor.org/stable/43299522.
200. 'Statement on Industrial Policy 1991', 24 July 1991, paras 24 and 25.
201. The Foreign Exchange Management Act, 1999, India Code, National Informatics Centre, Government of India, 29 December 1999, https://www.indiacode.nic.in/bitstream/123456789/1988/1/A1999_42.pdf.

202. Gautam Chikermane, *70 Policies that Shaped India: 1947 to 2017, Independence to $2.5 Trillion*, Observer Research Foundation (2018), pp. 109–110, https://www.orfonline.org/wp-content/uploads/2018/07/70_Policies.pdf.
203. Ibid., pp. 97–98.
204. Pradeep Thakur, 'Intel agencies favour making FEMA a criminal act like PMLA', *The Times of India*, 13 November 2019, https://timesofindia.indiatimes.com/india/intel-agencies-favour-making-fema-a-criminal-act-like-pmla/articleshow/72031020.cms.
205. Gautam Chikermane, '5G Infrastructure, Huawei's Techno-Economic Advantages and India's National Security Concerns: An Analysis', Observer Research Foundation, 10 December 2019, https://www.orfonline.org/research/5g-infrastructure-huaweis-techno-economic-advantages-and-indias-national-security-concerns-58644/.
206. K.R. Narayanan, 'Address by the President of India', Press Information Bureau, Government of India, Para 16, 25 October 1999, https://archive.pib.gov.in/archive/ArchiveSecondPhase/RASHTRAPATI%20BHAWAN/1999-JAN-DEC-NO-1-PRESIDENT-SECTT/PDF/RPB-1999-10-25_064.pdf: 'A Programme for Rural Connectivity through construction of all-weather roads to connect all villages will soon be started. Fifty per cent of the Diesel cess will be earmarked for this programme.'
207. 'Rural Roads Programme—A Novel Concept to Benefit Over 30 Crore Rural Population; Consultative Committee Meets to Discuss Schemes and Programmes of the Ministry of Rural Development', Press Information Bureau, Government of India, 10 August 2000, https://archive.pib.gov.in/archive/ArchiveSecondPhase/WORK%20AND%20HOUSING/2000-JAN-DEC-RURAL-AFFAIRS-EM-PAWARMENT/WOR-2000-08-10_103.pdf.
208. 'PM Launches Rural Roads Programme', Press Information Bureau, Government of India, 25 December 2000, https://archive.pib.gov.in/archive/ArchiveSecondPhase/WORK%20AND%20HOUSING/2000-JAN-DEC-RURAL-AFFAIRS-EM-PAWARMENT/WOR-2000-12-25_171.pdf.
209. The Central Road and Infrastructure Fund Act, 2000, India Code, 27 December 2000, https://www.indiacode.nic.in/bitstream/123456789/1931/1/A2000-54.pdf: '…for development and maintenance of National Highways, railway projects, improvement of safety in railways, State and rural roads and other infrastructure, and for these purposes to levy and collect by way of cess, a duty of excise and a duty of customs on motor spirit commonly known as petrol and high speed diesel oil and for other matters connected therewith.'
210. 'Background note on Rural Roads', Press Information Bureau, Government of India, 28 January 2000, https://archive.pib.gov.in/archive/

ArchiveSecondPhase/WORK%20AND%20HOUSING/2000-JAN-DEC-RURAL-AFFAIRS-EM-PAWARMENT/WOR-2000-01-28_010.pdf.

211. Ibid.

212. 'Status Report on the Pradhan Mantri Gram Sadak Yojana', Press Information Bureau, Government of India, 5 October 2001, https://archive.pib.gov.in/archive/ArchiveSecondPhase/WORK%20AND%20HOUSING/2001-SEP-DEC-RURAL-DEVEPLOPMENT/WOR-2001-10-05_005.pdf.

213. Rural Dashboard, Pradhan Mantri Gram Sadak Yojana, http://omms.nic.in/dbweb/, accessed 4 August 2021.

214. UNCITRAL Model Law on Electronic Commerce (1996), United Nations Commission on International Trade Law, United Nations, 12 June 1996, https://uncitral.un.org/en/texts/ecommerce/modellaw/electronic_commerce.

215. State Development Report on Punjab, Planning Commission, NITI Aayog, Government of India, 28 December 2002, p. 569, https://niti.gov.in/planningcommission.gov.in/docs/plans/stateplan/sdr_punjab/sdrpun_ch13.pdf.

216. The Indian Evidence Act, 1872, India Code, Government of India, https://www.indiacode.nic.in/bitstream/123456789/6819/1/indian_evidence_act_1872.pdf.

217. Indian Penal Code, 1860, Legislative Department, Ministry of Law and Justice, Government of India, 6 October 1860, https://legislative.gov.in/sites/default/files/A1860-45.pdf.

218. The Reserve Bank of India Act, Reserve Bank of India, 6 March 1934 https://rbidocs.rbi.org.in/rdocs/Publications/PDFs/RBIA1934170510.PDF.

219. The Information Technology Amendment Act, 2008, Legislative Department, Ministry of Law and Justice, The Gazette of India: Extraordinary, Government of India, 5 February 2009, https://www.meity.gov.in/writereaddata/files/itact2000/it_amendment_act2008.pdf.

220. Ibid., Section 66A.

221. Shreya Singhal versus Union of India, Para 119 (a), Supreme Court of India, Ministry of Electronics and Information Technology, Government of India, 24 March 2015, Para 119, https://www.meity.gov.in/writereaddata/files/Honorable-Supreme-Court-order-dated-24th-March%202015.pdf.

222. Ibid., Para 82.

223. 'Why Social Media Is the New Weapon in Modern Warfare', University of Pennsylvania, Wharton, 17 January 2019, https://knowledge.wharton.upenn.edu/article/singer-weaponization-social-media/.

224. 'Prime Minister Shri Atal Bihari Vajpayee's Independence Day Address', Press Information Bureau, Government of India, 15 August 2000, https://archivepmo.nic.in/abv/speech-details.php?nodeid=9113.
225. 'District Primary Education Programme: Guidelines', Department of Education, Ministry of Human Resource Development, Government of India, May 1995, http://14.139.60.153/bitstream/123456789/59/1/DPEP%20guidelines.pdf.
226. The Right of Children to Free and Compulsory Education Act, 2009, Legislative Department, Ministry of Law and Justice, Government of India, 26 August 2009, https://legislative.gov.in/sites/default/files/A2009-35_0.pdf.
227. The Constitution (Eighty-Sixth Amendment) Act, 2002, Legislative Department, Ministry of Law and Justice, Government of India, 12 December 2002, https://legislative.gov.in/constitution-eighty-sixth-amendment-act-2002: 'The State shall provide free and compulsory education to all children of the age of six to fourteen years in such manner as the State may, by law, determine.'
228. 'Universalization of Primary Education', Written answer by the Minister of Human Resource Development, Minister of Science and Technology and Minister of Ocean Development, Dr Murli Manohar Joshi, Lok Sabha Debates (Thirteenth Lok Sabha), Lok Sabha Secretariat, 7 August 2001, p. 368, https://eparlib.nic.in/bitstream/123456789/759761/1/lsd_13_07_07-08-2001.pdf.
229. 'About the Mid-Day Meal Scheme', Ministry of Education, Government of India, http://mdm.nic.in/mdm_website/.
230. CABE (Central Advisory Board of Education) Committee on 'Free and Compulsory Education Bill and Other Issues Related to Elementary Education', Background Paper on Free and Compulsory Education Bill, First Meeting, Department of Elementary Education and Literacy, Ministry of Human Resource Development, Government of India, 22 November 2004, http://14.139.60.153/bitstream/123456789/2371/1/CABE%20COMMITTEE%20ON%20FREE%20AND%20COMPULSORY%20EDUCATION%20BILL%20AND%20OTHER%20ISSUES%20RELATED%20TO%20ELEMENTARY%20EDUCATION%20FIRST%20MEETING%2c22%20ND%20NOV.2004%20_no%20accession%20number.pdf.
231. Ibid., Annexure VIII.
232. 'Order', Department of Secondary and Higher Education, Ministry of Human Resource Development, Government of India 8 September 2004, https://www.education.gov.in/sites/upload_files/mhrd/files/document-reports/Free%20and%20Compulsory%20Education%20Bill%20and%20other%20issues%20related%20to%20Elementary%20Education.pdf.

233. Right of Children to Free and Compulsory Education Act, 2009, Legislative Department, Ministry of Law and Justice, Government of India, 26 August 2009, https://legislative.gov.in/sites/default/files/The%20Right%20of%20Children%20to%20Free%20and%20Compulsory%20Education%20Act,%202009.pdf.
234. Anil Sadgopal, 'Right to Education vs. Right to Education Act', *Social Scientist* 38, No. 9/12 (September–December 2010), pp. 17–50, https://www.jstor.org/stable/27896288.
235. About Samagra Shiksha, Department of School Education and Literacy, Ministry of Education, Government of India, Undated, https://samagra.education.gov.in/about.html.
236. Rashtriya Madhyamik Shiksha Abhiyan, Department of School Education and Literacy, Ministry of Human Resource Development, Government of India, Undated, https://www.education.gov.in/en/rmsa.
237. 'The Forty Recommendations of the Financial Action Task Force on Money Laundering 1990', Financial Action Task Force, Undated, https://www.fatf-gafi.org/media/fatf/documents/recommendations/pdfs/FATF%20Recommendations%201990.pdf.
238. The Financial Action Task Force defines it thusly: 'The goal of a large number of criminal acts is to generate a profit for the individual or group that carries out the act. Money laundering is the processing of these criminal proceeds to disguise their illegal origin.' What Is Money laundering, Financial Action Task Force, Undated, https://www.fatf-gafi.org/faq/moneylaundering/.

    When a criminal activity generates substantial profits, the individual or group involved must find a way to control the funds without attracting attention to the underlying activity or the persons involved. Criminals do this by disguising the sources, changing the form, or moving the funds to a place where they are less likely to attract attention.

    In response to mounting concern over money laundering, the Financial Action Task Force on money laundering (FATF) was established by the G-7 Summit in Paris in 1989 to develop a co-ordinated international response. One of the first tasks of the FATF was to develop Recommendations, 40 in all, which set out the measures national governments should take to implement effective anti-money laundering programmes.
239. 'Swiss Bank Helped Launder Nazi Gold, Documents Show', *Los Angeles Times*, 13 January 1997, https://www.latimes.com/archives/la-xpm-1997-01-13-mn-18207-story.html.
240. 'Anti-money laundering and counter-terrorist financing measures: Pakistan, Mutual Evaluation Report', Asia/Pacific Group, 2019, https://www.fatf-gafi.org/media/fatf/documents/reports/mer-fsrb/APG-Mutual-Evaluation-Report-Pakistan-October%202019.pdf.

241. 'Political Declaration and Action Plan against Money Laundering adopted at the Twentieth Special Session of the United Nations General Assembly devoted to countering the world drug problem together', International Money Laundering Information Network, 10 June 1998, https://www.imolin.org/imolin/ungadec.html.
242. The Prevention of Money-laundering Act, 2002, Enforcement Directorate, Ministry of Finance, Government of India, 17 January 2003, https://www.enforcementdirectorate.gov.in/PreventionOfMoneyLaunderingAct2002.pdf?p1=117281489017600032.
243. Ibid., Chapter II, Section 3: 'Whosoever directly or indirectly attempts to indulge or knowingly assists or knowingly is a party or is actually involved in any process or activity connected proceeds of crime including its concealment, possession, acquisition or use and projecting or claiming it as untainted property shall be guilty of offence of money-laundering.'
244. 'FAQs (Frequently Asked Questions) on the Prevention of Money Laundering Act', Enforcement Directorate, Ministry of Finance, Government of India, Questions 5 and 16, 1 May 2013, https://www.enforcementdirectorate.gov.in/faqs_on_pmla.pdf.
245. The Prevention of Money-laundering (Amendment) Act, 2009, PRS Legislative Research, 6 March 2009, https://prsindia.org/files/bills_acts/acts_parliament/2009/the-prevention-of-money-laundering-(amendment)-act,-2009.pdf.
246. The Prevention of Money-laundering (Amendment) Act, 2012, Department of Revenue, Ministry of Finance, Government of India, 3 January 2013, https://dor.gov.in/sites/default/files/PML%20%28Amendment%29%20Act%2C%202012.pdf.
247. See Part VI, Sections 145–152 under the Finance Act, 2015, Legislative Department, Ministry of Law and Justice, Government of India, 14 May 2015, https://dor.gov.in/sites/default/files/Amendments%20to%20the%20Prevention%20of%20Money-Laundering%20Act%20vide%20Finance%20Act%202015_0.pdf.
248. See Part IX, Section 232 under The Finance Act, 2016, Legislative Department, Ministry of Law and Justice, The Gazette of India, Government of India, 14 May 2016, https://dor.gov.in/sites/default/files/Amendments%20to%20the%20Prevention%20of%20Money-Laundering%20Act%20vide%20Finance%20Act%202016_0.pdf.
249. The Prevention of Corruption (Amendment) Act, 2018, Legislative Department, Ministry of Law and Justice, The Gazette of India, Government of India, 26 July 2018, https://www.egazette.nic.in/writereaddata/2018/187644.pdf.

250. M.S. Krishna Kumar, 'Amendments to PMLA by Finance Act 2019 – Widening the Scope of the Legislation', Bar and Bench, 21 August 2019, https://www.barandbench.com/columns/amendments-to-pmla-by-finance-act-2019-widening-the-scope-of-the-legislation.
251. 'Cases under Prevention of Money-Laundering Act (PMLA), 2002', Unstarred Question No. 1665, Rajya Sabha Parliament Question-Answer Publishing System, 13 December 2019, https://pqars.nic.in/annex/250/AU1665.pdf.
252. Maneet Pal Singh, 'Are ED's Powers under FEMA, PMLA Arbitrary?', 21 August 2020, http://www.lawstreetindia.com/experts/column?sid=456
253. Securitisation and Reconstruction of Financial Assets and Enforcement of Security Interest Act, 2002, Ministry of Law and Justice, Government of India, https://legislative.gov.in/sites/default/files/A2002-54.pdf.
254. Notification, Ministry of Finance and Company Affairs (Department of Economic Affairs): Banking Division, The Gazette of India, 28 January 2003, https://financialservices.gov.in/sites/default/files/NOTIFICATION_CO-OPERATIVE_BANKS_28_1_2003E_86_2011_sw.pdf.
255. 'Table 64: Gross and Net NPAs of Scheduled Commercial Banks: Bank Group-Wise', *Handbook of Statistics on the Indian Economy: 2019–20*, Reserve Bank of India, p. 120, https://rbidocs.rbi.org.in/rdocs/Publications/PDFs/64T_HB150909.pdf.
256. Table 58: Gross and Net NPAs of Scheduled Commercial Banks: Bank Group-Wise, *Handbook of Statistics on the Indian Economy: 2009–10*, Reserve Bank of India, p. 109, https://rbidocs.rbi.org.in/rdocs/Publications/PDFs/0HBS202024D4CA0CC03F4674B040F7DEDE7E5360.PDF.
257. Ibid.
258. Shruti J. Pandey, Vishakha G. Tilak and Bipin Deokar, 'Non-Performing Assets of Indian Banks: Phases and Dimensions', *Economic and Political Weekly* 48, No. 24 (2013), pp. 91–93, https://www.jstor.org/stable/23527401.
259. 'Banking Sector in India—Issues, Challenges and the Way Forward Including Non-Performing Assets/Stressed Assets In Banks/Financial Institutions', Standing Committee on Finance (2017-2018), Ministry of Finance (Department of Financial Services), Lok Sabha Secretariat, August 2018, Para 14.10.3.: 'Written submission furnished by Indian Overseas Bank Enforcement of securities under SARFAESI Act', http://164.100.47.193/lsscommittee/Finance/16_Finance_68.pdf: 'It has become a practice on the part of the borrower to file application on the day of auction under SARFAESI to stay the auction/sale. These applications are being entertained and arguments are heard by the PO but the orders are not passed on the same day. This indirectly results into stay of the sale proceedings. Entire exercise of

the bank to put the properties on sale becomes futile since potential buyers are not interested in bidding for the properties due to pending litigation.'

260. Report of the Financial Sector Legislative Reforms Commission, Volume I: Analysis and Recommendations, Ministry of Finance, Government of India, March 2013, p. 187.
261. 'The Statement on Industrial Policy, July 24, 1991', Ministry of Industry, Government of India, Part 3, Paras 35–38, https://dpiit.gov.in/sites/default/files/IndustrialPolicyStatement_1991_15July2019.pdf.
262. Notably the 1984 amendment on false advertising and the 1991 amendment that expanded its scope to public sector enterprises.
263. It stated: 'The present MRTP Act is limited in its sweep and hence fails to fulfil the need of a competition law in an age of growing liberalization and globalization.'
264. The Competition Act, 2003, Competition Commission of India, Government of India, 13 January 2003, https://www.cci.gov.in/sites/default/files/cci_pdf/competitionact2012.pdf.
265. Brahm Dutt versus Union of India, Supreme Court, 20 January 2005, https://main.sci.gov.in/judgment/judis/26740.pdf.
266. Ibid., Para 6.
267. The Competition (Amendment) Act, 2007, Legislative Department, Ministry of Law and Justice, The Gazette of India: Extraordinary, Government of India, 24 September 2007, https://www.mca.gov.in/Ministry/actsbills/pdf/Competition_Amendment_Act_2007.pdf.
268. Notification S.Q. 1240 (E), Ministry of Corporate Affairs, The Gazette of India: Extraordinary, Government of India, 15 May 2009, https://www.cci.gov.in/sites/default/files/notification/cf_7.pdf.
269. Annual Report 2019–20, Competition Commission of India, p. xiii, https://www.cci.gov.in/sites/default/files/annual%20reports/ARENG2019-20.pdf.
270. The Finance Act, 2017, Section 171, 26 May 2017, amended the Competition Act, 2002, Chapter VIIIA, https://nclat.nic.in/Useradmin/upload/2204247425ae16b0ce8331.pdf.
271. 'Report of Competition Law Review Committee', Ministry of Corporate Affairs, Government of India, July 2019, https://www.ies.gov.in/pdfs/Report-Competition-CLRC.pdf.
272. 'Report of the Competition Law Review Committee submitted to Union Finance and Corporate Affairs Minister; Key recommendations include introduction of a "Green Channel" for combination notifications to enable fast-paced regulatory approvals of mergers and acquisitions', Ministry of Corporate Affairs, Press Information Bureau, 14 August 2019, https://pib.gov.in/PressReleasePage.aspx?PRID=1581956.

273. Karan Chandhiok and Deeksha Manchanda, 'A look at the Draft (Competition) Amendment Bill, 2020—Clarity, transparency, robustness, and bit more to be desired', Bar and Bench, 1 March 2020, https://www.barandbench.com/columns/a-look-at-the-draft-competition-amendment-bill-2020-clarity-transparency-robustness-and-bit-more-to-be-desired.
274. Deb Kusum Das, 'Trade Policy and Manufacturing Performance: Exploring the Level of Trade Openness in India's Organized Manufacturing in the Period 1990–2010', Development Research Group, Reserve Bank of India, 29 January 2016, https://rbidocs.rbi.org.in/rdocs/Publications/PDFs/41DRG33B9D69D7B6941B1A81ADEC2E172C71D.PDF.
275. 'Budget Speech of Shri Manmohan Singh, Minister of Finance', Ministry of Finance, Government of India, 24 July 1991, Para 107.
276. Arvind Virmani, 'Towards a Competitive Economy: VAT & Customs Duty Reform,' Planning Commission, March 2002, https://niti.gov.in/planningcommission.gov.in/docs/reports/wrkpapers/wp_vat.pdf: The 'peak' tariff rate also refers to the same 'basic' customs tariffs and is the highest general rate applying to a large majority of imports. Selected commodities (e.g. alcohol) have a 'basic' rate higher than the 'peak' rate. We define the 'maximum' rate as the highest rate including the goods with tariffs exceeding the 'peak' rate.'
277. Ibid., Deb Kusum Das.
278. 'Union Finance Minister says Every Possible Measure shall be taken to smoothen the GST; Custom duty structure to be overhauled, over 400 old exemptions to be reviewed; Customs duty hiked proposed on some mobile parts, auto parts and cotton; Phased manufacturing plan for Solar Cells/Panels to be notified; AIDC Cess proposed in the Union Budget to improve Agricultural Infrastructure; Taxation changes proposed to benefit MSMEs', Ministry of Finance, Press Information Bureau, Government of India, 1 February 2021, https://pib.gov.in/PressReleasePage.aspx?PRID=1693879.
279. 'Explanatory Memoranda to Notification Nos. 02/2021—Customs to 15/2021—Customs, dated 1st February 2021', Union Budget 2021–22, Ministry of Finance, Government of India, https://www.indiabudget.gov.in/doc/cen/explanatorynote.pdf.
280. The Project OASIS Report (Old Age Social and Income Security Project), Pension Fund Regulatory and Development Authority, 11 January 2000, https://www.pfrda.org.in/writereaddata/links/rep2d5d02004-a7c9-4875-be6e-f8b92744e210.pdf.
281. 'Resolution', Department of Economic Affairs, Ministry of Finance, The Gazette of India, Government of India, 10 October 2003, https://www.pfrda.org.in/myauth/admin/showimg.cshtml?ID=524.

282. 'Resolution', Department of Financial Services, Ministry of Finance, The Gazette of India: Extraordinary, Government of India, 14 November 2008, https://www.pfrda.org.in/myauth/admin/showimg.cshtml?ID=354.
283. The Pension Fund Regulatory and Development Authority Act, 2013, Legislative Department, Ministry of Law and Justice, The Gazette of India: Extraordinary, Government of India, 18 September 2013, https://www.pfrda.org.in/myauth/admin/showimg.cshtml?ID=353.
284. Notification, Department of Financial Services, Ministry of Finance, The Gazette of India: Extraordinary, Government of India, 1 February 2014, https://www.pfrda.org.in/myauth/admin/showimg.cshtml?ID=422.
285. 'List of State Governments Who have joined NPS', National Pension System Trust, Undated, http://www.npstrust.org.in/nps-state-governments.
286. 'Assets Under Management & No. of Subscribers', National Pension System Trust, Undated, http://www.npstrust.org.in/assets-under-management-and-subsribers.
287. 'Industrial Policy Resolution, New Delhi, the 30th April, 1956', The Gazette of India: Extraordinary, Part I—Section I, Cabinet Secretariat, Government of India, 30 April 1956, Para 8, p. 140, Para 8, https://ia800807.us.archive.org/24/items/in.gazette.e.1956.491/E-2182-1956-0039-99550.pdf.
288. 'Railways Sign Agreement for Adipur–Mundra Port line', Ministry of Railways, Press Information Bureau, Government of India, 6 November 2002, https://archive.pib.gov.in/archive/releases98/lyr2002/rnov2002/16112002/r161120024.html.
289. 'Notification', Railway Board, Ministry of Railways, The Gazette of India, Government of India, 26 September 2006, https://indianrailways.gov.in/railwayboard/uploads/directorate/traffic_tran/downloads/gazzette-TT.pdf.
290. 'Recommendations of Bibek Debroy Committee', Ministry of Railways, Press Information Bureau, Government of India, 11 March 2020, https://pib.gov.in/PressReleseDetailm.aspx?PRID=1606002.
291. 'Private Freight Terminal (PFT)', Railway Board, Ministry of Railways, Government of India, 31 March 2010, https://indianrailways.gov.in/railwayboard/uploads/directorate/traffic_comm/FREIGHT-MKTG-2K10/FM_14_10.pdf.
292. 'Master Circular on Private Freight Terminal (PFT) Scheme', Ministry of Railways, Press Information Bureau, Government of India, 23 June 2020, https://indianrailways.gov.in/railwayboard/uploads/directorate/traffic_comm/Freight_Marketing_2020/PFT%20Master%20Circular.pdf
293. 'Railways' Own Your Wagon Scheme', Press Information Bureau, Government of India, 22 May 1996, https://archive.pib.gov.in/archive/ArchiveSecondPhase/TOURISM%20&%20CIVIL%20AVIATION/1996-

JAN%20DEC%20MIN%20OF%20TOURISM%20CIVIL%20AVITION/TOU-1996-05-22_003.pdf.

294. 'Ro-Ro Freight Service in Indian Railways', Ministry of Railways, Press Information Bureau, Government of India, 24 March 2017, https://pib.gov.in/newsite/PrintRelease.aspx?relid=159898.
295. 'PIB's Bulletin on COVID-19', Ministry of Railways, Press Information Bureau, Government of India, 19 June 2021, https://www.pib.gov.in/PressReleseDetailm.aspx?PRID=1728604.
296. '151 Trains proposed to be run by Private operators once the selection process is over, would be OVER and ABOVE the already existing trains', Ministry of Railways, Press Information Bureau, Government of India, 8 July 2020, https://pib.gov.in/Pressreleaseshare.aspx?PRID=1637428.
297. 'Shri Piyush Goyal reviews the progress of Redevelopment of Railway Stations. Progress of upcoming Gandhinagar and Habibganj Railway Stations reviewed. Redevelopment of railway stations across India is a priority agenda of Ministry of Railways—Shri Goyal. Work on redevelopment of 123 stations is in progress', Ministry of Railways, Press Information Bureau, Government of India, 17 March 2021, https://pib.gov.in/PressReleseDetailm.aspx?PRID=1705568.
298. The excess of Government's revenue expenditure over revenue receipts constitutes revenue deficit of Government: 'Key to the Budget Documents: 2021–2022', Budget Division, Ministry of Finance, Government of India, Section H(i), https://www.indiabudget.gov.in/doc/Key_to_Budget_Document_2021.pdf.
299. The difference between the total expenditure of Government by way of revenue, capital and loans net of repayments on the one hand and revenue receipts of Government and capital receipts which are not in the nature of borrowing but which accrue to Government on the other, constitutes gross fiscal deficit: Ibid.
300. *Handbook of Statistics on Indian Economy 2019–20*, Reserve Bank of India, 18 September 2020, https://rbidocs.rbi.org.in/rdocs/Publications/PDFs/0HBS202024D4CA0CC03F4674B040F7DEDE7E5360.PDF.
301. The Fiscal Responsibility and Budget Management Act, 2003, Legislative Department, Ministry of Law and Justice, Government of India, 26 August 2003, https://legislative.gov.in/sites/default/files/A2003-39_1.pdf.
302. The Act defines the objectives thusly: 'An Act to provide for the responsibility of the Central Government to ensure inter-generational equity in fiscal management and long-term macro-economic stability by removing fiscal impediments in the effective conduct of monetary policy and prudential debt management consistent with fiscal sustainability through limits on the

Central Government borrowings, debt and deficits, greater transparency in fiscal operations of the Central Government and conducting fiscal policy in a medium-term framework and for matters connected therewith or incidental thereto.'

303. Economic Survey 2000–2001, Ministry of Finance, Government of India, pp. 48–49, https://www.indiabudget.gov.in/budget_archive/es2000-01/chap26.pdf.
304. Notification No. G.S.R. 395(E), The Gazette of India: Extraordinary, Part II, Section 3(i), Government of India, 5 July 2004.
305. Reserve Bank of India Annual Report: 2011–12, Reserve Bank of India, 23 August 2012, p. 189, https://rbidocs.rbi.org.in/rdocs/AnnualReport/PDFs/01ANR230812FL.pdf.
306. 'Speech by Vice-President Valdis Dombrovskis: 'The Transatlantic Economy Ten Years After the Crisis: Macro-Financial Scenarios and Policy Responses', European Commission, 23 April 2018, https://ec.europa.eu/commission/presscorner/detail/en/SPEECH_18_3510.
307. 'Thirteenth Finance Commission 2010–2015, Volume I: Report', Finance Commission of India, https://fincomindia.nic.in/writereaddata/html_en_files/oldcommission_html/fincom13/tfc/13fcreng.pdf.
308. 'FRBM Review Committee Report Volume – I, Responsible Growth: A Debt and Fiscal Framework for 21st Century India', FRBM Review Committee, January 2017, p. 72, https://dea.gov.in/sites/default/files/Volume%201%20FRBM%20Review%20Committee%20Report.pdf.
309. Gautam Chikermane, 'Response of the Indian state to Covid-19: All in', Observer Research Foundation, 28 March 2020, https://www.orfonline.org/expert-speak/response-of-the-indian-state-to-covid-19-63770/.
310. 'Policy responses to COVID-19: Policy Tracker', International Monetary Fund, Undated, https://www.imf.org/en/Topics/imf-and-covid19/Policy-Responses-to-COVID-19.
311. Cigdem Akin, Bruno Carrasco, Sudipto Mundle and Abhijit Sen Gupta, 'Fiscal Responsibility and Budget Management Act in India: A Review and Recommendations for Reform', ADB South Asia Working Paper Series, Asian Development Bank, No. 52 | July 2017, Para 117, https://www.adb.org/sites/default/files/publication/337306/swp-52.pdf.
312. 'India: Building Capacities for Public Private Partnerships', Energy and Infrastructure Unit and Finance and Private Sector Development Unit, South Asia Region, The World Bank Group, June 2006, p. 13, https://openknowledge.worldbank.org/bitstream/handle/10986/19446/368750IN0white1Partnership01PUBLIC1.pdf?sequence=1&isAllowed=y.

313. It is impossible to give a synopsis of definitions. Not only do the definitions of PPP vary across countries or multilateral institutions, they diverge across departments, organizations and universities. I believe a paper on simply defining the term and the sectors to which it applies is waiting to be written.
314. Facilitating Public–Private Partnership for Accelerated Infrastructure Development in India. Department of Economic Affairs, Ministry of Finance, Government of India, and Asian Development Bank, 2006, p. 15, https://www.adb.org/sites/default/files/project-document/66596/39659-ind-tacr.pdf: 'Public Private Partnership (PPP) Project means a project based on a contract or concession agreement, between a Government or statutory entity on the one side and a private sector company on the other side, for delivering an infrastructure service on payment of user charges. Private Sector Company means a company in which 51% or more of the subscribed and paid up equity is owned and controlled by a private entity.'
315. L. Lakshmanan, 'Public–Private Partnership in Indian Infrastructure Development: Issues and Options', *Reserve Bank of India Occasional Papers* 29, No. 1 (2008), p. 48, https://rbidocs.rbi.org.in/rdocs/Content/PDFs/ppp1.pdf.
316. 'The Infrastructure Report: Policy Imperatives for Growth and Welfare', Expert Group on the Commercialization of Infrastructure Projects, Ministry of Finance, Government of India, DIANE Publishing Company, 1998, p. 4.
317. 'The Report of the Committee on Infrastructure Financing', May 2007, Department of Economic Affairs (Infrastructure Division), Ministry of Finance, p. 3, https://icisa.cag.gov.in/resource_files/720dc44c3026a156dc886c1d3eaa0229.pdf.
318. 'Procedure for Approval of Public Private Partnership Projects – setting up of Public Private Partnership Approval Committee', Department of Economic Affairs, Ministry of Finance, Government of India, 29 November 2005, https://www.pppinindia.gov.in/documents/20181/45106/1.+Notifiation+29th+Nov%2C+2005.pdf/b16df4ed-6887-44dd-8fb8-5091863b8b5b.
319. 'Procedure for approval of Public Private Partnership projects', Department of Economic Affairs, Ministry of Finance, Government of India, 12 January 2006, https://www.pppinindia.gov.in/documents/20181/45106/6.+Procedure+for+approval+of+PPP+%28notification+dated+Jan+12%2C+2006%29.pdf/3ee22646-ca94-478f-9cae-695a3479d83c.
320. 'Projects recommended by the Public Private Partnership Appraisal Committee (PPPAC)', Public Private Partnerships in India, Department of Economic Affairs, Ministry of Finance, Government of India, 10 August 2021, https://www.pppinindia.gov.in/projects-summary?p_p_

id=projectsummarydisplay_WAR_PPPININDIAProjectportlet_INSTANCE_PXBY5cotkTHJ&p_p_lifecycle=0&p_p_state=normal&p_p_mode=view&p_p_col_id=column-1&p_p_col_count=2&_projectsummarydisplay_WAR_PPPININDIAProjectportlet_INSTANCE_PXBY5cotkTHJ_jspPage=%2Fhtml%2Fprojectsummarydisplay%2Fview.jsp&_projectsummarydisplay_WAR_PPPININDIAProjectportlet_INSTANCE_PXBY5cotkTHJ_curTabs=Overall+summary.

321. Ibid., 'Sector wise summary'.
322. 'English rendering of PM's reply to the Motion of Thanks on the President's address in Lok of Sabha', Prime Minister's Office, Press Information Bureau, Government of India, 10 February 2021, https://pib.gov.in/PressReleseDetail.aspx?PRID=1696958.
323. 'The Prime Minister Shri Narendra Modi addressed the Nation from the ramparts of the Red Fort on the 74th Independence Day; Following are the highlights from his Speech', Prime Minister's Office, Press Information Bureau, Government of India, 15 August 2020, https://pib.gov.in/PressReleseDetail.aspx?PRID=1646044.
324. 'National Infrastructure Pipeline Report of the Task Force', Department of Economic Affairs, Ministry of Finance, Government of India, Volume I, p. 36, https://www.pppinindia.gov.in/documents/20181/55954/Report+of+the+Task+Force+National+Infrastructure+Pipeline+%28NIP%29+-+volume-i_0.pdf/5f0c7cd5-3409-4267-8010-01ac5c2ab98e.
325. Sandeep G. Kudtarkar, 'Resetting PPP in Infrastructure Model in India Post-COVID-19 Pandemic', *The Indian Economic Journal* (2020), https://journals.sagepub.com/doi/pdf/10.1177/0019466220976678.
326. 'Air transport, passengers carried—India', World Bank Open Data, The World Bank, Undated, https://data.worldbank.org/indicator/IS.AIR.PSGR?locations=IN&most_recent_value_desc=true.
327. Ibid.
328. 'Report of the Committee on a Road Map for the Civil Aviation Sector', Ministry of Civil Aviation, Government of India, 30 November 2003, pp. 1 and 3, https://www.civilaviation.gov.in/sites/default/files/moca_000740.pdf.
329. 'The Airports Authority of India (Amendment) Act, 2003', Legal Information Institute of India, 7 September 2003, http://www.liiofindia.org/in/legis/cen/num_act/aaoia2003388/.
330. Gautam Chikermane, *70 Policies that Shaped India: 1947 to 2017, Independence to $2.5 Trillion*, Observer Research Foundation (2018), pp. 121–122, https://www.orfonline.org/wp-content/uploads/2018/07/70_Policies.pdf.

331. 'Cabinet approves leasing out six airports—Ahmedabad, Jaipur, Lucknow, Guwahati, Thiruvananthapuram and Mangaluru through PPP', Cabinet, Press Information Bureau, Government of India, 8 November 2018, https://pib.gov.in/Pressreleaseshare.aspx?PRID=1552165.
332. 'The Airports Economic Regulatory Authority of India Act, 2008', 5 December 2008, http://aera.gov.in/aera/upload/uploadfiles/files//AERAACT.pdf.
333. 'National Civil Aviation Policy, 2016', https://www.civilaviation.gov.in/sites/default/files/Final_NCAP_2016_15-06-2016-2_1.pdf.
334. 'Ude Desh Ka Aam Naagrik : Civil Aviation Ministry's Regional Connectivity Scheme "UDAN" Launched Today', Ministry of Civil Aviation, Government of India, Press Information Bureau, 21 October 2016, https://pib.gov.in/newsite/PrintRelease.aspx?relid=151850.
335. Smita Kashiramka, Radhika Banerjee, Anand Kumar and P.K. Jain, 'Efficiency Analysis of Airports in India in a Changing Environment', *Journal of Transport Economics and Policy* 50, No. 4 (2016), pp. 384–403, https://www.jstor.org/stable/10.2307/jtranseconpoli.50.4.384.
336. 'Trade Agreements', Department of Commerce, Ministry of Trade and Industry, Government of India, Undated, https://commerce.gov.in/international-trade/trade-agreements/.
337. 'Free Trade Agreement Between the Republic of India and the Democratic Socialist Republic of Sri Lanka', Department of Commerce, Ministry of Trade and Industry, Government of India, 28 December 1998, https://commerce.gov.in/international-trade/trade-agreements/india-sri-lanka-fta/free-trade-agreement-between-the-republic-of-india-and-the-democratic-socialist-republic-of-sri-lanka/.
338. 'Comprehensive Economic Cooperation and Partnership Agreement (CECPA) between the Republic of India and the Republic of Mauritius', Department of Commerce, Ministry of Trade and Industry, Government of India, 22 February 2021, https://commerce.gov.in/wp-content/uploads/2021/08/India-Mauritius-CECPA-Text-for-Upload.pdf.
339. 'Prime Minister witnesses signing of the India–Australia Economic Cooperation and Trade Agreement—"IndAus ECTA"', Ministry of External Affairs, 2 April 2022, https://www.mea.gov.in/virtual- meetings-detail.htm?35140/Prime+Minister+witnesses+signing+of+the+India Australia+Economic+Cooperation+and+Trade+Agreement IndAus+ECTA.
340. World Bank Data.
341. Dr V.K. Saraswat, Prachi Priya and Aniruddha Ghosh, 'A Note on Free Trade Agreements and Their Costs', NITI Aayog, https://www.niti.gov.in/writereaddata/files/document_publication/FTA-NITI-FINAL.pdf.

342. For a cultural-economic deep dive into this subject, read Amrita Narlikar and Aruna Narlikar, *Bargaining with a Rising India: Lessons from the Mahabharata*, Oxford University Press (2014).
343. Hardeep Singh Puri, 'India's Trade Policy Dilemma and the Role of Domestic Reform', Carnegie Endowment, 2017, https://carnegieendowment.org/files/CP_298_Puri_Trade_A5_Web.pdf.
344. Arvind Panagariya, 'India's Trade Reform', in *Indian Policy Forum 2004 – Volume 1,* eds. Suman Bery, Barry P. Bosworth and Arvind Panagariya (Brookings Institution, 2004), https://www.brookings.edu/wp-content/uploads/2016/07/2004_panagariya.pdf.
345. 'Figures on Regional Trade Agreements notified to the GATT/WTO and in force', Regional Trade Agreements Database, World Trade Organization, http://rtais.wto.org/UI/publicsummarytable.aspx.
346. 'Regional trade agreements notified to the GATT/WTO and in force: By country/territory', Regional Trade Agreements Database, World Trade Organization, http://rtais.wto.org/UI/publicPreDefRepByCountry.aspx.
347. 'Bay of Bengal Initiative on Multi-Sectoral Technical and Economic Cooperation (BIMSTEC)', Regional Trade Agreements Database, World Trade Organization, http://rtais.wto.org/UI/PublicShowMemberRTAIDCard.aspx?rtaid=373.
348. 'EFTA—India', Regional Trade Agreements Database, World Trade Organization, http://rtais.wto.org/UI/PublicShowMemberRTAIDCard.aspx?rtaid=598.
349. 'EU—India', Regional Trade Agreements Database, World Trade Organization, http://rtais.wto.org/UI/PublicShowMemberRTAIDCard.aspx?rtaid=158.
350. 'India—SACU', Regional Trade Agreements Database, World Trade Organization, http://rtais.wto.org/UI/PublicShowMemberRTAIDCard.aspx?rtaid=718.
351. The Mahatma Gandhi National Rural Employment Guarantee Act, 2005, Ministry of Rural Development, Government of India, 5 September 2005, https://nrega.nic.in/amendments_2005_2018.pdf.
352. Sanjeet Singh, 'Evaluation of world's largest social welfare scheme: An assessment using non-parametric approach', *Evaluation and Program Planning* 57 (2016), pp. 16–29, https://pubmed.ncbi.nlm.nih.gov/27153391/.
353. Suresh Babu, C. Dheeraja, G. Rajani Kanth and S.V. Rangacharyulu, 'Frequently Asked Questions (FAQs) on MNREGA Operational Guidelines – 2003', Centre for Wage Employment and Poverty Alleviation, Ministry of Rural Development, Government of India, June 2014, Question 8, https://nrega.nic.in/Circular_Archive/archive/nrega_doc_FAQs.pdf.

354. Keshap C. Sen, 'Le développement rural en Inde/Rural development in India', *Civilisations*, Vol. 13, No. 4 (1963), pp. 411–428, Institut de Sociologie de l'Université de Bruxelles, https://www.jstor.org/stable/41230767.
355. Chapter 11: Rural Development and Cooperation, 6th Five Year Plan, Planning Commission, NITI Aayog, 18 January 1981, Para 11.7, https://niti.gov.in/planningcommission.gov.in/docs/plans/planrel/fiveyr/6th/6planch11.html.
356. Rudra Prasad Roy, 'NREGA: Opportunity and Challenges', *IOSR Journal of Humanities and Social Science* Volume 19, Issue 10, Ver. II (October 2014), pp. 26–30, http://www.iosrjournals.org/iosr-jhss/papers/Vol19-issue10/Version-2/F0191022630.pdf.
357. Ibid.
358. Jawahar Rozgar Yojana, Ministry of Rural Development, Press Information Bureau, Government of India, 18 January 1993, https://archive.pib.gov.in/archive/ArchiveSecondPhase/WORK%20AND%20HOUSING/1993-JAN-DEC-MIN-OF-DEVELOPMENT/WOR-1993-01-19_005.pdf.
359. 'Prime Minister Launches National Rural Health Mission: Calls for a Monitoring System to Support Accountability at Community Level', Ministry of Health and Family Welfare, Press Information Bureau, Government of India, 12 April 2005, https://archive.pib.gov.in/newsite/PrintRelease.aspx?relid=8545.
360. Ibid.
361. Ibid. These included: Uttar Pradesh, Uttaranchal, Madhya Pradesh, Chhattisgarh, Bihar, Jharkhand, Orissa, Rajasthan, Himachal Pradesh, Jammu and Kashmir, Assam, Arunachal Pradesh, Manipur, Meghalaya, Nagaland, Mizoram, Sikkim, and Tripura.
362. Ibid.
363. Nachiket Mor, Diva Dhar and Sandhya Venkeswaran, 'Healthcare in India: A Fork in the Road', in *India Transformed: 25 Years of Economic Reforms*, ed. Rakesh Mohan (Penguin, 2017).
364. 'Mother and Child Tracking System', Ministry of Health and Family Welfare, Press Information Bureau, Government of India, 10 December 2013, http://pibmumbai.gov.in/scripts/detail.asp?releaseId=E2013PR2187.
365. 'National Health Mission', National Health Mission, Ministry of Health and Family Welfare, Government of India, http://nhm.gov.in/images/pdf/NHM/NHM_more_information.pdf.
366. 'Mortality rate, infant (per 1,000 live births)', World Bank Data, World Bank. For India, see: https://data.worldbank.org/indicator/SP.DYN.IMRT.IN?locations=IN. For the world average, see: https://data.worldbank.org/indicator/SP.DYN.IMRT.IN.

367. 'Cabinet apprised on progress under National Health Mission (NHM) 2019–20', Cabinet, Press Information Bureau, Government of India, 23 March 2021, https://pib.gov.in/PressReleasePage.aspx?PRID=1706902.
368. 'The Constitution (Seventy-fourth Amendment) Act, 1992', Legislative Department, Ministry of Law and Justice, 20 April 1993, https://legislative.gov.in/constitution-seventy-fourth-amendment-act-1992.
369. 'PM launches Jawaharlal Nehru National Urban Renewal Mission', Ministry of Housing and Urban Affairs, Government of India, 3 December 2005, http://mohua.gov.in/upload/uploadfiles/files/3Launch%20of%20Mission%20Speech%20of%20Honble%20PM%20English(1).pdf.
370. 'Jawaharlal Nehru National Urban Renewal Mission', Ministry of Housing and Urban Affairs, Government of India, Undated, http://mohua.gov.in/cms/jawaharlal-nehru-national-urban-renewal-mission.php.
371. 'Jawaharlal Nehru National Urban Renewal Mission: Overview', Ministry of Urban Employment and Poverty Alleviation, and Ministry of Urban Development, Government of India, Undated, p. 5, http://mohua.gov.in/upload/uploadfiles/files/1Mission%20Overview%20English(1).pdf.
372. Ibid. For UIF: 'This will be administered by the Ministry of Urban Development through the Sub-Mission Directorate for Urban Infrastructure and Governance. The main thrust of the Sub-Mission will be on infrastructure projects relating to water supply and sanitation, sewerage, solid waste management, road network, urban transport and redevelopment of old city areas with a view to upgrading infrastructure therein, shifting industrial and commercial establishments to conforming areas, etc.' For BSUP: 'This will be administered by the Ministry of Urban Employment and Poverty Alleviation through the Sub-Mission Directorate for Basic Services to the Urban Poor. The main thrust of the Sub-Mission will be on integrated development of slums through projects for providing shelter, basic services and other related civic amenities with a view to providing utilities to the urban poor.'
373. Annexure—I, 'List of Identified Cities/Urban Agglomerations (UAs) under Sub-Mission on Basic Services to the Urban Poor(BSUP)', Annual Report 2005–2006, Ministry of Urban Employment & Poverty Alleviation, Government of India, pp. 22–23, http://mohua.gov.in/upload/uploadfiles/files/12AR2005_06.pdf.
374. 'JNNURM: State wise Progress', Ministry of Urban Employment and Poverty Alleviation, Government of India, 8 February 2021, http://mohua.gov.in/upload/uploadfiles/files/17(5).pdf.
375. 'Report of the Comptroller and Auditor General of India on Performance Audit of Jawaharlal Nehru National Urban Renewal Mission', 4 September 2012, p. 5, https://cag.gov.in/uploads/download_audit_report/2012/

Union_Performance_Commercial_Jawaharlal_Renewal_Mission_Ministry_Housing_and_Urban_poverty_15_2012_Exe_Summ.pdf.

376. Reuben Abraham, 'Ubanization: India Finally Lives in Livable Cities', in *India 2030: The Rise of a Rajasic Nation,* ed. Gautam Chikermane (Penguin, 2021), pp. 150–162.
377. 'Identification of Benami Properties', Ministry of Finance, Press Information Bureau, Government of India, 2 July 2019, https://pib.gov.in/PressReleasePage.aspx?PRID=1576787.
378. 'The Benami Transactions (Prohibition) Amendment Act, 2016', The Gazette of India, Ministry of Law and Justice, Government of India, PRS Legislative, 11 August 2016, https://prsindia.org/files/bills_acts/acts_parliament/2016/the-benami-transactions-(prohibition)-amendment-act,-2016.pdf.
379. 'The Prohibition of Benami Property Transactions Act, 1988', Legislative Department, Ministry of Law and Justice, Government of India, https://legislative.gov.in/sites/default/files/A1988-45_1.pdf.
380. 'The Benami Transactions Prohibition (Amendment) Bill, 2015', Standing Committee on Finance (2015–16), Sixteenth Lok Sabha, Ministry of Finance (Department of Revenue), Twenty-Eighth Report, Lok Sabha Secretariat, 18 April 2016, http://164.100.47.193/lsscommittee/Finance/16_Finance_28.pdf.
381. 'Fifty-seventh Report: Benami Transactions', Law Commission of India, Ministry of Law, Justice and Company Affairs, Government of India, 7 August 1973, https://lawcommissionofindia.nic.in/51-100/report57.pdf.
382. 'Benami Transactions Informants Reward Scheme, 2018', Central Board of Direct Taxes, Department of Revenue, Ministry of Finance, Government of India, 23 April 2018, https://www.incometaxindia.gov.in/Documents/Feedback/Letter-Benami-Informants-Rewards-Scheme-1-5-18.pdf.
383. These were: Central Excise Duty; Duties of Excise (Medicinal and Toilet Preparations); Additional Duties of Excise (Goods of Special Importance); Additional Duties of Excise (Textiles and Textile Products); Additional Duties of Customs (commonly known as CVD); Special Additional Duty of Customs (SAD); Service Tax; Cesses and surcharges insofar as they relate to supply of goods or services.
384. These are: State VAT; Central Sales Tax; Purchase Tax; Luxury Tax; Entry Tax (All forms); Entertainment Tax (except those levied by the local bodies); Taxes on advertisements; Taxes on lotteries, betting and gambling; State cesses and surcharges insofar as they relate to supply of goods or services.
385. Speech of Shri Vishwanath Pratap Singh, Minister of Finance Introducing the Budget for the Year 1986–87, Ministry of Finance, 28 February 1986, Paras 113–119. MODVAT stands for Modified Value Added Tax.

386. Budget 2000–2001: Speech of Shri Yashwant Sinha, Minister of Finance, Ministry of Finance, Government of India, 29 February 2000, Paras 73–93.
387. Ibid., Para 74.
388. Introduction of VAT in the Country, Ministry of Finance, Press Information Bureau, Government of India, 15 March 2005, https://pib.gov.in/newsite/erelcontent.aspx?relid=7781.
389. 'Compensation to the States/UTs, in case of loss of revenue, on account of introduction of Value Added Tax (VAT)—Revised Consolidated Instructions', Department of Revenue, Ministry of Finance, Government of India, 19 July 2005, https://dor.gov.in/sites/default/files/VAT_Compentation_guidelines_dated_19th_July_2005.pdf.
390. 'First Discussion Paper on Goods and Services Tax in India', Empowered Committee of State Finance Ministers, Department of Revenue, Ministry of Finance, Government of India, 10 November 2009, https://dor.gov.in/sites/default/files/EC%27s_First_discussion_paper_on_GST.pdf.
391. The Foreign Contribution (Regulation) Act, 2010, Legislative Department, Ministry of Law and Justice, The Gazette of India: Extraordinary, Government of India, 26 September 2010, https://fcraonline.nic.in/home/PDF_Doc/FC-RegulationAct-2010-C.pdf.
392. The Foreign Contribution (Regulation) Act 1976, Legislative Department, Ministry of Law and Justice, Government of India, 31 March 1976, https://legislative.gov.in/sites/default/files/A1976-49.pdf.
393. Department-Related Parliamentary Standing Committee on Home Affairs on The Foreign Contribution (Regulation) Bill, 2006, October 2008, Rajya Sabha, Parliament of India, Hosted on PRS Legislative, Section 5.3, https://prsindia.org/files/bills_acts/bills_parliament/2006/scr1224826398_The_Foreign_Contribution__Regulation__Bill__2006.pdf. Section 5.3(i): 'The use of negative expression "to prohibit" has the potential to curb the freedom of voluntary sector, which works for the betterment of the poor.'
394. Ibid., Section 5.3(xi): 'One of the conditions for grant of registration stipulates that an organization has not indulged or involved in activities aimed at conversion through inducement or force, either directly or indirectly, from one religious faith to another. These expressions are not defined and if these undefined expressions become cause for rejecting an application for registration, then it will have negative effect.'
395. Ibid., Section 5.3(vii): 'The restriction of fifty per cent on administrative expenditure may not be practical and may have a negative effect on the utilization of funds. Further, administrative expenses cannot be clearly defined.'
396. 'Foreign Funding to NGOs', Ministry of Home Affairs, Press Information Bureau, Government of India, 15 September 2020, https://pib.gov.in/PressReleaseIframePage.aspx?PRID=1654601.

397. 'Human Rights cannot be an excuse for defying the law of the land', Ministry of Home Affairs, Press Information Bureau, Government of India, 29 September 2020, https://pib.gov.in/PressReleaseIframePage.aspx?PRID=1660095.
398. The Foreign Contribution (Regulation) Amendment Act, 2020, Legislative Department, Ministry of Law and Justice, The Gazette of India: Extraordinary, 28 September 2020, https://fcraonline.nic.in/Home/PDF_Doc/fc_amend_07102020_1.pdf.
399. Amendment to Section 8.
400. 'Dashboard', Ministry of Home Affairs, Government of India, https://fcraonline.nic.in/fc_dashboard.aspx.
401. Shruti Chandra, 'Retail & E-commerce', Invest India, Department of Industrial Policy and Promotion, Ministry of Commerce and Industry, Government of India, https://www.investindia.gov.in/sector/retail-e-commerce.
402. Ibid.
403. 'Statement on Industrial Policy', Chapter 1, Para B (iv), Department of Industrial Policy and Promotion, Ministry of Commerce and Industry, Government of India, 24 July 1991, http://dipp.nic.in/sites/default/files/chap001_0_0.pdf.
404. Press Note No. 3, Para 14 (iii), Guidelines for Consideration of Foreign Direct Investment Proposals by Foreign Investment Promotion Board, Department of Industrial Policy and Promotion, Ministry of Commerce and Industry, Government of India, 17 January 1997, http://dipp.nic.in/sites/default/files/chap008_1.pdf.
405. Press Note No. 4 (2012 Series), Department of Industrial Policy and Promotion, Ministry of Commerce and Industry, Government of India, 20 September 2012, http://dipp.nic.in/sites/default/files/pn4_2012_2.pdf.
406. Ibid., Para 6.2.16.4(2)(e).
407. Binoy Prabhakar, 'FDI in retail: Why 30% local rule is 100% trouble for MNCs', *The Economic Times*, 30 September 2012, https://economictimes.indiatimes.com/news/economy/policy/fdi-in-retail-why-30-local-rule-is-100-trouble-for-mncs/articleshow/16605481.cms?from=mdr.
408. Indivjal Dhasmana, 'Ikea application for single brand retail cleared by FIPB', *Business Standard*, 20 November 2012, https://www.business-standard.com/article/economy-policy/ikea-application-for-single-brand-retail-cleared-by-fipb-112112003016_1.html.
409. Press Note No. 5 (2013 Series), Department of Industrial Policy and Promotion, Ministry of Commerce and Industry, Government of India, 5 April 2013, http://dipp.nic.in/sites/default/files/pn5_2013_1.pdf.
410. Ibid., Para 6.2.16.5 (iii).
411. Ibid., Para 6.2.16.5 (iv).

412. Ibid., Para 6.2.16.5 (vi).
413. 'FDI policy further liberalized in key sectors, Cabinet approves amendments in FDI policy', Cabinet, Press Information Bureau, Government of India, 10 January 2018, http://www.pib.nic.in/PressReleseDetail.aspx?PRID=1516115#.
414. 'PM gives a clarion call for Atmanirbhar Bharat; PM announces special economic package; comprehensive package of Rs 20 lakh crore; Total package equivalent to 10% of India's GDP; PM gives a call for self-reliant India; lays down five pillars of Atmanirbhar Bharat; Bold reforms across sectors will drive the country's push towards self-reliance: PM; It is time to become vocal for our local products and make them global: PM', Prime Minister's Office, Press Information Bureau, Government of India, 12 May 2020, https://pib.gov.in/PressReleseDetail.aspx?PRID=1623391.
415. 'Petrol Prices Deregulated; Marginal Increase in HSD, PDS Kerosene and Domestic LPG Prices; Government to bear a large part of Under Recoveries', Ministry of Petroleum and Natural Gas, Press Information Bureau, Government of India, 25 June 2010, https://archive.pib.gov.in/archive2/erelease.aspx.
416. 'Deregulation of Diesel Prices', Ministry of Petroleum and Natural Gas, Press Information Bureau, 18 October 2014, https://archive.pib.gov.in/archive2/erelease.aspx.
417. Mehta articulates it with elegance: 'Petroleum engages multiple stakeholders: the politician who knows what should be done but does not know how to get re-elected thereafter; the government that appreciates the importance of fiscal prudence but does not have the legislative backing to stave off political pressure; the bureaucrat who will espouse the virtues of the free market but is loath to relinquish the power and patronage derived from control over a cash-rich industry; the management of the PSEs which want operational and financial autonomy but dare not ignore the demands of their government bosses; and the consumer who wants reliable, clean and affordable energy but does not object when the government pegs the logic for "bad economics" on its perception that the consumers desire nothing but subsidies and low prices.' Vikram Singh Mehta, 'Political Economy of Petroleum Sector Deregulation', in *India Transformed: Twenty-Five Years of Economic Reforms*, ed. Rakesh Mohan (Penguin), year)http://www.jstor.com/stable/10.7864/j.ctt20d8754.20.
418. Mukesh Kumar Anand, 'Reforming fossil fuel prices in India: Dilemma of a developing economy', *Energy Policy*, Elsevier, 2016, pp. 130–150: 'Empirical estimates show that every 10 per cent increase in global crude prices, if fully passed-through to domestic prices, could have a direct impact of 1 percentage point increase in overall WPI inflation and the total impact could be about 2

percentage points over time as input cost increases translate to higher output prices across sectors.'

419. Ashutosh Varshney, 'India's Democratic Challenge', *Foreign Affairs*, Vol. 86, No. 2 (March–April 2007), pp. 93–106, http://www.jstor.org/stable/20032286: '…economic issues are more likely to arouse mass opposition than others. Inflation, for example, quickly becomes a contentious matter in mass politics because it affects most segments of the population.'
420. PTI, 'India's oil import dependence jumps to 84 per cent', *The Economic Times*, 5 May 2019, https://economictimes.indiatimes.com/industry/energy/oil-gas/indias-oil-import-dependence-jumps-to-84-pc/articleshow/69183923.cms?from=mdr.
421. 'India Energy Outlook 2021', *International Energy Agency*, 2021, p. 11, https://iea.blob.core.windows.net/assets/1de6d91e-e23f-4e02-b1fb-51fdd6283b22/India_Energy_Outlook_2021.pdf.
422. 'India Energy Subsidy: December 2018', International Institute for Sustainable Development, 2018, http://www.jstor.com/stable/resrep22017.
423. Standing Committee on Finance (2009–2010), (Ministry of Corporate Affairs), The Companies Bill, 2009, Twenty-First Report, Lok Sabha Secretariat, August 2010, Para 6, https://www.icsi.edu/media/webmodules/linksofweeks/21_Report_Companies_Bill.pdf.
424. The Companies Act, 2013, Ministry of Corporate Affairs, Government of India, 29 August 2013, https://www.mca.gov.in/Ministry/pdf/CompaniesAct2013.pdf.
425. 'MCA initiates implementation of Companies Act in phased manner', *The Indian Express*, 13 September 2013, http://archive.indianexpress.com/news/mca-initiates-implementation-of-companies-act-in-phased-manner/1168395/.
426. Ibid., Section 135: Every company with a net worth of Rs 500 crore or more, or turnover of Rs 1,000 core or more, or a net profit of Rs 5 crore or more would have to spend at least 2 per cent of its average net profits made during the previous three years on social activities.
427. The Companies (Amendment) Act, 2019, Section 21(7), Legislative Department, Ministry of Law and Justice, The Gazette of India: Extraordinary, Government of India, https://www.mca.gov.in/Ministry/pdf/AMENDMENTACT_01082019.pdf.
428. 'Attracting investment in post-Covid Economy: Challenges and Opportunities for India', Department Related Parliamentary Standing Committee on Commerce, Rajya Sabha Secretariat, Parliament of India, 10 February 2021, Para 13.18, p. 59, https://rajyasabha.nic.in/rsnew/Committee_site/Committee_File/ReportFile/13/141/158_2021_2_13.pdf.

429. Development Challenges in Extremist Affected Areas: Report of an Expert Group to Planning Commission, Government of India, hosted on People's Archive of Rural India, April 2008, Para 1.12.3., https://ruralindiaonline.org/en/library/resource/development-challenges-in-extremist-affected-areas-report-of-an-expert-group-to-planning-commission/. The study cites a paper that says 50 million (not 60 million) people were displaced between 1947 and 2000, and 20 million hectares of land acquired between 1951 and 1995. See: Walter Fernandes, 'Rehabilitation Policy for the Displaced', *Economic and Political Weekly* 39, No. 12 (2004), pp. 1191–1193, https://www.jstor.org/stable/4414785.
430. The Land Acquisition Act, 1894, 2 February 1894, Revenue and Disaster Management Department, Government of Meghalaya, Undated, https://megrevenuedm.gov.in/acts/land-aquisition-act-1894.pdf.
431. These are: The Ancient Monuments and Archaeological Sites and Remains Act, 1958; The Atomic Energy Act, 1962; The Damodar Valley Corporation Act, 1948; The Indian Tramways Act, 1886; The Land Acquisition (Mines) Act, 1885; The Metro Railways (Construction of Works) Act, 1978; The National Highways Act, 1956; The Petroleum and Minerals Pipelines (Acquisition of Right of User in Land) Act, 1962; The Requisitioning and Acquisition of Immovable Property Act, 1952; The Resettlement of Displaced Persons (Land Acquisition) Act, 1948; The Coal Bearing Areas Acquisition and Development Act, 1957; The Electricity Act, 2003; and The Railways Act, 1989.
432. National Policy on Resettlement and Rehabilitation for Project Affected Families, 2003, Department of Land Resources, Ministry of Rural Development, The Gazette of India: Extraordinary, 17 February 2004, Hosted on Indian Railways, https://indianrailways.gov.in/railwayboard/view_section.jsp?lang=0&id=0,1,304,366,540,976.
433. The National Rehabilitation and Resettlement Policy, 2007, Land Reforms Division, Department of Land Revenues, Ministry of Rural Development, Government of India, 31 October 2007, https://dolr.gov.in/sites/default/files/National%20Rehabilitation%20%26%20Resettlement%20Policy%2C%202007.pdf.
434. The Right to Fair Compensation and Transparency in Land Acquisition, Rehabilitation and Resettlement Act, 2013, Legislative Department, Ministry of Law and Justice, Government of India, 26 September 2013, https://legislative.gov.in/sites/default/files/A2013-30.pdf.
435. Ibid., Section 2: These include but are not restricted to strategic purposes, infrastructure building, agricultural projects such as warehousing, industrial corridors, water harvesting, government research institutions, sports, healthcare, housing for certain income groups.

436. Ibid., Section 2(b)(i).
437. Ibid., Section 2(b)(ii).
438. Ibid., The Second Schedule: This lists out elements and entitlements.
439. Ibid., The Second Schedule, Serial No. 4.
440. The Right to Fair Compensation and Transparency in Land Acquisition, Rehabilitation and Resettlement (Amendment) Ordinance, 2015, Ministry of Rural Development, Press Information Bureau, Government of India, 30 May 2015, https://pib.gov.in/newsite/PrintRelease.aspx?relid=122150.
441. 'PM launches Pradhan Mantri Jan Dhan Yojana; End financial untouchability for freedom from poverty; "Vish-chakra se gareebon ki aazadi ka parv"—celebration of liberation of the poor from a poisonous cycle; A record unprecedented in economic history—1.5 crore bank accounts opened in one day', Prime Minister's Office, Press Information Bureau, 28 August 2014, https://pib.gov.in/newsite/PrintRelease.aspx?relid=109147.
442. Ibid.
443. Ibid.
444. CRISIL Inclusix: An index to measure India's progress on Financial Inclusion, CRISIL, June 2013, p. 12, https://www.crisil.com/content/dam/crisil/our-analysis/publications/crisil-inclusix/CRISIL-Inclusix-An-index-to-measure-indias-progress-on-financial-inclusion-vol1-june2013.pdf.
445. 'Financial inclusion surges, driven by Jan-Dhan Yojana', CRISIL Inclusix, Volume 4, CRISIL, February 2018, https://www.crisil.com/content/dam/crisil/our-analysis/reports/Research/documents/2018/march/crisil-inclusix-financial-inclusion-surges-driven-by-Jan-Dhan-yojana.pdf.
446. 'As per RBI Report on Trend and Progress of Banking in India 2017–18, the proportion of persons joining the Formal Financial System in terms of an account at Financial Institutions has more than doubled since 2011 and by 2017, it had reached 80 per cent of the Indian population', Ministry of Finance, Press Information Bureau, Government of India, 12 February 2019, https://pib.gov.in/Pressreleaseshare.aspx?PRID=1564085.
447. Demirguc-Kunt, Asli, Leora Klapper, Dorothe Singer, Saniya Ansar and Jake Hess, 'The Global Findex Database 2017: Measuring Financial Inclusion and the Fintech Revolution', International Bank for Reconstruction and Development/The World Bank, 2018, pp. 123–126, http://www.worldbank.org/globalfindex.
448. 'Finance Minister announces Rs 1.70 Lakh Crore relief package under Pradhan Mantri Garib Kalyan Yojana for the poor to help them fight the battle against Corona Virus', Ministry of Finance, Press Information Bureau, Government of India, 26 March 2020, https://pib.gov.in/PressReleseDetail.aspx?PRID=1608345.

449. 'Robust Digital Payment Infrastructure Enables Prompt Transfer of Cash Payment under Pradhan Mantri Garib Kalyan Package', Ministry of Finance, Press Information Bureau, Government of India, 12 April 2020, https://pib.gov.in/PressReleseDetail.aspx?PRID=1613686.
450. The Indian Arbitration Act, 1899, Thacker, Spink and Co. (1914), http://jkarchives.nic.in/Record_Holdings_PDF/Acc.%20No.%201149.pdf.
451. The Arbitration (Protocol and Convention) Act, 1937, Bombay High Court, 4 March 1937, https://bombayhighcourt.nic.in/libweb/actc/1937.06.pdf.
452. The Arbitration Act, 1940, Legislative Department, Ministry of Law and Justice, Government of India, 11 March 1940, https://legislative.gov.in/sites/default/files/legislative_references/1940.pdf.
453. The Arbitration and Conciliation Act, 1996, Legislative Department, Ministry of Law and Justice, Government of India, 16 August 1996, https://legislative.gov.in/sites/default/files/A1996-26.pdf.
454. UNCITRAL Model Law on International Commercial Arbitration (1985), United Nations, https://www.jus.uio.no/lm/un.arbitration.model.law.1985/portrait.pdf.
455. Law Commission of India: One Hundred and Seventy Sixth Report on the Arbitration and Conciliation (Amendment) Bill, 2001, Law Commission of India, Ministry of Law and Justice, Government of India, 12 September 2001, https://lawcommissionofindia.nic.in/arb.pdf.
456. 'Proposed Amendments to the Arbitration and Conciliation Act, 1996: A Consultation Paper', Ministry of Law and Justice, Government of India, https://districts.ecourts.gov.in/sites/default/files/Arbitration%20act%20amendments%20proposed.pdf.
457. The Arbitration and Conciliation (Amendment) Act, 2003, Ministry of Law and Justice, Government of India, 19 December 2003, http://164.100.47.4/billstexts/rsbilltexts/AsIntroduced/LXXV_2003.pdf
458. Ibid., 'Proposed Amendments', Para 142(a)(ii).
459. Law Commission of India: Report No. 246, 'Amendments to the Arbitration and Conciliation Act 1996', Law Commission of India, Ministry of Law and Justice, Government of India, August 2014, para 21, https://lawcommissionofindia.nic.in/reports/report246.pdf.
460. Ibid., para 23.
461. The Arbitration and Conciliation (Amendment) Act, 2015, Legislative Department, Ministry of Law and Justice, The Gazette of India: Extraordinary, Government of India, 31 December 2015, https://lawmin.gov.in/sites/default/files/ArbitrationandConciliation.pdf.
462. Ibid., through insertions of Section 29A and 29B.
463. Ibid., through insertion of the Fifth Schedule.

464. Ibid., through insertion of the Fourth Schedule.
465. The Arbitration and Conciliation (Amendment) Act, 2019, Legislative Department, Ministry of Law and Justice, The Gazette of India: Extraordinary, 9 August 2019, https://egazette.nic.in/WriteReadData/2019/210414.pdf: Through the insertion of Part IA.
466. Ibid., through insertion of Sub-section 3A.
467. Ibid., through insertion of Section 23(4).
468. The Arbitration and Conciliation (Amendment) Act, 2021, Legislative Department, Ministry of Law and Justice, The Gazette of India: Extraordinary, 11 March 2021, https://egazette.nic.in/WriteReadData/2021/225832.pdf.
469. 'India Skills Report 2021', Confederation of Indian Industry, 19 February 2021, https://cii.in/Publicationform.aspx?enc=kT7DlMaWYCzK69aRQVywrrorkStRIhhValP94HNVLsVv9zFWJx8/lVYX09jo9XUc.
470. 'PM's Independence Day Speech, 2007', Prime Minister's Office, 15 August 2007, https://archivepmo.nic.in/drmanmohansingh/speech-details.php?nodeid=551.
471. 'About Us', National Skill Development Corporation, Undated, https://nsdcindia.org/about-us.
472. 'National Skill Development Mission: A Framework for Implementation', Ministry of Skill Development and Entrepreneurship, Government of India, 15 July 2015, https://msde.gov.in/sites/default/files/2019-09/National%20Skill%20Development%20Mission.pdf.
473. 'National Policy for Skill Development and Entrepreneurship 2015', Press Information Bureau, Government of India, https://archive.pib.gov.in/documents/rlink/2015/jul/p201571503.pdf.
474. These include the flagship scheme, the Pradhan Mantri Kaushal Vikas Yojana, the Jan Shikshan Sansthan, the National Apprenticeship Promotion Scheme in the short-term skilling ecosystem, with long-term training being imparted by the Industrial Training Institutes under the Craftsmen Training Scheme. See 'Beneficiaries of National Skill Development Mission', Ministry of Skill Development and Entrepreneurship, Press Information Bureau, Government of India, 5 February 2021, https://pib.gov.in/PressReleasePage.aspx?PRID=1695631.
475. 'Overview', National Skill Development Corporation, Undated, https://nsdcindia.org/partners.
476. 'Sector Skill Councils', National Skill Development Corporation, Undated, https://nsdcindia.org/sector-skill-councils.
477. Ibid., About Us.

478. 'Beneficiaries of National Skill Development Mission', Ministry of Skill Development and Entrepreneurship, Press Information Bureau, Government of India, 5 February 2021, https://pib.gov.in/PressReleasePage.aspx?PRID=1695631.
479. 'New Exploration Licensing Policy (NELP)', Ministry of Petroleum and Natural Gas, Government of India, Undated, http://petroleum.nic.in/sites/default/files/2exp.policy.NELP2015.pdf.
480. 'Hydrocarbon Exploration and Licensing Policy (HELP)', Cabinet, Press Information Bureau, Government of India, 10 March 2016, https://pib.gov.in/newsite/printrelease.aspx?relid=137638.
481. Gautam Chikermane, *70 Policies that Shaped India: 1947 to 2017, Independence to $2.5 Trillion*, Observer Research Foundation (2018), pp. 141–142, https://www.orfonline.org/wp-content/uploads/2018/07/70_Policies.pdf.
482. See 1) 'Report of the Committee on Roadmap for Reduction in Import Dependency in Hydrocarbon Sector by 2030: Part I', Ministry of Petroleum and Natural Gas, Government of India, December 2013, http://petroleum.nic.in/sites/default/files/kelkar.pdf; and 2) 'Roadmap for Reduction in Import Dependency in the Hydrocarbon Sector by 2030: Final Report', Ministry of Petroleum and Natural Gas, Government of India, September 2014, http://petroleum.nic.in/sites/default/files/FinalReportKelkarCommittee2014.pdf.
483. Resolution No. 0-32011/4/2013-ONG-I, Ministry of Petroleum and Natural Gas, Government of India, 30 March 2016, http://petroleum.nic.in/sites/default/files/HELP.pdf.
484. 'Ministry of Petroleum and Natural Gas launches Open Acreage Licensing Programme Bid Round-VI; Area of approximately 35,346 sq. km. on offer to the investors', Ministry of Petroleum and Natural Gas, Press Information Bureau, Government of India, 6 August 2021, https://www.pib.gov.in/PressReleasePage.aspx?PRID=1743116.
485. 'A Presentation on Recent Policy Decisions', Ministry of Petroleum and Natural Gas, Government of India, Undated, Slide 3, http://petroleum.nic.in/sites/default/files/imppolicy.pdf.
486. Unstarred Question No. 3449, 'Unique Identification Authority', Home Affairs, Lok Sabha, 23 December 2008, https://eparlib.nic.in/bitstream/123456789/568576/1/67501.pdf.
487. Standing Committee on Finance (2014–15), Ministry of Planning, Demands for Grants (2015–16), Twelfth Report, Lok Sabha Secretariat, April 2015, Para 2.4, http://164.100.47.193/lsscommittee/Finance/16_Finance_12.pdf.
488. Ibid. The meetings occurred on 22 November 2007, 28 January 2008, 7 August 2008 and 4 November 2008.

489. 'Notification No. A.03011/02/2009-Admn.l, Planning Commission, Unique Identification Authority of India, Government of India, 28 January 2009, https://uidai.gov.in/images/notification_28_jan_2009.pdf.
490. 'Government of India's Resolution setting up the Planning Commission,' Resolution, Cabinet Secretariat, NITI Aayog, Government of India, 15 March 1950, https://niti.gov.in/planningcommission.gov.in/docs/aboutus/history/PCresolution1950.pdf.
491. Ibid. Standing Committee on Finance, Para 2.5.
492. 'PM constitutes Council of UIDAI', Prime Minister's Office, 3 August 2009, https://archivepmo.nic.in/drmanmohansingh/press-details.php?nodeid=971.
493. The National Identification Authority of India Bill, 2010, PRS Legislative Research, 3 December 2010, https://prsindia.org/files/bills_acts/bills_parliament/2010/The_National_Identification_Authority_of_India_Bill,_2010.pdf.
494. Standing Committee on Finance (2011–12), Ministry of Planning, The National Identification Authority of India Bill, 2010, Lok Sabha Secretariat, December 2011, https://uidai.gov.in/images/report_of_the_departmental_standing_committee_on_finance_on_the_bill_13012017.pdf.
495. The Aadhaar (Targeted Delivery of Financial and Other Subsidies, Benefits and Services) Act, 2016, Unique Identification Authority of India, Government of India, 25 March 2016, https://uidai.gov.in/images/Aadhaar_Act_2016_as_amended.pdf.
496. *Justice K.S. Puttaswamy (Retd.) and Another versus Union of India and Others*, Supreme Court of India, 26 September 2018, https://main.sci.gov.in/supremecourt/2012/35071/35071_2012_Judgement_26-Sep-2018.pdf.
497. Pranav Mukul, 'How Aadhaar grew from an idea into one of the world's largest identity platform', *The Indian Express*, 17 January 2021, https://indianexpress.com/article/books-and-literature/how-aadhaar-grew-from-an-idea-into-one-of-the-worlds-largest-identity-platform-7148103/.
498. 'Annual Report 2019–20', Unique Identification Authority of India, Undated, p. 18, https://uidai.gov.in/images/AADHAR_AR_2019_20_ENG_approved.pdf.
499. Ibid., p. 19.
500. The Insolvency and Bankruptcy Code, 2016, Legislative Department, Ministry of Law and Justice, The Gazette of India: Extraordinary, Government of India, 28 May 2016, https://www.mca.gov.in/Ministry/pdf/TheInsolvencyandBankruptcyofIndia.pdf.
501. Injeti Srinivas, 'The Story Behind Section 29A of IBC', in *Insolvency and Bankruptcy Regime in India: A Narrative*, Insolvency and Bankruptcy Board of India (2020), Government of India, pp. 97, https://www.ibbi.gov.in/uploads/

whatsnew/2020-10-01-210733-43cms-9224c9b668aac0d6149a5d866bfb4c79.pdf.

502. Ibid., IBC, Part I.
503. Ibid., IBC, Part IV.
504. Ibid., IBC, Part V.
505. National Company Law Tribunal.
506. The Insolvency and Bankruptcy Code (Amendment) Act, 2018, Legislative Department, Ministry of Law and Justice, The Gazette of India: Extraordinary, 18 January 2018, https://ibbi.gov.in//webadmin/pdf/legalframwork/2018/Jan/182066_2018-01-20%2023:35:29.pdf.
507. The Insolvency and Bankruptcy Code (Second Amendment) Act, 2018, Legislative Department, Ministry of Law and Justice, The Gazette of India: Extraordinary, https://ibbi.gov.in//webadmin/pdf/legalframwork/2018/Aug/The%20Insolvency%20and%20Bankruptcy%20Code%20(Second%20Amendment)%20Act,%202018_2018-08-18%2018:40:34.pdf.
508. The Insolvency and Bankruptcy Code (Amendment) Act, 2019, Legislative Department, Ministry of Law and Justice, The Gazette of India: Extraordinary, https://www.ibbi.gov.in/uploads/legalframwork/630af836c9fbbed047c42dbdfd2aca13.pdf.
509. The Insolvency and Bankruptcy Code (Amendment) Act, 2020, Legislative Department, Ministry of Law and Justice, The Gazette of India: Extraordinary, https://www.ibbi.gov.in/uploads/legalframwork/d36301a7973451881e00492419012542.pdf.
510. The Insolvency and Bankruptcy Code (Second Amendment) Act, 2020, Legislative Department, Ministry of Law and Justice, The Gazette of India: Extraordinary, https://ibbi.gov.in//uploads/legalframwork/c1d0cde66b213275d9cf357b59bab77b.pdf.
511. The Insolvency and Bankruptcy Code (Amendment) Act, 2021, Legislative Department, Ministry of Law and Justice, The Gazette of India: Extraordinary, https://ibbi.gov.in//uploads/legalframwork/0150ec26cf05f06e66bd82b2ec4f6296.pdf
512. 'Time to resolve insolvency (years)', World Bank, https://data.worldbank.org/indicator/IC.ISV.DURS
513. 'MacroeconomicImpactofDemonetisation:APreliminaryAssessment',Reserve Bank of India, 10 March 2017, https://rbidocs.rbi.org.in/rdocs/Publications/PDFs/MID10031760E85BDAFEFD497193995BB1B6DBE602.PDF.
514. Budget 1997–98 Speech of Shri P. Chidambaram, Minister of Finance, Ministry of Finance, Government of India, 28 February, 1997, Para 87.
515. Budget 1998–99 Speech of Shri Yashwant Sinha, Minister of Finance, Ministry of Finance, Government of India, 1 June, 1998, Para 92.

516. The High Denomination Bank Notes (Demonetisation) Act, 1978, Legislative Department, Ministry of Law and Justice, Government of India, 30 March 1978.
517. The Specified Bank Notes (Cessation of Liabilities) Act, 2017, Section 3, The Gazette of India, Ministry of Law and Justice, Government of India, 27 February 2017, https://rbidocs.rbi.org.in/rdocs/content/pdfs/SBNACT200417.pdf.
518. 'Voluntary Disclosure of Income Scheme, 1997: Notified Effective Date of Voluntary Disclosure of Income Scheme, 1997', Income Tax Department, Ministry of Finance, Government of India, 9 June 1997.
519. Budget 1992–93, Budget Speech of Shri Manmohan Singh, Minister of Finance, Ministry of Finance, Government of India, 29 February, 1992, Para 62.
520. 'Text of Prime Minister's address to the Nation', Prime Minister's Office, Press Information Bureau, Government of India, 8 November 2016, https://pib.gov.in/newsite/PrintRelease.aspx?relid=153404.
521. 'Status of the Return of SBNs – Reserve Bank of India (RBI) Annual Report 2016-17', Ministry of Finance, Press Information Bureau, Government of India, 30 August 2017, https://pib.gov.in/newsite/PrintRelease.aspx?relid=170379.
522. Gautam Chikermane, *70 Policies that Shaped India, 1947 to 2017, Independence to $2.5 Trillion*, Observer Research Foundation (2018), p. 148, https://www.orfonline.org/wp-content/uploads/2018/07/70_Policies.pdf.
523. 'Income Tax Department Time Series Data: Financial Year 2000–01 to 2018–19', Central Board of Direct Taxes, Ministry of Finance, Government of India, Undated. https://www.incometaxindia.gov.in/Documents/Direct%20Tax%20Data/IT-Department-Time-Series-Data-FY-2000-01-to-2018-19.pdf. A taxpayer is defined as 'a person who either has filed a return of income for the relevant Assessment Year (AY) or in whose case tax has been deducted at source in the relevant Financial Year but the taxpayer has not filed the return of income'.
524. Ibid.
525. Gautam Chikermane, *70 Policies that Shaped India: 1947 to 2017, Independence to $2.5 Trillion*, Observer Research Foundation (2018), pp. 149–150, https://www.orfonline.org/wp-content/uploads/2018/07/70_Policies.pdf.
526. The Real Estate (Regulation and Development) Bill, 2013, Rajya Sabha, Parliament of India, http://164.100.47.5/newcommittee/press_release/bill/Select%20Committee%20on%20the%20Real%20Estate%20(Regulation%20and%20Development)%20Bill,%202013/real%20estate-E.pdf.

527. The Real Estate (Regulation and Development) Act, 2016, Legislative Department, Ministry of Law and Justice, Government of India, 25 March 2016, https://legislative.gov.in/sites/default/files/A2016-16_0.pdf.
528. Ibid., Chapter V.
529. Ibid., Chapter VII.
530. Constitution of India, Seventh Schedule, List II—State List, Entry 18, Legislative Department, Ministry of Law and Justice, Government of India, https://legislative.gov.in/sites/default/files/COI_1.pdf.
531. Ibid., Chapter II, Section 3(2)(a).
532. Ibid., Chapter II, Section 9.
533. Ibid., Chapter III, Section 13.
534. Ibid., Chapter II, Section 4(2)(l)(D).
535. Real Estate (Regulation & Development) Act, 2016 [RERA] Implementation Progress Report (as on 07-08-2021), Ministry of Housing and Urban Affairs, Government of India, http://mohua.gov.in/upload/uploadfiles/files/RERA_Status_Tracker%20(07-08-2021).pdf.
536. Gautam Chikermane, *70 Policies that Shaped India: 1947 to 2017, Independence to $2.5* Trillion, Observer Research Foundation (2018), pp. 151–152, https://www.orfonline.org/wp-content/uploads/2018/07/70_Policies.pdf.
537. 'GST – Concept and Status: Updated as on 01st September 2017', Goods and Services Tax Council, Ministry of Finance, Government of India, p. 5, http://www.gstcouncil.gov.in/sites/default/files/gst%20rates/01092017-GST-Concept-and-Status%20english.pdf. These are: Central Excise Duty; Duties of Excise (Medicinal and Toilet Preparations); Additional Duties of Excise (Goods of Special Importance); Additional Duties of Excise (Textiles and Textile Products); Additional Duties of Customs (commonly known as CVD); Special Additional Duty of Customs (SAD); Service Tax; Cesses and surcharges insofar as they relate to supply of goods or services.
538. Ibid. These are: State VAT; Central Sales Tax; Purchase Tax; Luxury Tax; Entry Tax (All forms); Entertainment Tax (except those levied by the local bodies); Taxes on advertisements; Taxes on lotteries, betting and gambling; State cesses and surcharges insofar as they relate to supply of goods or services.
539. The Constitution (One Hundred and First Amendment) Act, 2016, Central Board of Indirect Taxes and Customs, Ministry of Finance, Government of India, 8 September 2016, https://cbic-gst.gov.in/constitution-amendment-act.html.
540. 'GST Law', Goods and Services Tax, Ministry of Finance, Government of India, Undated, https://services.gst.gov.in/services/gstlaw/gstlawlist. The five laws are: (i) Central Goods and Services Tax Act, 2017 including Central

Goods and Services Tax (Extension to Jammu and Kashmir) Act, 2017; (ii) State Goods and Services Tax Act, 2017 as notified by respective States; (iii) Union Territory Goods and Services Tax Act, 2017; (iv) Integrated Goods and Services Tax Act, 2017 including Integrated Goods and Services Tax (Extension to Jammu and Kashmir Act, 2017); (v) Goods and Services Tax (Compensation to States) Act, 2017. Following the laws, the Rules, Notifications, Amendments and Circulars issued under the respective Acts remain a work in progress.

541. For instance, and on the lines of, this law enacted by the Maharashtra and Uttar Pradesh Legislatures in June and May 2017 respectively: The Maharashtra Goods and Services Tax Act, 2017, Department of Goods and Services Act, 2017, Government of Maharashtra, 15 June 2017, https://www.mahagst.gov.in/sites/default/files/MGST%20Act%20updated%20till%20January%202021.pdf; and The Uttar Pradesh Goods and Services Tax Act, 2017, Department of Commercial Taxes, Uttar Pradesh, India Code, 27 July 2020, https://www.indiacode.nic.in/bitstream/123456789/15617/1/upgst2017.pdf.

542. For instance, and on the lines of, this law enacted by the Delhi Legislative Assembly: The Delhi Goods and Services Tax Act, 2017, India Code, 14 June 2017, https://www.indiacode.nic.in/bitstream/123456789/13625/1/delhi_gst_act.pdf.

543. 'Rate of GST on Goods', Goods and Services Tax Council, Ministry of Finance, Government of India, http://www.gstcouncil.gov.in/sites/default/files/goods-rates-booklet-03July2017.pdf.

544. 'Rate of GST on Services', Goods and Services Tax Council, Ministry of Finance, Government of India, http://www.gstcouncil.gov.in/sites/default/files/services-booklet-03July2017.pdf.

545. Speech of Shri Vishwanath Pratap Singh, Minister of Finance, Introducing the Budget for the Year 1986–87, Ministry of Finance, 28 February 1986, Paras 113–119. MODVAT stands for Modified Value Added Tax.

546. Shankar Acharya, 'Thirty Years of Tax Reform in India', *Economic and Political Weekly* 40, No. 20 (2005), pp. 2061, 2063–2070, https://www.jstor.org/stable/4416644.

547. 'All time high Gross GST collection in March 2022, breaching earlier record of `1,40,986 crore collected in the Month of January 2022; `1,42,095 crore gross GST revenue collected in the month', Ministry of Finance, Press Information Bureau, Government of India, 1 April 2022, https://pib.gov.in/PressReleasePage.aspx?PRID=1812315.

548. Entry 6, List II—State List, Seventh Schedule (Article 246), Constitution of India, Legislative Department, Ministry of Law and Justice, Government of India, https://legislative.gov.in/constitution-of-india.

549. 'Employees' State Insurance Act, 1948', Employees' State Insurance Corporation, Ministry of Labour and Employment, Government of India, 19 April 1948, https://www.esic.nic.in/attachments/actfile/ae036213fec2e5ca97e2c9314a1fc9e9.pdf.
550. D. Narayana, 'Review of the Rashtriya Swasthya Bima Yojana', *Economic and Political Weekly* 45, No. 29 (17–23 July 2010), pp. 13, 15–18, https://www.jstor.org/stable/20764304.
551. 'Resolution adopted by the General Assembly on 12 December 2017', Agenda item 127, Seventy-second session, United Nations General Assembly, 15 January 2018, https://undocs.org/a/res/72/138.
552. 'Cabinet approves Ayushman Bharat—National Health Protection Mission; Benefit cover of Rs. 5 lakh per family per year More than 10 crore families to be covered RSBY and SCHIS to be subsumed under Ayushman Bharat—NHPS', Cabinet, Press Information Bureau, Government of India, 21 March 2018, https://pib.gov.in/newsite/printrelease.aspx?relid=177816.
553. 'About Pradhan Mantri Jan Arogya Yojana (PMJAY)', National Health Authority, Government of India, Undated, Para 1, https://pmjay.gov.in/about/pmjay.
554. Ibid., Para 2.
555. Ibid., PIB 2018, Para 6.
556. 'Consolidated Report for the Week as on Date - 05-08-2021', Ayushman Bharat—Health and Wellness Centre, Ministry of Health and Family Welfare, Government of India, https://ab-hwc.nhp.gov.in/home/Consolidated_Weekly_Report?pmo_date=2021-08-05&state=0.
557. Gautam Chikermane and Oommen C. Kurian, 'Can PMJAY Fix India's Healthcare System? Crossing Five Hurdles on the Path to Universal Health Coverage', Observer Research Foundation, https://www.orfonline.org/wp-content/uploads/2018/10/ORF_OccasionalPaper_172_PMJAY.pdf.
558. 'Freedom from the Cobweb of Archaic Laws', *New India Samachar*, Press Information Bureau, Government of India, 1–15 January 2021, p. 32, http://newindiasamachar.pib.gov.in/WriteReadData/Magazine//2021/Jan/M202101011.pdf.
559. 'PM sets up Committee to identify obsolete laws within three months', Prime Minister's Office, Government of India, 27 August 2014, https://www.pmindia.gov.in/en/news_updates/pm-sets-up-committee-to-identify-obsolete-laws-within-three-months/?comment=disable.
560. 'Obsolete Laws: Warranting Immediate Repeal (Interim Report)', Report No. 248, Law Commission of India, Government of India, 12 September 2014, https://lawcommissionofindia.nic.in/reports/Report248.pdf.

561. 'Obsolete Laws: Warranting Immediate Repeal (Second Interim Report)', Report No. 249, Law Commission of India, Government of India, 13 October 2014, https://lawcommissionofindia.nic.in/reports/Second%20Interim%20Report%20on%20Obsolete%20Laws.pdf.
562. 'Obsolete Laws: Warranting Immediate Repeal (Third Interim Report)', Report No. 250, Law Commission of India, Government of India, 29 October 2014, https://lawcommissionofindia.nic.in/reports/Report_No.250_signed_copy.pdf.
563. 'Obsolete Laws: Warranting Immediate Repeal (Fourth Interim Report)', Report No. 251, Law Commission of India, Government of India, 14 November 2014, https://lawcommissionofindia.nic.in/reports/Report_No.251%20on%20Obsolete%20Laws%20-%20Warrnting%20immediate%20Repeal%20(Fourth%20%20%20%20%20%20%20%20%20%20%20%20Interim).pdf.
564. 'Report of the Committee to Identify the Central Acts Which are not Relevant or No Longer Needed or Require Repeal/Re-Enactment in the Present Socio-Economic Context', Volumes I, II, III and IV, Prime Minister's Office, Government of India, 5 November 2014, https://www.pmindia.gov.in/wp-content/uploads/2015/01/Extracts-of-the-Committee-of-the-Report-Vol.I-.pdf.
565. See 1) 'The Repealing and Amending Act, 2015', Legislative Department, Ministry of Law and Justice, The Gazette of India: Extraordinary, Government of India, 13 May 2015, https://legislative.gov.in/sites/default/files/Act17of2015.pdf; and 2) The Repealing and Amending (Second) Act, 2015, Legislative Department, Ministry of Law and Justice, The Gazette of India: Extraordinary, Government of India, 14 May 2015, https://legislative.gov.in/sites/default/files/Act%2019%20of%202015.pdf.
566. See 1) 'The Repealing and Amending Act, 2017', Legislative Department, Ministry of Law and Justice, The Gazette of India: Extraordinary, Government of India, 5 January 2018, https://www.egazette.nic.in/WriteReadData/2018/181637.pdf; and 2) 'The Repealing and Amending (Second) Act, 2017', Legislative Department, Ministry of Law and Justice, The Gazette of India: Extraordinary, Government of India, 5 January 2018, https://www.egazette.nic.in/WriteReadData/2018/181639.pdf.
567. 'The Repealing and Amending Act, 2019', Legislative Department, Ministry of Law and Justice, The Gazette of India: Extraordinary, Government of India, 8 August 2019, https://egazette.nic.in/WriteReadData/2019/210358.pdf.
568. 'National Monetisation Pipeline Volume I: Monetisation Guidebook', NITI Aayog, Government of India, July 2021, p. 5, https://www.niti.gov.

in/sites/default/files/2021-08/Vol_I_NATIONAL_MONETISATION_PIPELINE_23_Aug_2021.pdf.

569. 'National Monetisation Pipeline Volume II: Asset Pipeline', NITI Aayog, Government of India, July 2021, pp. 17–92, https://www.niti.gov.in/sites/default/files/2021-08/Vol_2_NATIONAL_MONETISATION_PIPELINE_23_Aug_2021.pdf.

570. Ibid. The sector-wise pipeline of the monetisation plan is: roads (Rs 1,60,200 crore, p. 18), railways (Rs 1,52,496 crore, p. 24), power transmission (Rs 45,200 crore, p. 38), telecom (Rs 35,100 crore, p. 45), power generation (Rs 39,832 crore, p. 51), natural gas pipelines (Rs 24,462 crore, p. 55), petroleum, petroleum product pipeline and others (Rs 22,504 crore, p. 60), telecom (Rs 35,100 crore, p. 45), warehousing (Rs 28,900 crore, p. 65), mining (Rs 28,747 crore, p. 71), airports (Rs 20,782 crore, p. 75), ports (Rs 12,828 crore, p. 81), stadiums (Rs 11,450 crore, p. 87), and urban real estate (Rs 15,000 crore, p. 92).

571. Ibid., pp. 39.

572. 'Lease Deed between Airports Authority of India and Delhi International Airport Private Limited', Ministry of Civil Aviation, Government of India, 25 April 2006, https://www.civilaviation.gov.in/sites/default/files/moca_000977.pdf.

573. 'Operation, Management and Development Agreement between Airports Authority of India and Mumbai International Airport Private Limited for Mumbai Airport', Ministry of Civil Aviation, Government of India, 4 April 2006, https://www.civilaviation.gov.in/sites/default/files/moca_000979.pdf.

574. 'Labour', Press Information Bureau, Government of India, 24 May 1990, https://archive.pib.gov.in/archive/ArchiveSecondPhase/FEATURE/1990-%20FEATURE%20ARTICLES%20JAN%20JUNE%20VOL1/PDF/FEA-1990-05-24_121.pdf.

575. 'Statement on Industrial Policy, July 24, 1991', Para 16.

576. 'List III—Concurrent List', Constitution of India, Legislative Department, Ministry of Law and Justice, Government of India, pp. 219–221, https://legislative.gov.in/sites/default/files/COI_1.pdf. Entries 22, 23 and 24 under the Concurrent List come under the joint jurisdiction; Entries 55, 61 and 65 under List I—Union List are covered by the Union.

577. 'Liberalisation not at the Cost of Workers—Shri Pilot', Press Information Bureau, Government of India, 20 November 1992, https://archive.pib.gov.in/archive/ArchiveSecondPhase/COMMUNICATION/1992-JAN-DEC-COMMUNICATIONS/COM-1992-11-20_193.pdf.

578. Gautam Chikermane and Rishi Agrawal, '8 reforms to end India's regulatory cholesterol', Observer Research Foundation, 24 July 2021, https://www.orfonline.org/expert-speak/8-reforms-to-end-indias-regulatory-cholesterol/.

579. 'The Code on Wages', Ministry of Law and Justice (Legislative Department), The Gazette of India, Government of India, 8 August 2019, https://labour.gov.in/sites/default/files/THE%20CODE%20ON%20WAGES%2C%20 2019%20No.%2029%20of%202019.pdf.
580. 'The Occupational Safety, Health and Working Conditions Code, 2020', Ministry of Law and Justice (Legislative Department), Gazette of India, Government of India, 28 September 2020, https://labour.gov.in/sites/default/files/OSH_Gazette.pdf.
581. 'The Code on Social Security, 2020', Ministry of Law and Justice (Legislative Department), The Gazette of India, Government of India, 28 September 2020, https://labour.gov.in/sites/default/files/SS_Code_Gazette.pdf.
582. 'The Industrial Relations Code, 2020', Ministry of Law and Justice (Legislative Department), The Gazette of India, Government of India, 28 September 2020, https://labour.gov.in/sites/default/files/IR_Gazette_of_India.pdf.
583. 'The Code on Wages (Central Advisory Board) Rules, 2021', Ministry of Labour and Employment, The Gazette of India, Government of India, 1 March 2021, https://labour.gov.in/sites/default/files/Code_on_Wages_%28Central_Advisory_Board%29_Rules%2C2021.pdf.
584. Gautam Chikermane and Rishi Agrawal, 'COVID-19: Shivraj Singh Chouhan initiates Reforms 2.0 in Madhya Pradesh', 8 May 2020, https://www.orfonline.org/expert-speak/covid19-shivraj-singh-chouhan-initiates-reforms-2-madhya-pradesh-65867/.
585. Gautam Chikermane and Rishi Agrawal, 'COVID-19: Yogi Adityanath attempts reforms, delivers regulatory chaos in Uttar Pradesh', Observer Research Foundation, 9 May 2020, https://www.orfonline.org/expert-speak/covid19-yogi-adityanath-attempts-reforms-delivers-regulatory-chaos-uttar-pradesh-65918/.
586. Gautam Chikermane, 'Farmer interests are missing in farm protest politics', Observer Research Foundation, 7 December 2020, https://www.orfonline.org/expert-speak/farmer-interests-are-missing-in-farm-protest-politics/.
587. Dhananjay Mahapatra, 'SC slams govt over farmers stir, wants laws kept on hold', *The Times of India*, 12 January 2021, https://timesofindia.indiatimes.com/india/sc-wants-to-keep-farm-laws-in-abeyance-form-expert-panel/articleshow/80223242.cms.
588. Harikishan Sharma and Liz Mathew, 'Centre blinks: Let us keep farm laws on hold for 18 months, form joint panel', *The Indian Express*, 21 January 2021, https://indianexpress.com/article/india/farm-laws-farmer-government-talk-protest-narendra-singh-tomar-supreme-court-7155148/.
589. Gautam Chikermane, 'Modi's U-turn on farm laws: A set back in the history of India's economic reforms', Observer Research Foundation, 19 November 2021, https://www.orfonline.org/expert-speak/modis-u-turn-on-farm-laws/.

590. 'Farmers' Produce Trade and Commerce (Promotion and Facilitation) Act, 2020', Ministry of Law and Justice, The Gazette of India, Government of India, 24 September 2020, https://egazette.nic.in/WriteReadData/2020/222039.pdf.
591. 'The Essential Commodities (Amendment) Act, 2020', Ministry of Law and Justice, The Gazette of India, Government of India, 26 September 2020, https://consumeraffairs.nic.in/sites/default/files/file-uploads/acts-and-rules/EC%28Amendment%29%20Act2020.pdf.
592. 'The e Farmers (Empowerment and Protection) Agreement on Price Assurance and Farm Services Act, 2020', Ministry of Law and Justice, The Gazette of India, Government of India, 24 September 2020, https://egazette.nic.in/WriteReadData/2020/222040.pdf.
593. 'Agriculture Marketing and Role of Weekly Gramin Haats', Standing Committee on Agriculture (2018-2019), Sixteenth Lok Sabha, Ministry of Agriculture and Farmers Welfare (Department of Agricultural, Cooperation and Farmers Welfare), Sixty-Second Report, Lok Sabha Secretariat, January 2019, p. 39, http://164.100.47.193/lsscommittee/Agriculture/16_Agriculture_62.pdf.
594. Sriram Iyer, '"APMC and MSP will continue"—why Indian farmers must not fear the new laws', *Business Insider India,* 21 September 2020, https://www.businessinsider.in/india/news/apmc-and-msp-will-continue-under-new-farm-bills-2020/slidelist/78230172.cms.
595. Gautam Chikermane, 'An intellectual biography of India's new farm laws', Observer Research Foundation, 11 December 2020, https://www.orfonline.org/research/intellectual-biography-india-new-farm-laws/?.
596. The Factories Act, 1948, Ministry of Labour and Employment, Government of India, 23 September 1948, https://labour.gov.in/sites/default/files/Factories_Act_1948.pdf.
597. The Contract Labour (Regulation and Abolition) Act, 1970, Legislative Department, Ministry of Law and Justice, Government of India, 5 September 1970, https://legislative.gov.in/sites/default/files/A1970-37_0.pdf.
598. The Food Safety and Standards Act, 2006, India Code, Government of India, 23 August 2006, https://www.indiacode.nic.in/bitstream/123456789/7800/1/200634_food_safety_and_standards_act%2C_2006.pdf.
599. Clauses relating to fraud or obstructing inspectors, for instance.
600. Clauses relating to not re-establishing a canteen committee, or not cleaning spittoons, for instance.
601. Bibek Debroy, Laveesh Bhandari, Swaminathan S. Anklesaria Aiyar, 'India's Segmented Labour Markets, Inter-State Differences, and the Scope for Labour

Reforms', *Economic Freedom of the States of India: 2012*, Academic Foundation (2013), https://cdn.cato.org/economic-freedom-india/Economic-Freedom-States-of-India-2012.pdf.

602. Companies (Amendment) Act, 2019, Legislative Department, Ministry of Law and Justice, The Gazette of India: Extraordinary, Government of India, 31 July 2019, https://www.mca.gov.in/Ministry/pdf/AMENDMENTACT_01082019.pdf.
603. The Companies (Amendment) Act, 2020, Legislative Department, Ministry of Law and Justice, The Gazette of India: Extraordinary, 28 September 2020, https://prsindia.org/files/bills_acts/bills_parliament/2020/Companies%20(Amendment)%20Act,%202020.pdf.
604. Notification, Ministry of Corporate Affairs, The Gazette of India, Government of India, 21 December 2020, https://www.mca.gov.in/Ministry/pdf/CommencementNotification_24122020.pdf.
605. Notification, Ministry of Corporate Affairs, The Gazette of India, Government of India, 21 December 2020, https://www.mca.gov.in/Ministry/pdf/CommencementNotification_23012021.pdf.
606. Notification, Ministry of Corporate Affairs, Government of India, 11 February 2021, https://www.mca.gov.in/Ministry/pdf/CommencementNotification_12022021.pdf
607. 'De-criminalization of penalties for Companies Law breaches', Ministry of Corporate Affairs, Press Information Bureau, Government of India, 4 February 2020, https://pib.gov.in/PressReleasePage.aspx?PRID=1601892.
608. Report of the Company Law Committee, Ministry of Corporate Affairs, Government of India, 14 November 2019, https://www.mca.gov.in/Ministry/pdf/CLCReport_18112019.pdf.
609. Gautam Chikermane and Rishi Agrawal, *Jailed for Doing Business: The 26,134 Imprisonment Clauses in India's Business Laws*, Observer Research Foundation, February 2022, https://www.orfonline.org/wp-content/uploads/2022/02/ORF_Monograph_JailedForDoingBusiness_Final-New-11Feb.pdf.
610. Samir Saran, '#Covid19: Made in China pandemic', Observer Research Foundation, 20 March 2020, https://www.orfonline.org/expert-speak/covid19-made-in-china-pandemic-63531/.
611. Vijay Laxman Kelkar, 'India and World Economy: Search for Self-Reliance', *Economic and Political Weekly*, Vol. 15, No. 5/7, Annual Number (February 1980), pp. 245, 247, 249, 251, 253, 255, 257-258, https://www.jstor.org/stable/4368372.
612. K.B., 'Indira Gandhi: An Attempt at a Political Appraisal', *Economic and Political Weekly* 20, No. 12 (23 March 1985), pp. 496–499, 502–503, https://www.jstor.org/stable/4374199.

613. 'India at Davos: PM Modi flags "protectionism" as a threat, says globalization is shrinking', *Financial Express*, 23 January 2018, https://www.financialexpress.com/economy/india-at-davos-pm-modi-flags-protectionism-as-a-threat-says-globalization-is-shrinking/1027021/.
614. 'PM gives a clarion call for Atmanirbhar Bharat; PM announces special economic package; comprehensive package of Rs 20 lakh crore; Total package equivalent to 10% of India's GDP; PM gives a call for self-reliant India; lays down five pillars of Atmanirbhar Bharat; Bold reforms across sectors will drive the country's push towards self-reliance: PM; It is time to become vocal for our local products and make them global: PM', Prime Minister's Office, Press Information Bureau, Government of India, https://pib.gov.in/PressReleasePage.aspx?PRID=1623391.
615. 'Finance Minister announces Government Reforms and Enablers across Seven Sectors under Aatma Nirbhar Bharat Abhiyaan', Ministry of Finance, Press Information Bureau, Government of India, 17 May 2020, https://pib.gov.in/PressReleasePage.aspx?PRID=1624661.
616. 'Implementation of Aatma Nirbhar Bharat Package pertaining to Ministries of Finance & Corporate Affairs —Progress So Far', Ministry of Finance, Press Information Bureau, Government of India, 13 September 2020, https://pib.gov.in/PressReleasePage.aspx?PRID=1653725.
617. 'Finance Minister announces measures on AatmaNirbhar Bharat 3.0', Ministry of Finance, Press Information Bureau, Government of India, 12 November 2020, https://pib.gov.in/PressReleasePage.aspx?PRID=1672321.
618. 'Finance Minister announces Government Reforms and Enablers across Seven Sectors under Aatma Nirbhar Bharat Abhiyaan', Ministry of Finance, Press Information Bureau, Government of India, 17 May 2020, https://pib.gov.in/PressReleasePage.aspx?PRID=1624661.
619. Press Trust of India, 'Rs 20-lakh cr stimulus package: At 10% of GDP, Narendra Modi's Atma-nirbhar Bharat Abhiyan ranks among biggest in world', *Firstpost,* 13 May 2020, https://www.firstpost.com/business/rs-20-lakh-cr-stimulus-package-at-10-of-gdp-narendra-modis-atma-nirbhar-bharat-abhiyan-ranks-among-biggest-in-world-8364191.html.
620. 'UPI Product Statistics', NPCI, https://www.npci.org.in/what-we-do/upi/product-statistics.
621. Sasanka Sekhar Maiti, Mint Street Memo No. 07, 'From Cash to Non-cash and Cheque to Digital: The Unfolding Revolution in India's Payment Systems', 24 November 2017, https://rbidocs.rbi.org.in/rdocs/MintStreetMemos/07MSM24112017.pdf.
622. 'The Payment and Settlement Systems Act, 2007', Ministry of Law and Justice (Legislative Department), The Gazette of India, Government of India, http://164.100.47.193/BillsPDFFiles/Notification/2006-50-gaz.pdf.

623. 'The e Payment and Settlement Systems Regulations, 2008', Reserve Bank of India, The Gazette of India, Government of India, https://financialservices.gov.in/sites/default/files/PSS%20Act%202007%20Regulations.pdf.
624. 'Product Overview: IMPS', NPCI, Undated, https://www.npci.org.in/what-we-do/imps/product-overview.
625. 'BHIM Product Overview', NPCI, Undated, https://www.npci.org.in/what-we-do/bhim/product-overview.
626. 'RuPay Product Overview', NPCI, Undated, https://www.npci.org.in/what-we-do/rupay/product-overview.
627. 'Cheque Truncation System Overview', NPCI, Undated, https://www.npci.org.in/what-we-do/cts/product-overview.
628. 'Product Overview', NPCI, Undated, https://www.npci.org.in/what-we-do/upi/product-overview.
629. Data charges are borne by consumers, but there are no transaction charges by banks.
630. The fintech adoption rates of India and China, both at 87 per cent between 2015 and 2019, are the highest in the world. 'Global FinTech Adoption Index 2019', EYGM, 2019, p. 8, file:///Users/gautam/Downloads/ey-global-fintech-adoption-index-2019.pdf.
631. 'Payment and Settlement Systems in India: Journey in the Second Decade of the Millennium', Department of Payment and Settlement Systems, Reserve Bank of India, Undated, p. 4, https://rbidocs.rbi.org.in/rdocs/Publications/PDFs/PSSBOOKLET93D3AEFDEAF14044BC1BB36662C41A8C.PDF.
632. Press Trust of India, '"Only 15 paise reaches the needy": SC quotes Rajiv Gandhi in its Aadhaar verdict', *Hindustan Times*, 11 June 2017, https://www.hindustantimes.com/india-news/only-15-paise-reaches-the-needy-sc-quotes-rajiv-gandhi-in-its-aadhaar-verdict/story-I8dniDGXF6ksulggTDgb9L.html.
633. 'Rollout of Direct Benefits: Transfer to begin from 1 January 2013', Department of Financial Services, Ministry of Finance, Government of India, https://financialservices.gov.in/sites/default/files/PIB%20Press%20Note.pdf.
634. 'Binoy Viswam versus Union of India and Others', Writ Petition (Civil) No. 247 of 2017, Supreme Court of India, Unique Identification Authority of India, Government of India, 9 June 2017, p. 138, https://www.uidai.gov.in/images/Pan-Aadhaar_Linking.pdf.
635. 'More than Rs 36,659 crore transferred by using Direct Benefit Transfer (DBT) through Public Financial Management System (PFMS) in the Bank accounts of 16.01 crore beneficiaries during COVID 2019 lockdown; Cash Benefits announced under Prime Minister Garib Kalyan Package also being transferred by using DBT Digital Payment Infrastructure; PFMS usage for

DBT Payments increased over last #3 FYs; total DBT amount disbursed increased from 22% in FY 2018–19 to 45% in FY 2019–20; DBT ensures Cash benefit directly credited into the account of the beneficiary, eliminates leakage and improves efficiency', Ministry of Finance, Press Information Bureau, Government of India, 19 April 2020, https://nidm.gov.in/covid19/PDF/covid19/Ministries/Ministry%20of%20Finance/5.pdf.

636. 'PM launches Pradhan Mantri Jan Dhan Yojana; End financial untouchability for freedom from poverty; 'Vish-chakra se gareebon ki aazadi ka parv'—celebration of liberation of the poor from a poisonous cycle; A record unprecedented in economic history—1.5 crore bank accounts opened in one day', Prime Minister's Office, Press Information Bureau, 28 August 2014, https://archive.pib.gov.in/archive2/erelease.aspx.
637. 'About UIDAI', Unique Identification Authority of India, Government of India, Undated, https://uidai.gov.in/about-uidai/unique-identification-authority-of-india/about.html.
638. According to Telecom Regulatory Authority of India, the country has more than 1.1 billion mobile phone subscribers in India: See 'Press Release No.35/2021', 29 June 2021, p. 5, https://trai.gov.in/sites/default/files/PR_No.35of2021.pdf.
639. 'About Us', Direct Benefit Transfer, Government of India, Undated, https://www.dbtbharat.gov.in/page/frontcontentview/?id=MTc=.
640. 'Direct Benefit Transfer Details (FY 2021–22)', Direct Benefit Transfer, Government of India, Undated, dbtbharat.gov.in/reportnew/scheme-group-report.
641. 'DBT Schemes', Direct Benefit Transfer, Government of India, Undated, https://www.dbtbharat.gov.in/scheme/scheme-list.
642. 'Estimated Gains: Estimated Benefits/Gains from DBT and Other Governance Reforms (upto March 2020)', Direct Benefit Transfer, Government of India, Undated, https://www.dbtbharat.gov.in/estimatedgain.
643. Jai Parkash Dalal, 'How DBT prevented arhatiyas from economically exploiting farmers and streamlined procurement of produce', *FirstPost,* 21 June 2021, https://www.firstpost.com/india/how-dbt-prevented-arhatiyas-from-economically-exploiting-farmers-and-streamlined-procurement-of-produce-9739471.html.
644. 'The National Highways Authority of India Act, 1988', Legislative Department, Ministry of Law and Justice, Government of India, 16 December 1988, https://legislative.gov.in/sites/default/files/A1988-68.pdf.
645. 'National Highways (Amendment) Act, 1995', 16 June 1995, Manupatra, http://www.indianlegislation.in/BA/BaActToc.aspx?actid=15865.

646. 'About NHDP', National Highways Authority of India, Ministry of Road Transport and Highways, Government of India, Undated, https://nhai.gov.in/#/about-nhdp.
647. Data sourced from: Basic Road Statistics: 2017–2018, Transport Research Wing, Ministry of Road Transport and Highways, Government of India, Table 2.1: Total Length of National Highways during 1951–2018, March 2021, p. 20, https://morth.nic.in/sites/default/files/BRS_Final.pdf.
648. Data sourced from: 'National Highway Summary', National Highways Authority of India, Ministry of Road Transport and Highways, Government of India, 1 March 2019, https://nhai.gov.in/nhai/sites/default/files/NationalHighwaySummary.pdf.
649. Budget 2000–2001: Speech of Shri Yashwant Sinha, Minister of Finance', Ministry of Finance, Government of India, 29 February 2000, Para 49, https://www.indiabudget.gov.in/doc/bspeech/bs200001.pdf.
650. Martin Melecky, Siddharth Sharma, Hari Subhash, 'Wider Economic Benefits of Investments in Transport Corridors and the Role of Complementary Policies', Policy Research Working Paper, World Bank Group, February 2018, https://documents1.worldbank.org/curated/en/982341519219762457/pdf/WPS8350.pdf.
651. 'NHAI achieves first milestone in Electronic Toll Collection: dedicated FASTag lane operationalized at every toll plaza from today', Ministry of Road Transport and Highways, Government of India, 1 September 2017, https://pib.gov.in/PressReleasePage.aspx?PRID=1501503.
652. 'Daily Toll Collection through FASTag Reaches the Level Recorded before the Second Wave of Covid19', Ministry of Road Transport and Highways, Press Information Bureau, Government of India, 2 July 2021, https://pib.gov.in/PressReleaseIframePage.aspx?PRID=1732321.
653. Ibid.
654. 'Indian Railways', Civil Engineering Portal, Ministry of Railways, Government of India, Undated, https://ircep.gov.in/AboutUs.html.
655. 'Text of Prime Minister's Independence Day address; PM's Independence Day Call—"Rozgar Badhao"; Text of Prime Minister's Independence Day Address', 15 August 2005, https://archive.pib.gov.in/archive2/AdvSearch.aspx.
656. 'Salient Features: Design Features', Dedicated Freight Corridor Corporation of India Ltd, Ministry of Railways, Press Information Bureau, Government of India, Undated, https://dfccil.com/Home/DynemicPages?MenuId=75.
657. 'Dedicated Freight Corridors in Railways', Ministry of Railways, Press Information Bureau, Government of India, 25 July 2018, https://pib.gov.in/newsite/PrintRelease.aspx?relid=181043.

658. 'Dedicated Freight Corridor: A Game Changer in Economic Development; Rewari–Madar Section on Western Corridor, Dedicated to the Nation by Prime Minister Shri Narendra Modi Today', Ministry of Railways, Press Information Bureau, Government of India, 7 January 2021, https://pib.gov.in/PressReleseDetailm.aspx?PRID=1686785.
659. 'Project Status: Dedicated Freight Corridor Projects (EDFC & WDFC)', Dedicated Freight Corridor Corporation of India Ltd, Ministry of Railways, Government of India, May 2021, https://dfccil.com/Home/ProgressStatusImage.
660. V. Anantha Nageswaran and Gulzar Natarajan, 'Can India Grow?: Challenges, Opportunities, and the Way Forward', Carnegie Endowment for International Peace (2016), https://www.jstor.org/stable/resrep26899.12.
661. Navroz K. Dubash and Sudhir Chella Rajan, 'The Politics of Power Sector Reform in India', World Resources Institute, 2 April 2001, http://pdf.wri.org/power_politics/india.pdf.
662. 'Mega Power Projects: Revised Policy Guidelines', Policy for Setting Up of Mega Power Projects in Pvt Sector, Ministry of Power, Government of India, 10 November 1995, https://powermin.gov.in/en/content/policy-setting-mega-power-projects-pvt-sector.
663. 'The Electricity Regulatory Commissions Act, 1998', The Gazette of India, Extraordinary, Part II, Central Electricity Regulatory Commission, Government of India, 2 July 1998, https://cercind.gov.in/electregucommiact1998.pdf.
664. 'The Electricity Act, 2003', Ministry of Law and Justice, Government of India, 26 May 2003, https://cercind.gov.in/Act-with-amendment.pdf.
665. See 1) 'Union Government for the first time lays down Rights to the Electricity Consumers through "Electricity (Rights of Consumers) Rules, 2020"; Beginning of an era of empowering Power Consumers in a paradigm shift bringing Consumers to Centre Stage: Shri R.K. Singh; Consumers to have the option to apply for new electricity connection and pay bills online; Consumers to get electricity connection in prescribed timeline which is 7 days in Metro cities, 15 days in other cities and 30 days in rural areas; Violations to result in penalties; Rules to benefit about 30 crores existing and prospective consumers in the country; These rules are important step towards furthering the ease of doing business across country: Power Minister Shri R.K. Singh', Ministry of Power, Press Information Bureau, Government of India, 21 December 2020, https://pib.gov.in/PressReleasePage.aspx?PRID=1682384; and 2) 'Electricity (Rights of Consumers) Rules, 2020', Notification, The Gazette of India: Extraordinary, 31 December 2020, https://powermin.gov.in/sites/default/files/uploads/Consumers_Rules_2020.pdf.

666. 'National Electricity Policy, 2021', Ministry of Power, Government of India, February 2021, https://powermin.gov.in/sites/default/files/webform/notices/Inviting_suggestions_on_draft_NEP_2021_0.pdf.
667. Ibid.

Conclusion: Beyond Compulsions and Convictions

1. For a deeper discussion on this, see Gautam Chikermane, 'Forces: Consolidation of a Rajasic India', in Gautam Chikermane, ed., *India 2030: The Rise of a Rajasic Nation* (Penguin 2021), pp. 1—20.
2. Peter F. Drucker, 'Beyond the Information Revolution', *The Atlantic* (October 1999), https://www.theatlantic.com/magazine/archive/1999/10/beyond-the-information-revolution/304658/: 'Almost everybody today believes that nothing in economic history has ever moved as fast as, or had a greater impact than, the Information Revolution. But the Industrial Revolution moved at least as fast in the same time span, and had probably an equal impact if not a greater one. In short order it mechanized the great majority of manufacturing processes, beginning with the production of the most important industrial commodity of the eighteenth and early nineteenth centuries: textiles. Moore's Law asserts that the price of the Information Revolution's basic element, the microchip, drops by 50 percent every eighteen months. The same was true of the products whose manufacture was mechanized by the first Industrial Revolution.'
3. Gautam Chikermane, 'Time for Democracies to Fix the UN: A View from India', Italian Institute for International Political Studies, 28 July 2020, https://www.ispionline.it/en/publication/time-democracies-fix-un-view-india-27078.
4. Shubhajit Roy, 'Canada's Justin Trudeau Backs Farmers' Protest; India Says Remarks "Ill-informed"', *The Indian Express*, 1 December 2020, https://indianexpress.com/article/india/situation-is-concerning-canadas-justin-trudeau-backs-farmers-protests-7075085/.
5. 'Prime Minister Announces Public Order Emergency Commission Following the Invocation of the *Emergencies Act*', Prime Minister of Canada Justin Trudeau, Government of Canada, 25 April 2022, https://pm.gc.ca/en/news/news-releases/2022/04/25/prime-minister-announces-public-order-emergency-commission-following.
6. Samir Saran, 'Big Tech Influence and It's solutions,' The Charvaka Podcast, YouTube.com, https://www.youtube.com/watch?v=-400XiJWSjY.
7. Gautam Chikermane, 'Towards a 21st Century Protest Playbook,' Observer Research Foundation, 6 February 2021, https://www.orfonline.org/expert-speak/towards-21st-century-protest-playbook/.

8. Gautam Chikermane, 'Attacks on India by Western Left Leaning Liberal Media Are Not as Much on India as They Are on Domestic Conservative Constituencies. India Is Just a Proxy: @stephenharper to @samirsaran at #Raisina2022,' Twitter, 27 April 2022, 11:39 pm, https://twitter.com/gchikermane/status/1519196903606431744?s=20&t=eBekR2-Crr79vga8Bha7iw.
9. 'India's Monthly Purchase of Russian Oil Less Than What Europe Does in an Afternoon: Jaishankar in US', *The Economic Times* (12 April 2022) https://economictimes.indiatimes.com/news/india/indias-monthly-purchase-of-russian-oil-less-than-what-europe-does-in-an-afternoon-jaishankar-in-us/videoshow/90791455.cms?from=mdr.
10. Pratik Parija, 'India Bans Wheat Exports as Food Security Comes under Threat', Bloomberg, 14 May 2022, https://www.bloomberg.com/news/articles/2022-05-14/india-says-wheat-exports-prohibited-with-immediate-effect.
11. Press Trust of India, 'Prime Minister Manmohan Singh Calls for Revival of "Animal Spirit" in Economy', *The Economic Times* (28 June 2012), https://economictimes.indiatimes.com/news/economy/finance/prime-minister-manmohan-singh-calls-for-revival-of-animal-spirit-in-economy/articleshow/14435229.cms?from=mdr.
12. 'Wealth creation is a great national service. Let us never see wealth creators with suspicion. Only when wealth is created, wealth will be distributed. Wealth creation is absolutely essential. Those who create wealth are India's wealth and we respect them: PM @narendramodi' Twitter, 15 August 2019, 8:40 am, https://twitter.com/PMOIndia/status/1161837526002229249?s=20&t=Sa6SMLC8ErynNirbibn3_Q. Read full speech on the Prime Minister's Office website here https://www.pmindia.gov.in/en/news_updates/pm-addressed-the-nation-from-the-ramparts-of-the-red-fort-on-the-73rd-independence-day/?comment=disable.
13. Uday S. Kotak, 'Private Enterprise and Nation-Building', in Bluekraft Digital Foundation, ed., *Modi@20: Dreams Meet Delivery* (Rupa Publications, 2022), p. 185.
14. 'Paul Krugman is Right, After All! CEA Arvind Subramanian Agrees with Him on This "jobs' issue"', *The Financial Express* (23 March 2018), https://www.financialexpress.com/economy/paul-krugman-is-right-afterall-cea-arvind-subramanian-agrees-with-him-on-this-jobs-issue/1108720/.
15. James Manyika, Jeff Sinclair, Richard Dobbs, Gernot Strube, Louis Rassey, Jan Mischke, Jaana Remes, Charles Roxburgh, Katy George, David O'Halloran, and Sreenivas Ramaswamy, 'Manufacturing the Future: The Next Era of Global Growth and Innovation', McKinsey and Co., 1 November 2012, p. 1, https://www.mckinsey.com/~/media/McKinsey/Business%20Functions/

Operations/Our%20Insights/The%20future%20of%20manufacturing/MGI_Manufacturing%20the%20future_Executive%20summary_Nov%202012.pdf.

16. World Bank Data, World Bank.
17. 'Production Linked Incentive (PLI) Scheme: For Large Scale Mobile and Component Manufacturing', Press Information Bureau, 17 November 2021, https://pib.gov.in/FactsheetDetails.aspx?Id=148581.
18. '20 Applicants Have Been Approved under "Champion OEM Incentive Scheme" of the Production Linked Incentive (PLI) Scheme for Automobile and Auto Component Industry in India', Ministry of Heavy Industries, Press Information Bureau, 11 February 2022, https://pib.gov.in/PressReleseDetail.aspx?PRID=1797610.
19. Gautam Chikermane and Rishi Agrawal, '8 Reforms to End India's Regulatory Cholesterol', Observer Research Foundation, 24 July 2021, https://www.orfonline.org/expert-speak/8-reforms-to-end-indias-regulatory-cholesterol/.
20. Gautam Chikermane and Rishi Agrawal, 'Jailed for Doing Business', Observer Research Foundation, 10 February 2022, https://www.orfonline.org/jailed-for-doing-business/.
21. Annual Report of Reserve Bank of India: 1990–91, 30 August 1991, Table 2.2, p. 5, https://rbidocs.rbi.org.in/rdocs/AnnualReport/PDFs/9032020AR1990_91.PDF.
22. Annual Report of Reserve Bank of India: 2020–21, 27 May 2022, Appendix Table 3, p. 289, https://rbidocs.rbi.org.in/rdocs/AnnualReport/PDFs/3T728C4D29F15B4DF8968643F5883730A1.PDF.
23. 'Indian Financial Code,' Department of Economic Affairs, Ministry of Finance, Government of India, 22 March 2013, https://dea.gov.in/sites/default/files/Revised_Draft_IFC.pdf.
24. 'English Rendering of PM's Address at Joint Conference of Chief Ministers and Chief Justices of High Courts', Prime Minister's Office, Press Information Bureau, 29 Aprill 2022, https://pib.gov.in/PressReleseDetail.aspx?PRID=1821534.
25. Gautam Chikermane, 'Canada's Plans for a No-China 5G is a Geoeconomic Ricochet of Rejection', Observer Research Foundation, 24 May 2022, https://www.orfonline.org/expert-speak/canadas-plans-for-a-no-china-5g/.
26. 'CBDT Eyes up to 20% Tax-GDP Ratio in 5–10 years from 12% now,' *The Hindu*, 26 April 2022, https://www.thehindu.com/business/Economy/cbdt-eyes-up-to-20-tax-gdp-ratio-in-5-10-years-from-12-now/article65357516.ece.
27. World Bank Data.

28. Gautam Chikermane and Rishi Agrawal, 'Jailed for Doing Business: The 26,134 Imprisonment Clauses in India's Business Laws', Observer Research Foundation, February 2022, https://www.orfonline.org/wp-content/uploads/2022/02/ORF_Monograph_JailedForDoingBusiness_Final-New-11Feb.pdf.
29. Ibid.
30. Pratim Ranjan Bose, 'Rajasthan and Chhattisgarh undo Pension Reforms; Why It Can Lead to a Bigger Fiscal Mess for the Country', *Swarajya*, 1 May 2022, https://swarajyamag.com/economy/rajasthan-and-chhattisgarh-undo-pension-reforms-why-it-can-lead-to-a-bigger-fiscal-mess-for-the-country.
31. Shantanu Gupta, *The Monk who Transformed Uttar Pradesh* (Garuda Prakashan, 2021), p. 30.
32. 'Ageing: Ageis', World Health Organization, 18 March 2021, https://www.who.int/news-room/questions-and-answers/item/ageing-ageism.
33. 'Cities as Engines of Growth: TA-9508: Strengthening the States for Broad Based Urban Development,' NITI Aayog and Asian Development Bank, May 2022, https://www.niti.gov.in/sites/default/files/2022-05/Mod_CEOG_Executive_Summary_18052022.pdf.
34. Ibid.
35. 'Net Direct Tax Collections for the F.Y. 2021-22 at Rs. 13,63,038 crore Showing a Growth of over 48.4%', Ministry of Finance, Press Information Bureau, 17 March 2022, https://pib.gov.in/PressReleaseIframePage.aspx?PRID=1807004.

Index

About the Author

Gautam Chikermane is vice president at Observer Research Foundation (ORF). His areas of expertise are economics, politics, foreign policy and the Mahabharata.